WORKSHOPS IN COMPUTING
Series edited by C. J. van Rijsbergen

Also in this series

continued on back page...

David J. Harper and Moira C. Norrie (Eds.)

Specifications of Database Systems

International Workshop on
Specifications of Database Systems,
Glasgow, 3–5 July 1991

Springer-Verlag London Ltd.

David Harper, BSc, PhD
Department of Computer Science
University of Glasgow
17 Lilybank Gardens
Glasgow G12 8QQ
Scotland

Moira Norrie, BSc, MSc
Department of Computer Science
University of Glasgow
17 Lilybank Gardens
Glasgow G12 8QQ
Scotland

ISBN 978-3-540-19732-4

British Library Cataloguing in Publication Data
International Workshop on Specifications of Database Systems (1st: 1991: Glasgow, Scotland)
Specifications of database systems. – (Workshops in computing)
I. Title   II. Harper, David J. (David John), *1952–*   III. Norrie, Moira C., (Moira Constable), *1953–*   IV. Series
005.74
ISBN 978-3-540-19732-4   ISBN 978-1-4471-3864-8 (eBook)
DOI 10.1007/978-1-4471-3864-8
Library of Congress Data available

34/3830-543210 Printed on acid-free paper

Preface

As researchers in the database field, we were convinced of the benefits of using formal specification techniques to describe our systems. However, we were faced with a whole host of specification techniques and languages from which to choose.

Should we start from basic set theory and first-order predicate logic and devise our own approach? Should we adopt one of the widely-used specification languages such as Z or OBJ? Should we use different techniques for different aspects of our system?

Arguments were prevalent within our research group (and surely among many other research groups) of the relative merits of model-based and algebraic techniques. We would ask our colleagues in the formal specifications community for their advice. As one might expect, this often left us more confused as each defended their own camp.

It is a debate that parallels the debates of which programming language to use on a particular project. Partly the decision is based on functionality; partly on familiarity and partly on politics.

From the literature, we could see that a number of researchers in the specifications community were using database systems as their application domain. Generally, the work was interesting and informative – but often the "database aspect" was over-simplified. At least, it didn't appear to tackle many of the current issues of interest to the database researchers.

It occurred to us that perhaps the specification community could assist us, and perhaps we could be of benefit to them by presenting them with interesting issues.

Further, we thought that it would be good to share experiences with others in the database community who had ventured into the same maze. Hopefully, by exchanging information and ideas, we could help each other reach our goals and avoid the pitfalls and dead-ends.

And so in July 1991, we held the first International Workshop on the Specification of Database Systems in Glasgow, Scotland. The workshop had 24 full participants. It was interesting to note that when asked to classify themselves on the first morning, half claimed to be "database people" and half "specifications people".

Attendance at the workshop was limited to ensure an active exchange of ideas. We are pleased to say that all of the participants contributed to the success of the workshop. We refer to it as the "first" workshop because there was a general feeling that the exercise was very worthwhile and should be repeated.

We have chosen to order the papers in the proceedings by the name of the first author. This was done because we did not want to impose any subject groupings on the papers – and thereby encourage readers to be restrictive in their reading. In truth, there are no clear groupings: two papers may use very different techniques for similar applications or similar techniques for different applications.

It was our wish that the workshop be a "working" workshop. We therefore arranged four small working group sessions. A brief summary of each session's discussion is included at the end of the proceedings. It should be stressed that the summaries were produced by those named at the end of the summary: we therefore acknowledge the contributions of all participants while apologising for any misrepresentations.

Our thanks go to all those who refereed papers for the workshop: we appreciate that it is often hard work for little reward. Finally, we give our thanks to all of the workshop participants: they gave us a very stimulating and enjoyable three days.

Glasgow   David Harper
September 1991   Moira Norrie

Contents

Transforming Functional Database Schemes to Relational Representations

A. T. M. Aerts[*], P. M. E. De Bra[†] and K. M. van Hee[‡]

Department of Mathematics and Computing Science

Eindhoven University of Technology

Eindhoven

The Netherlands

Abstract

Semantic database models have become a popular tool for designing database schemes, despite the lack of an exact and efficient way to transform these schemes into (relational) database schemes for which efficient implementations exist and are widely available. This paper presents a precise and linear-time algorithm for transforming functional database schemes into relational ones.

The functional database model has a graphical representation which is easily understood, but it also has a formal semantics based on set-theory. Hence comprehensible and mathematically exact database design can be combined using this model. By using our algorithm one can transform a functional database scheme into a relational scheme with a minimal number of relations (tables). The generated schemes are always in Fifth Normal Form (and hence also in Boyce-Codd Normal Form). Furthermore there is no need for artificially introduced primary keys to simulate the concept of "object-identity".

1 Introduction

The Relational Database Model [1, 2, 3] provides a solid theoretical background for reasoning about databases, for formulating queries and updates, and for describing constraints. However, modeling a real-world situation using a relational database model is non-trivial at best. One cannot easily and intuitively define relations and constraints that form a useful and efficient representation of the real-world situation. The Functional Database Model [4] does provide such an intuitive tool, and also has a formal basis [5]. It has been proven successful in many database-design projects performed (mostly by students) for small and medium-size companies [5, 6]. A graphical representation of objects, functions, and several types of constraints enable the designer to generate a visualization of the database scheme that can easily be understood by non-experts.

---

[*]email: wsinatma@win.tue.nl
[†]email: debra@win.tue.nl
[‡]email: wsinhee@win.tue.nl

In order to use the Functional Database Model in real applications, an algorithm has been developed to generate a relational database scheme from a functional scheme. This is possible because in our version of the Functional Database Model a clear distinction is made between two levels: an object oriented level where the major concern is the construction of a model of the real world situation of interest, and a value oriented level, where emphasis is placed on the construction of a database model for the information system. At the first level there are just object and property types, modeling the various kinds of objects in the real world and their (functional) relationships. At the second level the representations of these types in the information system are introduced. Such a separation of concerns—modeling versus representing—is not explicitly present in Shipman's FDM where in addition also 'printable' types, such as 'STRING' and 'INTEGER', occur in the model at the same level as entitytypes.

Given a functional database model at the object oriented level, we could opt for a functional representation model, i.e. construct representations in terms of sets of object(identifier)s and functions. In this paper a relational representation scheme is chosen, i.e. a representation in terms of sets of tuples. A third alternative would be to use a network database model. Note that at this stage representations are constructed in terms of the mathematical constructs underlying each model, not in terms of the data types available in some specific database management system.

The algorithm produces a relational database scheme in Boyce-Codd Normal Form. The generated scheme does not contain multivalued dependencies or join dependencies, hence it also is in Fifth Normal Form. In this respect our approach has a clear advantage over related approaches using for instance the Entity-Relationship Model (see [7]) in which functional dependencies are not made explicit at the semantic level and have to be given extensive consideration in a separate normalization step. We supplement our basic algorithm with a few optimization steps to avoid the generation of unnecessary relations.

On several occasions the 'pure' Functional Model [5, 6] has been a bit too restrictive because it only provides functional relationships between objects. Therefore, like in [4], we allow the use of set-valued functions, which we replace by an additional object type and two mono-valued functions during the transformation from a functional to a relational scheme.

By using a transformation algorithm which carefully selects the relations that are needed to represent the structure of the functional database scheme we can employ the functional database model as a modeling tool. Classical database applications, among others, can be modeled elegantly using FDM and for such applications relational database systems have proven to provide excellent performance. When using a high-performance relational database management system, with appropriate indices, one should not suffer a large performance penalty compared to the object-oriented database management systems that exist today.

2   The Functional Database Model

The *Functional Database Model (FDM)*[6, 4] is a member of the family of *Semantic Database Models* (see for example [8]). A database scheme in FDM has a mathematical definition, but also a graphical representation which is easier to understand.

Because the database scheme describes the structure of the part of the real world we wish to describe by means of a database, we call it a *Structure Scheme*. The equivalent graphical representation is called a *Structure Diagram*.

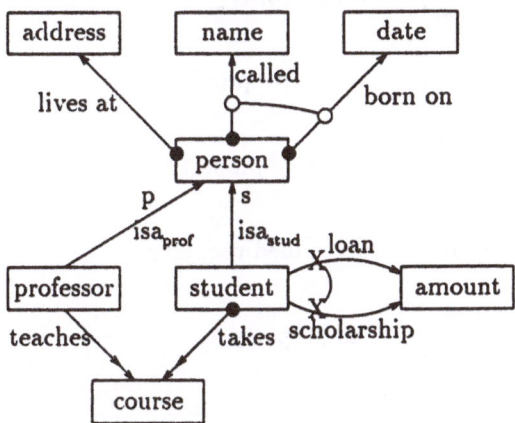

Figure 1: Structure Diagram for a University example

An example of a structure diagram is shown in Figure 1. It shows the structure of a small database concerning students, professors and courses. The diagram depicts a well known situation at a university, where professors teach courses that are taken by students. Both professors and students are persons with a name, who live at an address and are born on a certain date. No two persons at the university have the same name and date of birth. Students finance their education by means of either a scholarship or a loan.

The diagram is composed of rectangles and arrows of various kinds. A rectangle represents an object type. In any instance of the database it stands for a set of objects of that type. Sets of objects corresponding to different object types are disjoint. The arrows represent property types. A property type stands, in an instance of the database, for a (mono- or set-valued) function between the set of objects at the base of the property arrow and the set of objects at its tip.

The graphical conventions used in Figure 1 are given in Figure 2 and will be explained below. In addition to object types and their functional relations also a number of (common) constraints can be expressed graphically.

The information represented in Figure 1 may also be represented textually using a structure scheme. We will give the definition of this scheme first and then work it out for the University example.

Definition 2.1 *Structure Scheme*
A structure scheme is a 4-tuple $<O, P, C, W>$ where

O: a finite set of names of object types.

P: a triple specifying a finite set of property types; $P = <F, D, R>$, where

 F is a finite set of names of property types: $O \cap F = \emptyset$.

 D is a function which maps a property type to the object type which is called the *domain type* of the property type; so $D \in F \to O$.

4

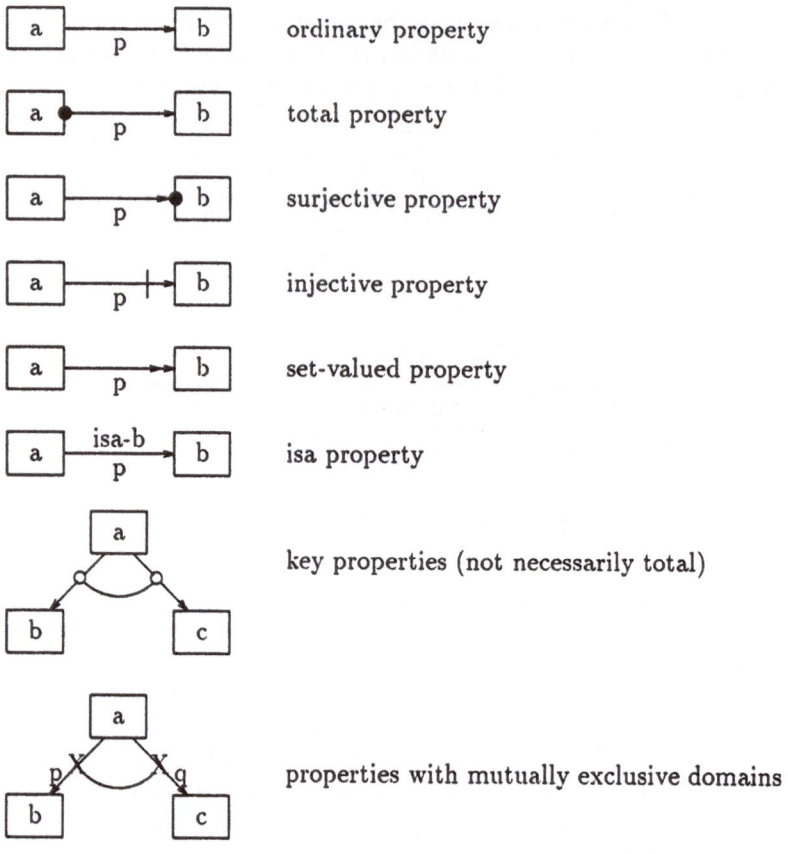

a ├────p────→ b	ordinary property
a ●────p────→ b	total property
a ├────p────●→ b	surjective property
a ├────p──┼──→ b	injective property
a ├────p────→→ b	set-valued property
a ├──isa-b──→ b	isa property
a / b ⌣ c	key properties (not necessarily total)
a / b ⌣ c	properties with mutually exclusive domains

Figure 2: Graphical Representation of Objects and Properties.

R is a function which maps a property type to the object type which is called the *range type* of the property type; so $R \in F \rightarrow O$.

When a property is set-valued we say that the range is O, not $\mathcal{P}(O)$.

$C = <Q, U, X>$, a triple specifying standard constraints:

Q: a function which assigns to every property type a number of attributes:
$Q \in F \rightarrow V_{is\_a} \cup$
$\prod(\{<total, \{\top, \bot\}>, <injective, \{\top, \bot\}>, <surjective, \{\top, \bot\}>,$
$<set-valued. \{\top, \bot\}>\}).$[1]

For set-valued properties we say that being *total* means that the property must not only be defined for every object of the domain type, but also that the corresponding set of objects in the range type is non-empty. For the injectivity and surjectivity we look at the objects in the range sets, not the range sets themselves. Injectivity then means that the property defines a partition on the range object type: $\forall a, b \in dom(f) : a \neq b \rightarrow f(a) \cap f(b) = \emptyset$. An injective set-

---

[1]The symbol $\prod$ denotes the *Generalized Product*: Let P be a set valued function, then $\prod(P) = \{ p \mid p \text{ is a function with domain } dom(P) \text{ and } \forall x \in dom(P) : p(x) \in P(x)\}$, also, $\top$ = true, $\bot$ = false; V_{is_a} is a set of (is_a-) labels, disjoint from F and O.

valued property f then can be thought of as the inverse of an ordinary property f' from $R(f)$ to $D(f)$. Surjectivity means that $R(f) = \bigcup \{f(a) \mid a \in dom(f)\}$.

U: a function which assigns to an object type $o \in O$ the subsets k of $D^{-1}(o)$ of names of property types, called the keys of this object type, that together form an injective function from o to k, so $U \in O \to \mathcal{P}(\mathcal{P}(F))$. We do include singletons—sets containing a single, injective property type—in U, although they are already represented by Q. However, in our examples we will not mention the singletons explicitly. The keys in U are minimal, of course.

X: a function which assigns to an object type $o \in O$ the subsets of $D^{-1}(o)$ of names of property types, that have mutually exclusive domains, so $X \in O \to \mathcal{P}(\mathcal{P}(F))$.

W: a set valued function with $dom(W) = O$, called the object world function. If for $f \in F$ it holds that $Q(f) \in V_{is\_a}$ then $W(D(f)) \subseteq W(R(f))$ $\square$

The components O and P together specify a labeled, directed graph that gives the structure of the database in terms of object and property types. Component C specifies a number of general constraints these types have to satisfy. W is a function which associates a set of real world objects with (the name of) an object type. These sets do not have to be disjoint. On the contrary, if two object types are related to one another by an is_a relationship, the set of real world objects corresponding to the subtype is required to be a subset of the set of objects for the supertype. A single real world object thus may be represented in the database model by two or more objects that are related by is_a-relationships and represent the various roles the real world object plays in the model. W allows one to make statements about the relation between sets of objects, but can, since it refers to real-world objects, not be formalized completely.

The O and P components of the structure scheme specify a labeled, directed graph, in which the object types are nodes and the property types correspond to labeled, directed edges. Not every graph specified this way is acceptable as a structure scheme. When we select the subgraph $< N, E >$ based on the property types with an is_a-label with edges $E = \{f \in F \mid Q(f) \in V_{is\_a}\}$ and nodes $N = \{o \in O \mid \exists \{f \in E \mid o = D(f) \vee o = R(f)\}\}$, this subgraph has to be free from cycles. Also, in $< N, E >$, if an object has 2 or more supertypes (i. e. has 2 or more outgoing is_a edges) then these must have a common supertype. Furthermore, if there is no directed path from an object type $o_1 \in N$ to an object type $o_2 \in N$ then o_1 and o_2 correspond to disjoint sets of real-world objects: $W(o_1) \cap W(o_2) = \emptyset$.

The is_a properties are required to be total, injective and not set-valued. Every subtype object thus is mapped to precisely one, unique supertype object. Is_a-properties are given an is_a-label l ($l \in V_{is\_a}$) in addition to a name. When two is_a-properties have a common supertype as range type and have the same is_a-label, their range sets are disjoint. The range sets of is_a-properties with a common supertype, but with different is_a-labels are allowed to overlap.

To illustrate the definition of a functional database scheme we give the scheme version of the structure of (part of) a university database.

Example 2.1 *University database (structure scheme)*
The components $< O, P, C, W >$ for the example of Figure 1 are:

$O = \{\text{address. name. date, person, professor, student. amount, course}\}$

$P = \,<F,D,R>$, where

  $F = \{\text{lives at, called, born on, p, s, loan, scholarship, teaches, takes}\}$

  $D = \{(\text{lives at, person}), (\text{called, person}), (\text{born on, person}), (\text{p, professor}),$
       $(\text{s, student}), (\text{loan, student}), (\text{scholarship, student}), (\text{teaches, professor}),$
       $(\text{takes, student})\}$

  $R = \{(\text{lives at, address}), (\text{called, name}), (\text{born on, date}), (\text{p, person}), (\text{s, person}),$
       $(\text{loan, amount}), (\text{scholarship, amount}), (\text{teaches, course}), (\text{takes, course})\}$

$C = \,<Q,U,X>$, where

  $Q = \{(\text{lives at}, (<\text{total}, \top>, <\text{injective}, \bot>, <\text{surjective}, \bot>, <\text{set-valued}, \bot>$
       $)),$
       $(\text{called}, (<\text{total}, \top>, <\text{injective}, \bot>, <\text{surjective}, \bot>, <\text{set-valued}, \bot>)),$
       $(\text{born on}, (<\text{total}, \top>, <\text{injective}, \bot>, <\text{surjective}, \bot>, <\text{set-valued}, \bot>$
       $)),$
       $(\text{p, isa}_{\text{prof}}), (\text{s, isa}_{\text{stud}}),$
       $(\text{teaches}, (<\text{total}, \bot>, <\text{injective}, \bot>, <\text{surjective}, \bot>, <\text{set-valued}, \top>$
       $)),$
       $(\text{takes}, (<\text{total}. \top>, <\text{injective}, \bot>, <\text{surjective}, \bot>, <\text{set-valued}, \top>)),$
       $(\text{loan}, (<\text{total}, \bot>, <\text{injective}, \bot>, <\text{surjective}, \bot>, <\text{set-valued}, \bot>)),$
       $(\text{scholarship}, (<\text{total}, \bot>, <\text{injective}, \bot>, <\text{surjective}, \bot>,$
       $<\text{set-valued}, \bot>)),$

  $U = \{(\text{person}, \{\text{called, born on}\})\}$

  $X = \{(\text{student}, \{\text{loan, scholarship}\})\}$

$W =$ the function linking every object in the database to the corresponding object
in the real world. This basically is the "meaning" of the database.

   We require the *takes* property to be total, meaning that the set of courses
taken by a student must be known and non-empty. We do not require the *teaches*
property to be total, mostly to show the difference.

   From U we see (as shown in Figure 1) that the key properties for a person are
his (her) name (property *called*) and date of birth (property *born on*).

   X tells us that a student cannot have both a loan and a scholarship at the
same time. In some sense, having such properties which exclude each other is an
alternative to creating subtypes (using is_a properties) in some simple cases. We
could have created subtypes student-with-loan and student-with-scholarship, both
with the same is_a label, and that would have meant that a student cannot have
both a loan and a scholarship. A person however can be both a professor and a
student at the same time, because the is_a labels isa$_{\text{prof}}$ and isa$_{\text{stud}}$ are different.

   The figure is fairly easy to understand, whereas a typical non-expert would
not even begin to read the formal mathematical definition. The two are completely
equivalent however. We use the figure to clarify the database design to the customer,
while the mathematical definition is used in the transformation algorithm. In addition to the mathematical definition corresponding to the figure one can define a
formal language for expressing constraints and queries. This has been done in [5]

for instance. The mathematical definition is what is typically stored in the data dictionary.

Note also that the structure scheme we have given for the university database does not describe all the details that will be present in an actual implementation. We have omitted properties which are unimportant for describing the overall structure of the database, such as the representation of a *course* by means of a number and/or title. (Such details are needed later on, regardless whether the implementation is based on a relational or a functional DBMS.) □

In order to transform a structure scheme into a relational scheme we first eliminate the set-valued functions.

Definition 2.2 *Purely Functional Structure Scheme*
A structure scheme is called *purely functional* if there are no set-valued properties (i. e. for all properties the *set-valued* attribute is ⊥). □

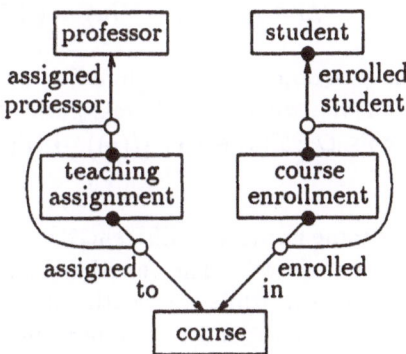

Figure 3: Purely Functional (part of the) University Database

A structure scheme can always be transformed into a purely functional scheme by replacing set-valued property types by an extra object type and two mono-valued total key-properties. Figure 3 shows how this is done in the university example. The figure shows that although we use a (double) arrow to draw a set-valued function the translation becomes symmetric: a professor may teach a number of courses, and a course may also be taught by a number of professors.

3 Relational Representation Schemes

Before we can present our transformation algorithm we need the definition of the target (or output) of that algorithm: a relational database scheme, which we call *relational representation scheme* because it is a representation of the structure scheme in an alternative but at least as powerful formalism. We first present the definition of a relational representation scheme and then discuss its components.

Definition 3.1 *Relational Representation Schema*
A relational representation scheme for a purely functional structure scheme $<O, P, C, W>$ is a 6-tuple $<E, A, V, I, H, T>$ where:

A : a finite set of names of attributes

V : a function with $\mathrm{dom}(V) = A$, which maps every attribute name $a \in A$ to a set of values $V(a)$, called *attribute range*, sometimes also called the *domain* of the attribute.

H : a (partial) function[2], which maps object types $o \in O$ to a corresponding set of attribute names $H(o) \subseteq A$, so $H \in O \nrightarrow \mathcal{P}(A)$.

I : a function, which maps each object type $o \in \mathrm{dom}(H)$ to a corresponding set of attribute names $I(o)$, which is called the *primary key* of o, so $I \in \mathrm{dom}(H) \rightarrow \mathcal{P}(A)$ and $\forall o \in \mathrm{dom}(H) : I(o) \subseteq H(o)$.

E : a (partial) function, which maps property types $f \in F$ to an injective function of attribute names to attribute names, such that :

$$\forall f \in \mathrm{dom}(E) : E(f) \in I(R(f)) \rightarrow H(D(f)) \text{ and}$$
$$\forall f \in \mathrm{dom}(E) : \forall a \in I(R(f)) : V(a) = V\big(E(f)(a)\big) .$$

T : a function which maps each object type to a function which maps the identifying (primary key-) part of the representation of a real world object to the object itself, so $\mathrm{dom}(T) = O$, and $\forall o \in O : T(o) \in \prod(V|I(o)) \rightarrow W(o)$.

□

This definition shows some important differences between the functional database model and the relational model. The functional model at the level of the structure scheme is *object-oriented*, while the relational model is *value-oriented*. V defines the *domain* of each attribute : a set of values. In the functional model we only have objects, although some objects do not correspond to physical real-world objects but rather to abstract objects (like a *date* for instance). The functional model does not say how to print or represent a date, whereas the relational model does indicate the set of possible values.

In the functional model an object type o may have several keys—$U(o)$ may have more than one element—whereas we need one *primary* key in the relational representation scheme, to act as an object identifier and to simulate the functional relationships between objects.

H represents the *heading* of the relation (or table) that corresponds to an object type. H is a partial function because we only want to create a relation for object types with properties. A table which only contains dates for instance usually is of little use and a relation for it can be omitted provided that does not cause any loss of information.

To represent a property of an object we will include a representation of the range object of that property in the tuple for the object. The heading of the relation for an object type thus will include a set of attributes for representing each of the property types of which that object type is the domain type. When the range type of a property of an object type is itself an object type with properties of its own (hence it will be represented by a table) then we need a link between the attribute(s) corresponding to that property and the attribute(s) that identify the objects in the

---

[2]The symbol $\nrightarrow$ is used to denote a *partial function*.

range type of that property. This link is provided by the renaming function E. Although the renaming is usually the identity this need not always be the case. In the purely functional university example we can use *enrolled in* as the attribute to indicate the course to which a *course enrollment* refers, whereas this attribute corresponds to some attribute of *course*, which we shall name *courseno* below. E indicates that *courseno* is renamed to *enrolled in* in the *course enrollment* relation.

Finally, T ensures that tuples in our relations correspond to objects in the real world, by mapping the primary key for an object of type o to an object in $W(o)$, the real-world object it represents.

Before turning to the algorithm we show a possible relational representation scheme for the university database. This representation scheme correponds to the structure diagram of Figure 4, the purely functional version of the diagram of Figure 1 which has been made more complete by adding a few more details, such as the title of a course, the name of the street, and the number of the house in the address. (The reader is invited to verify that this relational representation is indeed the output of the algorithm.) Some elements in this relational scheme may not represent the typical use of the university database. It is always possible to change some attributes or relations, for instance to select more appropriate primary keys.

Example 3.1 *Relational University database*
The components $< E, A, V, I, H, T >$ of a possible relational representation scheme are:

$A = $ {nr. street, state, zip, city, name, birthdate, SS#, empno, studno, loan,
 courseno. coursename, assigned professor, assigned to, enrolled student,
 scholarship, enrolled in}

These are the names of the attributes we will use in our relations. Some of these attributes are not represented in the structure diagram of Figure 1, but shown in Figure 4. Also, there is no need to use the same names for attributes as for their "corresponding" properties in the structure scheme. In particular we have chosen to use *birthdate* instead of *born on* and *name*—the name of an object type— instead of *called*.

$V = $ {(nr, *numbers*), (street, *strings*), (state, *char*[2]), (zip, *numbers*), (city, *strings*),
 (name, *strings*), (birthdate, *dates*), (SS#, *numbers*), (empno, *numbers*),
 (studno, *numbers*), (loan, *money*), (scholarship, *money*), (courseno, *numbers*),
 (coursename, *strings*), (assigned professor. *numbers*), (assigned to, *numbers*),
 (enrolled student, *numbers*), (enrolled in, *numbers*)}

where *strings, char*[2], *numbers, dates, money* denote the sets of all possible strings, strings of 2 characters, numbers, dates, and amounts of money. Again, the name of the domain of an attribute need not be the same as the name we used for the object type in the structure scheme. For instance, *dates* refers to the set of values we use to represent objects of type date, and values of type *money* represent an amount.

$H = $ {(person, {nr. street. state. zip, city, SS#, name, birthdate}),
 (student. {studno. SS#, loan. scholarship}), (course, {courseno, coursename}),
 (teaching assignment, {assigned professor, assigned to}),
 (professor, {empno. SS#}). (course enrollment, {enrolled student, enrolled in})}

H defines headings of the tables. We have chosen not to define relations for the object types *name, date* and *amount* since they have no properties. There is also no table for *address* because there is only one property which refers to *address* and there is no (nontrivial) key for *address*. In other words: all information about adresses can be represented in the *person* relation. Note also that we have added attributes (empno, studno, SS#, courseno and coursename) which are not present in the structure scheme. It is common to omit properties in a structure scheme to trim down the graphical representation.

$I =$ {(person, {SS#}), (professor, {SS#}), (student, {SS#}), (course, {courseno}),
(teaching assignment, {assigned professor, assigned to}),
(course enrollment, {enrolled student, enrolled in})}

I defines the primary keys. We have chosen the social security number to be the primary key of the *person* relation. Because *professor* and *student* are specializations of *person* (they are connected to *person* through an is_a relationship) they inherit the same primary key. In an implementation however one may wish to use the *empno* as primary key for *professor* and the *studno* for *student*. This means that a *teaching assignment* could consist of an *empno* and a *courseno*, or in other words that *empno* could be used as a foreign key in the *teaching assignment* relation.
Note that the objects in the structure scheme may have more than one key. Our relational representation scheme does not have an equivalent to U, the set of all keys for the objects, as present in the structure scheme. The constraints specified at the structure scheme level of course still hold at the representational level and do not have to be repeated there. In general one will describe the constraints in a formal language, like in [5]. These constraints are not essential for our transformation algorithm, since they do not affect the structure of the model.

$E =$ {(p, id({SS#})), (s, id({SS#})), (assigned professor, {(SS#, assigned professor)}),
(assigned to, {(courseno, assigned to)}), (enrolled in, {(courseno, enrolled in)}),
(enrolled student, {(SS#, enrolled student)})}

We see that in our example a renaming function has been defined only for property types relating object types for which a relation has been constructed. This usage of renaming is a reflection of the referential integrity constraints that functions between sets of objects have to satisfy. The renaming function for a property type p maps the attributes in the primary key of $R(p)$ to the corresponding attributes in $D(p)$. For the is_a-properties in our example this mapping turns out to be trivial. For a property type such as *enrolled in* it is a little less trivial. Renaming becomes necessary when one object type is related to another one by more than one property type. Consider for example an object type *period* which is related by property types *begin* and *end* to an object type *date*. The relation for *period* then may contain attributes such as *begin_of_period* and *end_of_period* which are renamed from the primary key attribute, say *date*, of the relation for the object type *date*. Attributes that are mapped to one another by a renaming function have the same attribute range.

$T =$ a complicated function which maps each object type to a function from the set of possible primary-key values for the representation of an object to the set of real-world objects. Basically, this is the equivalent of the object world function, but now for the relational representation. If the "person" object with name "John Doe", and born on 1/1/1950 refers to a real person, then the tuple in the person-table with name-value "John Doe" and date of birth "1/1/1950" must refer to the same real person.

□

4   The Transformation Algorithm

The transformation from a functional structure scheme to a relational representation scheme can only be completely automated if the structure scheme is complete. Often one omits a number of properties to keep the graphic representation small. Figure 4 shows a complete, purely functional structure scheme for the university database. We have chosen object names almost at random for (what will become) the attributes.

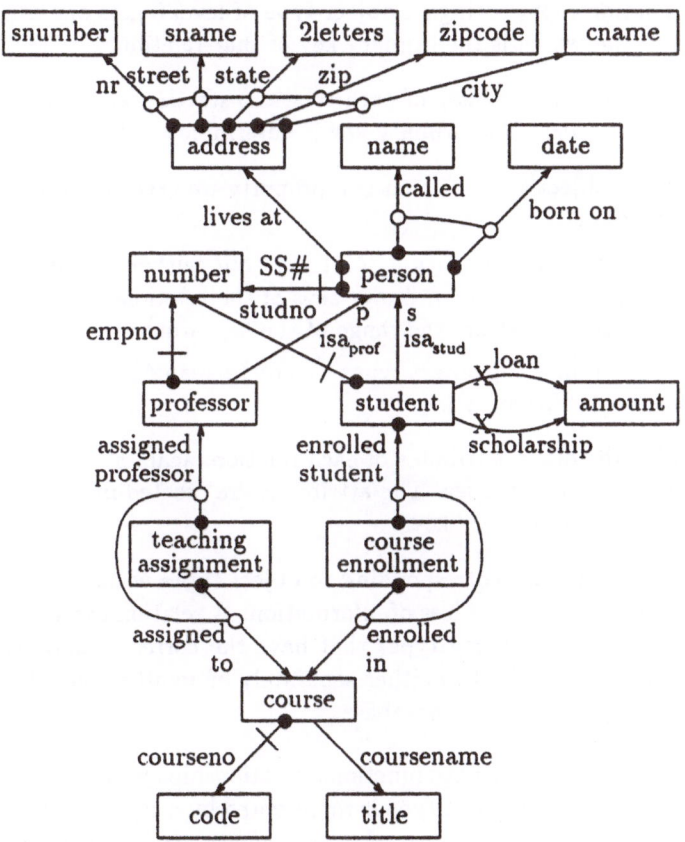

Figure 4: Complete, Purely Functional University Structure Diagram

We now turn to the exact description of the algorithm which takes as input a functional database scheme, and produces an equivalent relational scheme in Boyce-Codd Normal Form (and, because of the absence of multivalued dependencies and join dependencies, also in Fifth Normal Form, see also [9]). We will first present a summary of the algorithm. In the subsections that follow the most important steps in the algorithm are discussed in more detail.

4.1 Summary of the Algorithm

To summarize the algorithm we enumerate the basic steps and we apply them to the university example.

1. Create a purely functional scheme, equivalent to the given structure scheme. For the university example, see Figure 4.

2. Create a relation name o for each object type o.

3. Determine the level of each object type. The level determines the order in which primary keys can be assigned.

4. Every relation representing an object type of level 0 gets one attribute which we call o, and which is the primary key of that relation.

5. Determine the primary key of each relation, starting at level 1, and working in ascending order. The primary key is determined as follows:

   (a) For an object type with an is_a property we take the primary key of the superclass.

   (b) For an object type with a total key (but without an is_a property) we take the union of the primary keys of the relations corresponding to the object types that are the range of the key-properties.

   (c) For the remaining object types we create a single new attribute that will become the primary key.

6. Determine the other attributes of each relation, again starting at level 0, and working in ascending order. The attributes are created much in the same way as we did for the primary key.

7. Remove the relations corresponding to object types without properties, when this can be done without loss of information. A relation can be removed when the range sets of property types that have the corresponding object type as range type, are required to either separately or jointly cover the set of range objects in any state of the database.

Note that since we only have functional relationships between object types and that every (non-attribute) object type is represented by a separate relation there are no functional dependencies within a relation that are not key-dependencies. Hence the relational database schemes we generate are always in Fifth Normal Form.

4.2 Removing Set-Valued Properties

Because of the widely accepted (and enforced) First Normal Form all values that can occur in relation instances must be atomic. Structured (i. e. tuple-valued) and/or set-valued attributes are prohibited. In the transformation of a functional database scheme to a relational scheme we wish to represent functional relationships by (one or more) attributes. To avoid set-valued attributes we must eliminate set-valued functions from the structure scheme first. This is done by transforming the functional scheme into a purely functional scheme (see Definition 2.2) by replacing every set-valued function by a combination of an extra object type and two mono-valued total key-properties. The result of applying this transformation to the set-valued functions *teaches* and *takes* in Figure 1 is shown in Figure 3.

Let $o_1, o_2 \in O$ and let $f \in F$ be a property name such that $D(f) = o_1$, $R(f) = o_2$ and $Q(f)(\text{set-valued}) = \top$. Suppose first that f is not injective. The replacement of the set-valued function f then works as follows:

- Remove all information concerning f from the components $P = <F, D, R>$ and $C = <Q, U, X>$ of the structure scheme.

- Add a new object o to O. For example, an object type *teaching assignment* will be added as part of replacing the set-valued property *teaches*.

- Add two new property names f_1 and f_2 to F. In our example we introduced the property names *assigned professor* and *assigned to*.

- Add (f_1, o) and (f_2, o) to D.

- Add (f_1, o_1) and (f_2, o_2) to R.

- Add $(f_1, (<\text{total}, \top>, <\text{injective}, \bot>, <\text{surjective}, \alpha>, <\text{set-valued}, \bot>))$ to Q where $\alpha = \top$ if f is total and $\bot$ if it is not. According to Definition 2.1 being total means that the sets in the range must all be nonempty. In the university example the *teaches* property would only be total if every professor would be linked to a nonempty set of courses. In that case every professor would be the *assigned professor* for at least one *teaching assignment*.

- Add $(f_2, (<\text{total}, \top>, <\text{injective}, \bot>, <\text{surjective}, \alpha>, <\text{set-valued}, \bot>))$ to Q, where $\alpha = \top$ if f is surjective and $\bot$ if it is not. If every course occurs in the set of courses taught by some professor, then every course will be assigned to some professor in some teaching assignment.

- Add $(o, \{f_1, f_2\})$ to U. So for every course a professor teaches a unique teaching assignment has to be introduced.

By applying the composition of the inverse of *assigned professor* and *assigned to* to an object in the range of *assigned professor* (= dom(*teaches*)) we obtain the set of course-objects taught by the corresponding professor. The set-valued property *teaches* thus is effectively replaced by the equivalent set-valued composition $f \circ g^{-1}$ with $f = $ *assigned to* and $g = $ *assigned professor*.

From the example above it can be seen that the procedure may be simplified when f is injective. The injectivity constraint would be carried over to f_2 implying that every object in o corresponds to one, unique object in o_2. Property f_2 now does not contain any new information. It is therefore simpler to replace the set-valued property f by an ordinary property f' going in the opposite direction. So:

- Remove all information concerning f from the components $P = <F, D, R>$ and $C = <Q, U, X>$ of the structure scheme.

- Add one new property type name f' to F.

- Add (f', o_2) to D.

- Add (f', o_1) to R.

- Add $(f', (<\text{total}, \alpha>, <\text{injective}, \bot>, <\text{surjective}, \beta>, <\text{set-valued}, \bot>))$ to Q where $\alpha = \top$ if f is surjective and $\bot$ if it is not, and $\beta = \top$ if f is total and $\bot$ if it is not.

As an example consider the case where *teaches* in Figure 1 is required to be injective. This means that none of the courses taught by one professor are taught by any of the other professors. *Teaches* is then replaced by an ordinary property from *course* to *professor* with a suitable name such as *taught_by*.

The above procedure is repeated until all set-valued properties have been eliminated.

Some information (from U and X) is not accounted for during the elimination of set-valued properties. Using a formal constraint-language (see [5]) one can still describe the altered constraints, but we can no longer represent them using our graphical representation.

4.3   Selection of Relations

Perhaps the most crucial part in the transformation is the selection of the relations that are going to represent the object types of the structure scheme.

In order to automate this step it is important to have a complete structure scheme, i. e. a scheme in which all properties we wish to convert to attributes in the relational scheme are present. Whether one just keeps these properties in mind or actually draws them (like we did in Figure 4) is irrelevant. Also, in a more interactive version of this algorithm one may relax this constraint, as we in fact only need to know whether an object has properties, not which or how many of them.

In general all object types which are the domain of a property (i. e. which have outgoing arrows in the graphical representation) are candidates for being represented by a relation. However, some of these candidates may be uninteresting, and before actually implementing the relational scheme one must examine the scheme and eliminate the relations one considers useless. For instance, if the only key of an object type is the set of all its property types, then the only way to identify an object of that type is by giving (i. e. repeating) all its properties. In the university example the *person* object type has a *lives at* property which refers to an *address* object type. The only way to identify an *address* in our example is by giving all its properties. Hence in a relation instance all information about people's addresses would be contained in the *person* relation and also in the *address* relation. Furthermore, none of the properties of *address* have a range type that has properties of its own. Since there is no use for such a redundant *address* relation we do not generate it.

For the remainder of the algorithm we assume that we have a relation o for every object type $o \in O$. As a final step of the algorithm the relations corresponding to object types without properties are thrown away. So from H. E and I (defined below) we delete the elements that correspond to those relations.

4.4   Choosing Primary Keys

The most important problem in transforming functional schemes into relational representations is the identification of objects (and the translation of these id's into primary keys). In an object-oriented database (of which functional databases are a special kind) every object has an object-identity, which uniquely identifies it. In a relational database there are no "objects", only values (grouped into tuples). The aim of our transformation algorithm is to find a way to represent objects by means of tuples. This means that somehow the notion of object-identity has to be simulated using values. We do this by introducing primary keys. Depending on how the object-identity can be deduced from the structure scheme we will use different representations of the identity using primary keys.

The algorithm will be such that when an object type is a subtype of another object type, it will inherit the primary key of its supertype. When an object type is not a subtype, but satisfies a total key constraint, we choose to construct the primary key of this type on the basis of the primary keys of the range types of its key properties. If neither of the previous two cases is applicable the identity of the objects is considered to be internal to the object type, i.e. it can not be derived from that of other object types and an (artificial) one-attribute primary key is introduced. Note that we could apply this last alternative to every object type. This however we consider contrary to the semantics of the subtyping relations between object types and — in most cases — of the total key constraints.

To determine the order in which we assign primary keys to the relations representing object types we assign levels to the object types. In this way we in effect determine what is known as the "object identity graph" [10]. The assignment algorithm we use is an adapted version of the topological sort algorithm. The levels make it possible to introduce primary keys in a single pass through the structure diagram. In what follows we only need that part of the structure diagram consisting of the object types, the properties with an is_a-label and those total properties that are part of a key, provided this key contains only total properties. The object types without such properties are of level 0. The remaining object types fall into two categories: those with an is_a-property and those without. An object type with an is_a-property is assigned the level of its supertype increased by one. When an object type is directly related to more than one supertype it gets the largest of the supertype levels increased by one. Because of the restrictions we imposed following Definition 2.1 on specialization relations this procedure leads to an unambiguous level for every subtype.

The levels of the object types without is_a-properties but with a total key are in essence determined as follows. The object types with properties of which the range are object types of level 0 are of level 1. Those with properties of which the range are of level at most 1 are of level 2. We repeat this procedure until we have assigned a level to all object types of the structure scheme.

In case an object type is required to satisfy more than one total key constraint we take that key for which the levels of the associated range types are known. When there is more than one such key we choose arbitrarily among the keys with the smallest number of properties. Since we did not restrict the assignment of total key constraints in any way other than having to be minimal, we may run into a mutual dependency among several object types with a total key constraint.

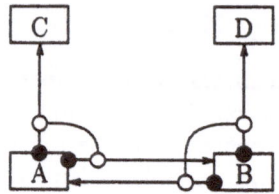

Figure 5: Mutually Dependent Keys

Figure 5, for example, shows a situation in which the level of object type A can not be determined before the level of B is known, which can only be determined after the level of A has been established. In such case we break the cycle by choosing arbitrarily among the object types involved with the largest number of key properties and assign it level 0.

Then we assign primary keys to the object types, starting with the objects of level 0 (in any order), then continuing with the object types of level 1 etc.[3]

For each object type there are three possible ways they can be identified. We can only assign one primary key to every relation, so we try each of the following possibilities in the order in which they are given below:

1. If there is an is_a property with name f from o to o' then $I(o) = I(o')$. Note that o' is of a lower level than o so $I(o')$ has been determined before we try to define $I(o)$.

   Note also that if there is another is_a property from o to an object type o'' then (see the remarks after Definition 2.1) o' and o'' must have a common supertype and inherit the same primary key (from the common supertype) regardless the is_a property we choose to use for determining $I(o)$.

2. If o has one or more total keys, i.e. $\exists k \in U(o) : \forall f \in k : Q(f)(\text{total}) = \top$ and one of these was chosen to assign a level to o, we generate a primary key for the relation o from that key. Let $k \in U(o)$ be the chosen key, then $I(o) = \bigcup_{f \in k} \{f - o' \mid o' \in I(R(f))\}$. So we copy the names of the attributes in the primary keys of the relations corresponding to the range of the properties in k, and add the name of the property to the names of these attributes, to keep names unique. We also add $\bigcup_{f \in k} \{(o', f - o') \mid o' \in I(R(f))\}$ to E to provide the link between the names of attributes in $R(f)$ and in o needed for keeping track of referential integrity constraints.

3. If o has no total key[4] or was assigned level 0, then there is no representation of the notion of object-identity of o by means of values. We then create a new

---

[3]The assignment of levels to object types is the reason why we need a complete structure scheme. In an interactive implementation of the algorithm one could ask for the level of object types that seem to be of level 0. The user could then tell the system that an object type is of a higher level because of properties that were omitted in the structure scheme.

[4]Even if o has a key one may choose to generate an "artificial" primary key consisting of only

artificial attribute, which we call o, with a sufficiently large domain (e. g. the natural numbers) and we let $I(o) = \{o\}$.

4.5 Naming Attributes and Domains

The object types of level 0 that don't have properties of their own, i.e. object types $o \in O \setminus \text{rng}(D)$, are not represented by relations. They are atomic, and represented by values. For every such object type we use the name of the object for the *domain*, i.e. the set of possible values representing the objects of this type. Therefore it is advisable to use meaningful names for these object types. When implementing the relational scheme one must associate types known to the DBMS to the domains. Different object types can be implemented using the same domain type.

For the assignment of attributes to relations we proceed in the same order as for the assignment of primary keys. For each object o we create attributes as follows:

For every property name f such that $o = D(f)$ we add the same number of attributes to $H(o)$ as are used in the primary key of the representation of $R(f)$, and, like we did for the primary keys, we add the name of the property f to the names of the attributes of the primary key of the relation representing $R(f)$. (If $R(f)$ is an object of level 0 then we need one attribute, if $R(f)$ is of a higher level then we need $| I(R(f)) |$ attributes.) Again, we add elements to E, describing the link between the attributes in $R(f)$ and in o.

4.6 Boyce-Codd Normal Form

Functional Structure Schemes only contain one type of "classical" constraints: *key-dependencies*. An object is identified by the values for its key attributes. Key dependencies are a special case of a more general constraint: the *functional dependency* (fd).

In relational database theory fd's have been studied extensively. The existence of some fd's can enable a database designer to identify redundancy, and by decomposing relations (vertically) one can eliminate this redundancy. Different *Normal Forms* have been defined which indicate that some kinds of redundancy cannot occur in databases that satisfy the normal form. The most popular normal form which only looks at fd's is the *Boyce-Codd Normal Form* (BCNF). A relational scheme satisfies the BCNF if all functional dependencies in the scheme are key-dependencies. Since our algorithm generates one relation for every object type, and the only fd's we can express in the functional model are key-dependencies, the constraints of the functional model roll over into key-dependencies in the relational representation scheme. Hence our representation schemes are in BCNF.

In literature [2, 3] other constraints are described, such as *multivalued dependencies* (mvd) and *join-dependencies* (jd), leading to other normal forms (4-th and 5-th normal form), which are all equivalent to BCNF plus some requirements for the mvd's and/or jd's. Since the relational schemes that are generated by our algorithm do not contain mvd's and jd's these schemes automatically also satisfy 4-th and 5-th normal form.

---

one attribute, by adding a key-property to the structure scheme. This is most useful when the existing total keys all consist of a large number of properties.

5   Conclusions and Future Research

We have presented an algorithm for transforming functional database schemes into relational representation schemes. This algorithm can be (and has been) implemented to run without user intervention. The generated relational database schemes are in Fifth Normal Form.

The relational representation schemes can be (and usually will be) modified before actually implementing them. We have given an example of redundant relations (the *address* relation), which one may wish to preserve or eliminate. We have also shown how to alter the functional scheme in order to avoid the duplication of keys with a large number of attributes.

In [5] a formal constraint language has been presented which can be used in conjunction with our graphical representation of database schemes, in order to capture constraints for which we have no graphical counterpart.

This transformation algorithm has been used successfully for designing and implementing relational database schemes while using functional schemes to present the design to non-experts (e. g. the customers).

In the near future our research will focus on the transformation of schemes in more general semantic database models to relational schemes. The IFO Model [10] is a prime candidate. We will also study the transformation to the Nested Relational Model [11, 12] which is a likely successor for the Relational Model as far as commercial database systems for the near future are concerned.

References

[1] Codd E.F., A Relational Model of Data for Large Shared Data Banks. Communications of the ACM 13:6, pp. 377–387, June 1970.

[2] Paredaens J., P. De Bra, M. Gyssens, D. Van Gucht, The Structure of the Relational Database Model. EATCS Monographs on Theoretical Computer Science 17, Springer Verlag, 1989.

[3] Ullman J.D., Principles of Database and Knowledge-Base Systems, Volume I. Computer Science Press, Rockville, MD, 1988.

[4] Shipman D., The Functional Data Model and the Data Language DAPLEX. ACM Transactions on Database Systems 6:1, pp. 140–173, 1981.

[5] Aerts A. T. M., P. De Bra, K. M. van Hee, Combining the Functional and the Relational Model. Proc. of the CSN-90 Conference, pp. 1–16, Utrecht, 1990.

[6] Aerts A. T. M., K. M. van Hee, Modelling with a Functional Database Model. Informatie 12.89, 1989 (in Dutch).
Aerts A. T. M., G. Alblas, K. M. van Hee, Conceptual Modelling of Information Systems. Academic Service, Schoonhoven, 1991 (in Dutch).

[7] Teorey T. J., D. Yang, J. P. Fry, A Logical Design Methodology for Relational Databases Using the Extended Entity-Relationship Model. Computing Surveys 18(2), pp. 197–222, 1986.

See also: Teorey T. J.. Database Modeling and Design, Morgan Kaufmann Publishers. Inc.. San Mateo. CA.. 1990.

[8] Hull R., R. King, Semantic Database Modeling: Survey, Applications, and Research Issues, ACM Computing Surveys, Vol. 19, No. 3, 1987.
Peckham J., F. Maryanski, Semantic Data Models, ACM Computing Surveys, Vol. 20, No. 3, 1988.

[9] De Troyer O. R. Meersman, Transforming Conceptual Schema Semantics to Relational Data Applications. Information Modelling and Database Management. Ed. H. Kangassallo. Springer Verlag, 1987.

[10] Abiteboul S., R. Hull, IFO: A Formal Semantic Model, ACM Transactions on Database Systems, 12, pp. 525–565, 1987.

[11] Arisawa H., K. Moriya, T. Miura, Operations and the Properties on Non-First-Normal-Form Relational Databases, Proc. of the 9th International Conference on Very Large Data Bases. Florence, pp. 197–204, 1983.

[12] Fisher P. C., S. T. Thomas, Operators for Non-First-Normal-Form Relations, Proc. of the IEEE Computer Software and Applications Conference, Chicago, pp. 464–475. 1983.

A   The University Example Revisited

In this appendix we present a DAPLEX formulation of the University Database Example from Figure 1. The structure of the object system is captured by a number of (stored) entity types:

```
DECLARE Person()  ⟶↦ ENTITY
DECLARE Address()  ⟶↦ ENTITY
DECLARE Name()  ⟶↦ ENTITY
DECLARE Date()  ⟶↦ ENTITY
DECLARE Amount()  ⟶↦ ENTITY
DECLARE Course()  ⟶↦ ENTITY,
```

two subtype relations:
```
DECLARE Professor()  ⟶ Person
DECLARE Student()  ⟶ Person,
```

and a number of single-valued and multivalued functions:
```
DECLARE Lives_at(Person)  ⟶ Address
DECLARE Called(Person)  ⟶ Name
DECLARE Born_on(Person)  ⟶ Date
DECLARE Loan(Student)  ⟶ Amount
DECLARE Scholarship(Student)  ⟶ Amount

DECLARE Teaches(Professor)  ⟶↦ Course
DECLARE Takes(Student)  ⟶↦ Course
```

The example of Figure 1 is at the level of objects. This feature is reflected in the DAPLEX-definition by the fact that no printable types such as STRING occur in the definition. We further note that the meaning of subtype in our version of the functional datamodel differs from the one used by Shipman. In our version a subtype-object is closely related (in fact synonymous) to, but distinct from the supertype-object it corresponds to and from which it inherits all the properties. These two objects however correspond to the same object in the real world (via the mapping W). In Shipman's conception this is modeled by declaring for example Student to be of type Person.

Every function has an inverse in the model; these are defined as derived functions:

DEFINE Lives_at_inv(Address) $\longrightarrow$ INVERSE OF Lives_at(Person)
DEFINE Called_inv $\longrightarrow$ INVERSE OF Called(Person)
DEFINE Born_on_inv $\longrightarrow$ INVERSE OF Born_on(Person)
DEFINE Loan_inv $\longrightarrow$ INVERSE OF Loan(Student)
DEFINE Scholarship_inv $\longrightarrow$ INVERSE OF Scholarship(Student)
DEFINE Taught_by $\longrightarrow$ INVERSE OF Teaches(Professor)
DEFINE Taken_by $\longrightarrow$ INVERSE OF Takes(Student)

In Figure 1 also a number of constraints have been specified; the totality constraints can be formulated as:

DEFINE CONSTRAINT Called_total() $\longrightarrow$ FOR ALL Person SOME Name
        SUCH THAT Name = Called(Person) EXISTS
DEFINE CONSTRAINT Born_on_total() $\longrightarrow$ FOR ALL Person SOME Date
        SUCH THAT Date = Born_on(Person) EXISTS
DEFINE CONSTRAINT Lives_at_total() $\longrightarrow$ FOR ALL Person SOME Address
        SUCH THAT Address = Lives_at(Person) EXISTS
and
DEFINE CONSTRAINT Takes_total() $\longrightarrow$ COUNT(Takes(Student)) > 0

The formulation of the exlusiveness and uniqueness constraints requires a few intermediate steps in the form of derived functions:

DEFINE LoanStudent() $\longrightarrow$ Student SUCH THAT FOR SOME Amount
        Loan(Student) = Amount
DEFINE SshipStudent() $\longrightarrow$ Student SUCH THAT FOR SOME Amount
        Scholarship(Student) = Amount
DEFINE LoanShip() $\longrightarrow$ INTERSECTION OF LoanStudent, SshipStudent
DEFINE CONSTRAINT ExclusiveFunds() $\longrightarrow$ COUNT(LoanShip) = 0

DEFINE NameDate() $\longrightarrow$ COMPOUND OF Name,Date
DEFINE NameDatePairs(Person) $\longrightarrow$ NameDate SUCH THAT
        FOR SOME Person Born_on(Person) = Date(NameDate)
        AND Called(Person) = Name(NameDate)
DEFINE CONSTRAINT UniqueNameDate() $\longrightarrow$
        COUNT(Person) = COUNT(NameDatePairs)

For the latter constraint definition to work the earlier totality constraints on Called and Born_on are needed.

Formal Development of Relational Database Applications

Roberto S. M. de Barros*
David J. Harper

Department of Computing Science
University of Glasgow
Glasgow G12 8QQ, Scotland, UK

Abstract

As a first step in the formal development of relational database applications, we present a method for the specification of such applications. The method prescribes how to capture the important aspects of a relational application, including the definition of relations, the specification of candidate and foreign keys, and querying and updating of relations, including error handling. Some features of the relational model itself are specified as pre-defined operators, which simplify the use of the method. We illustrate the method using a simple example application. The specification language used in this paper is Zc, a Z-like formalism.

1 Introduction

Basically, formal specification methods use mathematical expressions to describe, in a precise way, the properties the systems must satisfy, without any constraint on the way these properties will be guaranteed. They describe what the systems must do without saying how it will be done.

The main advantages of using formal specifications in software development are (1) the use of semantically precise notations that avoid the imprecision and ambiguity inherent in the use of natural languages, (2) the abstraction of implementation details, (3) the detection and correction of mistakes before the implementation, and (4) the possibility of generating prototypes and even full implementations of the systems from the formal specifications, based on (semi-)automatic methods.

In this paper we present a general method for the formal specification of relational databases [1, 2, 3] and applications. Such specifications could then be subject to translation processes that would transform them into implementations based on a specific Relational DBMS (RDBMS) and query language.

This work is being done using Zc [4, 5], a language based on Z [6, 7] that allows for modularization, and consequently a better organization, and reusability of the

---

*The author is a UFPE (Federal University of Pernambuco) Brazilian Civil Servant studying for a PhD degree at the Department of Computing Science, University of Glasgow.

specifications. Zc includes the main characteristics of Z such as the use of simple mathematical concepts (set theory and propositional and predicate logics) and the idea of Schemas, the basis for the incremental presentation of specifications. Zc, unlike Z, uses only standard keyboard symbols rather than mathematical symbols and hence its syntax is closer to traditional programming languages than that of Z.

The main strengths of our approach to the specification of relational databases and applications using Zc are:

- The method is formal.

- The method is based on a few simple concepts, which should make it easy to use in developing relational database applications.

- It allows the abstraction of several implementation details like the choice of types and domains, specific integrity rules over the attributes of the relations, treatment for errors, etc. These details may be added later and integrate well with the rest of the specification.

- The method also allows the specification of the systems independently of particular RDBMSs and query languages. This allows us to make use of the relational model features irrespective of whether they are supported by a specific RDBMS or not.

- We believe that translation processes for implementations using specific RDBMSs and query languages, from specifications written according to the method, are quite simple.

- When implementing database systems without having specified them before, people tend to concentrate their attention only on the correct behaviour of the operations, forgetting the situations when errors may occur. Our method also deals with the specification of the behaviour of the system when errors occur and prescribes how to get all possible errors for each of the operations.

- It seems likely that systems specified according to the method could also be implemented using either DBMSs based on other approaches, e:g. the inverted list approach, or even a file-based approach.

Firstly, we show how to specify relations with their attributes (whether null values are allowed or not), keys (candidate and foreign) and other constraints. Then, we present the specification of applications which include Select, Project, Join, Insert, Update and Delete operations. Finally, we extend the specification of applications to capture error handling.

Pre-defined operators are used in most parts of the specification in order to make it simpler to write and understand. These operators capture specific aspects of the relational model (e.g. keys, nulls, etc.), and some aspects of operations like deletes and updates. It is important that people read the specification of the operators carefully and understand exactly what they mean before using them. Using the operators makes the syntax closer to those of database languages, and, moreover, the specifications are formal.

The organization of the paper is as follows: Section 2 presents a description of the method(ology) for the specification of relational databases and applications. We also include in this section an informal description of the operators used in the method. The formal definition (specification) of the operators is presented in section 3. Then, in section 4, we present the specification of a simple example using the method. Finally, in section 5, we present our conclusions.

To conclude this section, we would like to say that a basic background on formal specifications would make the understanding of the method easier, even though it is not totally essential. On the other hand, a good knowledge of the relational model is indispensable.

2 The Method

Before we begin the presentation of the method, we would like to make some points clear. These are:

- Our method is for the specification of relational databases and applications and it requires the relations to be at least in first normal form (1NF). It is not a replacement for database design methodologies but, rather, complements such methodologies and enables the formalization of database designs.

- Our method is mainly intended to help database application designers in writing such specifications. However, database application programmers are expected to be able to read them. The aforementioned groups constitute the *users* of the method.

- The description presented in this paper does not cover all aspects of the method because of the limitation of space. A report [8] is in preparation containing a full description of the method. It includes the definition of all operators, the specification of composite attribute keys, updates of keys, transactions and views, and a complete treatment of error handling.

- The method is under development and may be changed subject to feedback from its users.

The description of the method will be split into three parts: the first one describes the specification of the database structures, i.e. the relations and their attributes, and of the constraints to be guaranteed. The second describes the specification of applications over the database, and the last deals with the extension of the applications to capture error handling, using two different approaches.

The rules of the method will be named using labels of the type **X**n, where **X** can be **D**, standing for database rules, **A** for application rules or **E** for extended application rules to capture error handling, and n will be a sequential number within each kind of rule, with subitems when necessary.

The reader may find it useful to refer to section 4 (the specification of a simple example) while reading the description of the method, in order to make its understanding easier.

2.1 Specification of the database structures and constraints

Relations will be specified as sets of tuples. The type record[1] was chosen to represent tuples because it makes the specification of the operations easier as it allows the access to the attributes using symbolic names as in most database manipulation languages.

Sets allow the abstraction of the real representation of the relations and make the association of the specification to the implementation easier, without enforcing any constraints on the way relations may be implemented.

D1 - Relations (Intention)

For each base relation there will be a corresponding Zc record definition, where the attributes (members of the record) must be of a simple type, i.e., either a predefined type or a given type. These types will represent the intention of the relations.

```
TYPE  Rel1  =  ( Att1 : TYPE1, Att2 : TYPE2, ... );
```

D2 - Relations (Extension)

For each record type defined, there will be a corresponding schema that declares a variable of type SET of the type defined earlier. These variables will represent the extension of the relations. These schemas will be referred to as the **D2** schemas elsewhere in the method.

```
SCHEMA Relat1;
VAR  rel1 : SET Rel1;
...
END Relat1;
```

D2.1 - Required attributes

The constraints which state that specific attributes of the relations are required will be specified in the predicates of each of these **D2** schemas, and will use the operator REQUIRED. This operator takes two parameters: the relation, and the attribute.

```
REQUIRED  rel1  Att1
```

In fact, REQUIRED is only a syntactic sugaring for a more general operator called NOT_NULL, that takes one attribute more as its first parameter: the null value corresponding to the type of the attribute.

```
NOT_NULL  <null>  rel1  Att1
```

As already mentioned, the specification of the operators, together with a more detailed explanation, are presented in section 3.

D2.2 - Candidate Keys

Candidate keys, i.e., attributes or groups of attributes that uniquely identify the tuples of the relations, will also be specified in the predicates of each of these **D2** schemas,

---

[1]In Z, schemas are used to specify types, records, constraints, operators, etc, and hence each record would be defined as a schema and the attributes would be variables in those schemas. This overuse of the schema concept makes some specifications unclear and is one of the disadvantages of Z.

and will use the operator KEY_OF. This operator takes two parameters: the relation, and the attribute that is a candidate key.

```
KEY_OF  rel1  Att1
```

D2.3 - Attribute constraints

The predicates of the **D2** schemas may also include any other intra-relation constraints, e.g. specific integrity rules over the attributes of the relations, using the universal quantifier FORALL to state that it must be true for all the tuples of the relation being defined.

```
( FORALL t : Rel1  |  t IN rel1  .  <condition> )
```

where <condition> is a boolean expression based on one or more attributes of t.

D3 - The "Database" schema

A schema, e.g. DB, that will represent the Database as a whole, will group all database definitions by including the **D2** schemas that define the relations.

```
SCHEMA DB;
INCLUDE  Relat1, Relat2, ..., Relatn;
...
END DB;
```

D3.1 - Foreign Keys

All foreign-keys will be defined in the predicate of the database schema, using the FOR_KEY operator. A foreign key in relation **rel2**, involving attribute **Fk2**, referring to relation **rel1** involving its primary key **Pk1**, is specified below.

```
FOR_KEY  rel2  Fk2  rel1  Pk1
```

In fact, FOR_KEY is, once again, a syntactic sugaring for a more general operator called FOREIGN_KEY, that takes one attribute more as its first parameter: the null value corresponding to the type of the attribute.

```
FOREIGN_KEY  <null>  rel2  Fk2  rel1  Pk1
```

D3.2 - Other constraints

The predicate of the database schema may also include other inter-relations constraints over the database. In particular, this includes the definition of inter-relation derived attributes.

D4 - The "Delta" schema

A schema that includes the database before and after the operations will be defined to be used in the update operations, in order to make possible the distinction between the relations before the operations and the relations after the operations. Its name will, by convention, be the name of the database schema with the prefix "Delta_".

```
Delta_DB  =  DB  AND  DB/'/;
```

D5 - The "Equiv" schema

The "Delta" schema will be extended by the definition of a new schema that will be used in the specification of the read-only operations. It adds an invariant stating that all its variables will be unchanged after the operations and its name will, once again by convention, be the prefix "Equiv_" added to the name of the original schema.

```
Equiv_DB  =  (Delta_DB  |  TUPLE DB  =  TUPLE DB/'/);
```

where TUPLE is an operator that, applied to a schema, gives the tuple formed by its variables.

2.2   Specification of the database applications

Now we begin the description of the rules of the method concerned with the specification of the applications. For organizational purposes, we will divide the applications into two groups, according to the type of operation they perform: read-only applications, that do not modify the database, and update applications, that modify the database by inserting, updating or deleting tuples of relations.

A1 - Read-only applications

Read-only applications will be specified by schemas such that (1) they include the "Equiv" schema (D5), (2) they declare the input (if any) and output variables of the operations, (3) their output variables will usually be relations, i.e., their types will be **SET A**, where **A** is a record type, and (4) their predicates describe the result of the operations according to at least one of the three following rules (A2, A3 and A4), and may use the aggregate functions **#** (number of elements), SUM, MAX, MIN and AVER.

A2 - Select

In the Select operation, we use the set constructor to describe the result as a set of tuples of a given type - a record type defined to represent the intention of some relation, taken from the corresponding relation - the variable that represents its extension, based on a select condition using its attributes.

```
res!  =  { t1 : Rel1  |  t IN rel1  AND  <condition> }
```

where <condition> is a boolean expression involving at least one of the attributes of t1, i.e., relation rel1.

A3 - Theta-Join

Theta-Joins, the most general form of joins, are described in a similar way but more than one relation is used and a join condition is specified, based on attribute(s) of all relations.

```
res!  =  { t1:Rel1; t2:Rel2 ...  |  t1 IN rel1  AND  t2 IN rel2 ...
                 AND   t1.Att1 <cop> t2.Att2   ... }
```

where <cop> is a comparison operator, and Att1 and Att2 are attributes of rel1 and rel2 respectively.

A4 - Project

The (extended) Project operation is similar to the select operation, the difference being the inclusion of the result, based on computations of some attributes of the qualifying tuples.

```
res!  =  { t1 : Rel1  |  t1 IN rel1  .  <result> }
```

where `<result>` is an expression that applied to **t1** gives a tuple of type **A**, such that all its attributes are attributes of **Rel1**. The type of **res!** is **SET A**.

A5 - Update applications

Update applications will be specified by schemas that (1) include the "Delta" schema (D4), (2) declare the input (if any) variables of the operations - normally there will be no output variables, and (3) their predicates describe the updates in one or more relations of the database according to one of the four following rules - A6 to A9.

A6 - Insert

A schema that describes inserting of tuples in a given relation will have one input variable - the set of tuples to be inserted - and its predicate will state that the updated relation is the set union (+) of the original relation and the input variable.

```
VAR  sr1? : SET Rel1;
rel1'  =  rel1  +  sr1?
```

A7 - Update

A schema that describes updating of tuples in a given relation will be specified in terms of (1) a select condition, that determines the set of tuples to be updated, and (2) an update rule, that gives the updated tuple for each tuple selected. The predicate will state that the relation after the operation is the union of the set of updated tuples with the set of tuples which were not selected.

```
rel1'  =  { t : Rel1  |  t IN rel1  AND  NOT <condition> }
       +  { t : Rel1  |  t IN rel1  AND  <condition>  .  <result> }
```

where `<condition>` is a boolean expression based on attributes of **rel1**, and `<result>` is an expression that, applied to **t**, gives the corresponding updated tuple. `<result>` may be any expression of type **Rel1** but usually is an expression like

```
t  BUT (Att1=v1, Att2=v2, ...)
```

such that **Att1**, **Att2**, etc are the modified attributes, and **v1**, **v2**, etc are expressions that give the updated values for these attributes. This is particularly useful because these specifications need not to be changed if, for instance, a new attribute is included in the corresponding relation.

A8 - Delete by primary key

For each relation, there will be a corresponding schema that specifies deletions based on its primary key. Such schemas will have one input variable - the primary keys of the tuples to be deleted - and their predicates will use the DELETE operator to describe the operation. DELETE from relation **rel1**, based on its primary key **Pk1**, the tuples with keys in the set **sk1?**, giving the relation after the operation **rel1'**, is presented below. Its result is a boolean, *true* when the operation is successful and *false* otherwise.

```
VAR  sk1? : SET Type1;
DELETE  rel1  Pk1  sk1?  rel1'
```

When the primary key of the relation is the target of one or more foreign keys, either in other relations or in the same relation, the predicates of these schemas must also specify what happens to all references for deleted tuples, in order to avoid violations of the referential integrity rule.

In general, there are at least three possibilities [3], *Restricted*, *Cascades* and *Nullifies*, that, for each foreign key, will be specified according to the rules A8.1, A8.2 and A8.3, respectively. For this purpose, assume that attribute **Fk2** of relation **rel2** is a foreign key for attribute **Pk1** of relation **rel1**, **rel2** not necessarily different from **rel1**, and that **sk1?** is the set of values of **Pk1** to be deleted.

A8.1 - Deletes restricted

When *Restricted* is chosen, deletes are performed only if there is no foreign reference to any of the tuples selected. In this case, the predicate of the schema that specifies deletes in relation **rel1** must include the following equation:

```
NOT ( EXIST  t2 : Rel2  |  t2 IN rel2  .  t2.Fk2 IN sk1? )
```

A8.2 - Deletes cascade

When *Cascades* is specified, every tuple where there is a foreign reference to a deleted tuple is also deleted. The way this constraint is specified depends on whether **rel2** is different from **rel1** or not.

If **rel2** is another relation - and usually this is the case, the schema that specifies deletes in relation **rel1** must include the expression

```
PRED  Delete_Rel2 [sdr2 / sk2?]   WHERE
        sdr2 = { t:Rel2 | t IN rel2 AND t.fk2 IN sk1?  .  t.pk2 }
```

where Delete_Rel2 is the schema that specifies deletes for relation **rel2** based on its primary key **Pk2**, **sk2?** is the input variable of that schema, the **WHERE** clause introduces a local variable, and the notation [a / b] refers to the substitution of variables **b** by **a** in the referred schema. In practice, the equation above means "use **Delete_Rel2** to delete the tuples of relation **rel2** that reference any of the deleted tuples of **rel1**".

When **rel1** and **rel2** are the same relation, there will be recursive deletions of tuples from the relation. To specify such deletions, we will use the operator CASC_DELETE, and the **WHERE** clause to state that the input relation for CASC_DELETE is the output relation of DELETE. CASC_DELETE takes five parameters: the foreign key **Fk2**, and the four parameters of delete. The resulting predicate is shown below.

```
CASC_DELETE  Fk2  r  Pk1  sk2  rel1'   WHERE
    ( DELETE  rel1  PK1  sk1?  r   AND
      sk2 = { t:Rel1 | t IN rel1  AND  t.Fk2 IN sk1?  .  t.Pk1 } )
```

The above predicate represents recursive deletions in **rel1** beginning with the set of keys originally selected for deletions (**sk1?**). Consequently, it is equivalent to

```
CASC_DELETE  Fk2  rel1  Pk1  sk1?  rel1'
```

which is simpler.

A8.3 - Deletes nullifies

Finally, *Nullifies* changes all foreign references for deleted tuples to contain the null value and this constraint will be specified using the operator UPDATE.

UPDATE takes four parameters: the relation to be updated and one of its attributes, a set of values of this attribute, and a new value for this attribute. Its effect is to update the attribute to the new value, in all tuples where its old value is a member of the set of values given.

```
rel2'  =  UPDATE  rel2  Fk2  sk1?  <null>
```

where <null> is the null value for the type of **Fk2** and, consequently, the type of **Pk1**.

When **rel1** and **rel2** are the same relation, we have to use the WHERE clause, and a local variable, to join the equation above with the one that specifies the deletions (A8) because, in this case, we want the result of one operation to be the input to the other. The order of the equations does not make any difference, and we chose the case in which the references are nullified first and, then, the tuples are deleted.

```
DELETE  r  Pk1  sk1?  rel1'   WHERE
        r  =  UPDATE  rel1  Fk2  sk1?  <null>
```

A9 - Other deletes

Any other deletes will be specified in terms of the ones defined by the schemas of rule A8, i.e., the deletes based on the primary key of the relations. This will be achieved by using a substitution of variables, the WHERE clause, and a selection of tuples of the relation, projected over its primary key.

```
PRED  Delete_Rel1  [sdr1 / sk1?]   WHERE
      sdr1 = { t:Rel1 | t IN rel1  AND  <condition>  .  t.Pk1 }
```

where <condition> is a boolean expression based on one or more attributes of t.

2.3   Specification of extended operations for error handling

Basically, the method provides two different ways for the specification of the extended operations including error handling. The first one, very simple, is suitable for more abstract specifications and states that the database is not modified if an error occur, and provides a variable (**result!**) that says whether the operation was successful or not. This possibility is described by rules E1, E2 and E3 below.

E1 - The schema OK

The Schema Ok, that will be used in both possibilities for error handling, is specified below. In fact, **Ok** may be provided together with the pre-defined operators and, so, there is no need to specify it again.

```
SCHEMA Ok;
VAR  result! : STRING;
PREDICATE
   result!  =  "Success"
END Ok;
```

E2 - The schema Error

The schema error states that there will be no change in the relations of the database and that the result is not "Success".

```
SCHEMA Error  =  Equiv_DB  AND  NOT Ok;
```

E3 - The extended operations

Now, the extended operations, e.g. Insert_rel1, are specified by extending their original specifications to describe what happens if any error occurs. Basically, we specify that, for correct inputs, there will be no change in the other relations and the result will be "success" (Ok). Otherwise, no change will be done in the database (Error) and a specific message will be put in result!.

```
SCHEMA Insert_rel1  =  (  Insert_rel1_Ok   AND    Ok      AND
                          ( Equiv_DB \ rel1 )  )
                OR  ( Error | result! = "Error in Insert_rel1" );
```

where Insert_rel1_Ok is the schema that describes inserts in relation rel1, Equiv_DB is the schema described in rule A5, and \ is the hiding operator.

Loosely speaking, hiding a variable from a schema means that this variable does not satisfy the predicate of the schema. Consequently, we should have hidden both variables (rel1 and rel1'). However, in this specific case (the "Equiv" schemas), it does not make any difference, and we decided to make it simpler for the user.

In the second possibility, suitable for more concrete specifications, i.e., specifications targeted at an implementation, the specifications explicitly state what are the possible errors[2] and give a specific message for each of them. The two following rules, E4 and E5, describe this second approach to error handling.

E4 - The error schemas

For each application using the database, there will be a corresponding error schema, that will describe the possible errors that may occur. Basically, each of these schemas will (1) include the "Equiv" schema, because no change is done in the relations when errors occur, (2) introduce the variable result! to keep the error message, (3) declare all input variables (if any) declared by the corresponding schema that deals with the correct behaviour of the operation, because they will be involved in some of the possible errors, and (4) describe. in its predicate, what are the possible errors, and which messages correspond to each of them. The main parts of such an error schema is presented below.

---

[2] In order to identify all possible error conditions, one must simplify, using logical equivalences, the negation of the preconditions of the corresponding schema that describes the correct behaviour of the operation. Limitations of space do not permit the presentation of this relatively simple process.

```
INCLUDE Equiv_DB;          (1)
VAR  result! : STRING;      (2)
     <input_variables>;     (3)
( <error_1>  AND  result! = "message_1" )   OR   ...   (4)
( <error_n>  AND  result! = "message_n" )
```

where `<input_variables>` is the declaration of all input variables of the corresponding schema that deals with the correct behaviour of the operation, `<error_1>`, etc are the possible errors, and `"message_1"`, etc, the corresponding error messages.

E5 - Application schemas

The schemas that describe the applications, e.g. Insert_rel1, will then be specified similarly to the ones prescribed by rule E3, but, now, the specific error schemas are used in substitution to the general schema Error.

```
SCHEMA Insert_rel1  =  (  Insert_rel1_Ok   AND   Ok      AND
                          ( Equiv_DB \ rel1 )  )
                   OR  Insert_rel1_Error;
```

where Insert_rel1_Ok, Ok and Equiv_DB are as described in E3, and Insert_rel1_Error is the schema described according to E4.

3 Defining operators formally

Now we show the definition of the operators that will be used in the specification of relational databases and of applications, informally introduced last section.

The specification follows the style of "Literate Specification", a style where comments are free and the lines of formal text begin with >. This style was originally advocated for programming [9] and will be adopted in the rest of the paper. Its main advantage is that it allows a natural merging of the specifications with the informal text in the same document, that could possibly be read by tools like a type-checker or a compiler without any modification.

3.1 Primary and candidate keys

The KEY_OF operator, used to specify that a specific attribute of a relation is a key (primary or candidate), is defined below and takes two parameters: a relation (its type is **SET A**) and an attribute of the tuple of this relation (its type is **(A->B)**, a function from the tuple to the value of the attribute). **A** and **B** are generic types.

```
> OP KEY_OF [A, B]  :  SET A  ->  (A->B)  ->  BOOL;
>
> PREDICATE
>
>    ( FORALL  rel : SET A;  Att : (A->B)  .
>
>          KEY_OF  rel  Att   <=>
>
>                    ( FORALL  t1, t2 : A  |  {t1, t2} <= rel  .
>
>                         Att t1 = Att t2   <=>   t1 = t2 )  )
>
> END KEY_OF;
```

The predicate of KEY_OF states that, for every pair of tuples of the relation having the same value for the attribute, the tuples are identical, i.e., they are in fact the same tuple. This means that every tuple of the relation must have a different value for the chosen attribute.

3.2 Foreign keys

The operator FOREIGN_KEY will be used to define Foreign Keys. This operator takes five arguments: a value of type C, that represents the null value for this type, the relation where the foreign key is, the foreign key attribute, and the relation and its primary key referred by the foreign key.

```
> OP FOREIGN_KEY [A, B, C]  :  C  ->  SET A  ->  (A->C)  ->
>
>                                         SET B  ->  (B->C)  ->  BOOL;
>
> PREDICATE
>
>    (  FORALL  null : C;  rel2 : SET A;  Fk2 : (A->C);
>
>                              rel1 : SET B;  Pk1 : (B->C)  .
>
>          FOREIGN_KEY  null  rel2  Fk2  rel1  Pk1    <=>
>
>            ( KEY_OF  rel1  Pk1                         AND
>
>              ( FORALL t2 : A  |  t2 IN rel2  .
>
>                   Fk2  t2  =  null                    OR
>
>                   ( EXIST  t1 : B  |  t1 IN rel1  .
>
>                        Pk1  t1  =  Fk2  t2 )  )  )  )
> END FOREIGN_KEY;
```

The above predicate states that attribute **Fk2** of relation **rel2** is a foreign key targeted at attribute **PK1** of relation **rel1**, and that **Pk1** is a key (in fact the primary key) of **rel1**. **rel1** is not necessarily different from **rel2**.

3.3 Null values

We are not going to dedicate too much time to the treatment of missing information, nulls, null values, marks or whatever, for the following reasons:

- There is no universally accepted approach for the treatment of nulls and it is not our aim to give a different treatment for each possible approach. On the contrary, our aim is simply to show one basic approach and leave the possibility of the specification of other approaches by different users of the method.

- The treatment for nulls is in general dependent on the specific DBMS and we intend our method to be independent of specific DBMSs.

- A number of proposals such as [2] consider the extension of the boolean type for a 4-boolean values type. However, no DBMS actually supports this approach, it is not completely accepted, and its specification would involve a large number of types and operators definitions and is beyond the scope of this paper.

Independently of the approach chosen for nulls, we will use an operator called NOT_NULL to specify that a specific attribute of a relation is mandatory, i.e., it cannot be null (missing). NOT_NULL, presented below, takes three arguments: a value of type **B**, that represents the null value for this type, a relation, and an attribute of the relation.

```
> OP NOT_NULL [A, B]  :  B -> SET A -> (A->B) -> BOOL;
> PREDICATE
>
>     ( FORALL null : B; rel : SET A; Att : (A->B)    .
>
>          NOT_NULL rel Att   <=>
>
>               ( FORALL t : A | t IN rel . Att t <> null ) )
>
> END NOT_NULL;
```

We would like to state that we are not advocating that this operator is universal and does not need to be changed, independently of the approach chosen. However, it seems likely that this is true, at least for several approaches.

In this paper, we are going to adopt Date's proposal called the default values approach [3], slightly modified to avoid the choice of different values for different attributes that are based on the same basic type. It was chosen because is very simple, and is presented below.

(A) Null values

There will be one constant definition for each basic type. These constants named NULLINT, NULNAT, NULLREAL, NULLSTR and NULLCHAR will represent the null values for the types INT, NAT, REAL, STRING and CHAR, respectively. We assume that their values will be zero, for types INT, NAT and REAL, the empty string for STRING and space for CHAR, but their definitions may be changed by the users.

```
> CONST  NULLINT  : INT     = 0;
>
>        NULLNAT  : NAT     = 0;
>
>        NULLREAL : REAL    = 0;
>
>        NULLSTR  : STRING  = "";
>
>        NULLCHAR : CHAR    = ' ';
```

(B) The REQUIRED operators

In order to simplify the specification of constraints that state that specific attributes cannot be missing, we introduce the operator REQUIRED below. In fact there will be five definitions (overloaded) that, for each of the basic types, instantiate the operator NOT_NULL (already defined) by giving the corresponding constant as the first parameter.

```
> OP REQUIRED [A]  =  NOT_NULL [A,INT]      NULLINT;
>
> OP REQUIRED [A]  =  NOT_NULL [A,NAT]      NULLINAT;
>
> OP REQUIRED [A]  =  NOT_NULL [A,REAL]     NULLREAL;
>
> OP REQUIRED [A]  =  NOT_NULL [A,STRING]   NULLSTR;
>
> OP REQUIRED [A]  =  NOT_NULL [A,CHAR]     NULLCHAR;
```

One of the REQUIRED operators resulting from these definitions is presented below to facilitate its understanding, and must be seen as a comment only. It corresponds to the instantiation of the first parameter of NOT_NULL using the constant NULLINT of type INT.

```
! OP REQUIRED [A]  :  SET A  ->  (A->INT)  ->  BOOL;
! PREDICATE
!    ( FORALL  rel : SET A;  Att : (A->INT)    .
!        REQUIRED  rel  Att   <=>
!            ( FORALL  t : A  |  t IN rel  .  Att t  <>  NULLINT )  )
! END REQUIRED;
```

Obviously, the REQUIRED operators are only syntactic sugar. However, using them allows the specification of this type of constraints to be done uniformly and independently of the types of the attributes [2].

(C) The FOR_KEY operators

Similarly, we define overloaded operators called FOR_KEY by partial parametrizations of FOREIGN_KEY on its first parameter.

```
> OP  FOR_KEY [A,B]  =  FOREIGN_KEY [A,B,INT]     NULLINT;
>
> OP  FOR_KEY [A,B]  =  FOREIGN_KEY [A,B,NAT]     NULLNAT;
>
> OP  FOR_KEY [A,B]  =  FOREIGN_KEY [A,B,REAL]    NULLREAL;
>
> OP  FOR_KEY [A,B]  =  FOREIGN_KEY [A,B,STRING]  NULLSTR;
>
> OP  FOR_KEY [A,B]  =  FOREIGN_KEY [A,B,CHAR]    NULLCHAR;
```

In this approach, nulls are in fact valid values that are used for this specific purpose. Consequently, the users must be aware that comparison operators treat these null values identically to all other values. So, these values must be explicitly excluded of the context of the comparisons, when necessary.

In particular, joins based on attributes that both allow nulls, or not based on the equality, usually require the explicit exclusion of nulls. However, because most joins are equi-joins based on a primary-key, and primary-keys do not accept nulls, this will rarely be necessary.

3.4 Other operators

Now we show auxiliary operators that will be used to simplify the specification of operations such as update and delete.

The first of them, UPDATE, simplifies the specification of updates for a specific attribute **Att** of a given relation **rel**. It will be used in the specification of the *Nullifies* effect on foreign key references - rule A8.3, and in the update of primary keys, which is not presented in this paper.

The effect of UPDATE is to change the value of attribute **Att** to **new** for those tuples in **rel** where the value of **Att** is a member of **old**.

```
> OP UPDATE [A, B]  :  SET A  ->  (A->B)  ->  SET B  ->  B  ->  SET A;
> PREDICATE
>    ( FORALL  rel : SET A;  Att : (A->B);  old : SET B;  new:B  .
>         UPDATE  rel  Att  old  new  =
>                 { t : A  |  t IN rel   AND   Att t  NOTIN  old } +
>                 { t : A  |  t IN rel   AND   Att t  IN  old  .
>                                            t BUT (Att=new) }  )
> END UPDATE;
```

The next one, DELETE, will be used to specify deletes in a given relation (**rel**) based on a given set of values (**sv**) of a specific attribute (**Att**), usually the primary key of the relation. The result (**rel'**) is the relation after the operation.

```
> OP DELETE [A, B] : SET A  ->  (A->B)  ->  SET B  ->  SET A  ->  BOOL;
> PREDICATE
>    ( FORALL  rel, rel' : SET A;  Att : (A->B);  sv : SET B  .
>         DELETE  rel  Att  sv  rel'  <=>
>             ( ( FORALL  v : B  |  v IN sv  .
>                  ( EXIST t :A  |  t IN rel  .  Att t = v ) )  AND
>             rel'  =  { t:A | t IN rel   AND   Att t NOTIN sv } )  )
> END DELETE;
```

The operator CASC_DELETE, specified below, is recursive and will be used to represent recursive cascade deletes over a relation, i.e., when there is a foreign key for the relation where it is defined and *Cascades* are specified for deletes.

```
> OP CASC_DELETE [A, B]  :  (A->B)  ->  SET A  ->  (A->B)  ->
>                                      SET B  ->  SET A  ->  BOOL;
> PREDICATE
>    ( FORALL  F:(A->B);  rel, rel' : SET A;  P:(A->B);  sb : SET B  .
>         ( EXIST  sb1 : SET B  |
>                 sb1  =  { t:A  |  t IN rel
>                                      AND   F t IN sb  .  P t }  .
>             ( sb1 = { }  =>  CASC_DELETE F  =  DELETE )   AND
>             ( sb1 <> { }  =>
>                   CASC_DELETE  F  rel  P  sb  rel'  =
>                        ( CASC_DELETE  F  r  P  sb1  rel'
>                           WHERE   DELETE  rel  P  sb  r ) ) ) )
> END CASC_DELETE;
```

Basically, CASC_DELETE represents recursive applications of DELETE such that the set of foreign key references in each step (sb1) will be the set of primary keys of tuples to be deleted in the following step. The recursion stops when there is no foreign reference to delete (sb1 is the empty set).

4 Specifying a simple example using the method

In this section we are going to apply the method to the specification of a simple **Department-Employee** Relational Database and its applications. In order to make the understanding of the method easier, the formal specification of the example is merged with informal comments that describe the specifications and make references to the rules of the method used in each step.

The section is subdivided into three subsections: the first one shows the specification of the database itself, the second specifies the applications, and the last deals with the extension of the specification of the applications to deal with error handling.

4.1 Specification of a simple Department-Employee Database

Now we begin the specification of the Database itself, what includes the definition of the relations, with their attributes, and the specification of the constraints that must be guaranteed. The types of the tuples, of each relation of the database being specified, are defined below, according to rule D1 in the description of the method.

```
> TYPE
>
>    Dept  = ( Code : NAT,      Name : STRING,      Num_emp : NAT );
>
>    Empl  = ( Num  : NAT,      Name : STRING,      Age : NAT,
>
>              Dept : NAT,      Sup  : NAT                       );
```

Each relation is specified in a separate schema as a set of tuples of the appropriate type (D2) and including the specification of invariants. The departments relation and constraints are specified in the schema Depart, using the operators REQUIRED and KEY_OF, according to rules D2.1 and D2.2, respectively.

```
> SCHEMA Depart;                          // Invariants of Departments
>
> VAR  depts  :  SET Dept;
>
> PREDICATE
>
>    REQUIRED  depts  Code      AND      REQUIRED  depts  Name      AND
>
>    KEY_OF    depts  Code
>
> END Depart;
```

The Schema Employee is defined in a similar way, below, and adds an extra invariant about the Age of employees (it must be less than 120), following D2.3.

```
> SCHEMA Employee;                          // Invariants of Employees
>
> VAR  empls  :  SET Empl;
>
> PREDICATE
>    REQUIRED  empls  Num      AND      REQUIRED  empls  Name      AND
>
>    REQUIRED  empls  Dept                                         AND
>
>    KEY_OF    empls  Num                                          AND
>
>    ( FORALL  e : Empl  |  e IN empls  .  e.Age < 120  )
>
> END Employee;
```

The Schema DB aggregates all the definitions (D3) and specifies all the constraints that involve more than one relation. This includes the definitions of the foreign keys, using the operator FOR_KEY (D3.1) and of derived attributes (D3.2).

```
> SCHEMA DB;                      //  The specification of the Database State
>
> INCLUDE Depart, Employee;
>
> PREDICATE
>    FOR_KEY   empls  Sup    empls  Num                                  AND
>    FOR_KEY   empls  Dept   depts  Code                                 AND
>    ( FORALL d : Dept  |  d IN depts  .
>          d.Num_emp  =  # { e:Empl  |  e IN empls
>                                    AND   e.Dept = d.Code }  )
> END DB;
```

According to rules D4 and D5, the schemas Delta_DB are EQUIV_DB are defined below. Delta_DB groups the database states before (DB) and after (DB/'/) the operations over the database. Equiv_DB uses Delta_DB to add the constraint that no change is done in the database, i.e., the database states before and after the operation are the same.

```
> SCHEMA Delta_DB  =  DB  AND  DB/'/;

> SCHEMA Equiv_DB  =  ( Delta_DB  |  TUPLE DB = TUPLE DB/'/ );
```

4.2 Specification of the Applications using the Database

Now, we are going to specify a number of applications (operations) using the Database. Initially, we present read-only operations (A1) using the set constructor to describe the result of the query and illustrate the specification of selects, joins and projects, according to the rules A2, A3 and A4, respectively.

The first of these specifies a simple select (employees of department d?) and is presented below. The meaning of the first equation of its predicate is: "Exists d1 of type Dept, taken from depts, such that its Code is d?".

```
> SCHEMA Employees_dept_Ok;      // Employees of department d? (Select)
>
> INCLUDE Equiv_DB;
>
> VAR  d? : NAT;
>      empl_d! : SET Empl;
>
> PREDICATE
>    ( EXIST d1 : Dept  |  d1 IN depts  .  d1.Code = d?  )        AND
>    empl_d!  =  { e : Empl  |  e IN empls   AND   e.Dept = d? }
> END Employees_dept_Ok;
```

The schema Names_empl_Ok gives the names of all employees from department whose name is name? and illustrates the use of Selects, Joins and Projects in a single query.

```
> SCHEMA Names_empl_Ok;        //  Names of all empls from dept whose name
>                              //  is  name?  ->  Select, Join and Project
> INCLUDE Equiv_DB;
>
> VAR  name? : STRING;
>
>     names_empl! : SET (Name : STRING);
>
> PREDICATE
>    ( EXIST  d1 : Dept  |  d1 IN depts  .  d1.Name = name?  )        AND
>
>    names_empl!  =  { d:Dept; e:Empl | d IN depts  AND  e IN empls
>
>                                 AND   d.Name = name?      // Select
>
>                                 AND   d.Code = e.Dept     // Join
>
>                                  .    (Name=e.Name)    }   // Project
>
> END Names_empl_Ok;
```

The next schema specifies the insertion of new departments and is presented below. It is the first of the update operations (A5) and uses the set union to add new tuples (input) to the relation, as prescribed by rule A6.

```
> SCHEMA Insert_dept_Ok;                          //  Insert  a  department
>
> INCLUDE Delta_DB;
>
> VAR  sd? : SET Dept;
>
> PREDICATE
>    depts'  =  depts + sd?
>
> END Insert_dept_Ok;
```

The schema Move_ empl_Ok, presented below, changes the department of a given employee e? to d?, and exemplifies the specification of updates of tuples, according to rules A5 and A7.

```
> SCHEMA Move_empl_Ok;             //  Move employee e? to department d?
>
> INCLUDE Delta_DB;
>
> VAR  e?, d? : NAT;
>
> PREDICATE
>    ( EXIST   e1 : Empl  |  e1 IN empls  .  e1.Num = e?         )  AND
>
>    ( EXIST   d1 : Dept  |  d1 IN depts  .  d1.Code = d?        )  AND
>
>    empls'  =  { e1 : Empl  |  e1 IN empls   AND   e1.Num <> e? }
>
>             + { e1 : Empl  |  e1 IN empls   AND   e1.Num = e?  .
>
>                                            e1 BUT (Dept = d?) }
>
> END Move_empl_Ok;
```

Now we show the specification of a schema to delete a set of tuples of depts based on its primary key (Code), rules A5 and A8. The schema also specifies what happens to tuples of other relations (empls in this case) where there is a foreign reference to deleted departments - rules A8.1, A8.2 and A8.3.

```
> SCHEMA Delete_depts_Ok;          // Delete  one  or  more  departments
>
> INCLUDE Delta_DB;
>
> VAR  sd? : SET NAT;         // Set of keys of departments to be deleted
>
> PREDICATE
>
>    DELETE  depts  Code  sd?  depts'                                AND
>
>
>    //  We chose (Deletes) CASCADES, for the foreign key Dept in empls
>
>    PRED Delete_empls_Ok  [sde / se?]    WHERE
>
>         sde = {e:Empl | e IN empls  AND  e.Dept IN sd? . e.Num}
>
!    //  If RESTRICTED were chosen, the specification would be:
!
!    NOT ( EXIST e : Empl |  e IN empls  .  e.Dept IN sd? )
!
!
!    //  Finally, if NULLIFIES were chosen, the specification would be:
!
!    empls'  =  UPDATE  empls  Dept  sd?  NULLNAT
>
> END Delete_depts_Ok;
```

Because we are using literate specification, the lines beginning with ! are simply comments.

In a similar way, we specify deletions of employees. The only difference is the fact that, in this case, there is a foreign key whose target is in the same relation. In spite of this, this special case is also described by rules A8.1, A8.2 and A8.3.

```
> SCHEMA Delete_empls_Ok;            // Delete  one  or  more  employees
>
> INCLUDE Delta_DB;
>
> VAR  se? : SET NAT;         // Set of keys of employees to be deleted
>
> PREDICATE
>
>    // We chose (Deletes) NULLIFIES, for the foreign key Sup  in empls
>
>    ( DELETE  e  Num  se?  empls'   WHERE
>
>              e  =  UPDATE  empls  Sup  se?  NULLNAT )
>
!    // If CASCADES were chosen, the specification would be:
!
!    CASC_DELETE  Sup  empls  Num  se?  empls'
!
!
!    // Finally, if RESTRICTED were chosen, the specification would be:
!
!    DELETE  empls  Num  se?  empls'                                 AND
!
!    NOT ( EXIST  e : Empl |  e IN empls  .  e.Sup IN se? )
>
> END Delete_empls_Ok;
```

Any other deletions on either of these relations may be specified in terms of the schemas already defined (rule A9). For example, the deletion of all employees of a given department is presented below in terms of Delete_empls_Ok.

```
> SCHEMA Delete_empl_dept_Ok;      // Delete employees of department d?
>
> INCLUDE Delta_DB;
>
> VAR  d? : NAT;
>
> PREDICATE
>
>    ( EXIST  d1 : Dept  |  d1 IN depts  .  d1.Code = d?  )          AND
>
>    PRED  Delete_empls_Ok  [sde / se?]   WHERE
>
>           sde = {e:Empl | e IN empls  AND  e.Dept = d? . e.Num}
>
> END Delete_empl_dept_Ok;
```

4.3   Extending the Specifications to capture Error Handling

Now we are going to show the specification of schemas that extend the operations to capture error handling. We will extend only one of the applications - in particular the schema Insert_dept_Ok, using both approaches described in subsection 2.3.

In order to use the first approach, we introduce the schema Error, below (E2), that is specific for this database but general in the sense that it is used to extend all applications. We assume that the schema Ok (E1) is provided together with the operators.

```
> SCHEMA Error  =  Equiv_DB  AND  NOT Ok;
```

Then, we present the specification of Insert_dept, by extending the specification of Insert_dept_Ok to describe what happens if any error occurs. As described in E3, we specify that, for correct inputs, there will be no change in the other relations and the result will be "success" (Ok). Otherwise, no change will be done in the database (Error) and a specific message will be put in **result!**.

```
> SCHEMA Insert_dept  =  (  Insert_dept_Ok   AND   Ok    AND
>
>                          ( Equiv_DB \ depts )  )
>
>                 OR  ( Error | result! = "Error in Insert_dept" );
```

As explained before, we did not hide **depts'**, together with **depts**, because, in this case (the schema Equiv_DB), it does not make any difference and we decided to make it simpler for the user.

For the second approach, we specify a specific error schema for the operation being extended, Insert_dept_Error in this example, according to E4.

```
> SCHEMA Insert_dept_Error;
>
> INCLUDE Equiv_DB;
>
> VAR  result! : STRING;
>
>      sd? : SET Dept;
>
> PREDICATE
>
>    ( ( EXIST  d : Dept  |  d IN sd?  .  d.Code = NULLNAT )  AND
>
>      result!  =  "Code_is_missing"                          )  OR
>
```

```
>     (  ( EXIST  d : Dept  |  d IN sd?  .  d.Name = NULLSTR )  AND
>
>       result!  =  "Name_is_missing"                        )    OR
>
>     (  ( EXIST  d : Dept  |  d IN sd?  .
>
>           ( EXIST  d1 : Dept  |  d1 IN (depts + sd?)
>
>                                      d1.Code = d.Code )  )  AND
>
>       result!  =  "Duplicated_department_primary_key"       )    OR
>
>     (  ( EXIST  d : Dept  |  d IN sd?  .  d.Num_emp <> 0 )   AND
>
>       result!  =  "Invalid_number_of_employees"            )
>
> END Insert_Dept_Error;
```

These four possible errors, specified in the predicate of the above schema, are the result of the simplification of the equation NOT (PRE Insert_dept_Ok), as prescribed by the method.

Now, the extended schema Insert_dept is specified, according to rule E5.

```
> SCHEMA Insert_dept  =  (  Insert_dept_Ok   AND   Ok      AND
>
>                              ( Equiv_DB \ depts )  )
>
>                    OR  Insert_dept_Error;
```

5 Conclusion

In general, the utilization of mathematical methods in formal specification allows the description of the fundamental properties of the system without regard to a particular implementation strategy. Our method, however, is specifically intended to be used in the formal specification of relational applications and, consequently, it should lead to specifications which are amenable to implementation using relational DBMSs. Even so, the specification does not address issues of system performance or indeed difficulty of implementation for a particular RDBMS.

We believe this method for the specification of relational databases and their applications achieves the proposed objectives. Firstly, it provides a simple way of specifying relational database applications formally. Secondly, it is generic and may be the first step in the direction of the formal development of database applications and of specification standardization in this context. Thirdly, it deals not only with the correct behaviour of the operations, but with the specification of errors also. Finally, because of its ease-of-use, it may be applied to the specification and documentation of relational database systems.

We note that the choice of Zc in this paper does not preclude using Z. The method is fully compatible with Z, i.e., there is a corresponding Z specification to every Zc specification prescribed by the method. This means that the method is generic and that different users may use different specification languages to specify their applications.

One possible extension to our method refers to the modularization of the specifications that result from the application of the method. This can be achieved by using the modularization structures **Document** and **Chapter** of Zc, also proposed for incorporation in Z [10], that were used to modularize the specification of real life systems, such as a Student Records Control System [11] and the Interface of a Hypertext System [12], with good results.

The idea is to split the specification of systems (documents) into several modules (chapters) based on the connections between objects. Specifically, the specification of complex databases should be split into several Chapters based on the connections between the relations, and this would result in a specification which is modular and, therefore, easier to understand. The problems that may arise from such a separation and a detailed explanation of what is needed to avoid these problems are subject of current work.

The full treatment for error handling, including the summarization of all possible errors for each operation, together with an example of the simplification process involved, is also subject of current work.

There are a number of other possible directions in which this research could be advanced. We will investigate generating database prototypes directly from the formal specifications that result from using the method. Specifically, we are investigating the problems involved in the generation of prototype database applications, through a simple translation process, for RDBMSs offering SQL [13] as their data-sublanguages, e.g. DB2 [14], and intend to do the same for RDBMSs offering QUEL [15].

We also intend investigating whether the method could be adapted for specifying O-O DBMS [16] applications. It may be that a "family" of specification methods are required, starting with a very general method for specifying applications (systems) according to some very-high level data model, e.g. enhanced ER model [17, 18]. Such a specification would then be subject to refinement into a specification targeted at a particular data model, e.g. relational or object-oriented, expressed in terms of its own specification method.

6 Acknowledgements

We would like to thank John Hughes and Moira Norrie, for many useful comments and suggestions on previous versions of this paper, and Silvio Meira, who was co-author of the first paper on this work.

References

[1] Codd E. F.; "A Relational Model of Data for Large Shared Data Banks", Communications of ACM, Vol. 13, June 1970.

[2] Codd E. F.; "The Relational Model for Database Management", Version 2, Reading, Mass: Addison-Wesley, 1990.

[3] Date C. J.; "An Introduction to Database Systems", vol. 1, Fifth Edition, Addison-Wesley, 1990.

[4] Sampaio A. C. and Meira S. L.; "Zc: A Notation for Complex Systems Specification" (In portuguese), XV SEMISH, SBC Brazilian Congress, Rio de Janeiro, July 1988.

[5] Sampaio A. C.; "Zc: A Notation for Complex Systems Specification" (In portuguese). M.Sc. Thesis, Depto. de Informática, UFPE, Brazil, November 1988.

[6] Hayes I. (ed); "Specification Case Studies", Prentice Hall International (UK) Ltd, 1987.

[7] Spivey J. M.; "The Z Notation: A Reference Manual", Prentice Hall International (UK) Ltd, 1989.

[8] Barros R. S. M. and Harper D. J.; "Formal Specification of Relational Database Applications: A Methodology", Report, Department of Computing Science, University of Glasgow, In preparation.

[9] Knuth D.; "Literate Programming", Computer Journal, Vol. 17, May 1984.

[10] Sampaio A. C. and Meira S. L.; "Modular Extensions to Z", proceedings of VDM'90 - VDM and Z!, Springer-Verlag, 1990.

[11] Barros R. S. M.; "Formal Specification of very large Software: A Real Example" (In portuguese), M.Sc. Thesis, Depto. de Informática, UFPE, Brazil, October 1988.

[12] Vasconcelos A.; "Specifying the Interface of a Hypertext System" (In portuguese). M.Sc. Thesis, Depto. de Informática, UFPE, Brazil, August 1989.

[13] American National Standards Institute; "The Database Language SQL", Document ANSI X3.135, 1986.

[14] Date C. J. and White C. J.; "A Guide to DB2", Third Edition, Addison-Wesley, 1989.

[15] Relational Technology Inc.; "INGRES/QUEL Reference Manual", Alameda, California, 1988.

[16] Zdonik S. B. and Maier D. (Eds); "Readings in Object-Oriented Databases Systems", Morgan Kaufmann Pub. Inc., 1990.

[17] Chen P. P. S.; "The Entity-Relationship Model - Toward a Unified View of Data", ACM TODS 1, No. 1, March 1976.

[18] Elmasri R. and Navathe S. B.; "Fundamentals of Database Systems", The Benjamin/Cummings Publishing Company Inc., 1989.

Formal Definition of Nested Relations by Syntactical Mappings[1]

Stefano Ceri   and   Stefano Crespi Reghizzi
Dipartimento di Elettronica
Politecnico di Milano
Piazza Leonardo, 32 - Milano, Italy 20133

Abstract

A new approach to the formal definition of nested relational data-structures and operators is proposed, based on syntactical mappings. Schemes of relations are viewed as Extended BNF, non-recursive grammars, and instances of the database as sentences generated by the grammar. Then most algebraic operators are conveniently expressed as syntax-directed translations. The method is applied to a large subset of ALGRES, an extended relational system, and compared with more traditional definitional techniques.

1 Introduction

In order to apply the relational data-base model to more complex application areas, the original model of Codd has been recently extended in several directions: complex attribute domains have been allowed, moving away from the 1st normal form assumption, new operators (such as transitive closure) have been introduced to obtain computational completeness, ordering and repetition of tuples have been considered, and null or undefined values of several types have been proposed.

Here we focus on the first extension, where relations are considered as valid attribute domains; this leads to the so called *non-1st-normal-form* or *nested relational model* (NRM). This has been proposed and studied by several groups, including the IBM-Heidelberg project [1], the INRIA's project [2], as well as others [3, 4, 5]. A collection of papers on the NRM is [6].

A few actual systems have been built which implement the NRM: the IBM-Heidelberg project is an integrated DBMS for nested relations [7]; INRIA has developed a DB machine for a restricted class of nested relations, the Verso model [2]; ALGRES [8], a core-resident nested relational DB programming language and system, offers all the mentioned extensions, and is used for rapid evolutionary prototyping of data-intensive systems.

Most query and data-manipulation languages of the NRM are derived from

[1].This work was supported by ESPRIT Project "Meteor" , by MPI 40% and by ESPRIT basic research action ASMICS. Applications are supported by ESPRIT Project "Stretch".

Codd's relational algebra, by suitably extending the classical algebraic operators (union, difference, projection, selection, join) and by introducing the data-structuring operators, *nest* (or *group by*, or *create structure*) and *unnest* (or *delete structure*). This results in an algebra for nested relations. The concrete syntax can vary from a SQL extension, to a polish prefix notation (with explicit algebraic operators) or to a graphical interactive interface; ALGRES allows all three forms, but this presentation will concentrate only on the second one, as user interfaces are beyond the scope of this paper. In the case of ALGRES the NRM algebra is enriched with tuple functions (to compute the value of an attribute as a function of the attributes in the same tuple), aggregate functions (e.g. union of a set valued attribute over all tuples of a relation), coercion operations for sets, sequences and multisets, and a generalized transitive closure operator (or a fixed point).

In order to formalize the rather complex data-structures and operations of the NRM we have followed an original syntax-oriented approach which is here presented for a large subset of ALGRES. A parallel formalization effort using algebraic specification methods is described in [9], and shortly compared in the conclusion. The syntax-directed method was inspired by the similarity between the nesting hierarchy of NRM and the tree structure of context-free (CF) grammars. More precisely a NRM schema is isomorphic to a CF grammar, if attribute names are made to correspond to nonterminal symbols. This analogy has been independently noticed by Gyssen et al. [10] (where the idea is attributed to Gonnet and Tompa [11]), who propose a data manipulation language based on syntactical transformations.

Actually the nested relations of most NRM models are of finite nesting depth, a fact excluding recursive schema definitions (but see the conclusion for a short discussion of possible extensions to recursively nested relations). As a consequence, the schema is a non-recursive CF grammar generating a regular language. When the DB schema is defined by a grammar, an instance of the schema is a sentence (string) generated by the grammar. Here comes a significant difference of our approach w.r.t. [10]: we use CF grammars with regular right parts (also called Extended BNF), i.e. productions allow the Kleene star operator in their right-hand sides. This allows a direct modeling of the essential set-oriented property of relational DB's: a relation is a collection of tuples with identical schema, and such a collection can be expressed as <schema>*, where <schema> is the nonterminal symbol defining the schema. A relational operator, say a projection, is then modeled as a syntactic mapping which can be specified in two steps. First the schema of the result is defined as a second EBNF grammar. Then the operand and result grammars are viewed as a sort of syntax-directed translation scheme (SDTS), as defined in compilation theory (a reference is Aho and Ullman [12]). The instance of the result is then defined as the image of the operand instance under the SDTS transformation. For most NRM algebraic operators this approach provides rather elegant, readable definitions.

We have worked out in detail many operators for set valued relations. As grammars generate strings, that are ordered sets, the description of (unordered) set operations require some additional device[2], in order to identify two strings which contain the same elements but in different order. Permutation equivalence is not needed for NRM models based on ordered sets, such as [5] and the sequence constructor of ALGRES itself, which would be straightforward to formalize by this method.

In addition to clarifying several problems with our original definitions of ALGRES operations, this definitional effort was exploited for designing the actual compiler and interpreter, using an attribute-grammar. The operators as here specified are essentially equivalent to the set operators of the ALGRES system [13]), which is available on Unix and OS/2 platforms. Sequence and multi-set operators have not been specified, but do not seem to present additional problems.

2 Definition of objects of ALGRES

An ALGRES object consists of two parts: the *schema* describes the object's structure, the *instance* describes the value (usually a set of tuples) assumed by the object at a certain time. Objects are of two classes: *scalar* and *complex*. The former, a simplified case of the latter, will be introduced afterwards.

2.1 Schema of Complex Objects

As an object is a tree of finite depth its schema is conveniently represented as a non-recursive context-free grammar with regular right-parts. Nonterminal symbols of the grammar are names of objects and subobjects (or attributes). Terminal symbols of the grammar are predefined elementary data types, e.g. integer, real, boolean, string; in this paper we are not concerned with the selection of a particular set of elementary types. Grammatical productions of a schema are of the following types:

1. Object $\rightarrow$ [Attribute$_1$ Attribute$_2$ ... Attribute$_n$]
2. Attribute$_i$ $\rightarrow$ [Attribute$_{i_1}$ Attribute$_{i_2}$ ... Attribute$_{i_m}$]
3. Attribute $\rightarrow$ Predefined_Elementary_Type
   with $n, m \geq 1$, n, m finite.

We assume that the grammar is nonrecursive, that all LHS names are distinct [3], and that all nonterminals in the RHS's are distinct and occur as the LHS of some

---

2. Alternatively one could consider commutative or partially commutative grammars.

production. Square brackets denote iteration (zero or more times). There is exactly one production of type 1 per object, whose LHS is the axiom. Attributes appearing as left part of productions of type 2 are called *complex* attributes or complex objects. More properly an attribute occurring in the RHS of production p is a *subobject* of LHS(p); the subobject relation is transitive. Attributes appearing as left part of productions of type 3 are called *elementary* attributes. We denote as RHS(p) the ordered set of attribute names appearing in the RHS of a production p of types 1 or 2.

Formally, the *schema* of a complex object is a quadruple: $G_O = (V_O, T_O, P_O, O_O)$ where V_O is the nonterminal alphabet, T_O is the terminal alphabet, P_O is the production set, and $O \in V_O$ is the axiom. The nonterminal alphabet V_O of the grammar is partitioned into:

V_O', the set of complex attributes (used in LHS of productions of type 1 or 2).

V_O'', the set of elementary attribute names (used in LHS of productions of type 3).

The subscript will be dropped whenever possible; the terminal alphabet T_O can be also omitted, as it is not affected by the operations on the object.

Consider a production of type 1 or 2:

$O_h \rightarrow [A_1 \ A_2 \ ... \ A_n]$

Attributes $A_1 \ A_2 \ ... \ A_n$ are called *sibling attributes*; they immediately derive from O_h (informally they are "the attributes of" O_h, their *generator*). Consider an object O having a schema defined by grammar G_O and let O' be a sub-object of O; then the schema $G_{O'}$ of O' is defined as the set of all productions $P_{O'} \subseteq P_O$ which can be reached (derive) from O' in one or more derivation steps. As the grammar is non-recursive, any derivation from the axiom has finitely many steps.

Two objects in the database not included one by the other are called *external*. Conceptually external objects are similar to sibling attributes of a global object, the database *DB*, which includes all existing external objects $O_1, O_2, ...$. The schema G_{DB} of the database includes the schemas of all objects, plus the production

$O_{DB} \rightarrow O_1 | O_2 | ...$

Example 1. Defines a set of classes; a class has 3 attributes (Room#, Teacher, Pupils). The first two are elementary, the third is a set of Pupils; a pupil is a complex subobject with 3 elementary attributes.

$G:$ Classes $\rightarrow$ [Room# Teacher Pupils]

---

3. This is done for the sake of simplicity in a formal definition, while in practice it is sufficient requiring that all names in the RHS of productions of type 1 and 2 be distinct.

$$
\begin{aligned}
&\text{Room\#} \rightarrow \text{INTEGER} \\
&\text{Teacher} \rightarrow \text{STRING} \\
&\text{Pupils} \rightarrow [\,\text{Name Sex Age}\,] \\
&\text{Name} \rightarrow \text{STRING} \\
&\text{Sex} \rightarrow \text{STRING} \\
&\text{Age} \rightarrow \text{INTEGER}
\end{aligned}
$$

$T = \{\text{INTEGER, STRING}\}$
$V' = \{\text{Classes, Pupils}\} \quad V'' = \{\text{Room\#, Teacher, Name, Sex, Age}\}$

Room#, Teacher, Pupils are attributes of Classes. Name, Sex, Age are attributes of Pupils. The schema of Pupils includes the last four productions. Sex derives in two steps from the axiom Classes:

Classes $\Rightarrow$ Room# Teacher Pupils $\Rightarrow$ Room# Teacher Name Sex Age
also written as: Classes $\Rightarrow^*$ Room# Teacher Name Sex Age

As customary with syntactic definitions, each terminal element (e.g. INTEGER) stands for any value in its domain. Terminal domains are all finite.

In order to define object compatibility we introduce the *skeleton parenthesized grammar* G_0' obtained from G_0 by replacing brackets with terminal curly brackets and by interpreting INTEGER, STRING, etc. as terminals, instead of value descriptors. Then, $L(G_0')$, the *language generated* by G_0', contains just one string called *signature* of the complex object O. The definition of signature is similarly extended to subobjects.

Example 1 (continued)
G':

$$
\begin{aligned}
&\text{Classes} \rightarrow \text{'\{' Room\# Teacher Pupils '\}'} \\
&\text{Pupils} \rightarrow \text{'\{' Name Sex Age '\}'} \\
&\text{Room\#} \rightarrow \text{'INTEGER'} \\
&\text{Teacher} \rightarrow \text{'STRING'} \\
&\text{Name} \rightarrow \text{'STRING'} \\
&\text{Sex} \rightarrow \text{'STRING'} \\
&\text{Age} \rightarrow \text{'INTEGER'}
\end{aligned}
$$

The signature of Classes is
{INTEGER, STRING, {STRING, STRING, INTEGER}}.
The signature of Pupils is {STRING, STRING, INTEGER}.
The signature of Name is STRING.

Two objects C1 and C2 have *structure compatibility* if their signatures are equal.

In the following, we denote nonterminals by capital letters, terminals by lower case letters $a...e$, terminal strings by lower case letters $o...z$, nonterminal or mixed strings by greek lower case letters. The null string is denoted ε. We use a standard notation for syntactic operations as in [12], with extension to regular right-part grammars as for instance in [14].

2.2 Instance of objects

Intuitively, an instance o of a complex object O with schema $G = (V, T, P, O)$ is a terminal string generated by G such that no object in o contains replicated elements. Thus, the *set of valid instances of O, $I(O)$,* is included by the *language* $L(G)$ of strings generated by G:

$$I(O) \subseteq L(G) = \{x \in T^* \mid O \Rightarrow^* x\}$$

Consider a production of types 1 or 2 of G:

$$O_h \rightarrow [A_1 \; A_2 \; ... \; A_n]$$

A non-null string δ is a *tuple* of O_h (denoted $O_h \vdash \delta$) if the following conditions hold:

$$O_h \vdash \delta \text{ iff } O \Rightarrow^* y \, O_h \, z \Rightarrow ya \, A_1 \; A_2 \; ... \; A_n \, \beta z \Rightarrow^* ya \, \delta \, \beta z$$

with a and $\beta \in (A_1 \; A_2 \; ... \; A_n)^*$. Notice that $\Rightarrow$ (resp. $\Rightarrow^*$) is the usual relation of immediate (resp. transitively closed) derivation. We also say that $O_h \vdash \delta$ *occurs* in the derivation $O \Rightarrow^* ya\delta\beta z$, and in any string $u\delta v$ such that $O \Rightarrow^* ya\delta\beta z \Rightarrow^* u\delta v$. If δ is a terminal string, it is a *terminal tuple* of O_h: this is the default. Fig.1 shows the derivation of a terminal tuple.

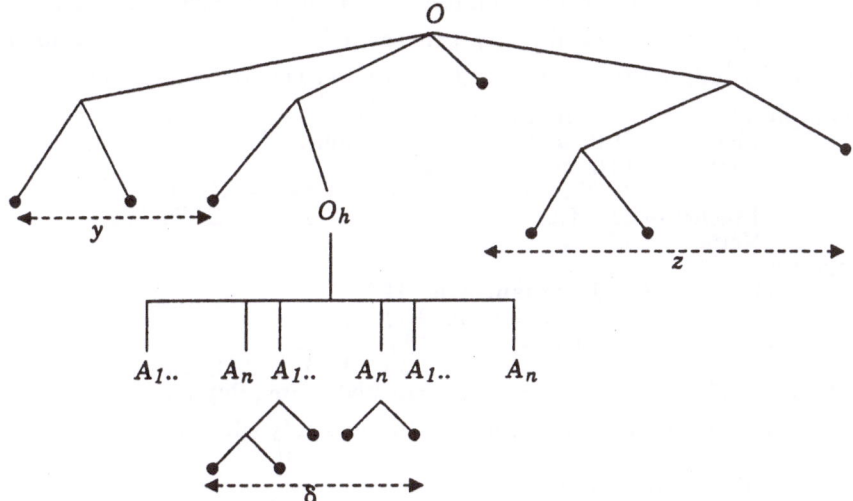

Fig.1 - Definition of a tuple δ of a complex (sub)object O_h. Notice the graphical difference between strings generated by iteration ($A_1 \; ... \; A_n \; ... \; A_1 \; ... \; A_n$), and by rewriting.

The set of *valid instances* of a complex object O with schema G is formally defined as follows:

$$I(O) = \{x \in L(G) \mid \forall O_i \in V :$$
$$((O_i \vdash y \text{ occurs in } x \text{ and } O_i \vdash z \text{ occurs in } x) \Leftrightarrow y \neq z)\}$$

We denote by *unic* the mapping from terminal strings into terminal strings that recursively removes duplicated tuples from each (sub)object of $L(G)$. Therefore:

$$I(O) = \{ unic(y) \mid y \in L(G) \}$$

Note: in the implementation of ALGRES *unic* corresponds to the routine that removes duplicates, a very frequently occurring action.

As strings represent sets, two strings identical up to a permutation of their tuples are considered equal. More precisely, two (terminal) *tuples* t_1 and t_2

occurring in the same (sub)object o are *equal*, $t_1 \approx t_2$

if $O \rightarrow [A_1 \; A_2 \; ... \; A_n] \in P$ and $\forall i \in 1...n$

if $A_i \in V''$, with $A_i \Rightarrow a_1$ occurring in t_1, $A_i \Rightarrow a_2$ occurring in t_2,
then $a_1 = a_2$.

if $A_i \in V'$, with $A_i \Rightarrow^* u_1$ occurring in t_1, $A_i \Rightarrow^* u_2$ occurring in t_2,
then $u_1 \approx u_2$.

Notice that this recursive definition terminates because O has a finite-depth tree.

Inclusion between two structurally compatible objects o_1 and o_2 with schemas O_1 and O_2 is evaluated as follows:

$$o_1 \subseteq o_2 \text{ iff } \forall t_1 \colon (O_1 \vdash t_1 \; \exists t_2 \colon (O_2 \vdash t_2 \wedge t_1 \approx t_2)).$$

The representation of instances through strings can be made more clear through the use of syntactic delimiters, i.e. brackets enclosing sets and tuples. These delimiters can be directly generated by a *parenthesized grammar G''* obtained by adding parentheses (and punctuation) to productions of G.

Example 1 (continued, parenthesis grammar).

G'' Classes → '{' [Room# ',' Teacher ',' Pupils] '}'
Pupils → '{' [Name ',' Sex ',' Age] '}'
Room# → INTEGER   Sex → STRING
Teacher → STRING   Age → INTEGER
Name → STRING

Instance:
{ (N1 , Tom , { (Jonathan, male , 12)
                    (Alicia, female , 15)   }
   (N2 , Jim , { (Tommy, male , 13)
                    (Annie, female , 15)   }   } ∈ *I*(Classes)
Pupils ⊢ (Tommy, male , 13) occurs in (N2 , Jim , Pupils).

In the following, we indicate instance delimiters only when useful.

2.3   Further definitions

Scalar objects

Scalar objects have a simpler schema and instance. The schema of a scalar object is a single production of type 3, the instance of a scalar object is a single value of the suitable elementary type.

Example 2.
Constant1 → INTEGER
3 ∈ *I*(Constant1)

Structured constants

In the specification of ALGRES expressions, one can use *structured constants*, i.e. strings built by using elementary data types and brackets. C must be a valid instance of a grammar G_C and is compatible with an object (or sub-object) O if G_C and G_O are compatible.

Example 3.
A structured constant which is structurally compatible with the object Pupils of
Ex.1 is:
{   (John , male , 14)
    (Ann , female , 6)}

Quantification rule

A database contains a number of objects, each one possibly containing subobjects.
Before introducing the operations and relations to manipulate the database
objects, we give a general rule specifying which (sub)objects can be combined by an
operator, and where the results is placed in the database.

The quantification rule states that two (sub)objects O_1 and O_2 can be combined by
an operator provided that *the father F of one of them* (say O_1) *is an ancestor of the
other one* (O_2). This rule ensures that there is (at most) a one-to-many
correspondence between a tuple t_1 of O_1 and the tuples t_{2_1}, t_{2_2}, ... of O_2 occurring
in the same object. Let A be the ancestor of O_2 which is a brother of O_1; then for
an instance of F where $F \vdash t_1$ we have:

$$F \Rightarrow \alpha\, O_1\, \beta\, A\, \gamma \Rightarrow^* \alpha\, t_1\, \beta\, A\, \gamma \Rightarrow^* \alpha\, t_1\, \beta\, \eta\, O_2\, \theta\, \gamma \Rightarrow^* \alpha\, t_1\, \beta\, \eta\, t_{2_1}, t_{2_2}, ...\ \theta\, \gamma$$

In particular if O_1 and O_2 are sibling, the correspondence is one-to-one. The result
of an operation is a new subobject which is placed at the level of the lower one of
the operands. Fig.2 shows legal and illegal combinations. The two operands of an
operation (e.g. union or join) are marked in Fig.2 by equal digits; positive (resp.
negative) digits mark legal (resp. illegal) operations. For legal operations the
object produced as result is also indicated in the schema with the same underlined
digit. Combinations like (-3, -3') are illegal as there is a many-to-many relations
between the tuples of the operands. Insteads the result of a (binary) operator
having as arguments the two objects marked by 2 and 2' is an object marked by 2̲
(in this case a sibling attribute of 2). Two subobjects satisfying the quantification
rule are *well quantified*.

Predicates

Predicates are functions from tuples of objects to boolean values {T,F}. The
following types of elementary predicates are valid:

   a. Scalar predicates, built through scalar comparison operators (e.g. =, <, ≤)
between two compatible well quantified attributes A_1 and $A_2 \in V''$.

   b. Set comparison predicates; built through set comparison operators (e.g. =,
⊆, ⊂) between two compatible well quantified attributes A_1 and $A_2 \in V'$.

   c. Membership predicates. Consider the following productions:

$p: O_h \rightarrow [C_1\ C_2\ ...\ C_n\ A_1\ A_2\ ...A_m\ O_k]$ [3]
$q: O_k \rightarrow [B_1\ B_2\ ...\ B_m]$ where $m \geq 1$ and $n \geq 0$.

52

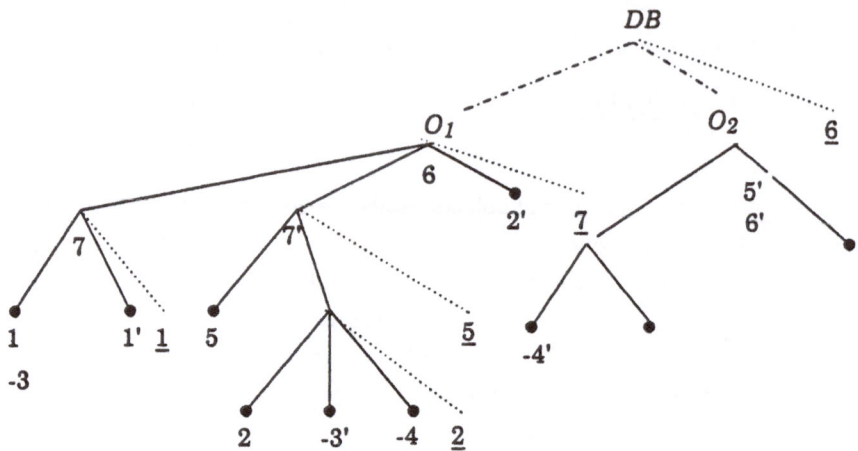

Fig.2 - Legal and illegal combinations of the arguments of an operation in predicates or expressions, and position of the result. O_1 and O_2 are external objects of the DB. Legal (resp. illegal) operands of an operation are marked by two equal positive (resp. negative) digits j and j; the result of a legal operation is marked by an underlined digit $\underline{j}$, and connected by a dotted arc to the tree.

Let the signatures of $A_1\ A_2\ ...\ A_m$ be ordered in the same way as the signatures of $B_1\ B_2\ ...\ B_m$. Then, an elementary membership predicate testing ($\in$ and $\neg\in$) between $A_1\ A_2\ ...\ A_m$ and O_k is defined as follows. Let o be an instance of O.

$(A_1\ A_2\ ...\ A_m) \in O_k$ iff
$(\exists w : (O_h \vdash w$ occurs in $o) \wedge (w = xy) \wedge (A_1\ A_2\ ...\ A_m \Rightarrow^* x$ occurs in $w) \wedge (O_k \vdash z$ occurs in $y) \wedge (x \approx z)$

The definition says that w is a tuple of O_h made of two strings x and y, the former deriving from $A_1\ A_2\ ...\ A_m$ and the latter from O_k. Then y has a tuple z which is equal to x (up to a permutation).

Elementary predicates have the obvious interpretation of defining a truth value over the tuples of the object O_h which generates the attributes appearing in the predicate itself; we denote O_h as the *target* of the elementary predicate. A legal predicate is built through any boolean combination of elementary predicates applied to the same target. More generally each elementary predicate must have well quantified targets, and the result is a truth value having the lower operand as its target. In elementary predicates, any operand can be replaced by a compatible constant; after introducing expressions in Section 4, we shall allow operands of a predicate to be suitable expressions.

3. We allow membership testing between attributes appearing in particular positions of RHS(p); however, the formulation is general enough, because projection (later defined) allows displacement of attributes. In practice ALGRES does not impose this constraint.

Example 4.
A predicate with target Pupils is:
  (Name = 'Tommy') $\vee$ (Age > 8)
A predicate with target Classes is:
  (Room# = 5) $\wedge$ ((Tommy, male, 13) $\in$ Pupils)
A predicate with targets Classes and Pupils satisfying the quantification rule is:
  (Room# = 5) $\wedge$ (Age > 8)
(true for the children of room 5 who are older than 8). Note that the truth valued result is an attribute of Pupils, in contrast to the previous case where it is an attribute of Classes.

3 Traditional algebraic operations

Traditional relational operations as from [15] are here extended to complex objects and a renaming operation is presented. Operations are unary or binary; they are presented by indicating their syntax, correctness constraints, and semantics. The latter is the specification of the schema $G_R = (V_R, P_R, R)$ and instance $r \in I(G_R)$ of the result R. G_R (resp. r) is typically constructively defined from grammar(s) G_O (resp. instance(s) o) of operand(s); we omit indicating that the axiom R systematically replaces axiom(s) of operand(s) in the LHS of the production of type 1 of G_R.

Operations are written in prefix as three fields (the second is not needed by some operators):

  Operator-code [Specification] Operand(s).

3.1 Selection

Syntax: SEL [p] $O = R$

Constraint: p is a legal predicate with target a subobject O_h (possibly coincident with O).

Semantics:

a. $G_R = G_O$.

b. The transformation from $I(O)$ to $I(R)$ is described by the following string homomorphism h defined for any tuple of O_h:

  $h(w) = \varepsilon$ if $O_h \vdash w \wedge \neg p(w)$; $h(w) = w$ otherwise.

Then the instance of r is $r = h(o)$. Note that if $p(w)$ is false for all tuples of O_h then $O_h \Rightarrow^* \varepsilon$ occurs in r; this means that the set O_h is empty.

3.2 Projection

Syntax: PRJ [Δ] $O = R$

Constraint: Δ is an ordered set of sibling attributes[4]. Hence there is a production p in G_O of type 1 or 2:

---

4. Projection is easily generalized to allow non-sibling attributes in Δ, e.g. PRJ [Room# Age] Classes .

$$p: A \rightarrow [B_1 \ B_2 \ ... \ B_n]$$

such that, for each $A_i \in \Delta : A_i \in RHS(p)$, i.e. $A_i = B_h$ for some h.

Semantics:

a. G_R is obtained from G_O by replacing p with a new production

$$p': A \rightarrow [\ \Delta\ ]$$

and eliminating all productions which are reachable from B_i, with $B_i \in (RHS(p) - \Delta)$. In this difference, we regard $RHS(p)$ and Δ as unordered sets.

b. Let τ be the syntax-directed translation (SDT) [12] defined by the above schema translation $(G_O, \ G_R)$; then $r = unic(\ \tau(o))$.[5]

3.3 Cartesian product

Syntax: CAR $O_1 \ O_2 \ = R$

Constraints: $V_{O_1} \cap V_{O_2} = \emptyset$

Semantics:

a. Let $O_1 \rightarrow [A_1 \ A_2 \ ... \ A_n]$ and $O_2 \rightarrow [B_1 \ B_2 \ ... \ B_n]$ be the productions of type 1 of the twooperands. Then the production of type 1 of R is:

$$R \rightarrow [A_1 \ A_2 \ ... \ A_n \ B_1 \ B_2 \ ... \ B_n]$$

All other productions of G_{O_1}, G_{O_2} are also productions of G_R.

b. r derives from o_1 and o_2 as follows:

$$R \vdash x \text{ occurs in } r \text{ iff } (O_1 \vdash y \text{ occurs in } o_1) \wedge (O_2 \vdash z \text{ occurs in } o_2)$$
$$\wedge \ (x \approx yz)$$

3.4 Union

Syntax: UNI $O_1 \ O_2 = R$

Constraints: O_1 and O_2 are structurally compatible

Semantics:

a. $G_R = G_{O_1}$

b. $r = unic \ (o_1 \ o_2)$, (the catenation of the two strings).

3.5 Rename

Syntax: REN[$A_j \leftarrow A_i$]$O = R$

Constraints:

1. $A_i \in V_O$.

2. $A_j \notin V_O$ (is a new name).

Semantics:

a. G_R is isomorphic to G_O, obtained by renaming as A_j the attribute A_i.

b. $r = o$

---

5. A SDT is usually defined by a pair of context-free grammars such that source and target productions are paired. For each pair, the same nonterminals occur in both productions Here we allow the target production to have a subset of the nonterminals of the corresponding source production. This has no consequence on the translation defined by the SDT. In addition the SDT is here defined on Extended BNF grammars, as in [14].

We allow a syntactic variation with multiple renaming within the same specification:

$$REN[A_1 \leftarrow B_1,..., A_j \leftarrow B_j] \, O \; = \; REN[\, A_1 \leftarrow B_1] \, ... \, REN[A_j \leftarrow B_j\,] \, O$$

3.6 Join

Syntax: $JOI[p] \, O_1 \, O_2$

Constraint: p is a legal predicate for $CAR \, O_1 \, O_2$.

Derivation: $JOI[p] \, O_1 \, O_2 \; = \; SEL \, [p] \, (CAR \, O_1 \, O_2 \,)$

Intersection and difference can be similarly defined.

4 New algebraic operations

In this section, we introduce operations for nesting and unnesting which are fundamental for the nested relational model: nesting groups together tuples sharing some common value; unnesting flatten the schema. Schema transformations produced by nest and unnest operations are shown in Fig. 3.

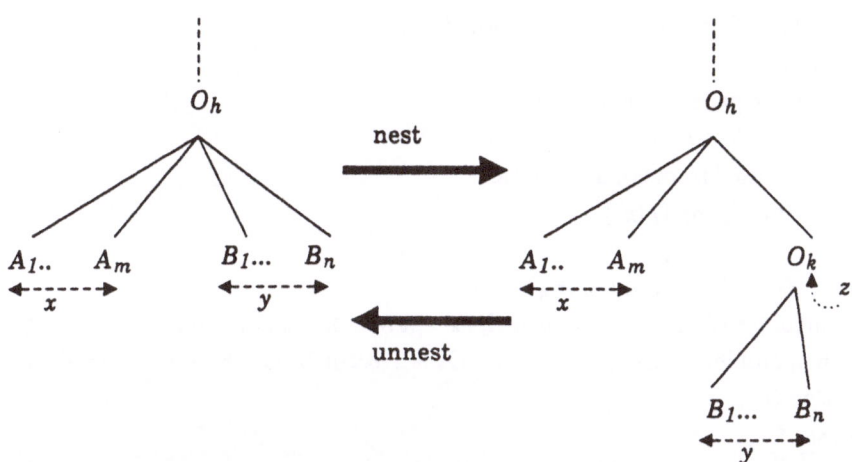

Fig. 3. Schema transformations for nest and unnest operations.

4.1 Nest (or create structure)

Syntax: $NST \, [\, O_k \rightarrow B_1... \, B_n\,] \, O = R$

Constraint:

1. There exists a production p of type 1 or 2 in G_O such that $B_1... \, B_n$ are the last sibling attributes in $RHS(p)$:

   $p: \; O_h \rightarrow [\,A_1...A_m \, B_1...B_n\,] \, , \; m \geq 0, \, n \geq 1.$

2. $O_k \notin V_O$ (O_k is a new name).

Semantics:

a. G_R is defined from G_O as follows:

$\quad P_R = P_O - \{p\} \cup \{p', q\}$

where:

$\quad p': \quad O_h \rightarrow [A_1...A_m O_k]$

$\quad q: \quad O_k \rightarrow [B_1...B_n]$

b. The instances o and r are identical, except in subtrees rooted in O_h. Let $O_h \vdash w$ occur in o, with $w = xy$ such that $A_1...A_m \Rightarrow^* x$ and $B_1...B_n \Rightarrow^* y$ occur in w. Then in r the derivation occurs: $O_h \vdash xz$, with $O_k \vdash y$ occurring in z.

Note that NST can be used to perform coercions of scalar values into singleton sets.

4.2 Unnest (or delete structure)

Syntax: UNN$[O_k]O = R$

Constraint:

a. There exists a production p of type 1 or 2 in G_O such that $O_k \in V_O'$ is the last attribute of RHS(p):

$\quad p: O_h \rightarrow [A_1...A_m O_k], m \geq 0, n \geq 1$.

b. No tuple of O_k is the empty set (null string)[6].

Semantics:

a. Let q be the production of type 2:

$\quad q: O_k \rightarrow [B_1...B_n]$

$\quad G_R$ is obtained from G_O as follows:

$\quad P_R = P_O - \{p, q\} \cup \{p'\}$

where:

$\quad p': \quad O_h \rightarrow [A_1...A_m B_1...B_n]$

b. The instances o and r are identical, except in subtrees rooted in O_k. Let $O_h \vdash w$ occur in o, and let $A_1...A_m \Rightarrow^* x$ and $O_k \vdash z$ occur in w. Then, there exists in r a derivation $O_h \vdash xz$[7]

Example 5.
R1 = UNN[A₂] O
R2 = NST[A₂ →A₃] R1
$\quad G_O: \quad O \rightarrow [A_1\ A_2]$
$\quad\quad\quad A_2 \rightarrow [A_3]$
$\quad\quad\quad A_1 \rightarrow$ CHAR
$\quad\quad\quad A_3 \rightarrow$ INTEGER
$\quad o = \{ \ (a, \{(1)(2)(3)\})$
$\quad\quad\quad (a, \{(2)(3)(4)\})\}$
$\quad G_{R1}: R1 \rightarrow [A_1\ A_3]$
$\quad\quad\quad A_1 \rightarrow$ CHAR
$\quad\quad\quad A_3 \rightarrow$ INTEGER

$\quad G_{R1}: R2 \rightarrow [A_1\ A_2]$
$\quad\quad\quad A_1 \rightarrow$ CHAR
$\quad\quad\quad A_2 \rightarrow [A_3]$

6. We add this constraint because here we do not deal with null values for elementary attributes.

7. In general the subsequent application of unnest and nest operation to an object yields a different object (see Example 5).

$$r1 = \{(a,1)(a,2)(a,3)(a,4)\} \qquad r2 = \{(a,\{(1)(2)(3)(4)\})\}$$

with $A_3 \to$ INTEGER above $r2$.

5 Algebraic expressions

ALGRES derives much of its generality and expressive power from treatment of algebraic expressions. We allow traditional use of algebraic expressions as the composition of basic operations applied to complex objects, which must be well quantified. Further, we allow using algebraic expressions within specificators of operations.

Let $R(O_1 \ldots O_n)$ be a generic algebraic expression; the result of the expression is an object with schema $G_R = (V_R, P_R, R)$ and instance r ; G_R and r are evaluated starting from the schema and instance of objects O_i and applying the operations of ALGRES.

Example 6.

$$R = \exp(O_1, O_2, O_3) = \text{JOI}[A_1 = A_4] \quad O_1$$
$$\text{UNI} \quad O_2$$
$$\text{PRJ}[A_7\ A_8] \quad \text{UNN}[A_6]\ O_3$$

$G_{O_1}: O_1 \to [A_1\ A_2]$
  $\quad A_2 \to [A_3]$
  $\quad A_1 \to$ STRING
  $\quad A_2 \to$ INTEGER

$G_{O_2}:$
  $\quad O_2 \to [A_4\ A_5]$
  $\quad A_4 \to$ STRING
  $\quad A_5 \to$ INTEGER

$G_{O_3}: O_3 \to [A_6\ A_7]$
  $\quad A_6 \to [A_8]$
  $\quad A_7 \to$ STRING
  $\quad A_8 \to$ INTEGER

$G_R: \quad R \to [A_1\ A_2\ A_4\ A_5]$
  $\quad A_1 \to$ STRING
  $\quad A_2 \to [A_3]$ $\qquad A_3 \to$ INTEGER
  $\quad A_4 \to$ STRING $\qquad A_5 \to$ INTEGER

$o_1 = \{(\text{abc}, \{(1)(2)(3)\})$
  $\quad (\text{def}, \{(4)(5)(6)\})\}$
$o_2 = \{(\text{abc}, 1)(\text{rst}, 7)\}$
$o_3 = \{(\{(1)(3)\}, \text{bcd})\}$

$r = \{(\text{abc}, \{(1)(2)(3)\}, \text{abc}, 1)\}$

5.1 Inner expressions

The above expression has external objects O_1, O_2, O_3 as operands; in ALGRES *inner expressions* can be built also over subobjects within an object O. A legal inner expression is built over well quantified objects. For simplicity here we consider only sibling attributes generated by an object O_h (called the *target* of the expression) as operands. The expression is iteratively applied to each tuple of O_h, which is extended with the result of the expression's evaluation. Inner expressions can occur in several contexts: in selection or join predicates; tuple extension operations are later used in order to derive data from computation over complex objects and include these data into the object structure.

The types of inner expressions allowed in ALGRES are the following:

a. Scalar expressions are built over sibling elementary attributes $A_1 \ldots A_m$ generated by O_h, using conventional scalar operations (sum, subtraction, product, and, or, etc.). The result of the scalar expression:

$O_h = \exp(A_1 \dots A_m)$

is a scalar object whose grammar is a single production:

$O_h \rightarrow$ elementary-basic-type

and whose instance is the result of the expression.

b. *Set expressions* are all legal algebraic expressions which can be built over sibling complex attributes $A_1 \dots A_m$ of O_h using traditional algebraic operations of ALGRES (selection, projection, cartesian product, union, difference, join, intersection, rename). Schema and instance of their result are thus properly defined.

c. *Scalar aggregate expressions* are given by the application of a scalar aggregate function *aggr* $\in$ {summation, average, min, max,...} to the set of values of one elementary attribute B_{ij} of a subobject A_i generated by O_h , and return a single value.

The result of a scalar aggregate expression:

$O_h = \text{aggr}(B_{ij} \text{ in } A_i)$

is a scalar object whose grammar is a single production:

$O_h \rightarrow$ elementary-basic-type

and whose instance is the result of the expression.

d. *Set aggregate expressions* are given by the application of a set aggregate function

saggr $\in$ {union, intersection,...}

to sets of sets of values obtained by projecting a complex object A_i generated by O_h over one of its complex attributes B_{ij} .

The result of a set aggregate expression:

$O_h = \text{saggr}(B_{ij} \text{ in } A_i)$

is a complex object (e.g., the union or intersection of all sets), whose grammar is given by the production:

$O_h \rightarrow B_{ij}$

and by all productions of G_O which are reachable from B_{ij}, and whose instance is the result of the expression.

Example 7.
```
   G: O  → [A₁ A₂ A₃]
      A₁ → [ A₄ ]                A₄ → INTEGER
      A₂ → [ A₅ ]                A₅ → INTEGER
      A₃ → [ A₆ ]                A₆ → INTEGER
```
a) scalar expression: $A_4 + 1$ -- a sibling of A_4
b) set expression: UNI A_2 A_1 -- a sibling of A_1
c) aggregate scalar expression: SUM(A_4 in A_1)   -- a sibling of A_1
d) aggregate set expression: UNION(A_1 in O)   -- a sibling of O in the DB.

5.2   Tuple extension

This operation adds an attribute (elementary or not) to the RHS of a type I or 2 production. We introduce two syntactic variations of the algebraic unary EXT (extend) operation. The latter applies to aggregate expressions applied to first-level attributes, i.e. attributes directly generated by the grammar's axiom. The former applies to all other cases.

Syntax 1 : $\text{EXT} [O_h \leftarrow O_k = \exp(A_1, ..., A_m)] O = R$

Constraints:

1. $V_O \cap V_{O_k} = \varnothing$ (all attribute names in the schema of $\exp(A_1, ..., A_m)$ including O_k are new).

2. There is a production p of G_O, $\text{LHS}(p) = O_h$ is the generator of $A_1, ..., A_m$, and exp is a legal inner expression of $A_1, ..., A_m$:

   $p: O_h \rightarrow B_1, ..., B_n \ A_1, ..., A_m$ [8]

a. G_R is derived from G_O as follows:

   $P_R = P_O - \{p\} \cup \{q\} \cup P_{O_k}$

   where:

   $q: \text{LHS}(p) \rightarrow [\ \text{RHS}(p)\ O_k\ ]$ (i.e. the string catenation)

   P_{O_k} is the set of productions defining the schema of O_k, as resulting from the exp.

b. The instances o and r are identical, except in subtrees rooted in O_h. Let $O_h \vdash x$ occur in o and let $y = \exp(x)$ denote the result of the expression evaluation over attributes $A_1, ..., A_m$ of x. Then there is a derivation $O_h \vdash xy$ in r.

Consider now separately the case of aggregate expressions applied to the axiom:

Syntax 2: $\text{EXT} [O_k = \text{aggr}(B_i \text{ in } O)] O = R$

Constraints:

1. $V_O \cap V_{O_k} = \varnothing$

2. Attribute B_i is generated by axiom O and *aggr* is a legal aggregate expression.

Semantics:

a. G_R is derived from G_O as follows:

   $G_R = G_O \cup \{q\} \cup G_{O_k}$

   where:

   $q: R \rightarrow [O\ O_k]$

b. Let $y = \exp(o)$ denote the result of the expression evaluation over attributes $A_1, ..., A_m$ of o. Then, object R has a single tuple:

   $R \vdash r$ with $r = oy$.

Finally, we allow the use of expressions within predicates, thus extending our previous definition.

---

8. The arguments $A_1, ..., A_m$ appear in fixed positions of RHS(p); however, the formulation is general, because projection allows displacement of attributes. In practice ALGRES does not impose this constraint.

Example 7 (continued).

G: $O \rightarrow [A_1 \ A_2 \ A_3]$

  $A_1 \rightarrow [A_4]$ $A_4 \rightarrow INTEGER$
  $A_2 \rightarrow [A_5]$ $A_5 \rightarrow INTEGER$
  $A_3 \rightarrow [A_6]$ $A_6 \rightarrow INTEGER$

  $o:\{$ $(\{(1) (2) (3)\} , \{(2) (3) (4)\} , \{(2) (3)\})$
      $(\{(1) (2) (3) (4)\} , \{\varepsilon\} , \{(2)\})$ $\}$

a) Scalar expression:

  $R = EXT [A_1 \leftarrow A_7 = A_4 + 1] O$ -- A_7 is the new integer attribute,
                            -- generated by A_1

  $r: \{ (\{(1,2) (2,3) (3,4)\} , \{(2) (3) (4)\} , \{(2) (3)\})$
       $(\{(1,2) (2,3) (3,4) (4,5)\} , \{\} , \{(2)\})$ $\}$

b) Set expression:

  $R = EXT [O \leftarrow A_8 = DIF \ A_2 \ A_1] O$ -- DIF is set difference
  $r: \{$ $(\{(1) (2) (3)\} , \{(2) (3) (4)\} , \{(2) (3)\} , \{(4)\})$
       $(\{(1) (2) (3) (4)\} , \{\} , \{(2)\} , \{\})$ $\}$

c) Scalar aggregate expression:

  $R = EXT [A_4 \leftarrow A_7 = SUM(A_4 \ in \ A_1)] O$ -- summation over the set A_1
                                -- of A_4

  $r: \{ (\{(1) (2) (3)\} , \{(2) (3) (4)\} , \{(2) (3)\} , 6)$
       $(\{(1) (2) (3) (4)\} , \{\} , \{(2)\} , 10)$ $\}$

d) Set aggregate expression :

  $R = EXT [O \leftarrow A_7 = U (A_4 \ in \ A_1)] O$ -- union over the set A_1 of A_4

  $r: \{$ $\{$ $(\{(1) (2) (3)\} , \{(2) (3) (4)\}, \{(2) (3)\})$
          $(\{(1) (2) (3) (4)\} , \{\} , \{(2)\}$ $\},$
       $\{(1) (2) (3) (4)\}$ $\}$

e) Expression within predicates:

  $R = SEL [A_3 \subseteq DIF \ A_1 \ A_2] O$
  $r: \{ (\{(1) (2) (3) (4)\} , \{\} , \{(2)\}) \}$

6 Closure operation

The transitive closure (also called fixed point) operation is introduced to enhance the computational power of ALGRES, which becomes equivalent to that of languages which offer recursion.

Syntax: $R = CLO [O_i] EXP(O_1 ... O_i ... O_n) = R$, where $n \geq 1$.

Constraint: O_i and the expression are structurally compatible.

Semantics:

a. $G_R = G_{O_i}$.

b. Tuples of $r \in I(G_R)$ are defined by the following condition:

  $R \vdash x \Leftrightarrow S \vdash x$ where S is recursively defined by:

  $S^{(0)} = EXP(O_1 ... O_i ... O_n)$

  $S^{(h)} = EXP(O_1 ... S^{(h-1)} ... O_n)$

Because of this definition, if $S^{(h)}$ is contained in the union $U_{j<h} \ S^{(j)}$, then the evaluation of $S^{(k)}$, with $k \geq h$, will contribute no additional tuples to the result Hence, the closure operation can be implemented by an iterative algorithm, using

the above test as termination condition; however, in general, termination is not assured .

7 Conclusions

We have presented a formal definition of a database language for nested (or non-1st-normal-form) relations. A rather original definition method has been proposed and applied to a large representative subset of ALGRES. By exploiting the isomorphism between a schema and a context-free extended-BNF grammar, we have described the effect of the operations as syntax-directed translations. This allowed us to exploit established concepts and notations from formal languages and compiler theory.

This formalization served as a guideline for the actual compiler, that was designed as an attribute grammar based translator. The compiler translates ALGRES expressions into an ad hoc intermediate language (called RA), which is then interpreted. Instances of NRM relations are represented as normalized relations in the intermediate representation. The run-time representation of relation instances in the ALGRES system [8] is thus rather traditional, and does not exploit the formal language model. On the other hand, one could alternatively represent instances as syntax-trees, or parenthesized strings: this would be attractive for certain operations that can be implemented by syntactic transducers (automata), but the experience of the Verso system [2], which took a similar approach, casts some doubts on the attainable performance.

The ALGRES system is used in several projects as a rapid prototyping environment and as a tool for designing DB applications. Examples are an intelligent training system for helicopter maintenance, a software engineering database, and *Grammatica*, a collection of tools for artificial language analysis; the experimental logic data-base language LOGRES [16], and the object-oriented database language SOL have been built on top of ALGRES.

Another formal definition [9] of ALGRES was obtained with algebraic axiomatic methods, which can be compared with the work of Wong [17]. Nested relations and operators were axiomatized as a complex abstract data type, using the RAP system [18], resulting in an executable specification. Then, in order to improve execution efficiency, the axioms were translated into Prolog by hand. Comparing the two approaches we found that the syntactical one is more readable and operational, and is useful as a blueprint of the ALGRES compiler. On the other hand the algebraic specification is more rigorous, uses established concepts, and can be turned into an executable prototype; but the prototype is extremely slow and its structure is so distant from the actual compiler and interpreter, that is not suitable for evolutionary prototyping.

Finally, we briefly discuss the issue of extending nested relational data-structures to allow recursive schema definitions. Recursive schemes are a rather expressive model, to represent the part-of relation, when its chains are of unbounded length. An example is a genealogy tree, where a complex object *Person* has an attribute *Son*, and *Son* is again a *Person*. In such a situation the context-free grammar is recursive, which is of course the normal case for usual applications of grammars. Extending our formalism to recursive schemes would cause no major technical complication, as syntactical mappings are hardly affected by recursion in the grammar. But practical difficulties would arise in a purely value-based (relational) model and query language, since two instances of the same recursive schema could be of arbitrarily different nesting depths, and the expressive power of traditional relational operators for such multiform structures is uncertain. Such difficulties are overcome by identity-based models and reference mechanisms (object identifiers), which enable the definition of recursive database instances, while providing finite schema structures. The extension of relational algebras to deal with object identity is outside the scope of this paper and is regarded as a promising evolution of ALGRES, which is actively investigated in ESPRIT project "Stretch".

Aknowledgments: The ALGRES project is a joint effort of Politecnico di Milano (F.Cacace, R.Zicari, L.Tanca) and TXT-Ingegneria Informatica (A.Di Maio and L.Lamperti). We thank the many other participants who have implemented ALGRES and are using and extending the system.

8 Bibliography

[1] H.Schek and M.Scholl "The relational model with relational-valued attributes, *Information Syst.*, 1986.

[2] S. Abiteboul, M.Scholl, G.Gardarin and E.Simon. "Towards DBMSs for supporting new applications", *Proc. 12th VLDB*, 1986.

[3] D.Van Gucht and P.C.Fisher "Multilevel nested relational structures", *Journ. Comp. and Syst. Sc.*, 36, 77-105, 1988

[4] S.J.Thomas and P.C.Fisher "Nested relational structures" in *Advances in Computing research, Vol.3*, P.C.Kanelakis (ed), JAI Press, 269-307, 1986.

[5] R.Gueting, R.Zicari and D. Choy "An algebra for structured office documents", *ACM Trans. on Office Info. Syst.*, 7, 4, 121-157, 1989.

[6] S.Abiteboul, P.Fischer and H.Schek (eds), *Nested relations and complex objects in databases*, Springer-Verlag, LNCS 361, 1989.

[7] H.J.Scheck and P.Pistor "Data structures for an integrated data base management and information retrieval system", *Proc. VLDB*, 197-207, 1982.

[8]   S.Ceri, S.Crespi Reghizzi, L.Lamperti, L.Lavazza and R.Zicari. "ALGRES: an advanced database for complex applications", *IEEE Software*, 68-78, July 1990 .

[9]   L.Lavazza and S.Crespi Reghizzi, "Algebraic ADT specifications of an extended relational algebra and their conversion into a working prototype", in M.Wirsing and J.A.Bergstra (Eds) *Algebraic methods: theory, tools and applications*, Springer-Verlag, LNCS 394, 1989.

[10]   M.Gyssen, J.Paredaens and D.Van Gucht "A grammar-based approach towards unifying hierarchical data models", Rept. 88-33, Universiteit Antwerp, 1989.

[11]   G.Gonnet and F.Tompa "Mind your grammar: a new approach to modelling text", Rept., University of Waterloo, 1988.

[12]   A.Aho and J.Ullman *The theory of parsing, translation and compiling*, Prentice-Hall, 1972.

[13]   F.Cacace and G.Lamperti "ALGRES user manual", Dipt. Elettronica, Politecnico di Milano, Jan. 1989.

[14]   J.Lewi, K. De Vlaminck, J.Huens and M.Huybrechts, *A programming methodology in compiler construction: Part 1*, North-Holland, 1979.

[15]   J.Ullman, *Principles of database systems*, Computer Sc. Press, 1983.

[16]   F.Cacace et al. "Integrating object-oriented data-modeling with a rule-based programming paradigm" in *Proc. ACM SIGMOD*, New York 1990.

[17]   E.Wong and W.B.Samson "The specification of a relational database (PRECI) as an abstract data type and its realization in HOPE", *Comp. Journ*, 29, 1986.

[18]   A.Geser and H.Hussman, "Experiences with the RAP system - a specification interpreter combining term rewriting and resolution", in B.Robinet and R.Wilhelm (eds) *Proc. ESOP 86*, Springer LNCS 213, 339-350, 1986.

Specifying Deductive Databases and Integrity Constraints in Meta-logic

Subrata Kumar Das

Computer Science Department, Heriot-Watt University

Edinburgh, Scotland

Abstract

A meta-logic statement over a language is characterised by a formula in typed ω-order λ-calculus. The head of the λ-term corresponding to a meta-logic statement is always a constant when it is in normal form. It is shown that both deductive database statements and integrity constraints, particularly those involving aggregate operations, can be represented conveniently in meta-logic statements. A special case of Huet's unification algorithm is considered on the domain of meta-logic terms and a proof procedure based on this unification is presented to answer database queries and to verify integrity constraints. Although, the main focus is to handle deductive databases problems, the results of this paper deal indirectly with a metalevel extension of first-order logic programming.

1. Introduction

A *deductive database* $[1, 2, 3, 4, 5, 6]$ is considered as a finite set of database clauses (or statements) of the form

$$A_1 \vee \cdots \vee A_m \leftarrow L_1 \wedge \cdots \wedge L_n, \qquad m \geq 1, n \geq 0 \qquad (1.1)$$

where each A_i is an atom and each L_j is a literal. The free variables are assumed to be universally quantified over the whole clause. A database is *definite* if, for each clause in the database, $m = 1$ and each L_i is an atom. The following is an example deductive database.

Example: $Postgraduate(x) \leftarrow MSc(x)$
$Postgraduate(x) \leftarrow PhD(x)$
$Student(x) \leftarrow Undergraduate(x)$
$MSc(x) \vee PhD(x) \leftarrow Student(x) \wedge \neg Undergraduate(x)$
$Student(a)$
$Supervisor(b, a)$
$Undergraduate(c) \vee MSc(c)$

Integrity constraints [7, 8, 9] are properties that the data of a database are required to satisfy. In the context of deductive databases, integrity constraints [10, 11, 12, 13, 14, 15, 16, 17] are expressed as closed first-order formulae. In the context of the above database, the constraint

$$\text{Every postgraduate student must have a supervisor} \qquad (1.2)$$

can be expressed as a closed first-order formula as

$$\forall x \, (Postgraduate \, (x) \rightarrow \exists y \, Supervisor \, (y, x)) \qquad (1.3)$$

Confining database statements and integrity constraints to the above mentioned forms of first-order formulae excludes some important statements and constraints [18] from considerations which are not first-order. However, dealing with a database system which is beyond first-order raises the question of far the extension should be stretched from first-order. Unlike the first-order case, the unification in the higher-order logic is undecidable [19]. Furthermore, implementing a database system on a general purpose higher-order theorem prover would not be useful for practical purposes because of its inefficiency. Hence, it is impractical to deal with the whole higher-order logic in a database.

The paper proposes an extension of first-order logic, called a *meta-logic*, to include many important database statements and integrity constraints which cannot otherwise be represented conveniently in first-order logic. A formal study of logic within the domain of these statements will be regarded as a meta-logic. It is shown that theoretical issues regarding the formal study of the proposed meta-logic can be dealt by a subsystem of typed λ-calculus [20]. An unification procedure is presented for such logic.

For all practical purpose, integrity constraints have so far been considered as range-restricted closed first-order formulae [21] which are an important subset of domain-independent formulae. Confining the definition of integrity constraints to closed first-order formulae excludes some important kinds of constraints from consideration. For example, consider the constraint

The total number of employees in a particular department may not exceed 100 (1.4)

The above constraint is obviously dependent on the domain of the set of employee identifications. Using the two relation schema Emp (Identification, Department) and $Dept$ (Department), no range-restricted first-order formulae can conveniently represent the above constraint. Given a higher-order predicate $Count$, which relates a set to its cardinality, the above constraint can be written in a typed formula as

$$\forall x_{str} \forall y_{int}(Dept\,(x_{str}) \wedge Count\,(\Gamma(x_{str}), y_{int}) \rightarrow y_{int} \leq 100 \qquad (1.5)$$

where $\Gamma(x_{str})$ (i.e., the value of the function Γ at the department x_{str}) denotes the set of all employees in the department x_{str}. The symbols str and int represent the types of string and integer respectively. The set $\Gamma(x_{str})$ can now be represented by the abstraction $\lambda z_{id}\,Emp\,(z_{id}, x_{str})$ of a function symbol, where id is the type symbol for identification. The domain of this function is the set of all objects of type id and the range is the set $\{true, false\}$ of truth values. The formula (1.5) can now be converted as

$$\forall x_{str} \forall y_{int}(Dept\,(x_{str}) \wedge Count\,(\lambda z_{id}\,Emp\,(z_{id}, x_{str}), y_{int}) \rightarrow y_{int} \leq 100 \qquad (1.6)$$

This leads one to think of allowing abstraction of a function, e.g., higher order λ-calculus terms, as arguments of predicates representing relations to the database. Since there is an equivalence in the representations of functions and relations, the predicate symbols appearing in (1.6) can be replaced by their equivalent function representation. Hence, by treating $\forall$, $\wedge$ and $\rightarrow$ as functions with appropriate domains and ranges, (1.6) can be replaced by its equivalent λ-term of the form

$$\forall_{(\alpha o)o}(\lambda x_\alpha(\forall_{(\beta o)o}(\lambda y_\beta((\rightarrow_{ooo}(((\wedge_{ooo}(DEPT_{\alpha o}\,x_\alpha))$$

$$((COUNT_{(\gamma o)\beta o}\,(\lambda z_\gamma(EMP_{\gamma\alpha o}\,z_\gamma)\,x_\alpha))\,y_\beta))))\,((\leq_{\beta\beta o}\,y_\beta)\,100)))))) \qquad (1.7)$$

where the suffix of a symbol denotes its type and $\alpha = str$, $\beta = int$, $\gamma = id$. For the sake of readability, the initial level of a λ-term will be expanded to a first-order predicate calculus like syntax such as (1.6) which can be thought of as an abbreviation of the λ-term (1.7)

By keeping the syntax within the typed first-order logic, another way of representing the constraint (1.4) is to replace $\Gamma(x_{str})$ in (1.5) by the variable x_{str} itself and rewrite (1.5) as

$$\forall x_{str} \forall y_{int}(Dept\,(x_{str}) \wedge Count\,(x_{str}, y_{int}) \rightarrow y_{int}\leq 100) \qquad (1.8)$$

One obvious disadvantage is then the predicate *Count* relates an integer to a department name of the *Emp* relation only. If one wants to impose a similar constraint on the number of students in a particular class, then either an extra procedure for *Count* relation has to be added to the database or the predicate *Count* has to be broken up into two predicates, *Count_Emp* and *Count_Stud*. This process of modifying the database state and schema will continue whenever a similar sort of aggregate operation is needed on an attribute domain of a new relation. Since the first argument position of *Count* in (1.5) can have any abstraction of a function whose domain is the set of *id*s and range is the set of truth values, the constraint (1.4)in the case of students can be represented in the form of (1.5) as

$$\forall x_{str} \forall y_{int}(Class\,(x_{str}) \wedge Count\,(\lambda z_{id}\,Stud\,(z_{id}, x_{str}), y_{int}) \rightarrow y_{int}\leq 100) \qquad (1.9)$$

Formulae in propositional calculus are considered as meta-logic statements of zero-order and formulae in first-order predicate calculus are mets-logic statements of first-order. The formulae (1.6) and (1.9) are meta-logic statements [22, 23] of second-order. A meta-logic statement can occur within another meta-logic statement. To represent a constraint like

No more than two tests may have an average mark of less than 50   (1.10)

one requires a meta-logic statement of third-order as

$$\forall x_{id} \forall y_{int} \forall z_{int}(Stud\,(x_{id}) \wedge Count\,($$

$$\lambda p_{str}\,(Avr\,(\lambda q_{int}\,Mark\,(x_{id}, p_{str}, q_{int}), y_{int}) \wedge y_{int}<50), z_{int}) \rightarrow z_{int}\leq 2) \qquad (1.11)$$

Even after a simplification process [24] , verification of the above kinds of constraints is sometimes expensive as they are evaluated as a query over the whole domain. For example, arrival of a new employee in a particular department will require counting of the total number of employee in that department by fetching each employee record. This is also the case when there are frequent queries to the database relating to the counting a domain or calculating an average on a domain. Efficiency in these cases can be increased by storing facts as λ-terms, for example

$$Count\,(\lambda y_{id}\,\,Stud\,(y_{id},\,Math\,),\,95) \qquad\qquad (1.12)$$

which stores the present number of students, which is 95, in the mathematics (Math) department. These kinds of facts, of course, may have to be updated after each transaction to the database.

The above discussion suggests the use of higher order facts in a database. Rules of this kind are also necessary as is evident from the following example which counts the total number of students in the science faculty (SF), which consists of, say, mathematics and computer science (CS).

$$\forall x_{int}\forall y_{int}\forall z_{int}(Count\,(\lambda p_{id}\,\,Stud\,(p_{id},\,SF\,),\,x_{int}) \leftarrow Count\,(\lambda q_{id}\,\,Stud\,(q_{id},\,Math\,),\,y_{int})\,\wedge$$

$$Count\,(\lambda r_{id}\,\,Emp\,(r_{id},\,CS\,),\,z_{int})\,\wedge x_{int}{=}y_{int}{+}z_{int}) \qquad\qquad (1.13)$$

The approach that has been adopted here is to consider meta-logic statements as database statements and some closed meta-logic statements as integrity constraints. This generalises first-order database statements and first-order range-restricted constraints. Although this approach increases flexibility for representing problems, some complexities arise regarding unification, simplification of constraints etc. unification can be tackled as a subsystem of typed w-order λ-calculus and Huet's unification procedure [25] is decidable in this subsystem. The simplification theorem for first-order range-restricted cases has to be generalised.

Taking into account of some of the problems discussed so far, the organisation of the paper is organised as follows. The following section introduces typed λ-calculus syntax. The definition of interpretation and model of typed λ-calculus is given in section 3. Meta-terms, meta-program, etc. are defined in 4 and the unification algorithm for two meta-terms is described in section 5. By defining a specific language and also by introducing some abbreviations, in section 6, a meta-program is transformed to a familiar syntax and a generalized definition of deductive database is given. A type theoretic view of a deductive database is presented in section 7. Integrity constraints aspects, i.e. representation, satisfaction and simplification, are discussed in section 8. Section 9 outlines a proof-procedure for deductive databases.

2. Typed λ-calculus

The syntax adopted in this section is much similar to ones in [26, 27]. In the notation, the suffix of a symbol representing a λ-term will denote the type of the symbol.

Given a finite set T_0 of elementary types (for example, int, str, $bool$), the set of types T is inductively defined as follows:

(a) if $\alpha \in T_0$ then $\alpha \in T$,

(b) if $\alpha, \beta \in T$ then $\alpha \rightarrow \beta \in T$,

(c) no other elements, other than those generated by the above two steps, are members of T.

The type $\alpha \rightarrow \beta$ denotes the type of a function with domain of elements of type α and range of elements of type β.

Given an at most countable set C of constants of arbitrary given types and a countably infinite set of variables V_α of each type $\alpha \in T$, the set of all atoms A is defined as $V \cup C$, where $V = \bigcup_{\alpha \in T} V_\alpha$. The set Λ of λ–*terms* (or *well-formed formulae*, or simply *formulae*) is inductively defined as follows:

(a) if $e \in A$ then $e \in \Lambda$,

(b) if $e^1 \in \Lambda$ has type $\alpha \rightarrow \beta$ and $e^2 \in \Lambda$ has type α, then the *application* $(e^1 e^2)$ is a member of Λ of type β,

(c) if $e \in \Lambda$ has type β and $x \in V_\alpha$, then the abstraction $\lambda x e$ is a member of Λ of type $(\alpha \rightarrow \beta)$,

(d) no other elements, other than those generated by the above three steps, are members of Λ.

A type symbol of the form $(\alpha_1 \rightarrow (\alpha_2 \rightarrow \cdots (\alpha_n \rightarrow \beta) \cdots))$ is written as $(\alpha_1, \alpha_2, ..., \alpha_n \rightarrow \beta)$. If a λ-term has the suffix $\alpha_1 \alpha_2 \cdots \alpha_n \beta$, then its type is

$(\alpha_1, \alpha_2, ..., \alpha_n \rightarrow \beta)$

A *subterm* of a term e are defined as follows:

(a)   the term e is a subterm of itself,

(b)   if e is of the form $(e^1 e^2)$, then both e^1 and e^2 are subterms of e,

(c)   if e is of the form $\lambda xe'$, then e' is a subterm of e,

(d)   if e^1 is a subterm of e and e^2 is a subterm of e^1, then e^2 is a subterm of e.

A *proper subterm* e' of a term e is a subterm of e such that $e \neq e'$. A *unit* term is a term without any subterm. All occurrences of x in a term λxe are said to be *bound* and the abstraction λxe is said to bind x and its *scope* is said to be e. An occurrence of a variable x in a term is *free* if it is not in the scope of an abstraction that binds x. A term in which no variables occur free is said to be a *closed* term. A term t is free for a variable x in a term e if there is no abstraction in e in whose scope x appears free and which also binds the free variables of t. $e[t/x]$ is used to denote the result of replacing each free occurrence of x in e by t (if $\tau(x) = \tau(t)$).

The computation rules of the λ-calculus are the following three λ-conversions:

(a) $(\lambda y \, e[y/x])$ follows from $(\lambda x \, e)$ by *α–conversion* provided y is free for x in e.

(b) $(e[t/x])$ follows from $(\lambda x \, e)t$ by *β–conversion* and vice versa provided t is free for x in e.

(c) $\lambda x\,(ex)$ follows from e by *η–conversion* and vice versa if e and x have appropriate type, provided x is not free in e.

α-conversion renames the bound variable in an abstraction; β-reduction replaces the formal argument by the actual one in an application.

Suppose, $e[s]$ denotes a term having a subterm s. Then let $e[t]$ denote the result of replacing the distinguished occurrence of s by a term t, where $\tau(s) = \tau(t)$. Define the relation $\rightarrow_\alpha$, $\rightarrow_\beta$ and $\rightarrow_{\alpha\beta}$ as follows:

$e[s] \rightarrow_\alpha e[t]$ *iff* t follows from s by α conversion,

$e[s] \rightarrow_\beta e[t]$ *iff* t follows from s by β conversion,

$e[s] \rightarrow_{\alpha\beta} e[t]$ *iff* either $e[s] \rightarrow_\alpha e[t]$ or $e[s] \rightarrow_\beta e[t]$.

The relation $\rightarrow_{\alpha\beta}^{*}$ is the reflexive and transitive closure of the relation $\rightarrow_{\alpha\beta}$. By λ-*conversion*, the relation $\rightarrow_{\alpha\beta}^{*}$ is meant. The reason for not considering η-conversion is to have a clear syntax by writing a function with all its arguments.

3. Interpretation and model of typed λ-calculus

An *interpretation* I of a meta-language L consists of the following:

(a) A collection $\{D_\alpha\}_\alpha$ of nonempty domains D_α, one for each type symbol α, called the *frame* of interpretation I.

(b) $D_o=\{T, F\}$.

(c) $D_{\alpha\beta}$ is a collection of functions mapping D_α into D_β.

(d) For each primitive constant of type α, the assignment of a fixed element of D_α.

Let I be an interpretation with frame $\{D_\alpha\}_\alpha$. Let $\{\Sigma_\alpha\}_\alpha$ be the set of all sequences of elements of D_α. For a given collection of sequences $\{S_\alpha=(s_\alpha^1, s_\alpha^2, ...)\in \Sigma_\alpha\}_\alpha$ and for a λ-term e consider the following *term assignment* ϕ_S of e with respect to I and S_α as follows:

(a) If e is a variable x_α^i then its assignment is s_α^i.

(b) If e is a constant then its assignment is according to I.

(c) If e is application $e_{\alpha\beta}^1 e_\alpha^2$ and if $e'^1_{\alpha\beta}$ and e'^2_α are the term assignments of $e_{\alpha\beta}^1$ and e_α^2 respectively then $e'^1_{\alpha\beta}e'^2_\alpha\in D_\beta$ is the term assignment of e.

(d) If e is an abstraction $\lambda x_\gamma^i e_\beta$ then the assignment of e is a member of $D_{\gamma\beta}$ whose value at each argument e_γ is e'_β, where e'_β is the term assignment of e_β corresponding to a set of sequences same as $\{\Sigma_\alpha\}_\alpha$ except the i-th position of the sequence S_γ in it is e_γ

A lambda term with some free variables can be assigned to different values with respect to different sequences. When a term is closed it is always assigned to the same value without regard to any sequence.

The definition of *satisfaction* of a formula e_o with respect to sequence $S \in \Sigma$ and an interpretation can be inductively defined as follows:

(e) S *satisfies* e_o iff $\phi_S(e_o) = T$.

(f) I *satisfies* e_o (or e_o is satisfiable in I) iff there is a sequence S such that S satisfies e_o.

(g) e_o is *valid* in I iff every sequence S satisfies I.

(h) I is a *model* of e_o iff e_o is valid in I.

(i) I is a *model* for a set F of wffs of type o iff I is a model for each e_o in F.

4. Meta-programs

A term is said to be in *normal form* if it does not contain a subterm of the form $(\lambda x e^1)e^2$.

Using the following two abbreviation:

$$e(e^1, e^2, ..., e^n) \equiv (\cdots ((ee^1)e^2), ..., e^n)$$
$$\lambda x^1 \cdots x^n\, e \equiv \lambda x^1 \cdots \lambda x^n\, e, \text{ where } x^1, ..., x^n \text{ are distinct.}$$

and by using λ-conversion, any term t can be converted to a normal form (unique upto α-conversion)

$$\lambda x^1 \cdots x^n.e(e^1, e^2, ..., e^m) \qquad\qquad (4.1)$$

where e is called the *head* of t, $\{e^1, ..., e^m\}$ are *arguments* of t, $\{x^1, ..., x^n\}$ called the *binder* of t. It can also be assumed that each x^i does not occur bound in any e^j. This property can be achieved by introducing new variables through α-conversions. When $m=0$, the term is written as $\lambda x^1 \cdots x^n.e$. When $n=0$, the term is written as $e(e^1, e^2, ..., e^m)$. The above term t is *rigid* if its head e is either a constant or a member of $\{x^1, ..., x^n\}$; otherwise t is *flexible*. The (equivalence) relation $=_\alpha$ between two terms e^1 and e^2 holds if and only if $e^1 \to_\alpha e^2$ and $e^2 \to_\alpha e^1$.

A *program* is a λ-term. A *meta-term* is a λ-term which does not contain a non-unit subterm with the head a variable. A *meta-program* is a meta-term. In the rest of the paper, meta-terms are assumed to be in their normal forms.

5. Unification of two meta-terms

The unification algorithm described in this section is a particular case (when the head of each non-unit λ-term is a constant) of Huet's unification algorithm [25].

A *disagreement set* is any finite set of pairs of terms of the same type:

$$\{<e^1_{\alpha_1}, e'^1_{\alpha_1}>, <e^2_{\alpha_2}, e'^2_{\alpha_2}>, ..., <e^n_{\alpha_n}, e'^n_{\alpha_n}>\}$$

Let e and e' are two meta-terms to be unified. Let N denotes a disagreement set and initially $N = \{<e, e'>\}$.

Step 1: If there does not exist in N a pair $<e^1, e^2>$ such that e^1 and e^2 are both rigid then perform step 2; otherwise, let $N = <e^1, e^2> \cup N'$ and e^1 and e^2 have the following form:

$$e_1 = \lambda x^1 \cdots x^{n_1} . t^1(g^1, ..., g^{m_1}) \qquad n_1 \geq 0, \ m_1 \geq 0,$$
$$e_2 = \lambda y^1 \cdots y^{n_2} . t^2(h^1, ..., h^{m_2}) \qquad n_2 \geq 0, \ m_2 \geq 0.$$

If $n_1 \neq n_2$ then e^1 and e^2 are not unifiable and algorithm stops here, else let $n = n_1 = n_2$, if $t^1 \neq_\alpha (\lambda y^1 \cdots y^n . t^2)(x^1, ..., x^n)$ then also e^1 and e^2 are not unifiable and algorithm stops here;
Otherwise, let $m = m_1 = m_2$ and replace N by $N' \cup \{<g'^1, h'^1>, ..., <g'^m, h'^m>\}$, where $g'^i =_\alpha \lambda x^1 \cdots x^n . g^i$, $h'^i =_\alpha \lambda y^1 \cdots y^n . h^i$, and repeat step 1.

Step 2: Replace in N every pair $<e^1, e^2>$, where e^1 is rigid and e^2 is flexible, by the pair $<e^2, e^1>$; perform Step 3.

Step 3: If there exists in N a pair $<e^1, e^2>$ such that e^2 is rigid then the two terms e and e' are not unifiable; otherwise each element in N is a substitution pair and N is a substitution which is an mgu of e_1 and e_2.

Consider an *Emp* relation whose first attribute is an identification and the second attribute is age. Consider the two λ-terms $\lambda x.Emp(x, y)$ and $\lambda y.Emp(x, y)$. If identification and age are two different types (e.g. string and integer respectively) then the term $\lambda x.Emp(x, B)$ has type $str \rightarrow o$ and the term $\lambda y.Emp(A, y)$ has type $int \rightarrow o$. Hence they are not unifiable. If identification and age are of same type then also they are not unifiable. The two lambda terms $\lambda x.Emp(x, y)$ and $\lambda x.Emp(x, A)$ are unifiable and unifier in this case is $\{y/A\}$.

6. Meta-programs and deductive databases

A specific familiar language is considered here for representing deductive database statements and integrity constraints in λ-terms. Using some abbreviations, each λ-term constructed in this language is converted to a first-order like syntax rather than always to their normal forms. The set of primitive symbols is considered as follows:

(a) The set T_0 of basic type symbols contains only ι and o. The type symbols o is the type of truth values. All database attribute domains have been considered to be a part of the same set of elements of type ι. This is introduced for simplicity reason and does not impose any restriction on a variety of attribute domains as all the subsequent results hold on any number of domains.

(b) The variables are as before $x_\alpha, y_\alpha, z_\alpha, ...$

(c) The improper symbols are λ, (,).

(d) The logical constants are $\neg_{oo}, \vee_{ooo}, \forall_{ioo}, =_{\alpha\alpha o}$, where α has the form $(\iota, \iota, \cdots (i\ times) \rightarrow o)$, $i = 0, 1, 2,....$ This set of logical constants is countable.

(e) A set of nonlogical constants of type ι which is the called the attribute domain of the database.

(f) A set of nonlogical constants each of type $\iota, \iota, ..., \iota$ ($n\ times$) $\rightarrow o$, for some n (≥ 0), and called an n-ary relation.

(g) A set of nonlogical constants each of type $\iota, \iota, ..., \iota$ ($n\ times$) $\rightarrow \iota$, for some n (≥ 0), and called an n-ary function.

The following conventions of abbreviations are introduced:

$$\neg_{oo} e_o \equiv (\neg e_o)$$

$$=_{\alpha\alpha o}(e_o^1, e_o^2) \equiv (e_o^1 =_{\alpha\alpha o} e_o^2)$$

$$\vee_{ooo}(e_o^1, e_o^2) \equiv (e_o^1 \vee e_o^2)$$

$$\neg((\neg e_o^1) \vee (\neg e_o^2)) \equiv (e_o^1 \wedge e_o^2)$$

$$e_o^1 \rightarrow e_o^2 \ (\text{or}, \ e_o^2 \leftarrow e_o^1) \equiv \neg e_o^1 \vee e_o^2$$

$$\forall_{(\alpha o)o}(\lambda x_\alpha e_o) \equiv \forall x_\alpha (e_o)$$

$$\neg(\forall x_\alpha(\neg e_o)) \equiv \exists x_\alpha e_o$$

It is always clear from the context whether the symbol '$\rightarrow$' is used in specifying a type symbol or used as a logical connective in specifying a meta-term.

A *meta-atom* is a meta-term of type o with the head is not a logical constant. A *positive meta-literal* is a meta-atom. A *negative meta-literal* has the form $\neg_{oo} e_o$, where e_o is a meta-atom. A *meta-literal* is either a positive or a negative meta-literal.

Considering an n-ary first-order typed predicate P as a function of type $(\alpha_1, ..., \alpha_n \rightarrow o)$, where $\alpha_1, ..., \alpha_n$ are types of the attribute domains of P, and also considering each logical connective as a function with appropriate domain and range (for example, $\wedge$ is a function of type (o, o $\rightarrow$ o), a first-order typed database statement can be taken as a special case of a meta-term.

A database meta-statement is a statement about a database statement; a database meta-meta-statement is a statement about a database meta-statement; and so on. In general, a database meta-statement can occur within another meta-statement and any meta-statement can be represented by a meta-term. With this view, the definition of a *meta-database* is considered as follows.

A *meta-database statement* (or *meta-database clause*) is a meta-term of the form

$$A_1 \vee \cdots \vee A_m \leftarrow L_1 \wedge \cdots \wedge L_n \qquad m \geq 1, n \geq 0 \qquad (6.1)$$

where each A_i is an atom and each L_j is a literal. The free variables in the clause, called the *global variables*, are assumed to be universally quantified over the whole clause. The structure of any proper subterm (of type o) of each of the atom occurring in the clause has the form

$$\exists y_1 \cdots \exists y_p (B_1 \wedge \cdots \wedge B_q) \qquad p \geq 0, q \geq 1 \qquad\qquad (6.2)$$

where each B_i is an atom.

The above definition of a meta-database clause generalises the definition of the first-order database clause of the form (1.1). When $m=1$ in clause (6.1), the meta-clause is reduced reduced to a *definite clause*. When $m=1$ and $n=0$ in clause (6.1), the meta-clause is reduced reduced to a *fact*. The set of all facts characterise all the functions corresponding to the nonlogical constants.

A *deductive meta-database* (or simply *meta-database*) is a closed meta-term of the form

$$((\cdots (e^1 \wedge e^2) \wedge \cdots) \wedge e^n) \qquad\qquad (6.3)$$

where e^i is a clause. In the intended interpretation (introduced in the next section), the logical constants are given their usual meanings and hence the truth value $(e^1 \wedge (e^2 \wedge e^3))$ is same as $((e^1 \wedge e^2) \wedge e^3)$, for any three terms e^1, e^2, e^3 of type o. Hence, the order of parentheses in (6.3) is irrelevant. For this reason the deductive database represented by (6.3) is written as a set $\{e^1, ..., e^n\}$ of clauses.

A *meta-goal* is a closed meta-term of the form

$$\leftarrow L_1 \wedge \cdots \wedge L_n \qquad n \geq 1 \qquad\qquad (6.4)$$

where each L_j is a literal and free variables are assumed to be universally quantified over the whole goal. The structure of any proper subterm (of type o) of each of the atom occurring in the goal is of the form (6.2). the goal (6.4) is *definite* when each L_i is an atom.

A meta-clause is *range-restricted* if each global variable occurring either in a negative literal of its condition or in an atom of its conclusion, should also occur in a positive literal of its condition. A deductive meta-database is *range-restricted* if each of its clauses is range-restricted.

Unless otherwise stated, the terms 'term', 'atom', 'literal', 'clause', 'statement', 'goal' and 'database' are read along with the prefix 'meta-'.

7. A type theoretic view of deductive databases

The type theoretic view of a deductive database D described in this section helps to define formally the answer to a goal and also the satisfiability of an integrity constraint in D.

Let D be a deductive database and $L(D)$ be a language defined as follows:

(1) The variables are as before x_α, y_α, z_α, ...

(2) The improper symbols are λ, (,).

(3) The logical constants are $\neg_{oo}$, $\vee_{ooo}$, $\forall_{(\iota o)o}$, $=_{\alpha\alpha o}$, where α has the form $(\iota, \iota, \cdots (i\ times) \rightarrow o)$, $i = 0, 1, 2,....$

(4) $L(D)$ contains the two nonlogical constants T and F of type o.

(5) $L(D)$ contains a set of nonlogical constants of type ι, one for each element of S_C, where S_C is the set of all constants of type o appearing in D.

(6) $L(D)$ contains a set of nonlogical constants of type $(\iota \rightarrow (\iota, \iota, ..., \iota\ (n-i\ times) \rightarrow \iota))$, $i=1,,2, ..., n$, one for each element of S_F, where S_F is the set of all nonlogical constants of $F^{(a^1, ..., a^i)}$ of type $(\iota \rightarrow (\iota, \iota, ..., \iota\ (n-i\ times) \rightarrow \iota))$, $i=1,,2, ..., n$, for all possible a^1, ..., a^i of S_C.

(7) $L(D)$ contains a set of nonlogical constants of type $(\iota \rightarrow (\iota, \iota, ..., \iota\ (n-i\ times) \rightarrow o))$, $i=1,,2, ..., n$, one for each element of S_R, where S_R is the set of all nonlogical constants of $R^{(a^1, ..., a^i)}$ of type $(\iota \rightarrow (\iota, \iota, ..., \iota\ (n-i\ times) \rightarrow o))$, $i=1,,2, ..., n$, for all possible a^1, ..., a^i of S_C.

The symbols $R^{(a^1, ..., a^i)}$ or $F^{(a^1, ..., a^i)}$ do not convey any special meaning. Each such symbol is unique to their representation if an order among the elements of S_C is defined in prior.

An *intended interpretation* I of the above language $L(D)$ is an interpretation of $L(D)$ with the following property:

(1) Each nonlogical constant in $L(D)$ is assigned to itself under the interpretation I.

(2) For each nonlogical constant a with appropriate type, if the value of $F^{(a_1, \dots, a_i)}(a)$ is a function then it is considered identical to the function $F^{(a_1, \dots, a_i, a)}$ $(0 \le i \le n-2)$; otherwise, the value of $F^{(a_1, \dots, a_{n-1})}(a)$ and $F(a^1, \dots, a^{n-1}, a)$ are identical.

(3) The logical constants are interpreted with their usual meanings.

The symbols F^0 and R^0 (i.e. when $i=0$) corresponds to F and R respectively. Any further reference to the term 'interpretation' will be referred to as 'intended interpretation'.

In the intended interpretation, the usual transformations (for example, distributivity of $\wedge$ over $\vee$, commutativity of $\vee$, etc.) hold. Using these transformation, any subterm of type o of a term (hence a database clause too) can be transformed to the familiar clausal notation

$$\Pi x^1 \cdots \Pi x^n ((l^{11} \vee \cdots \vee l^{1p}) \wedge \cdots \wedge (l^{q1} \vee \cdots \vee l^{qp})), \quad p \ge 0, q \ge 1 \quad (7.1)$$

where Π is either $\forall$ or $\exists$ and each l^{ij} is a literal. Parentheses in $\Pi x^1 \cdots \Pi x^n e$ is assumed as $(\Pi x^1 (\cdots (\Pi x^n (e)) \cdots))$ and the parentheses positions in a conjunction or in a disjunction is irrelevant as far as functional value is concerned.

Let D be a database and I is an interpretation of $L(D)$. Then I is said to be a *model* for D if and only if I is a *model* in the sense of section 3.

The type theory T_D of the database D, in other words the *meta-logic* T_D underlying the database D, is defined as follows (the symbol '=' assumes appropriate types at different places):

(a) The language of T_D is $L(D)$

(b) The proper axioms of T_D are as follows:

(1) Clauses of D other than the atomic facts are proper axioms of T_D.

(2) For each n-ary function F in the database schema and nonlogical constants a, $a^1, \dots, a^i$ with appropriate types, T_D includes

$$F^{(a^1, \dots, a^i)}(a) = F^{(a^1, \dots, a^i, a)}, \quad 0 \le i \le n-2.$$

$$F^{(a^1, \dots, a^{n-1})}(a) = F(a^1, \dots, a^{n-1}, a)$$

(3) For each n-ary relation R in the database schema and nonlogical constants a, $a^1, \dots, a^i$ with appropriate types, $\mathcal{T}_D$ includes

$$R^{(a^1, \dots, a^i)}(a) = R^{(a^1, \dots, a^i, a)}, \quad 0 \le i \le n-2.$$

(4) For each atomic fact $R(a^1, \dots, a^n)$, $\mathcal{T}_D$ includes

$$R^{(a^1, \dots, a^{n-1})}(a^n) = R(a^1, \dots, a^n).$$

(5) The logical axioms are defined as follows:

(1) $e_o^1 \to (e_o^2 \to e_o^1)$

(2) $(e_o^1 \to (e_o^2 \to e_o^3)) \to ((e_o^1 \to e_o^2) \to (e_o^1 \to e_o^3))$

(3) $(\neg e_o^1 \to \neg e_o^2) \to ((\neg e_o^1 \to e_o^2) \to e_o^1)$

(4) $\forall x_\alpha\, e_o \to e_o[x_\alpha/t]$ provided that t is free for x_α in e_o

(5) $\forall x_\alpha(e_o^\alpha \to e_o^\beta) \to (e_o^\alpha \to \forall x_\alpha e_o^\beta)$

(6) $e_\alpha = e_\alpha$

(7) $e_\alpha^1 = e_\alpha^2 \to e_\alpha^2 = e_\alpha^1$

(8) $e_\alpha^1 = e_\alpha^2 \to (e_\alpha^2 = e_\alpha^3 \to e_\alpha^1 = e_\alpha^3)$

(9) $e_\alpha^1 = e_\alpha^2 \to e_{\alpha\beta} e_\alpha^1 = e_{\alpha\beta} e_\alpha^2$

(10) $e_{\alpha\beta}^1 = e_{\alpha\beta}^2 \to e_{\alpha\beta}^1 e_\alpha = e_{\alpha\beta}^2 e_\alpha$

(11) $e_{\alpha\beta}^1 = e_{\alpha\beta}^2 \to e_\alpha^3 = e_\alpha^4 \to e_{\alpha\beta}^1 e_\alpha^3 = e_{\alpha\beta}^2 e_\alpha^4$

(12) $\forall x_\alpha(e_{\alpha\beta}^1 x_\alpha = e_{\alpha\beta}^2 x_\alpha) \to e_{\alpha\beta}^1 = e_{\alpha\beta}^2$

(13) Rules of inference [27] are as follows:

(1) *Conversions*: α, β and η.

(2) *Substitution*: From $e_{\alpha o}x_\alpha$ to infer $e_{\alpha o}t_\alpha$, provided x_α is not a free variable of $e_{\alpha o}$.

(3) *Modus ponens*: From $e_o \rightarrow e'_o$ and e_o, to infer e'_o.

(4) *Generalization*: From $e_{\alpha o}x_\alpha$ to infer $\forall x_\alpha(e_{\alpha o})$, provided that x_α is not a free variable of $e_{\alpha o}$.

A *theorem* is a formula obtainable from the set of axioms by a succession of applications of the rules of inference. A *proof* of a theorem is a finite sequence of formulae, the last of which is a theorem, and each of which is a formal axioms obtainable from the preceding formulae in the sequence by an application of a rule of inference.

Example :

Database:

$$P(x,y) \leftarrow Q(x,F(y)) \wedge R(y)$$
$$Q(a^1, a^2)$$
$$Q(a^1, a^3)$$
$$R(a^2)$$
$$S(a^2, a^1, a^3)$$
$$F(a^2) =_{uo} a^3$$
$$F(a^1) =_{uo} a^2$$
$$F(a^3) =_{uo} a^1$$

The nonlogical constants of L are a^1, a^2 and a^3. The function symbols with their types are as follows:

Function	Type
F	$(\iota \rightarrow \iota)$
P	$(\iota, \iota \rightarrow o)$
Q	$(\iota, \iota \rightarrow o)$
R	$(\iota \rightarrow o)$
S	$(\iota, \iota, \iota \rightarrow o)$
$P^{(a^i)}, Q^{(a^i)}$	$(\iota \rightarrow o)$
$S^{(a^i)}$	$(\iota, \iota \rightarrow o)$
$S^{(a^i a^j)}$	$(\iota \rightarrow o)$
$i, j = 1, 2, 3$	

The proper axioms are defined as follows:

$$P(x,y) \leftarrow Q(x, F(y)) \wedge R(y)$$
$$F(a^2) =_{\iota o} a^3$$
$$F(a^1) =_{\iota o} a^2$$
$$F(a^3) =_{\iota o} a^1$$
$$P(a^i) =_{(\iota o)(\iota o)o} P^{(a^i)}, \text{ for } i=1, 2, 3$$
$$Q(a^i) =_{(\iota o)(\iota o)o} Q^{(a^i)}, \text{ for } i=1, 2, 3$$
$$Q^{(a^1)}(a^2) =_{ooo} Q(a^1, a^2)$$
$$Q^{(a^1)}(a^3) =_{ooo} Q(a^1, a^3)$$
$$R(a^2)$$
$$S(a^i) =_{(\iota\iota o)(\iota\iota o)o} S^{(a^i)}, \text{ for } i=1, 2, 3$$
$$S^{(a^i)}(a^j) =_{(\iota o)(\iota o)o} S^{(a^i, a^j)}, \text{ for } i, j=1, 2, 3$$
$$S^{(a^2, a^1)}(a^3) =_{ooo} S(a^2, a^1, a^3)$$

8. Integrity constraints

This section discusses how integrity constraints are represented by closed meta-terms. Also, a definition of constraint satisfiability is introduced and constraint simplification issue is discussed.

8.1. Constraint representation

An *integrity constraint* is defined as a closed meta-term. For the sake of convenience, an integrity constraint is considered as a closed meta-term Γ of the form

$$\forall x_1 \cdots \forall x_p (e^1_{\alpha_1} \wedge \cdots \wedge e^n_{\alpha_n} \rightarrow e'^1_{\beta_1} \vee \cdots \vee e'^m_{\beta_m}) \qquad (8.1)$$

where $e^1_{\alpha_1} \wedge \cdots \wedge e^n_{\alpha_n}$ is the *condition* of Γ and $e'^1_{\beta_1} \vee \cdots \vee e'^m_{\beta_m}$ is the *conclusion*. Each $e^i_{\alpha_i}$ and $e'^j_{\beta_j}$ is a meta-atom and $x_1, ..., x_p$ are all the free variables of the condition and the conclusion of Γ. The above form does not impose any significant restriction on expressing constraints. In the first-order case, any arbitrary closed first-order formula expressing a constraint can be transformed to the form (8.1) by using the transformations in [28]. The constraints (1.6) and (1.11) are already in the form of (8.1). Also, the following two constraints

A student obtaining an average

$$\text{mark greater than or equal to 50, passes the examination} \qquad (8.2)$$

The maximum of the average salary of the departments must be less than 15000 $\qquad (8.3)$

can be expressed in the form of (8.1) as, respectively,

$$\forall x_{id} \forall y_{int}(Stud(x_{id}) \wedge Avr(\lambda z_{int} Mark(x_{id}, z_{int}), y_{int}) \wedge y_{int} \geq 50 \rightarrow Pass(x_{id})) \qquad (8.4)$$

$$\forall x_{int} \forall y_{int}(Max(\lambda v_{str}(Dept(v_{str}) \wedge$$

$$Avr(\lambda u_{id} \lambda w_{int} Emp(u_{id}, v_{str}, w_{int}), x)), y) \rightarrow y \leq 15000) \qquad (8.5)$$

8.2. Constraint satisfiability

Analogous to the definition of constraint satisfiability in the case of first-order constraints and first-order database, the definition of constraint satisfiability in the case of meta-database can be generalized as follows:

A database D is said to satisfy a constraint Γ if Γ is a theorem of the type theory T_D of D; otherwise, D violates Γ. The database D is said to satisfy a set of constraints I if D satisfies each of the constraints in I.

8.3. Constraint simplification

An important assumption regarding constraint checking is that a database satisfies constraints prior to its update. Hence, upon each update to the database, only a subset of the set of all constraints needs to be verified to guarantee the constraint satisfaction in the updated database. Also, a constraint can be simplified by the transaction before its verification towards the database. Inserting a tuple $P(a^1, ..., a^n)$ to a database D means the axiom

$$P^{(a^1, ..., a^{n-1})}(a^n) =_{ooo} P(a^1, ..., a^n) \qquad (8.6)$$

is added to the type theory $\mathcal{T}_D$ of D. Naturally, in the new theory some constraints may not be theorems any more. Similar argument is applicable in the case of deletion and update.

9. Proof procedure for definite clauses

This section will present a proof procedure for querying definite deductive databases. The procedure is an extension of SLD-resolution [29] which is based on the unification algorithm presented in section 5 and a particular case of the scheme proposed in [30]. The proposed proof procedures handles only definite clauses and definite goals.

Suppose D be a definite database and G a definite goal. Then a *definite derivation* of $D \cup \{G\}$ consists of a (finite or infinite) sequence $G_0 = G, G_1, G_2, ...$, a sequence of substitution $\theta_1, \theta_2, ...$ of mgu's such that G_{i+1} is derived from $G_i = \leftarrow B_1 \wedge \cdots B_n$ using θ_{i+1} if one of the following conditions hold:

(a) The selected atom B_k from G_i is a variable x, then θ_{i+1} is $\{x/true\}$ and G_{i+1} is

$$\leftarrow (B_1 \wedge \cdots \wedge B_{k-1} \wedge B_{k+1} \wedge \cdots \wedge B_n)\theta_{i+1}.$$

(b) The selected atom B_k from G_i is *true*, then θ_{i+1} is an empty substitution and G_{i+1} is

$$\leftarrow B_1 \wedge \cdots \wedge B_{k-1} \wedge B_{k+1} \wedge \cdots \wedge B_n.$$

(c) The selected atom B_k from G_i has a non-logical constant as its head and let $A \leftarrow A_1 \wedge \cdots \wedge A_m$ be a clause in D such that A and B_k unifies with an mgu θ, then θ_{i+1} is θ and G_{i+1} is

$$\leftarrow (B_1 \wedge \cdots \wedge B_{k-1} \wedge A_1 \wedge \cdots \wedge A_m \wedge B_{k+1} \wedge \cdots \wedge B_n)\theta$$

The definition of *derivation tree, finitely failed derivation tree, refutation,* etc. are defined in a usual manner.

10. Conclusion

An extension of first-order logic, called meta-logic, is presented here. Each statement of a meta-logic is characterised by a typed λ-calculus term whose head (when it is normal form) is a constant. It is also shown how some particular database statements and integrity constraints can be expressed conveniently by this system. A proof procedure is developed to answer definite queries in definite databases. Much of the theoretical work, for example, the equivalence of model theory and proof theory of this meta-logic, soundness and completeness of the proof procedure, are yet to be established. An efficient implementation of this logic (for example, through a Prolog meta-interpreter) is also an important issue.

Acknowledgements

I acknowledge Steve, Greg and Norman for their helpful comments on this paper.

References

1. H.Gallaire, J.Minker, and J.-M.Nicolas, "Logic and databases - a deductive approach," *ACM Computing Surveys,* **Vol. 16, No.2,** pp. 153-185, (1984).

2. H.Gallaire, "Logic databases vs deductive databases," *Proceedings of Logic Programming Workshop,* pp. 608-622, Algarve, Portugal, (1983).

3. A.Thayse (ed.), *From Modal Logic to Deductive Databases,* John Wiley & Sons, (1989).

4. Y.Y.Leung and D.L.Lee, "Logic approaches for deductive databases," *IEEE Expert*, (Winter 1988).

5. J.W.Lloyd, "An introduction to deductive database systems," *The Australian Computer Journal*, **Vol. 15, No.2**, pp. 52-57, (May 1983).

6. J.Minker, "Perspectives in deductive databases," *Journal of Logic Programming*, **Vol. 5**, pp. 33-60, (1988).

7. C.J.Date, *An Introduction to Database Systems, Vol2*, Addison Wesley, (1985).

8. E.B.Fernandez, R.C.Summers, and C.Wood, *Database Security and Integrity*, Addison Wesley, (1981).

9. J.D.Ullman, *Principles of Database Systems, 2nd edition*, Computer Science Press International, Inc, Maryland, USA, (1984).

10. R.A.Kowalski, "Logic programming with integrity constraints," *Workshop on Logic Programming, Imperial College, London*, (1989).

11. S.K.Das and M.H.Williams, "Integrity checking methods in deductive databases: A comparative evaluation," *Proceedings of the 7th British National Conference on Databases*, pp. 85-116, Cambridge University Press, (1989).

12. J.W.Lloyd and R.W.Topor, "A basis for deductive database systems," *Journal of Logic Programming*, **Vol. 2, No.2**, pp. 93-109, (1985).

13. H.Decker, "Integrity enforcements on deductive databases," *L.Kerschberg (ed.): Proceedings of the First International Conference on Expert Database Systems*, pp. 271-285, Charleston, South Carolina, (April 1986).

14. F.Sadri and R.A.Kowalski, "An application of general purpose theorem-proving to database integrity," *J.Minker (ed.): Proceedings of the Workshop on Foundations of Deductive Databases and Logic Programming*, (1987).

15. T.-W.Ling, "Integrity constraint checking in deductive databases using the Prolog not-predicate," *Data & Knowledge Engineering*, **Vol. 2**, pp. 145-168, (1987).

16. P.Asirelli, M.D.Santis, and M.Martelli, "Integrity constraint in logic databases," *Journal of Logic Programming*, **Vol. 3**, pp. 221-232, (1985).

17. S.K.Das and M.H.Williams, "A path finding method for checking integrity in deductive databases," *Data & Knowledge Engineering*, **Vol. 4**, pp. 223-244, Elsevier Science Publishers B.V. (North-Holland), (1989).

18. S.K.Das and M.H.Williams, "Extending integrity maintenance capability in deductive databases," *Proceedings of the UK ALP-90 Conference*, Intellect, Oxford, Bristol, (March 1990).

19. W.Snyder and J.Gallier, "Higher-order unification revisited: Complete sets of transformations," *Journal of Symbolic Computation*, **Vol. 8**, pp. 101-140, (1989).

20. H.P.Barendregt, "The lambda calculus: its syntax and semantics," *J.Barwise et al.(ed.): Studies in Logic and The Foundations of Mathematics, Vol.103*, North-Holland, (1984).

21. S.K.Das, *Integrity constraints in deductive databases*, Department of Computer Science, Heriot-Watt University, PhD Thesis, (1990).

22. P.M.Hill and J.W.Lloyd, "Analysis of meta-programs," *H.Abramson and M.H.Rogers (eds.): Meta-programming in Logic Programming*, pp. 23-51, MIT Press, (1989).

23. V.S.Subrahmanian, "A simple formulation of the theory of metalogic programming," *H.Abramson and M.H.Rogers (eds.): Meta-programming in Logic Programming*, pp. 65-101, MIT Press, (1989).

24. J.-M.Nicolas, "Logic for improving integrity checking in relational databases," *Acta Informatica*, **Vol. 18**, pp. 227-253, (1982).

25. G.P.Huet, "A unification algorithm for typed lambda-calculus," *Theoretical Computer Science*, **Vol. 1**, pp. 27-57, (1975).

26. P.B.Andrews, *An Introduction to Mathematical Logic and Type Theory: To Truth Through Proof*, Academic Press, Inc., (1986).

27. A.Church, "A formulation of the simple theory of types," *Journal of Symbolic Logic*, **Vol. 5**, pp. 56-68, (1940).

28. J.W.Lloyd and R.W.Topor, "Making Prolog more expressive," *Journal of Logic Programming*, **Vol. 1, No.3**, pp. 225-240, (1984).

29. K.R.Apt and M.H.Van Emden, "Contributions to the theory of logic programming," *Journal of the Association for Computing Machinery*, **Vol. 29**, pp. 841-862, (July 1982).

30. D.A.Miller and G.Nadathur, "Higher-order logic programming," *E.Shapiro (ed.): Proceedings of the 3rd International Conference on Logic Programming*, pp. 448-462, Springer-Verlag, London, U.K, (July 1986).

A Denotational Approach to Object-Oriented Query Language Definition

Karen C. Davis

Electrical and Computer Engineering
University of Cincinnati
Cincinnati, OH, USA

Lois M.L. Delcambre

The Center for Advanced Computer Studies
University of Southwestern Louisiana
Lafayette, LA, USA

Abstract

A denotational semantics approach to object-oriented database query language definition provides an elegant formalism for specifying the syntax and semantics of the query language. The challenge is to characterize an object-oriented database (OODB) as a semantic domain, so that query expressions can be mapped to their meaning in terms of the OODB. In this research, a high-level, conceptual view of OODBs and an algebraic query language that support query processing studies are proposed. The model is applicable to structurally similar database models, which includes most object-oriented and semantic databases; it can support complex objects, inclusion dependencies (the isa relationship), exclusion dependencies (the disjoint relationship), direct associations (properties) between complex objects, multi-valued properties, and modification of inherited properties. The query algebra is a closed and complete language in the spirit of relational algebra, supporting both value-oriented and object-oriented query processing in a single language. A contribution of the denotational definition of the model and query language is the precise characterization of both the rich intension and the extension of an OODB and of the results of queries on the OODB. In this paper, the conceptual model and query algebra are discussed and formalized, followed by an illustration of how the formal definition enables proofs of algebraic transformations for logical query optimization.

1 Introduction

Perhaps the most significant obstacle to object-oriented query processing research is the lack of agreement on a data model; this seriously impedes the development of a formal foundation for query language, query optimization, and view processing research. To overcome the data model problem, this research embraces a high-level, conceptual model of complex objects and presents a formally-defined, algebraic query language for the model. The results reported here apply to a wide variety of object-oriented and semantic database data models, requiring only that the database support strict inheritance through the isa relationship.

Using a formal technique for defining a language offers several advantages. Because formal definitions have a machine representation, they can be mechanically processed; applications include automatic prototyping and accessing the formal definition to support natural language interfaces and software tools [1]. A formal definition also provides a precise standard for implementation [2]. The particular formalism employed in this research is denotational semantics. Denotational semantics allows a language designer to specify an abstract, mathematical characterization of state, which is not tied to a particular machine or computation sequence. In this research, denotational semantics provides the framework for characterizing a conceptual query evaluation environment (both intension and extension) that is independent of any object-oriented database system implementation. The formal definition supports:

1. specification of the schema-level structure of complex objects,

2. precise characterization of the interaction of the algebra with the structural description and database,

3. formal reasoning about the meaning of queries, enabling proofs that syntactic transformations for logical query optimization are meaning-preserving,

4. formal specification of view definition, view integration, and view materialization, and

5. a framework for extending the model and query language.

The contribution of this paper is a theoretical framework for object-oriented query processing studies, with an example of the use of the formal definition for proving the equivalence of two algebraic expressions.

A conceptual model for object-oriented query processing is discussed in Section 2. The formal definition of an algebraic query language is presented in Section 3. To illustrate the formal basis for object-oriented logical query optimization, proof of an algebraic transformation using the denotational definition is given in Section 4. Conclusions and discussion are offered in Section 5.

2 A conceptual model for object-oriented query processing

In this section, features of an object-oriented database system that are relevant to abstract query processing studies are identified and synthesized into a conceptual data model. Updates and view materialization are discussed as topics for future research in Section 5. A more general description of OODBs may be found elsewhere, e.g., [3, 4, 5].

Query processing, from a query writer's point of view, is concerned with the conceptual level of a database. Physical details, such as whether data is stored or derived, are invisible to the user. Encapsulation of structure and behavior can be preserved, since a user need only retrieve data visible through the interface defined for a class. Since queries view the states of objects, which may be obtained through *observer* or *reporter* methods [5], methods that change the state of objects (*mutators* [5]) will not be considered here. In other words, a high-level query language based on the abstractions provided by a conceptual data model can serve as a query language for an OODB.

The proposed conceptual data model, essentially a semantic data model (e.g. [6]), provides the following:

1. object identity (a unique identifier regardless of values of objects),

2. complex state (the ability to reference other objects through properties),

3. the isa relationship with strict inheritance (encompassing both type and collection hierarchies [5]), and

4. inheritance of observer methods or attributes (both conceptually modeled as properties) through the isa relationship on types.

The semantics associated with these features supports the intensional specification of complex objects and provides the fundamental framework for the query language presented here.

Extension and *intension* are used to distinguish between data and schema information, respectively. *Class* is used here to refer to both a collection of objects (extension of the class) and the template for or type of the objects (intension of the class).

In this research, the notion of *property* embodies several concepts. A property associates complex objects in a class to data objects in another class. The data objects are called the *image* of the object for a property, and the image may contain either complex objects or values. A property between two classes containing complex objects directly relates object identifiers. A property which associates complex objects to values (possibly tuples) from an explicitly defined set of values is analogous to an attribute with an associated domain. The intensional aspect of the association may be viewed as the signature of a method which associates objects of one class to objects/values of another class. The extensional aspect of a property is modeled abstractly as a binary relation between the object identifier of the complex object and the appropriate data object (either a value or complex object identifier).

The notion of strict inheritance is critical to the correct processing of queries and is commonly embraced for object-oriented and semantic database data models in their structural descriptions. This means that once a property is defined, it cannot be extended by a subclass; the subclass may only accept or further restrict the range/cardinality restrictions on an inherited property. For example, if a class of automobiles is defined as vehicles having 4 wheels, then its subclasses may have 4 or fewer wheels, but not more. New local properties may be introduced at a subclass, and inherited by its subclasses. With regard to the overriding/replacing of methods, this research requires only that the signature for a method be accepted or further restricted. Observer methods are represented only by their external interface, i.e., their signature. This supports the participation of derived data in query processing and preserves encapsulation. The code in methods may be overridden at the subclass level, but for the purposes of this query language the signatures must conform to a subclass hierarchy. In other words, signatures for inherited methods must respect strict inheritance. For example, an *Integer* class may be a subclass of *Real*, where real addition is coded in an *add* method. The *add* method is inherited by *Integer*, but the code is replaced by integer addition. The signature for real addition is: *add: Real × Real → Real*, while the signature for integer addition is *add: Integer × Integer → Integer*. Thus, each class in the signature respects the class hierarchy. Other issues relating to behavioral abstraction beyond signatures are outside the scope of this research.

The fundamental tenet of the query algebra presented here is the notion of automatic membership [7] in classes. *Automatic* or *definitional* membership refers to membership in a class that is described by an intensional rather than extensional specification (e.g., enumeration or user-controllable membership). Early semantic data models suggested definitional subclasses as part of their data definition language (DDL), notably SDM [6]. The conceptual model used here does not require definitional subclasses in the DDL but adheres to the notion that query algebra operators are always class-forming and always definitional. Queries are definitional in the sense that the query is an abstract specification of precisely which objects from the database classes constitute the query answer. OODBSs such as GemStone [8, 9], Iris [10, 11], O_2 [12, 13], and ORION [14, 15] present no obstacles to using this conceptual model for query processing. Each supports a class hierarchy that allows structure and behavior to be inherited. None of them support automatic membership, but since queries are definitional in nature, query processing against these OODBSs are supported because queries induce an isa relationship with inheritance and definitional membership.

The structural abstraction provided by the conceptual model is sufficient for exploring query language issues in object-oriented data models, since the algebra presented here can be used to express information such as access paths. The algebra proposed here can bridge the gap between implementations and query interfaces, since it provides object-oriented and value-oriented query power, support for views, and the basis for logical query optimization; the use of a conceptual data model and algebra represents a step toward developing a theoretical foundation for object-oriented query and view processing.

3 A denotational definition of an algebraic query language

Several sources provided inspiration for the research reported here. The original goal was to bring the functionality of relational algebra to a data model with rich semantics. At the inception of the research, the structural data model was well-understood, the operators of the algebra were informally sketched, and denotational semantics was chosen to represent the concepts formally. Denotational semantics provides an elegant means for expressing the essential features of language semantics: the syntax of the language, the domains (environment) where the syntactic constructs have meaning, and the mapping from expressions in the language to meaningful results in the environment. The unresolved issues included:

1. How can the rich semantics of the conceptual data model be captured in the simple set-theoretic constructs of denotational semantics?

2. How can a single environment (in denotational semantics) represent both the intensional description (schema) and extensional description (data) of the database?

3. What is the result of a query? Further, will the processing of the query modify the extensional and/or intensional description of the database?

4. How can a query be mapped to a query result?

5. How can the algebra support closure? That is, how can the algebra support repeated application of operators as part of an arbitrarily complex query?

The query algebra is presented in Section 3.1, and the denotational definition developed to address these issues is presented in Section 3.2. A review of the intensional and extensional environment to support a query algebra with closure is given here.

Codd's original definition of the relational algebra was only an extensional account of the operators [16]. Extensional semantics alone do not completely describe a query result; it is conceptually accurate to view each query result as an actual relation with a name and attributes. For this research, all operators are class-forming and the resulting classes are described intensionally as well as extensionally in the denotational definition. Another important observation is that the query answer (the result relation) is precisely specified by the relational query. Thus, tuples are in the answer if and only if they satisfy the declarative specification in the query. The analogous notion for this research is support for classes with a membership definition (i.e., automatic membership).

In the data model developed for this research, the intensional portion of the database state contains structural information about classes such as details of their properties and membership definitions. The extensional portion of the database state includes the extension of classes (sets of object identifiers) and mappings of objects to their values (called *images* here) under properties. Each user-defined class has both an intension and an extension; each query result is a class with intension and extension *derived* from existing classes and query specifications. A query result can be viewed as a system-generated class, the details of which are appended to the database state. The formal definition of the query operators includes semantics for determining the inherited properties and membership definitions of query answers, as well as the data objects in the query answer.

Defining a query result in terms of the database state directly addresses one of the previously unresolved problems in object-oriented query-processing: the need for a query language with the closure property. Bancilhon and Kim describe the closure property as that feature of a query language which takes a schema and database as input, and produces a schema and database as the

Operator	Properties of Query Result	Membership Definition of Query Result
$e_1 \cup e_2$	most general version of common properties	"or" membership definitions $(wff(e_1) \vee wff(e2))$
$e_1 \cap e_2$	all properties with most specific common properties	"and" membership definitions $(wff(e_1) \wedge wff(e2))$
$e_1 - e_2$	properties of e_1	"difference" of membership definitions $(wff(e_1) \wedge \neg(wff(e2)))$
$\rho_{re}\ e$	properties of e	"and" membership definition and restrict expression $(wff(e) \wedge re)$
$\sigma_{se}\ e$	properties of e	"and" membership definition and select expression $(wff(e) \wedge se)$
$\pi_{pnl}\ e$	properties in property list (pnl); generated property with e as a range class	generated membership definition
$e_1 \times e_2$	two generated properties with e_1 and e_2 as range classes	generated membership definition

Figure 1: Intensional Query Results

result of a query [17]. The process of formally defining the object-oriented, algebraic query language described here led to defining the query evaluation environment in terms of schema and data, and to the natural extension of defining query results in terms of schema and data.

3.1 The query algebra

The core of the query language is the ability to form subclasses of existing classes by restricting inherited properties. In this case, all attributes and values of a query result are derived from existing database objects (both schema and data); retaining connections to the schema provides logical access paths to data. The algebra includes subclass-forming operators ($\cup, \cap, -, \rho$, and σ) and class-forming operators (π and $\times$). In both cases, the connection with the underlying database objects is preserved and thus query materialization is directly supported.

The operators of the algebra are listed in Figures 1 and 2, along with an informal summary of their semantics. A query expression is denoted by e, and a membership definition is denoted by wff. The intensional effects of the operators (Figure 1) are described in terms of the inherited or derived properties of the query result and its membership definition. The extensional effects (Figure 2) describe which objects are in the query answer.

The first group of operators ($\cup$, $\cap$, $-$, ρ, σ) are the identity-preserving, subclass-forming operators. (The union operator ($\cap$) actually produces a superclass or generalization of its argument classes, but the query result will be a subclass of the arguments' common superclass.) Intersection ($\cap$) is discussed in detail in the next section.

The restrict (ρ) and select (σ) operators form subclasses with membership based on objects' values. In other words, an object belongs in the extensional query result of a ρ or σ query if its image conforms to the property modifications given in the query. Both operators modify inherited properties by limiting the

Operator	Extensional Effect
$e_1 \cup e_2$	union of object identifiers
$e_1 \cap e_2$	intersection of object identifiers
$e_1 - e_2$	difference of object identifiers
$\rho_{re}\ e$	subset of object identifiers based on entire image of objects for restricted properties
$\sigma_{se}\ e$	subset of object identifiers based on partial image of objects for selected properties
$\pi_{pnl}\ e$	new object identifiers assigned to distinct values
$e_1 \times e_2$	new object identifiers assigned to each pair of object identifiers in cross product

Figure 2: Extensional Query Results

range class values and/or the cardinality constraints of properties. Range class modifications limit the values that an object's image may have to a subclass of the property's original range class values; cardinality modifications limit the number of values that an object's image may have. Two operators are used since properties may be multi-valued.

The restrict operator, ρ, is based on universal quantification; objects in a class defined by ρ must have entire images within the cardinality and range restrictions of the properties specified in the restrict expression. For example, let a *Ships* class have a *CargoType* property, which may have multiple images (a ship may carry 1 or more types of cargo). If the range is **restricted** to the class *TextilesUS* in a query using the ρ operator, then the objects in the query result are ships which carry only US textile products, and no other types of cargo. The semantics of the ρ operator are discussed in detail in the next section.

The select operator, σ, represents existential quantification; it allows objects to be selected based on part of their images for properties, without specifying all of the possible images containing that part. For example, if a query is defined by **selecting** the range of the *CargoType* property as *TextilesUS*, then ships which carry at least one US textile product, and possibly other types of cargo, would be in the query result.

The two remaining operators of the query algebra, project (π) and cross product ($\times$), form classes that are derived from existing classes; the members of these classes are new objects whose images are existing objects. The project operator defines a class with intension like that of a base class (i.e., a class with no superclasses that contains complex objects). Its properties are derived from the projected properties, its images are the set of images resulting from the projection (duplicates are removed), and new identifiers are assigned for each resulting image. For example, a class *Ships'* may be formed by projecting *CargoType* and *HomePort* from *Ships*. Each unique cargo type/home port combination appearing in the database is assigned a new object identifier, forming the membership in *Ships'*. There is a dilemma associated with an object-oriented project operator: what sort of a class does it form? A class formed by projection is not a subclass (e.g., of *Ships*), because it does not have all of the properties of the original class, nor is it a superclass since it may contain fewer objects due to the elimination of duplicate images. In this research, a class formed by the project operator is handled as if it were a new base class added to the schema, with an additional system-generated property that connects each newly generated object identifier with the set of objects from the original class that have its image value for the projected properties. The project operator (π) described here differs from the project operator of ORION's query language [15], since any number of properties of a class may be projected.

The cross product operator ($\times$) forms a new class with two properties whose range classes are the abstract classes involved in the cross product. A new object is generated for each pair of objects in the Cartesian product of the two range classes. Each new object is associated with an object in each range class via the two new properties, where the pair of associations corresponds to the Cartesian product. This operator is useful for unstructured joins (previously unestablished associations between objects), overcoming a weakness of object-oriented databases [18].

3.2 The formal definition

The denotational definition discussed here uses terminology and style similar to that employed by Schmidt [2]. The discussion focuses on the structure of the semantic domains (Figure 3) and the semantic algebras. The valuation functions (Figure 4) map the abstract syntax of the query algebra to semantic domains. The operations over domains are described using equational definitions of sets [2], where LISP-like syntax specifies a function whose actual value can be determined by substitution and simplification. The extensional and intensional effect of each query operator is defined in the semantic algebra for the domain of classes containing complex objects.

The domains of the query evaluation environment are outlined in Figure 3. The domains are arranged in a top-down, modular fashion, so that the structure of a domain and its associated operations can be understood and modified more easily. The highest-level domain is *QueryResult*, which shows that a query answer is composed of an abstract class name and a database state. A query expression is evaluated against an initial database state, producing an abstract class whose intension and extension is conceptually appended to the database state.

The database state is composed of intensional information (the domain *Schema*) and extensional information (the domain *Data*). Structural information about classes such as details of their properties is kept in the *Schema* domain. Membership definitions for classes are stored here, also. Queries always have membership definitions, whether or not the underlying database supports defined membership in schemas through its DDL. The formal definitions of the query operators include semantics for determining the inherited properties and membership definitions of query answers.

The domain *Data* includes the extension of classes (sets of object identifiers) and mappings of objects to their images (values) under properties. Subclasses formed by query operators contain a subset of their superclass's extension, but the operators do not affect the images in any way. In other words, the only modification to the extensional database state is to include the new subclass and the object identifiers of its contents; since the new class inherits properties of its superclass, the images of the objects are the same.

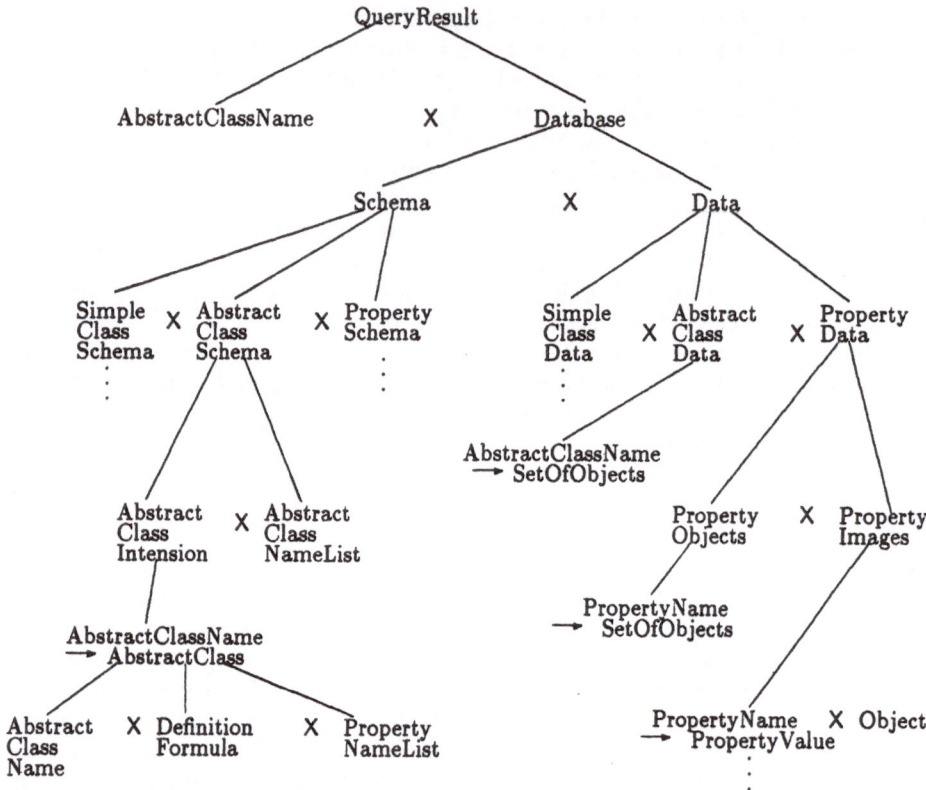

Figure 3: Domains of the Query Evaluation Environment

$\mathcal{Q}$: Expression $\rightarrow$ Database $\rightarrow$ QueryResult

$\quad \mathcal{Q}[\![e]\!] = \lambda$ db. $\mathcal{E}[\![e]\!]($initialQR db$)$

$\mathcal{E}$: Expression $\rightarrow$ QueryResult $\rightarrow$ QueryResult

$\quad \mathcal{E}[\![\text{abstract\_class\_name}]\!] = \lambda$ qr. $<$abstract_class_name, (database qr)$>$

$\quad \mathcal{E}[\![e_1 \cup e_2]\!] = \lambda$ qr. (**union** $\mathcal{E}[\![e_1]\!]$qr $\mathcal{E}[\![e_2]\!]$qr)

$\quad \mathcal{E}[\![e_1 \cap e_2]\!] = \lambda$ qr. (**intersect** $\mathcal{E}[\![e_1]\!]$qr $\mathcal{E}[\![e_2]\!]$qr)

$\quad \mathcal{E}[\![e_1 - e_2]\!] = \lambda$ qr. (**minus** $\mathcal{E}[\![e_1]\!]$qr $\mathcal{E}[\![e_2]\!]$qr)

$\quad \mathcal{E}[\![\rho_{re}\, e]\!] = \lambda$ qr. (**restrict** re $\mathcal{E}[\![e]\!]$qr)

$\quad \mathcal{E}[\![\sigma_{se}\, e]\!] = \lambda$ qr. (**select** se $\mathcal{E}[\![e]\!]$qr)

$\quad \mathcal{E}[\![\pi_{pnl}\, e]\!] = \lambda$ qr. (**project** pnl $\mathcal{E}[\![e]\!]$qr)

$\quad \mathcal{E}[\![e_1 \times e_2]\!] = \lambda$ qr. (**cross** $\mathcal{E}[\![e_1]\!]$qr $\mathcal{E}[\![e_2]\!]$qr)

Figure 4: Valuation Functions

In this research, queries have meaning based on the meaning of subqueries, which have meaning via valuation functions that map the algebraic operators to a modified database state. The valuation functions are given in Figure 4. The effect of evaluating an expression is defined in terms of intermediate query answers that result from subquery evaluation. The functions in boldface in Figure 4 are defined in λ-calculus [19] and selected functions are described below.

The formal definition of $\cap$ is given in Figure 5, in terms of the function **intersect**. Parentheses are used to indicate function expressions, and angle brackets are used to indicate the product constructor on semantic domains. The bracketed numbers are explained below. The function **intersect** defines the effect of the $\cap$ operator on the semantic domain *QueryResult*, since $\cap$ involves two intermediate query results. That is, evaluation of the subexpressions may not be as simple as looking up two classes in the same database state. There may be two different database states from the evaluation of nested subqueries, in which case a uniform, integrated view of the two states is needed.

To build intuition, consider an example. Let a query describe ships whose only cargo is oil. Its membership definition restricts a property (*CargoType*) inherited from a superclass *Ships*. For the purpose of this example, call the query result *OilTanker*. The extension of the class (objects from *Ships* which satisfy the restriction of *CargoType*) and the intension of the class (essentially its membership definition and inherited properties) are appended to the current database state. The query result consists of the class name created during query evaluation (*OilTanker* for this example, but in the formal definition it is assumed that a unique internal name is generated) and the modified database state containing its intension and extension. Consider that the description of *OilTanker* is a subexpression in an intersection query: *OilTankers* $\cap$ *Banned-Ships*, where *BannedShips* is a class defined by another query expression. Information appended to the original database state during both subexpression evaluations must be present in the database state against which the intersection is evaluated.

intersect: QueryResult $\rightarrow$ QueryResult $\rightarrow$ QueryResult
  intersect = λ qr_1 qr_2.
    ((let c_1 = (class_name qr_1))
    (let c_2 = (class_name qr_2))
    (let db = (integrateDB (database qr_1) (database qr_2)))   [1]
    (let newname = (newCN))   [2]
    (let pl = (most_specific (properties c_1 db) (properties c_2 db) db newname))   [2]
    (let newclass = (newAC newname (and (wff c_1 db) (wff c_2 db))
        (propertynames pl)))   [2]
    (let newACschema = (updateACS (acschema (schema db)) newclass))   [3]
    (let newmembers = (setint (members c_1 db) (members c_2 db)))   [4]
    (let newACdata = (updateACD newname newmembers (acdata (data db)))) [5]
    (let newPschema = (updatePRSlist (pschema (schema db)) pl))
    (let newschema = <(scschema (schema db)), newACschema, newPschema>)
    (let newdata = <(scdata (data db)), newACdata, (pdata (data db))>)
    <newname, <newschema, newdata>>)   [6]

Figure 5: Definition of ∩

An informal description of the definition of ∩ is described here. The numbered descriptions correspond to the numbers shown in the right margin of Figure 5.

1. Integrate the databases of the previous query results, since temporary results from separate expression evaluations may be appended to both databases.

2. Create a new class intension for the answer of the query; the new intension specifies a class name, the properties of the class, and a definition formula for the new class. Both inheritance and automatic membership are determined at this point. The properties of a class resulting from an intersect operator are the most specific version of common properties. For example, if *OilTankers* restricts the range of the *CargoType* property and *BannedShips* inherits it from *Ships* without modification, the intersection of the two would have the most restricted version of *CargoType*, the version present at *OilTankers*. The membership definition is the conjunction of the membership definitions of the two previous query results.

3. Add the new class to the database intension.

4. Intersect the members of the previous query result classes.

5. Add the new members to the database extension for the new class.

6. Construct the new query result which consists of the new class and the new database state.

The remaining set-theoretic operators, union (∪) and difference (−), have similar definitions.

To illustrate the extensional semantics of a class formed by property modification, Figure 6 contains an excerpt from the definition of **restrict** (Figure 4). (The extension for a σ subclass is defined similarly.) The extension of a subclass defined by ρ consists of the objects in the superclass which satisfy the restrict expression (i.e., a definition formula containing only property restrictions). The restrict expression is written in Membership Normal Form (MNF) for processing, a notation similar to conjunctive normal form for logic sentences [19]. The membership can be found by examining each object from the superclass, and determining whether the object satisfies each conjunct in the restrict expression. To satisfy a conjunct, one disjunct in each conjunct must be satisfied. For example, a query to find ships whose home port is Lisbon, and which carry only oil or are commanded by an admiral, has two conjuncts: a restriction of the *HomePort* property (*HomePort = "Lisbon"*) and an expression with two disjuncts (*CargoType = "oil"* or *Seniority(Captain) = "admiral"*). A ship appears in the query answer if it satisfies both conjuncts, which it may do by satisfying at least one disjunct in each conjunct. A ship whose home port is Lisbon which carries only oil satisfies the expression, as well as a ship whose home port is Lisbon and whose captain is an admiral. A disjunct is satisfied if the object's entire image is a subset of the range class for the restricted property and the cardinality of the object's image falls within the cardinality constraints of the restricted property.

The subclass-forming operators ($\cup, \cap, -, \rho, \sigma$) allow complex objects to be manipulated as a whole. Objects remain intact and retain their identity. The operators merely create new subclasses whose membership is derived from that of existing objects in abstract classes. This is in contrast to Encore's Query Algebra [20], where new object identifiers are always assigned to objects, even for set-theoretic queries where the original identifiers could be used. The disadvantage of generating new object identifiers for every query result is that answers to queries are disconnected from the classes in the schema. In the approach presented here, queries and subexpressions of queries which produce true subclasses are retained at the appropriate location in the isa hierarchy of the database schema. The other two operators (π and $\times$) produce new objects to represent distinct values but they retain connection with existing objects via system-generated properties. This approach retains the strengths of the schema, enabling the use of the isa relationship for providing logical access paths to data, and the use of the algebra for formal view materialization research.

4 Formal algebraic transformations

The formal definition of the algebraic query language and database state allows for reasoning about what queries in the language *denote* (i.e., the meaning of the queries), so that syntactic transformations for logical query optimization can be proven to be meaning-preserving. If query results are identical (same intension and extension), then the identity holds. Denotations of expressions can be used to show that their intension and extension are the same. For defined classes, identical intension implies that extension is the same, since a non-trivial membership definition completely describes the objects that have membership in the class.

restrictsubclass: SetOfObjectIDs → Database → DefinitionFormula → SetOfObjectIDs
  restrictsubclass = λ oids db df.
    (empty? oids)
      → emptyset
      [] ((let oid = (element oids))
        (satisfyconjunct? df oid db)
          → (union (set oid) (restrictsubclass (oids - (set oid)) db df))
          [] (restrictsubclass (oids - (set oid)) db df)))

satisfyconjunct?: Conjunct → ObjectID → Database → Boolean
  satisfyconjunct? = λ cj oid db.
    ((null? cj)
      → true
      [] (and (satisfydisjunct? (car cj) oid db)
        (satisfyconjunct? (cdr cj) oid db)

satisfydisjunct?: Disjunct → ObjectID → Database → Boolean
  satisfydisjunct? = λ dj oid db.
    ((null? dj)
      → false
      [] ((satisfyrestr? (car dj) oid db)
        → true
        [] (satisfydisjunct? (cdr dj) oid db)))

satisfyrestr?: RestrictPredicate → ObjectID → Database → Boolean
  satisfyrestr? = λ rp oid db.
    ((let pi = (propertyimages (pdata (data db))))
    (let pn = (restrpropname rp))
    (let pv = (imageP pn oid pi))
    (let ic = (imageC pn oid pi))
    ((and (subset? pv (members (restrrange rp) db)) (member? ic (restrcard rp)))
      → true
      [] false))

Figure 6: Formal Definition of Extensional Effect of ρ

To illustrate a proof of identity using the formal definition, consider the distributivity of a unary operator over a binary operator:

$$\rho_\theta(c_1 \cap c_2) = \rho_\theta c_1 \cap \rho_\theta c_2.$$

The query on the left restricts the class resulting from the intersection of c_1 and c_2 according to some condition θ. The query on the right restricts each class according to θ prior to intersecting the restricted classes.

To be shown: $\mathcal{Q}[\![\rho_\theta(c_1 \cap c_2)]\!]\mathrm{db} = \mathcal{Q}[\![\rho_\theta c_1 \cap \rho_\theta c_2]\!]\mathrm{db}$. Since identity is to be proven, the intension of the two classes comprising the query results must be shown to be identical. If the properties and definition formulas are the same, then the identity holds.

Consider the lefthand-side of the equation, which is evaluated according to the formal definition as follows:

$\mathcal{Q}[\![\rho_\theta(c_1 \cap c_2)]\!]\mathrm{db}$

$= \mathcal{E}[\![\rho_\theta(c_1 \cap c_2)]\!]\mathrm{qr}$, where qr $=$ (initialQR db)

$= $ (restrict θ $\mathcal{E}[\![c_1 \cap c_2]\!]\mathrm{qr}$)

$= $ (restrict θ (intersect $\mathcal{E}[\![c_1]\!]\mathrm{qr}$ $\mathcal{E}[\![c_2]\!]\mathrm{qr}$))

$= $ (restrict θ (intersect $<c_1$, db$>$ $<c_2$, db$>$))

The intersection subquery gives $<$gen_class$_1$, db'$>$, where gen_class$_1$ has membership definition $\mathit{wff}_{lhs_1} = \mathit{wff}_1 \wedge \mathit{wff}_2$ and $\mathit{properties}_{lhs_1} = $ (most_specific (properties c_1 db) (properties c_2 db)). The $\mathit{restrict}$ expression (restrict θ $<$gen_class$_1$, db'$>$) $= <$gen_class$_2$, db''$>$, where gen_class$_2$ has $\mathit{wff}_{lhs} = \theta \wedge \mathit{wff}_{lhs_1} = \theta \wedge \mathit{wff}_1 \wedge \mathit{wff}_2$ and $\mathit{properties}_{lhs} = \mathit{properties}_{lhs_1}$.

Consider the righthand-side of the equation, which is evaluated according to the formal definition as follows:

$\mathcal{Q}[\![\rho_\theta c_1 \cap \rho_\theta c_2]\!]\mathrm{db}$

$= \mathcal{E}[\![\rho_\theta c_1 \cap \rho_\theta c_2]\!]\mathrm{qr}$, where qr $=$ (initialQR db)

$= $ (intersect $\mathcal{E}[\![\rho_\theta c_1]\!]\mathrm{qr}$ $\mathcal{E}[\![\rho_\theta c_2]\!]\mathrm{qr}$)

$= $ (intersect (restrict θ $\mathcal{E}[\![c_1]\!]\mathrm{qr}$) (restrict θ $\mathcal{E}[\![c_2]\!]\mathrm{qr}$))

$= $ (intersect $<$gen_class$_3$, db'''$>$ $<$gen_class$_4$, db''''$>$

$= <$gen_class$_5$, db'''''$>$

The membership definition formula of gen_class$_3$ is $\mathit{wff}_{rhs_1} = (\theta \wedge \mathit{wff}_1)$; the definition of gen_class$_4$ is $\mathit{wff}_{rhs_2} = (\theta \wedge \mathit{wff}_2)$. The membership definition formula of the final query result is $\mathit{wff}_{rhs} = (\mathit{wff}_{rhs_1} \wedge \mathit{wff}_{rhs_2}) = ((\theta \wedge \mathit{wff}_1) \wedge (\theta \wedge \mathit{wff}_2))$. Since $\wedge$ is associative, $\mathit{wff}_{rhs} = (\theta \wedge \mathit{wff}_1 \wedge \mathit{wff}_2) = \mathit{wff}_{lhs}$. The properties of gen_class$_3$ and gen_class$_4$ are those of c_1 and c_2, respectively. The properties of gen_class$_5$ are $properties_{rhs}$ = (most_specific (properties c_1 db) (properties c_2 db)) = $properties_{rhs}$.

Thus, the two classes comprising the query results have the same intension, so the identity $\rho_\theta(c_1 \cap c_2) = \rho_\theta c_1 \cap \rho_\theta c_2$ holds. ■

5   Conclusions and future work

The algebra introduced here is an object-oriented, algebraic query language; thus, it has applications in view processing, language development and analysis, and logical query optimization. Any data model which supports complex objects with strict inheritance can use the algebra presented here for query specification, due to the definitional nature of queries. It is especially well-suited for data models which support the isa relationship, properties between classes, and strict inheritance of properties. Similar query algebras have been proposed [20, 21], but neither gives a formal definition. One important contribution of this research is its broad applicability; the generic nature of the algebra is made possible by the high-level conceptual model.

The algebra provides complete relational algebra functionality in an object-oriented setting. Just as relational algebra is closed over relations, the object-oriented algebra is closed over classes. The algebra supports both value-oriented and object-oriented query processing by providing operators which preserve object identity and allow complex objects to be manipulated as a whole, as well as operators which allow objects to be manipulated based on the values of their attributes. The ability to specify unstructured joins is provided via the cross product operator. The ability to create new objects representing only the values derived from existing objects is provided through the project operator.

The denotational semantic specification of the algebra precisely defines the operators; it makes the types of the data model and the behavior of the operators over them explicit. The definition of the algebra contributes a formal description of both the intension and extension of a conceptual model for object-oriented query processing, including a characterization of both intensional and extensional query results. Since each query describes a class, which has intension (e.g., inherited properties and a membership definition) and extension (data values), the results of a query may be stored in the database. The formal definition provides the basis for implementation as well as the basis for provably correct logical query optimization.

Plans for future research are outlined here. Based on the specification of Membership Normal Form, work is in progress to define a calculus and prove its equivalence to the algebra using the formal definition. Membership definitions provide the basis for the calculus, since they include ∧, ∨, ¬, as well as restrict (universal quantification) and select (existential quantification). The formal definition has been used to prove the correctness of logical transformations of queries [19]. Work is in progress to develop optimization heuristics for the algebraic transformations. This involves determining which expression is better in terms of performance than the other, and in which situations. Work is also in progress to expand the semantic domains of the denotational definition to include complete intensional information. Currently, only the information needed to support query evaluation is included (properties and membership definition formulas). Support for different collection types could be investigated; currently, values may be atomic, tuples, or sets of atomic values or tuples, while abstract classes contain sets of object identifiers.

Future plans include investigating the use of a tool for discovering structural relationships implicit in a schema, called the Classifier [19, 22, 23, 24], as a technique for query processing [26, 27]. The Classifier implements a set of sound and complete rules of inference, and is used to infer all inclusion (isa) and exclusion (disjoint) dependencies, as well as identify inconsistent (empty) and redundant (trivial) classes. The Classifier places a class resulting from a query in its correct place in the schema, and thus can be applied to finding all logical access paths. The Classifier can also be used for query simplification (e.g., elimination of redundant subexpressions in a query). The generic nature of the query language can be investigated; plans in this area include mapping the conceptual model and the algebra to a suitable user query language, such as OSQL [10, 11, 28].

Another promising area of investigation is the use of the query algebra for updating materialized views. Views can be expressed as queries, and materialized in the database intensionally and extensionally, as specified in the denotational definition of the query algebra. The main issue in updating a materialized view is deciding whether objects are retained or not, depending on updates to the membership of the base class. Since queries (and thus views) are specified intensionally in this research, updating a view is a straightforward membership definition check for the subclass-forming operators. The project and cross product operators can be maintained using the system-generated properties that provide a direct logical connection to the underlying objects. For example, when the last object that contributes to a project image is deleted, then the project object and image can be deleted. Further study is currently underway.

References

[1] Boom, H.J. (ed.), C.B. Nielsen, A.D. McGettrick, P.D. Mosses, C. Rattray, R.D. Tennent, and D.A. Watt, "A View of Formal Semantics," *Computer Standards and Interfaces*, 9, 1989.

[2] Schmidt, D.A., *Denotational Semantics: A Methodology for Language Development*, Allyn and Bacon, 1986.

[3] Bancilhon, F., "Object-Oriented Database Systems," *Proceedings of the Seventh ACM SIGACT-SIGMOD-SIGART Symposium on Principles of Database Systems*, Austin, TX, March 21-23, 1988.

[4] Atkinson, M., F. Bancilhon, D. DeWitt, K. Dittrich, D. Maier, and S. Zdonik, "Object-Oriented Database System Manifesto," *Deductive and Object-Oriented Databases*, Elsevere Science Publishers, Amsterdam, Netherlands, 1990.

[5] Zdonik, S.B., and D. Maier, "Introduction," in *Readings in Object-Oriented Database Systems*, Morgan Kaufmann, 1990.

[6] Hammer, M., and D. McLeod, "Database Description with SDM: A Semantic Database Model," *ACM Transactions on Database Systems,* Vol. 6, No. 3, Sept. 1981.

[7] The Committee for Advanced DBMS Function, "Third-Generation Database System Manifesto," Memorandum No. UCB/ERL M90/28, Electronics Research Laboratory, University of California, Berkeley, CA, April, 1990.

[8] Maier, D., A. Otis, and A. Purdy, "Object-Oriented Database Development at Servio Logic," *Database Engineering,* Vol. 8, No. 4, December, 1985.

[9] Maier, D., J. Stein, A. Otis, and A. Purdy, "Development of an Object-Oriented DBMS," *Proceedings of the First ACM OOPSLA Conference,* Portland, OR, Sept., 1986.

[10] Fishman, D., *et al.,* "Iris: an Object-Oriented Database Management System," *ACM Transactions on Office Information Systems,* Vol. 5, No. 1, January, 1987.

[11] Fishman, D., *et al.,* "Overview of the Iris DBMS," Database Technology Department, Hewlett-Packard Laboratories, Palo Alto, CA, 94304, June, 1988.

[12] Bancilhon, F., G. Barbedette, V. Benzaken, C. Delobel, S. Gamerman, C. Lecluse, P. Pfeffer, P. Richard, and F. Velez, "The Design and Implementation of O$_2$, an Object-Oriented Database System," in *Advances in Object-Oriented Database Systems: Second International Workshop on Object-Oriented Database Systems,* Dittrich, K., ed., Bad Munster am Stein, West Germany. Also appears as *Lecture Notes in Computer Science,* No. 334, Springer Verlag, 1988.

[13] Lecluse, C., P. Richard, F. Velez, "O$_2$, An Object-Oriented Data Model," *Proceedings of the ACM SIGMOD 1988 International Conference on Management of Data,* Chicago, IL, 1988.

[14] Banerjee, J., H.T. Chou, J. Garza, W. Kim, D. Woelk, N. Ballou, and H.J. Kim, "Data Model Issues for Object-Oriented Applications," *ACM Transactions on Office Information Systems,* January, 1987.

[15] Banerjee, J., W. Kim, K.-C. Kim, "Queries in Object-Oriented Databases," *Proceedings of the Fourth International Conference on Data Engineering,* Los Angeles, February, 1988.

[16] Codd, E.F., "A Relational Model of Data for Large Shared Data Banks," *Communications of the ACM,* Vol. 13, No.6, 1970.

[17] Bancilhon, F., and W. Kim, "Object-Oriented Database Systems: In Transition," *SIGMOD Record,* Vol. 19, No. 4, 1990.

[18] Laguna Beach Participants, "The Laguna Beach Report: Future Directions in DBMS Research," *SIGMOD Record,* Vol. 18. No. 1, March, 1989.

[19] Davis, K.C., "A Formal Foundation for Object-Oriented, Algebraic Query Processing," Ph.D. Dissertation, The Center for Advanced Computer Studies, University of Southwestern Louisiana, Lafayette, LA, May, 1990.

[20] Shaw, G., and S. Zdonik, "An Object-Oriented Query Algebra," *Database Engineering*, Vol. 12, No. 3, 1989.

[21] Osborn, S.L, "Identity, Equality, and Query Optimization," in *Advances in Object-Oriented Database Systems: Second International Workshop on Object-Oriented Database Systems*, Dittrich, K., ed., Bad Munster am Stein, West Germany. Also appears as *Lecture Notes in Computer Science*, No. 334, Springer Verlag, 1988.

[22] Davis, K.C., "The Theoretical Foundation for Inferencing on a Semantic Schema," M.S. Thesis, The Center for Advanced Computer Studies, University of Southwestern Louisiana, Lafayette, LA, June, 1987.

[23] Delcambre, L.M.L, and Davis, K.C., "Automatic Validation of Object-Oriented Database Structures," *Proceedings of the Fifth International Conference on Data Engineering*, Los Angeles, February, 1989.

[24] Delcambre, L.M.L, and Davis, K.C., "The Design and Validation of Object-Oriented Schemas," CACS Technical Report No. TR-89-6-2, accepted contingent upon revision, *Information Systems*.

[25] Borgida, A., R.J. Brachman, D.L. McGuinness, and L.A. Resnick, "CLASSIC: A Structural Data Model for Objects," *Proceedings of the 1989 SIGMOD Conference*, Portland, Oregon, 1989.

[26] Davis, K.C., and L.M.L. Delcambre, "Foundations for Object-Oriented Query Processing," *The Proceedings of the X3/SPARC/DBSSG Object-Oriented Database Task Group Workshop*, National Institute of Standards and Technology, October, 1990, held in conjunction with OOPSLA 1990; to appear in *Computer Standards and Interfaces*.

[27] Davis, K.C., and L.M.L. Delcambre, "A Classifier for Object-Oriented Schema and Query Processing," invited chapter to appear in *Progress in Object-Oriented Databases*, Volume 1, J.B. Prater, editor, Ablex Publishing Corporation.

[28] Derrett, N., W. Kent, and P. Lyngbaek, "Some Aspects of Operations in an Object-Oriented Database," *Database Engineering*, Vol. 8, No. 4, December, 1985.

Reasoning about a Modular Model-Oriented Formal Specification

John S Fitzgerald

Dept. of Computer Science, The University of Manchester
Manchester M13 9PL, United Kingdom*

Abstract

The object of this paper is to illustrate the interaction of modular structuring with formal reasoning in a model-oriented specification. The need for modular structuring facilities in model-oriented specifications is discussed. It is argued that structuring mechanisms in specification languages should pay due regard to the theories associated with the units of structure in a modular specification. Taking part of a model-oriented (VDM) specification of the well-known CAVIAR database as an example, some elementary modular structuring facilities are introduced, and their effects on formal reasoning illustrated. Issues specific to model-oriented specification, such as the status of the state and representation hiding, are discussed. Though the paper is primarily about formal specification, a brief discussion of the relationship of the work described here to implementation is included.

1 Introduction

Techniques for the formal specification of computing systems are increasingly viewed as credible technology, applicable to realistic industrial problems. The movement towards standardisation of notations (e.g. [1]) and requirements for certain classes of government contract [2], as well as the developing market in specification and proof support tools, bear this out. A natural consequence of this growth is an increase in the complexity of the problems to which formal specification techniques are applied.

An important weapon against complexity is the exploitation of *modularity*: that property of a problem which permits its decomposition onto simpler sub-problems, which may then be tackled relatively independently. Consider a software development project in which rigorous specification and proof are to play a major role. After a number of initial attempts at writing a specification, a structured informal description of the problem will have been derived. The structure of this description is to be reflected in the formal specification. The specifiers may be split into separate teams to consider the specifications of parts of the problem. These separate specifications may be encapsulated as modules.

Managers who have learned the lessons of Brooks [3] will be conscious of the overheads of communication on a large project and will require the use of a specification structuring mechanism which allows the teams to work relatively independently

---

*From August 1991, the author's address will be: The Computing Laboratory, University of Newcastle upon Tyne, Newcastle upon Tyne, NE1 7RU, U.K.

of one another. This suggests that interfaces between modules must be carefully delineated: some restriction of the use made by one module of another's facilities may be necessary. Each module's dependencies on others should be recorded. It would be naïve to expect inter-module interfaces to be fixed correctly at the beginning of the specification phase. They would evolve via negotiation between teams.

As each team works on its specification, its members may observe commonly occurring subsystems in their specification. Specifications for such subsystems may already exist, so that they can be taken "off-the-shelf" and instantiated to the particular needs of the point of use. Specifications for such subsystems may not already exist, in which case they may be generated and added to a library. This use of structuring emphasises the need for generic components.

The scenario given above suggests that four objectives should be met by a mechanism for structuring a specification:

Encapsulation: The structuring mechanism should allow the specification to be constructed from (possibly named) separate sub-specifications. These will be the modules of the specification.

Restriction: It should be possible to restrict the view of a module's contents granted to other modules. This helps change control and aids the separate construction of modules.

Genericity: It should be possible to write modules which can be used at several points within a specification, and possibly in other specifications.

Dependencies: So that the problem's structure is reflected in its specification, there should be a mechanism for recording exactly which other modules a given module may use.

Note that the discussion above and the bulk of this paper are primarily concerned with modular *specification* rather than formal *development*. Some comments on the latter are contained in Section 5.3.

Support for a module-based approach to programming has been present in programming languages for many years. In property-oriented specification languages such as Clear [4], Larch [5] and Extended ML [6], structuring facilities play a key role. However, model-oriented languages which meet the above objectives have only recently been developed (e.g. the Bear proposals for BSIVDM [7], VVSL [8], RSL [9]).

One of the most significant activities associated with formal specification is formal or rigorous reasoning. It may be necessary to discharge proof obligations about the well-formedness of a specification, or show that the specification is satisfiable. It will be necessary to prove certain properties about specified objects in order to gain conviction that the specification describes the expected system. Tools to support construction and reasoning about model-oriented formal specifications (e.g. [10] and [11]) are a current research topic. It is reasonable to expect that modular structuring facilities in specification languages should be designed to assist formal reasoning.

There is a need for recorded experience in structuring and reasoning about modular model-oriented specifications. Database-related problems have proved fruitful as a source of material for this purpose. Such problems frequently exhibit a structure which makes them suitable for decomposition into modules based on data types. An initial effort to determine requirements for structuring facilities in a specification language is reported in [12] via a specification of NDB, a commercial database system[1]. More recently, [14] defines some simple structuring facilities and describes their effects on formal reasoning. In this paper, the simplest elements of the facilities described in [14] are introduced and applied to a well-known database application. The presentation here is relatively informal. More detail may be obtained from [14].

Section 2 introduces CAVIAR, the system to be specified, and indicates the lines along which its specification may be split into modules. Section 3 introduces basic concepts of specification and theory before describing facilities which meet the four objectives derived in this section. Section 4 applies these facilities to (part of) a specification of CAVIAR. The reader is assumed to be familiar with the Meta-IV specification language of VDM ([15], [1]), the associated Logic of Partial Functions ([16]) and the style of Natural Deduction proofs and inference rules employed in [15] (and [10]).

2   CAVIAR: The Problem and its Structure

In this section, the problem of specifying the CAVIAR system is introduced. The problem is seen to exhibit a clear structure which could form the basis of a modular specification using some "off-the-shelf" generic specifications. In later sections, structuring techniques to allow the expression of this modular specification will be developed.

The CAVIAR (Computer Aided Visitor Information And Retrieval) system, described in [17], holds information about a conference centre. Meetings are attended by a number of visitors. Each visitor is registered and may be supplied with hotel and transport reservations. Each meeting has an associated conference room and may have an associated dining room.

This suggests a number of major subsystems which can be described relatively independently. In [17] these subsystems are specified separately in Z, though they are semantically part of a single Z specification. In this paper, the subsystems correspond to separate modules. Some of the advantages and disadvantages of this approach in comparison to that employed in [17] are discussed in Section 5.2.

The main subsystems suggested are:

1. *M-V*, **the Meeting – Visitor subsystem:** For each session, the meetings currently being held and the visitors attending are recorded. A minor subsystem records information about particular visitors.

2. *HR-V*, **the Hotel Reservation – Visitor subsystem:** Each visitor's hotel reservations are recorded for the dates on which they are visiting.

3. *TR-V*, **the Transport – Visitor subsystem:** This is similar to *HR-V*, but transport reservations are recorded for each visitor.

4. *CR-M*, **the Conference Room – Meeting subsystem:** This concerns the allocation of rooms to meetings at each session.

5. *DR-M*, **the Dining Room – Meeting subsystem:** This records the allocation of dining rooms to meetings for lunch on each day.

---

[1]A number of responses to the problem posed in that paper have been received: [13] using COLD-K has already been published; other responses using Z, VVSL, RSL and Extended ML will be published in the Formal Aspects of Computing Journal (Springer/BCS) in 1992.

Certain features are recurrent in this system. For example, *HR-V* and *TR-V* are similar in that they both record relationships between users (visitors) and some resource (e.g. hotel reservations) which vary over time. Time-varying pools of values are also common (e.g. the pool of registered visitors). These concepts are candidates for specification as generic modules. Some specifications of subsystems, such as *HR-V*, can be viewed as single instances of these modules. Others, such as *M-V*, involve instances of several generic modules in combination. The overall CAVIAR specification can be seen as a module dependent on the modules describing these subsystems.

The specification is only of the application-level view of a database system, but this is regarded as well worth specifying before trying to express the system in any particular (relational, object-oriented, hierarchical etc.) database formalism. The apparatus for writing this structured specification is built in the following section.

3   Basic Structuring Concepts

In Section 1, four objectives for modular structuring facilities in a specification language were set out. In this section, a syntax for module definitions is built up by examining each objective in turn and adding to the emerging syntax a facility which meets, to some degree, the objective. At each stage, the effect of the new facility on the notion of theory associated with each module is considered. The essential apparatus will then be in place to permit an attempt at structuring part of the CAVIAR specification. First, however, the basic concepts of an unstructured ("flat") specification and its associated theory are considered.

3.1   Flat Specifications and Theories

In a model-oriented, state-based specification, a distinguished type (the *state*) is specified via a model, along with other *visible* types, also specified via models. The models are defined via type expressions, which may include invariants. Operations are specified which work on a single argument of the state type and any number of arguments of the visible types. An operation specification denotes a relation between states as well as between input and output values. The behaviour specified is described in terms of the visible input and output values produced by sequences of applications of the operations. For example, consider a simple specification of a pool of values which changes over time. This specification will be used as a running example. It is also of use in specifying CAVIAR. Time is defined by a visible type T, the definition of which is not given in full here. The values are all of type X, the definition of which is similarly not given in full:

$$T = \dots$$

$$X = \dots$$

A state type *Pool* defines the timed pool of resources as a mapping between times and sets of values:

$$Pool :: pl : T \xrightarrow{m} X\text{-set}$$

The function *exists* returns the contents of the pool at a given time. In VDM terminology, it is an *auxiliary function*, i.e. it need not be implemented, but is defined for convenience in writing and reasoning about the other specified types and operators.

$exists : Pool \times T \to X\text{-set}$

$exists(p, t) \quad \triangleq \quad pl(p)(t)$

pre $t \in \text{dom } pl(p)$

Two simple operations are specified implicitly via pre-/post-conditions: *CREATE* adds a value to the pool for a given time period; *DESTROY* removes a resource for a given time period.

$CREATE\ (ts{:}\ T\text{-set}, x{:}\ X)$

ext wr $pl\ :\ T \xrightarrow{m} X\text{-set}$

pre $ts \subseteq \text{dom } pl$

post $pl = \overleftarrow{pl} \dagger \{t \mapsto \overleftarrow{pl}(t) \cup \{x\} \mid t \in ts\}$

$DESTROY\ (ts{:}\ T\text{-set}, x{:}\ X)$

ext wr $pl\ :\ T \xrightarrow{m} X\text{-set}$

pre $ts \subseteq \text{dom } pl$

post $pl = \overleftarrow{pl} \dagger \{t \mapsto \overleftarrow{pl}(t) - \{x\} \mid t \in ts\}$

In the formalism discussed here, that of Meta-IV, a flat specification has a signature containing the names of the types and operators defined in the specification, along with the input and output types of the operators themselves. The signature of the pool specification above is

$$
\begin{aligned}
T \quad &: \quad \text{Type} \\
X \quad &: \quad \text{Type} \\
Pool \quad &: \quad \text{State} \\
mk\text{-}Pool \quad &: \quad (T \xrightarrow{m} X\text{-set}) \to Pool \\
pl \quad &: \quad Pool \to (T \xrightarrow{m} X\text{-set}) \\
exists \quad &: \quad Pool \times T \to X\text{-set} \\
pre\text{-}exists \quad &: \quad Pool \times T \to \mathbf{B} \\
CREATE \quad &: \quad T\text{-set} \times X \xrightarrow{o} () \\
DESTROY \quad &: \quad T\text{-set} \times X \xrightarrow{o} ()
\end{aligned}
$$

The $\xrightarrow{o}$ notation for the operations implies that each operation has pre- and post-conditions which may be viewed as Boolean functions on states or pairs of states. For *CREATE*, for example, there are defined functions:

$$
\begin{aligned}
pre\text{-}CREATE \quad &: \quad Pool \times T\text{-set} \times X \to \mathbf{B} \\
post\text{-}CREATE \quad &: \quad Pool \times T\text{-set} \times X \times Pool \to \mathbf{B}
\end{aligned}
$$

A flat specification such as this has a meaning in some semantic domain. For specification languages such as Meta-IV and Z this is often given by a denotational semantics producing, for each specification, a class of models (see [1], [18]). This paper is, however, mainly concerned with the theory in which reasoning about a specification is conducted. For the purposes of this paper, a theory is a collection of *rules* in the style of [10], which is based on [15]. A rule contains a number of hypotheses and a single conclusion. The hypotheses and conclusion are formulae of a logic appropriate to the specification language, in this paper the Logic of Partial Functions, LPF ([16]). In addition to the logical operators, primitive types, type constructors and operators specific to the specification language may be used. *Axiomatic* rules give fundamental characterisations of the behaviour of the operators and types in their formulae. *Derived* rules follow from axioms via formal proofs and may be subsequently used in proofs of other derived rules.

A specification gives rise to a collection of axioms defining the properties of the specified types and operators. From these, the theory of a specification can be derived. A satisfaction relationship must exist between the theorems derived from a specification and its model-based semantics.

As an example, consider the theory due to the pool specification above. The simplest rules in this theory are axiomatic. They give definitions of the types, operations and auxiliary function. For example, the following rules define the formation of the constructor and selector functions on the state type:

$$\text{mk-Pool-form} \quad \frac{pl \in T \xrightarrow{m} X\text{-set}}{mk\text{-}Pool(pl) \in Pool}$$

$$pl\text{-form} \quad \frac{p \in Pool}{pl(p) \in T \xrightarrow{m} X\text{-set}}$$

The following rule defines the *exists* function:

$$\text{exists-def} \quad \frac{\begin{array}{c} p \in Pool; t \in T; \\ pre\text{-}exists(p, t); \\ pl(p)(t) \in X\text{-set} \end{array}}{exists(p, t) = pl(p)(t)}$$

The operations yield axioms defining their pre- and postconditions. For example:

$$\text{pre-CREATE-def} \quad \frac{\begin{array}{c} p \in Pool; ts \in T\text{-set}; x \in X; \\ (ts \subseteq \text{dom}\, pl(p)) \in \mathbf{B} \end{array}}{pre\text{-}CREATE(p, ts, x) \iff ts \subseteq \text{dom}\, pl(p)}$$

Work on Mural ([10]) has shown how axioms such as those illustrated can be automatically derived from a flat specification. Given such an axiomatisation, a collection of results about the basic data types of the specification language, and inference rules for the logic of the specification language, it is possible to infer more advanced properties of the specified constructs. For example, an obvious result about the addition of *x* at time *t* via the *CREATE* operation is:

$$\text{CREATE-1} \quad \frac{\begin{array}{c} \overleftarrow{p}, p \in Pool; ts \in T\text{-set}; x \in X; \\ pre\text{-}CREATE(\overleftarrow{p}, ts, x); post\text{-}CREATE(\overleftarrow{p}, ts, x, p); \\ t \in T; t \in ts \end{array}}{pl(p)(t) = pl(\overleftarrow{p})(t) \cup \{x\}}$$

This would be used in a proof that *CREATE* increases the number of existing resources:

$$\overleftarrow{p}, p \in Pool; ts \in T\text{-set}; x \in X;$$
$$pre\text{-}CREATE(\overleftarrow{p}, ts, x); post\text{-}CREATE(\overleftarrow{p}, ts, x, p);$$
$$t \in T;$$

CREATE-2

$$\dfrac{pre\text{-}exists(\overleftarrow{p}, t); pre\text{-}exists(p, t)}{exists(\overleftarrow{p}, t) \subseteq exists(p, t)}$$

A more advanced result is the satisfiability of *CREATE*, which states that for every $\overleftarrow{p}$, *ts* and *x* satisfying *pre-CREATE*, there is a result pool so that the relation denoted by *post-CREATE* is satisfied:

$$\overleftarrow{p} \in Pool; ts \in T\text{-set}; x \in X;$$
$$pre\text{-}CREATE(\overleftarrow{p}, ts, x)$$

CREATE-sat

$$\exists p \in Pool \cdot post\text{-}CREATE(\overleftarrow{p}, ts, x, p)$$

In subsequent sections, simple modular structuring facilities for the specification language are introduced. Their effects on the notions of specification and theory are considered. To aid the definition of these facilities, the following types are introduced. They will be used in constructing the abstract syntax of module definitions and discussing their theories:

1. *FlatSpecSig* is the class of all signatures of flat specifications;

2. *FlatSpec* is the class of all flat specifications;

3. *Theory* is the class of all theories. A theory is just a set of inference rules, so *Theory = Rule*-set, where *Rule* is the class of rules.

Now it is possible to move on to a consideration of some elementary structuring facilities based on the objectives listed in Section 1.

3.2   Encapsulation: Module Definitions

The previous section gave a flat specification and some representative theorems from its theory. Modules are to be (named) encapsulated specifications. In terms of a Meta-IV abstract syntax, a module name definition (of type *ModNameDef*) consists of a module
name (*ModName*) and a module definition (*ModDef*):

   ModNameDef :: *name* : *ModName*
                    def : *ModDef*

A module definition just consists of a flat specification which constitutes the module's *body*:

   ModDef :: *body* : *FlatSpec*

This abstract syntax will be developed further in later sections.

For the specification of the timed pool, it is a simple matter to use this abstract syntax, naming the specification and calling the result a module (named *POOL1*):

POOL1 $\triangleq$

   $T = ...$

$X = \ldots$

$Pool :: pl : T \xrightarrow{m} X\text{-set}$

$exists: Pool \times T \rightarrow X\text{-set} \ldots$
$CREATE(ts: T\text{-set}, x: X) \ldots$
$DESTROY(ts: T\text{-set}, x: X) \ldots$

The theory due to the module $POOL1$ is exactly the collection of rules described above for the flat specification. All that has happened is that the specification and theory are now named.

This simple notion of module does not allow for the recording of restrictions on the use of the constructs defined in $POOL1$. Genericity is not supported and dependencies on other modules cannot be recorded. The provision of features to support these objectives are considered below.

3.3   Restriction: The Export Clause

Which of the constructs defined in $POOL1$ will a user of that module be permitted to use? Recall that the specification is being written purely for the purposes of defining the problem. It does not (necessarily) describe an implementation. Hence the writer of $POOL1$ should be prepared to make available anything in the module which is of use in reasoning about its contents.

The constructs made available by $POOL1$ are said to be *exported*. To the simple syntax for modules developed so far, an *export clause* is added. The export clause lists constructs which may be utilised by another module. In the developing abstract syntax, a *FlatSpecSig* called *exps* is added to the notion of module definition:

$ModDef :: body : FlatSpec$
$\qquad\qquad exps : FlatSpecSig$

In the case of $POOL1$, it is decided to make available all the types and operations specified. The auxiliary function is also made available. This results in the module $POOL2$:

$POOL2 \triangleq$

$T = \ldots$

$X = \ldots$

$Pool :: pl : T \xrightarrow{m} X\text{-set}$

$exists: Pool \times T \rightarrow X\text{-set} \ldots$
$CREATE(ts: T\text{-set}, x: X) \ldots$
$DESTROY(ts: T\text{-set}, x: X) \ldots$

Export $Pool, X, T, exists, CREATE, DESTROY$

The export clause defines a signature which must be closed: it would not, for example, be appropriate to export $CREATE$ without exporting the visible types X and T since any arguments to $CREATE$ in modules using $POOL2$ would have to use these types.

How does this restriction affect the formal theory due to the module? The theory due to the body of a module is as discussed above. However, not all the rules in this theory will be made available to a user of *POOL2*. A *reduct operator*:

$$\_ \downarrow \_ : \textit{Theory} \times \textit{FlatSpecSig} \to \textit{Theory}$$

is applied to the theory due to the body of *POOL2* to remove unwanted rules. Thus, if $\mathcal{R}$ is the theory due to a module body, $(\mathcal{R} \downarrow exps)$ is the theory due to the whole module definition.

Which rules in a theory are to be removed by $\downarrow$? This is a matter of language philosophy for the writer of the structuring language semantics. One possibility out of many is considered here.

Since the specifications in the bodies of modules are model-oriented and potentially state-based, the first requirement on the reduct defined here is that it should distinguish the state from the non-state types, hiding the representing model of the state and exposing the representing models of the non-state types. Here "hide" means removing from the theory of the body any results which "reveal" the definition of the representing model.

Consider a flat specification signature containing the name of a state $\mathcal{S}$, a collection of names of types $\mathcal{T}$, signatures of functions $\mathcal{F}$ and signatures of operations $\mathcal{O}$. Consider its application to a theory $\mathcal{R}$. Some assumptions have to be made about the well-formedness of the export signature:

- If the state type $\mathcal{S}$ is exported, its invariant inv-$\mathcal{S}$ is not in the export clause;

- For any non-state type T in $\mathcal{T}$, inv-T is in the export clause (in $\mathcal{F}$). If T is defined as a composite type, then its selectors and constructor are exported (i.e. are in $\mathcal{F}$).

All pre- and postconditions are considered included in the export clause by virtue of the fact that the functions or operations employing them are included.

The reduct $\downarrow$ removes from $\mathcal{R}$ all rules which do not satisfy all of the following criteria:

1. The state type is used only in typing judgements (of the concrete form '$\sigma \in \Sigma$') using the typing operator '$\in$' [2].

2. Variables of the state type (like σ above) defined within a rule appear only as arguments to explicitly exported operators (i.e. pre- or postconditions of operations or auxiliary functions).

3. Only primitive and exported constructs appear in the rule.

Restrictions 1 and 2 ensure that only rules which make assertions about the state using exported operators get through the reduct. Rules involving the state type in type constructions, for example:

$$\text{Non-exported-rule} \frac{x \in \mathsf{N} \xrightarrow{m} \Sigma}{\dots}$$

---

[2] '$\in$' is an overloaded symbol here, as in [15]. It refers both to the typing judgement and the membership of sets. Some texts (e.g. [10]) make the distinction by using ':' for the typing assertion. Here the convention of the standard text on the subject will be followed.

are not exported. Nor are rules where variables of the state type are supplied as arguments to primitive operators of the specification language. For example:

$$\boxed{\text{Non-exported-rule}} \quad \frac{\overleftarrow{\sigma}, \sigma \in \Sigma; \, post\text{-}OP(\overleftarrow{\sigma}, \sigma)}{\overleftarrow{\sigma} \cup \sigma = \overleftarrow{\sigma}}$$

The primitive operators of the specification language include equality. This does not prevent the specification writer defining an equivalence relation on states and exporting it.

The effect of $\downarrow$ on the *POOL2* example is that rules which mention non-exported constructs (e.g. *Pool*-form, *pl*-form, *exists*-def, *pre-CREATE*-def and *CREATE*-1) are excluded from the public theory of *POOL2*. Rules which use only exported constructs (e.g. *CREATE*-2 and *CREATE*-sat) are published. Note that a published rule may use non-published rules in its proof: exclusion is based on the rule statements alone. The representation of the state type is hidden in the sense that a module which uses *POOL2* may not use the *pl* selector function or *mk-Pool* constructor on a variable of type *Pool*. The representations of *T* and *X* are not hidden.

3.4 Genericity: Module Parameters

The *POOL2* module is not very general. It contains its own particular definitions of the types for time and value. A more generally useful module would be parameterised over these types. To permit such parameterisation, the emerging abstract syntax for module definitions is extended:

$$\begin{aligned} ModDef :: \quad & parms : ModName \xrightarrow{m} FlatSpecSig \\ & body : FlatSpec \\ & exps : FlatSpecSig \end{aligned}$$

The parameters are defined by a mapping from parameter names to *restrictions* which are flat specification signatures. Any arguments to the parametric specification must provide constructs matching those listed in the restriction. Applying this to *POOL2* yields the final version of the timed pool module, called *POOL*:

$POOL \triangleq$
Parameters T: Type T,
$\qquad\qquad X$: Type X

$Pool :: pl : T.T \xrightarrow{m} X.X\text{-set}$

$exists : Pool \times T.T \to X.X\text{-set}$

$exists(p, t) \triangleq pl(p)(t)$

pre $t \in \operatorname{dom} pl(p)$

$CREATE \ (ts: T.T\text{-set}, x: X.X)$

ext wr $pl : T.T \xrightarrow{m} X.X\text{-set}$

pre $ts \subseteq \operatorname{dom} pl$

post $pl = \overleftarrow{pl} \dagger \{t \mapsto \overleftarrow{pl}(t) \cup \{x\} \mid t \in ts\}$

$DESTROY$ (ts: $T.T$-set, x: $X.X$)

ext wr p : $T.T \xrightarrow{m} X.X$-set

pre $ts \subseteq \operatorname{dom} pl$

post $pl = \overleftarrow{pl} \dagger \{t \mapsto \overleftarrow{pl}(t) - \{x\} \mid t \in ts\}$

Export $Pool, X.X, T.T, exists, CREATE, DESTROY$

The module $POOL$ may be instantiated by any two modules which supply a type called T and a type called X respectively. The formal parameters, themselves modules, are also called T and X.

Note the change in naming of constructs used in the body. The type T is now referred to as $T.T$, and likewise for X. Since a construct with the same name could be supplied by two parameters, constructs acquired from parameters have their names qualified by the name of their formal parameter.

The notion of theory due to a module now needs to be updated to reflect the introduction of parameters. A module now no longer denotes a single theory, but a function from arguments to the theory of the body interpreted in an environment due to the theories of the arguments, and restricted by the export signature. The meaning of a module definition in terms of theories is of type $TDen^3$:

$$TDen = (ModName \xrightarrow{m} Theory) \rightarrow Theory$$

The rules in the theory due to any given instance of $POOL$ are affected by the qualification of names. For example, the $CREATE$-2 rule is now:

$$\overleftarrow{p}, p \in Pool;$$
$$ts \in T.T\text{-set}; x \in X.X;$$
$$pre\text{-}CREATE(\overleftarrow{p}, ts, x); post\text{-}CREATE(\overleftarrow{p}, ts, x, p);$$
$$t \in T.T;$$

$$\boxed{CREATE\text{-}2} \quad \frac{pre\text{-}exists(\overleftarrow{p}, t); pre\text{-}exists(p, t)}{exists(\overleftarrow{p}, t) \subseteq exists(p, t)}$$

3.5 Recording Dependency: The Import Clause

How might one module be used by another? Already it has been seen that one module may instantiate another's formal parameters. Direct dependencies must also be recorded. This is done via an *import clause* which contains the names of other defined modules:

$ModDef$ :: $parms$: $ModName \xrightarrow{m} FlatSpecSig$
 $imps$: $ModName$-set
 $body$: $FlatSpec$
 $exps$: $FlatSpecSig$

The body may use the exported constructs of (instances of) the imported modules. The theory of the body may use the theories of the imported modules.

For example, suppose a module is to be written describing a resource management system which involves a timed pool and a collection of unallocated resources. The

---

[3]In the rest of this paper the term "theory of M" (for some module M) is used loosely to refer to the theory due to any *instance* of M. Where a particular instance is considered, this is stated in the text.

module is parametric over modules S and R supplying time (T) and resource (X) types. An operation *SHIFT* moves a resource out of the collection and into the timed pool:

POOL-RES $\triangleq$
Parameters S: Type T,
$\qquad\quad$ R: Type X
Import *POOL*

$\quad$ *PR* :: pl : $POOL(S,R).Pool$
$\qquad\quad$ rec : $R.X$-set

$\quad$ *SHIFT* $(r\text{:}\,R.X, ss\text{:}\,S.T\text{-set})$

$\quad$ ext wr pl $\;$: $\;POOL(S,R).Pool$
$\qquad\;$ wr rec : $\;R.X$-set

$\quad$ pre $POOL(S,R).pre\text{-}CREATE(pl, ss, r) \wedge r \in rec$

$\quad$ post $POOL(S,R).post\text{-}CREATE(\overleftarrow{pl}, ss, r, pl) \wedge rec = \overleftarrow{rec} - \{r\}$

$\quad$ ...

The *PR* state is defined partly in terms of the state type specified by an instance of *POOL*. The *CREATE* operation from the imported module *POOL* is used via its pre- and postconditions. The operation *SHIFT* is said to *promote CREATE* to operate on the *PR* state. All constructs acquired from *POOL* must be qualified by the instance of *POOL* from which they originate, to differentiate them from the identically-named constructs acquired from other instances. Note that only the constructs exported by *POOL* can be used in the body of *POOL-RES*.

$\quad$ Consider now the effects of import on the theory associated with a module. Imported modules contribute their theories to the environment in which the body of the importing module is interpreted. The theory due to a module is a function from arguments to the theory of the body interpreted in an environment due to the theories of the arguments and imports, the result being restricted by the export signature.

$\quad$ In the current example, for the sake of textual brevity, let "*P*" stand for "*POOL(S,R)*". The following theorem is the *POOL-RES* equivalent of *CREATE*-2 (as defined in Section 3.4):

$$\overleftarrow{pr}, pr \in PR;$$
$$r \in R.X; ss \in S.T\text{-set};$$
$$pre\text{-}SHIFT(\overleftarrow{pr}, r, ss); post\text{-}SHIFT(\overleftarrow{pr}, r, ss, pr);$$
$$s \in S.T;$$

$$\boxed{\text{SHIFT-1}}\quad \frac{P.pre\text{-}exists(pl(\overleftarrow{pr}), s); P.pre\text{-}exists(pl(pr), s)}{P.exists(pl(\overleftarrow{pr}), s) \subseteq P.exists(pl(pr), s)}$$

In proving this rule, access is available to the theory of *POOL(S,R)*, from where the result *CREATE*-2 is used. Obviously, before *CREATE*-2 can be used, the construct names in it must be properly qualified to refer to the correct instances of *POOL* for use in the theory of the body of *POOL-RES*. This yields (again with "*P*" standing for "*POOL(S,R)*"):

$$\overleftarrow{p}, p \in P.Pool;$$
$$ts \in P.T.T\text{-set}; x \in P.X.X;$$
$$P.pre\text{-}CREATE(\overleftarrow{p}, ts, x); P.post\text{-}CREATE(\overleftarrow{p}, ts, x, p);$$
$$t \in P.T.T;$$

P.CREATE-1
$$\frac{P.pre\text{-}exists(\overleftarrow{p}, s); P.pre\text{-}exists(p, s)}{P.exists(\overleftarrow{p}, s) \subseteq P.exists(p, s)}$$

This rule can be applied in the context of the body of *POOL-RES* with $pl(\overleftarrow{pr})$ and $pl(pr)$ matching $\overleftarrow{p}$ and p respectively. Note also that the rule *P.CREATE*-1 refers to the type *P.T.T*, the type exported by *P*, whereas *SHIFT*-1 refers to *S.T*, the type local to *POOL-RES*, derived from its formal parameter. Since *P* is *POOL(S, R)*, these two types are exactly the same, though their names are different. The same applies to *P.X.X* and *R.X*. This commonality of origin must be borne in mind when using acquired constructs in rules. The issue of construct origins is too detailed to warrant a discussion here, but is further discussed in a similar context in [14] and in a more general context in [19] and [8]. The issue of inherited substructure appears very directly in the semantics of the algebraic specification language Clear ([20]).

Further examples of module import and its effect on formal reasoning can be found in Section 4.

4 Some Modules from the CAVIAR Specification

Section 2 introduced the CAVIAR problem. Section 3 introduced elementary structuring technology for model-oriented formal specifications. This section describes the application of that technology to part of the specification of CAVIAR. Limitations of space mean that only a small part of the specification can be discussed here. A more comprehensive version is given as a case study in [14]. The *POOL* module described above is used as part of the specification. First, however, another reusable module is described.

4.1 Resource – User System

One of the commonest concepts in the CAVIAR specification is that of a relationship between a collection of resources and its users, where the relationship changes with time. For example, conference rooms are resources used by meetings, different conference rooms being used by different meetings during each session. This observation yields a reusable module specifying a timed resource–user system. The specification describes a relation between resources and users for each time slot. The time unit, class of resources and class of users may vary between instances of the resource–user system, so these are all parameters to the module describing the system.

Constraints may be placed on the cardinality of the relations in a resource–user system. They may be one-to-one, one-to-many etc..

The module is generic over three modules, each of which supplies a type: *T* supplies a type representing time values; *R* a type representing resources and *U* a type representing users. The timed resource-user relationship is specified by a map from times to resource-user relations:

$$RU :: ru : T \xrightarrow{m} (R \times U)\text{-set}$$

An additional parameter *RESTR* will contribute a single value *restr* from the type {1-1, 1-M, M-1, M-M} which indicates the cardinality of the relationship. Hence the invariant added to *RU*:

$RU :: ru : T \xrightarrow{m} (R \times U)$-set

inv $(ru) \triangleq$

$\forall t \in$ dom $ru \cdot$cases *restr* of

$1\text{-}1 \rightarrow \forall (r_1, u_1), (r_2, u_2) \in ru(t) \cdot r_1 = r_2 \Leftrightarrow u_1 = u_2$

$1\text{-}M \rightarrow \forall (r_1, u_1), (r_2, u_2) \in ru(t) \cdot u_1 = u_2 \Rightarrow r_1 = r_2$

$M\text{-}1 \rightarrow \forall (r_1, u_1), (r_2, u_2) \in ru(t) \cdot r_1 = r_2 \Rightarrow u_1 = u_2$

others true

end

The header to the module is therefore (with names now properly qualified):

RES-USR $\triangleq$

Parameters T: Type T,

R: Type R,

U: Type U,

RESTR: Value *restr*: {1-1, 1-M, M-1, M-M}

State *RU*

$RU :: ru : T.T \xrightarrow{m} (R.R \times U.U)$-set

inv $(ru) \triangleq$

$\forall t \in$ dom $ru \cdot$cases *RESTR.restr* of

$1\text{-}1 \rightarrow \forall (r_1, u_1), (r_2, u_2) \in ru(t) \cdot r_1 = r_2 \Leftrightarrow u_1 = u_2$

$1\text{-}M \rightarrow \forall (r_1, u_1), (r_2, u_2) \in ru(t) \cdot u_1 = u_2 \Rightarrow r_1 = r_2$

$M\text{-}1 \rightarrow \forall (r_1, u_1), (r_2, u_2) \in ru(t) \cdot r_1 = r_2 \Rightarrow u_1 = u_2$

others true

end

A number of basic auxiliary functions return the domain and range of the relation at a particular time:

$in\text{-}use : RU \times T.T \rightarrow R.R$-set

$in\text{-}use(ru, t) \triangleq$ Dom $ru(t)$

pre $t \in$ dom ru

$users : RU \times T.T \rightarrow U.U$-set

$users(ru, t) \triangleq$ Rng $ru(t)$

pre $t \in$ dom ru

and the inverse relation at a particular time:

$ur : RU \times T.T \rightarrow (U.U \times R.R)$-set

$ur(ru, t) \triangleq ru(t)^{-1}$

pre $t \in$ dom ru

Operations allow the booking of a resource to a user over a range of times, the cancellation of such a booking, the deletion of a resource and the deletion of a user from the relations over a given time period. For example, the booking operation is:

$BOOK$ $(ts\colon T.T\text{-set}, r\colon R.R, u\colon U.U)$

ext wr ru : RU

pre $\forall t \in ts \cdot t \in \text{dom}\, ru \land (r, u) \notin ru(t) \land$
$\qquad$ inv-$RU(ru \dagger \{t' \mapsto ru(t') \cup \{(r, u)\} \mid t' \in ts\})$

post $\forall t \in ts \cdot ru(t) = \overleftarrow{ru}(t) \cup \{(r, u)\} \land ts \triangleleft ru = ts \triangleleft \overleftarrow{ru}$

The remaining operations are specified in Appendix A.1, where the module is presented in full. The module exports all its types, auxiliary functions and operations. It also re-exports the types supplied by the parameters because these are needed to ensure closure of the signature due to the export clause.

Note that some additional constructs are defined to help Meta-IV cope cleanly with relations. For $\alpha \in (A \times B)$-set:

$$
\begin{aligned}
\text{Dom}\, \alpha \quad &\triangleq \quad \{a \in A \mid \exists b \in B \cdot (a, b) \in \alpha\} \\
\text{Rng}\, \alpha \quad &\triangleq \quad \{b \in B \mid \exists a \in A \cdot (a, b) \in \alpha\} \\
\alpha^{-1} \quad &\triangleq \quad \{(b, a) \in B \times A \mid (a, b) \in \alpha\} \\
as \triangleleft \alpha \quad &\triangleq \quad \{(a, b) \in \alpha \mid a \notin as\} \\
\alpha \triangleright bs \quad &\triangleq \quad \{(a, b) \in \alpha \mid b \notin bs\}
\end{aligned}
$$

4.2 Hotel and Transport Reservation Subsystems

The modules describing hotel room (*HR-V*) and travel reservation (*TR-V*) are simply instances of *RES-USR*, since they consist of time-varying relationships between resources (hotel/transport reservations) and users (visitors):

$HR\text{-}V \triangleq RES\text{-}USR(DATE, HR, V, 1\text{-}1)$

$TR\text{-}V \triangleq RES\text{-}USR(TIME, TR, V, 1\text{-}1)$

These are instantiations of *RES-USR* by primitive modules defined elsewhere in the CAVIAR specification. *DATE* and *TIME* each supply a type T. Hotel reservations vary by date. Travel arrangements vary by time. *HR* supplies hotel reservation information via an exported type R. *TR* supplies travel reservation information via an exported type R. *V* supplies visitor information via a type U. The constant names 1-1, 1-M etc. are overloaded: they refer to the module supplying the *restr* constant as well as the value of the constant itself. The same is true of the T, R, and U parameter modules and the types they supply.

Instantiations like those defining *HR-V* and *TR-V* define *TDens* mapping the empty argument map to a single theory due to the body of the instantiated module interpreted in an environment of theories due to the arguments and imported modules.

4.3 The Meeting-Visitor Subsystem

The meeting-visitor subsystem is described as a composite containing a *Pool* of meetings and a resource-user system relating meetings and visitors. This is as far as the CAVIAR structure will be taken in this paper. The *POOL* module is that of Section 3.4.

Appropriate instantiations of *RES-USR* and *POOL* are defined first. Note that *M* is not a proper second argument to *POOL*, in that it supplies a type called *R*, not a type called *X*. An appropriate renaming is applied to resolve this:

$$R_{M\text{-}V} \triangleq RES\text{-}USR(SESS, M, V, 1\text{-}M)$$

$$M_X \triangleq M[X/R]$$

$$P_{M\text{-}V} \triangleq POOL(SESS, M_X)$$

The *M-V* module can now be written. $R_{M\text{-}V}$ and $P_{M\text{-}V}$ will be imports to *M-V*. Since they take only the empty map of arguments, the abbreviation "$R_{M\text{-}V}$" will stand for "$R_{M\text{-}V}()$". Likewise for "$P_{M\text{-}V}$". An invariant on the composite state ensures that all the meetings for which visitors are recorded for a certain session are recorded in the pool for the same session:

$M\text{-}V \triangleq$
Import $R_{M\text{-}V}, P_{M\text{-}V}$
State $M\text{-}V\text{-}S$

    $M\text{-}V\text{-}S ::\ ru\ :\ R_{M\text{-}V}.RU$
               $p\ :\ P_{M\text{-}V}.Pool$
    inv $(ru, p) \triangleq$
        $\forall t \in R_{M\text{-}V}.T.T \cdot (R_{M\text{-}V}.pre\text{-}in\text{-}use(ru, t) \wedge P_{M\text{-}V}.pre\text{-}exists(p, t)) \Rightarrow$
           $R_{M\text{-}V}.in\text{-}use(ru, t) \subseteq P_{M\text{-}V}.exists(p, t)$

It is not necessary to define $R_{M\text{-}V}$ and $P_{M\text{-}V}$ as separate modules outside *M-V*. *M-V* could equally well import *RES-USR* and *POOL* directly (along with *SESS*, *M*, *V* and 1-*M*) and provide the instantiation at each use of RU_M or P_M in the body of *M-V*. The approach employed here is primarily for notational convenience.

The functions *exists* and *users*, which come from the imported $R_{M\text{-}V}$ module, are promoted to work on the composite state:

    $exists : M\text{-}V\text{-}S \times P_{M\text{-}V}.T \rightarrow P_{M\text{-}V}.X\text{-set}$

    $exists(mvs, t) \triangleq P_{M\text{-}V}.exists(p(mvs), t)$

    pre $P_{M\text{-}V}.pre\text{-}exists(p(mvs), t)$

    $users : M\text{-}V\text{-}S \times R_{M\text{-}V}.T \rightarrow R_{M\text{-}V}.U\text{-set}$

    $users(mvs, t) \triangleq R_{M\text{-}V}.users(ru(mvs), t)$

    pre $R_{M\text{-}V}.pre\text{-}users(ru(mvs), t)$

The operations from the imported modules are also promoted. For example, *CREATE* from $P_{M\text{-}V}$ is promoted by *CREATE-MEETING*:

$CREATE\text{-}MEETING$ $(ts\text{:}\,P_{M\text{-}V}.T.T\text{-}set, x\text{:}\,P_{M\text{-}V}.X.X)$

ext wr p : $P_{M\text{-}V}.Pool$

pre $P_{M\text{-}V}.pre\text{-}CREATE(p, ts, x)$

post $P_{M\text{-}V}.post\text{-}CREATE(\overleftarrow{p}, ts, x, p)$

Sometimes an additional conjunct must be added to the precondition to preserve the invariant on the importing state. For example, $BOOK$ from $R_{M\text{-}V}$ is promoted by $ADD\text{-}VIS\text{-}TO\text{-}MEETING$:

$ADD\text{-}VIS\text{-}TO\text{-}MEETING$ $(ts\text{:}\,R_{M\text{-}V}.T.T\text{-}set, r\text{:}\,R_{M\text{-}V}.R.R, u\text{:}\,R_{M\text{-}V}.U.U)$

ext wr ru : $R_{M\text{-}V}.RU$
    rd p : $P_{M\text{-}V}.Pool$

pre $R_{M\text{-}V}.pre\text{-}BOOK(ru, ts, r, u)\,\wedge$
    $\forall t \in ts \cdot P_{M\text{-}V}.pre\text{-}exists(p, t)\wedge r \in P_{M\text{-}V}.exists(p, t)$

post $R_{M\text{-}V}.post\text{-}BOOK(\overleftarrow{ru}, ts, r, u, ru)$

Another operation promotes two acquired operations simultaneously:

$CANCEL\text{-}MEETING$ $(ts\text{:}\,R_{M\text{-}V}.T.T\text{-}set, r\text{:}\,R_{M\text{-}V}.R.R)$

ext wr ru : $R_{M\text{-}V}.RU$
    wr p : $P_{M\text{-}V}.Pool$

pre $R_{M\text{-}V}.pre\text{-}DEL\text{-}RES(ru, ts, r)\wedge P_{M\text{-}V}.pre\text{-}DESTROY(p, ts, r)$

post $R_{M\text{-}V}.post\text{-}DEL\text{-}RES(\overleftarrow{ru}, ts, r, ru)\wedge P_{M\text{-}V}.post\text{-}DESTROY(\overleftarrow{p}, ts, r, p)$

The state type, all operations and auxiliaries are exported, along with the types of their parameters.

4.4 A Simple Proof in the $M\text{-}V$ Module

It is now possible to consider the use of the structuring mechanism developed here in proving theorems about the constructs defined in the body of $M\text{-}V$. Recall that the theory due to the body is interpreted in an environment of theories due to the imported modules and arguments.

Consider satisfiability of $CREATE\text{-}MEETING$. This should be a rule in the theory of $M\text{-}V$. The rule is:

$$\frac{\begin{array}{c}\overleftarrow{\sigma} \in M\text{-}V\text{-}S;\\ ts \in P_{M\text{-}V}.T.T\text{-}set; x \in P_{M\text{-}V}.X.X;\\ pre\text{-}CREATE\text{-}MEETING(\overleftarrow{\sigma}, ts, x)\end{array}}{\exists \sigma \in M\text{-}V\text{-}S\cdot post\text{-}CREATE\text{-}MEETING(\overleftarrow{\sigma}, ts, x, \sigma)}\ \boxed{\text{C-M-sat}}$$

It should therefore be possible to construct a proof for $C\text{-}M$-sat using the theories due to the imported modules. A rigorous (not fully formal) proof, using the Natural Deduction style and inference rules of [15] is given in Figure 1. The proof is not fully formal because the definedness results for the bodies of functions used have not been taken into account.

The proof hinges on the rule:

from $\overleftarrow{\sigma} \in M\text{-}V\text{-}S$
  $ts \in P_{M\text{-}V}.T.T\text{-set}; x \in P_{M\text{-}V}.X.X;$
  $pre\text{-}CREATE\text{-}MEETING(\overleftarrow{\sigma}, ts, x)$

1	$\exists p \in P_{M\text{-}V}.Pool \cdot post\text{-}CREATE(p(\overleftarrow{\sigma}), ts, x, p)$	C-sat-1, hyps

2   from $p' \in P_{M\text{-}V}.Pool;\ post\text{-}CREATE(p(\overleftarrow{\sigma}), ts, x, p)$
2.1   from $t \in R_{M\text{-}V}.T.T$
2.1.1   from $R_{M\text{-}V}.pre\text{-}in\text{-}use(ru(\overleftarrow{\sigma}), t) \wedge P_{M\text{-}V}.pre\text{-}exists(p', t)$
2.1.1.1 $R_{M\text{-}V}.pre\text{-}in\text{-}use(ru(\overleftarrow{\sigma}), t) \wedge P_{M\text{-}V}.pre\text{-}exists(p(\overleftarrow{\sigma}), t) \Rightarrow$
                      $R_{M\text{-}V}.in\text{-}use(ru(\overleftarrow{\sigma}), t) \subseteq P_{M\text{-}V}.exists(p(\overleftarrow{\sigma}), t)$
                      inv-M-V-S-def
2.1.1.2 $R_{M\text{-}V}.pre\text{-}in\text{-}use(ru(\overleftarrow{\sigma}), t)$ $\wedge$-E(h2.1.1)
2.1.1.3 $P_{M\text{-}V}.pre\text{-}exists(p(\overleftarrow{\sigma}), t)$
                      exists-1(h2.1, p-def)
2.1.1.4 $R_{M\text{-}V}.in\text{-}use(ru(\overleftarrow{\sigma}), t) \subseteq P_{M\text{-}V}.exists(p(\overleftarrow{\sigma}), t)$
                      $\Rightarrow$ -E(2.1.1.2,2.1.1.3)
2.1.1.5 $P_{M\text{-}V}.exists(p(\overleftarrow{\sigma}), t) \subseteq P_{M\text{-}V}.exists(p', t)$ M-V-S-3
                infer $R_{M\text{-}V}.in\text{-}use(ru(\overleftarrow{\sigma}), t) \subseteq P_{M\text{-}V}.exists(p', t)$
                      $\subseteq$-trans(2.1.1.4,2.1.1.5)
            infer $R_{M\text{-}V}.pre\text{-}in\text{-}use(ru(\overleftarrow{\sigma}), t) \wedge P_{M\text{-}V}.pre\text{-}exists(p', t) \Rightarrow$
                $R_{M\text{-}V}.in\text{-}use(ru(\overleftarrow{\sigma}), t) \subseteq P_{M\text{-}V}.exists(p', t)$
                      $\Rightarrow$ -I(2.1.1), B
2.2   inv-M-V-$S(ru(\overleftarrow{\sigma}), p')$
                      $\forall$-I(2.1), inv-M-V-S-def
2.3 $mk\text{-}M\text{-}V\text{-}S(ru(\overleftarrow{\sigma}), p') \in M\text{-}V\text{-}S$
                      2.2, mk-M-V-S-def
2.4 $post\text{-}CREATE\text{-}MEETING(\overleftarrow{\sigma}, ts, x, mk\text{-}M\text{-}V\text{-}S(ru(\overleftarrow{\sigma}), p'))$
                      2.3, h2, $post$-$CREATE$-$MEETING$-def
    infer $\exists \sigma \in M\text{-}V\text{-}S \cdot post\text{-}CREATE\text{-}MEETING(\overleftarrow{\sigma}, ts, x, \sigma)$ $\exists$-I(2.3,2.4)
  infer $\exists \sigma \in M\text{-}V\text{-}S \cdot post\text{-}CREATE\text{-}MEETING(\overleftarrow{\sigma}, ts, x, \sigma)$ $\exists$-E(1,2)

Figure 1: Proof of C-M-sat

$$\begin{array}{l} \overleftarrow{p} \in P_{M\text{-}V}.Pool; \\ ts \in P_{M\text{-}V}.T.T\text{-set}; x \in P_{M\text{-}V}.X.X; \\ P_{M\text{-}V}.pre\text{-}CREATE(\overleftarrow{p}, ts, x) \end{array}$$

$$\boxed{C\text{-sat-1}} \quad \exists p \in P_{M\text{-}V}.Pool \cdot P_{M\text{-}V}.post\text{-}CREATE(\overleftarrow{p}, ts, x, p)$$

Considering the theory identified by $P_{M\text{-}V}$, the following rule is found:

$$\begin{array}{l} \overleftarrow{p} \in Pool; \\ ts \in T.T\text{-set}; x \in X.X; \\ pre\text{-}CREATE(\overleftarrow{p}, ts, x) \end{array}$$

$$\boxed{C\text{-sat-2}} \quad \exists p \in Pool \cdot post\text{-}CREATE(\overleftarrow{p}, ts, x, p)$$

This must be qualified before it can be used in the proof. It therefore appears as C-sat-1 in the theory of M-V's body.

The rest of the proof depends on showing invariant preservation on M-V-S:

$$\begin{array}{l} \overleftarrow{p}, p \in P_{M\text{-}V}.Pool; ts \in P_{M\text{-}V}.T.T\text{-set}; x \in P_{M\text{-}V}.X.X; \\ P_{M\text{-}V}.pre\text{-}CREATE(\overleftarrow{p}, ts, x); P_{M\text{-}V}.post\text{-}CREATE(\overleftarrow{p}, ts, x, p); \\ \overleftarrow{ru} \in R_{M\text{-}V}.RU; \\ mk\text{-}M\text{-}V\text{-}S(\overleftarrow{ru}, \overleftarrow{p}) \in M\text{-}V\text{-}S \end{array}$$

$$\boxed{M\text{-}V\text{-}S\text{-}1} \quad mk\text{-}M\text{-}V\text{-}S(\overleftarrow{ru}, p) \in M\text{-}V\text{-}S$$

i.e., by definition of inv-M-V-S:

$$\begin{array}{l} \overleftarrow{p}, p \in P_{M\text{-}V}.Pool; ts \in P_{M\text{-}V}.T.T; \text{-set} x \in P_{M\text{-}V}.X.X; \\ P_{M\text{-}V}.pre\text{-}CREATE(\overleftarrow{p}, ts, x); P_{M\text{-}V}.post\text{-}CREATE(\overleftarrow{p}, ts, x, p); \\ \overleftarrow{ru} \in R_{M\text{-}V}.RU; \\ mk\text{-}M\text{-}V\text{-}S(\overleftarrow{ru}, \overleftarrow{p}) \in M\text{-}V\text{-}S; \\ t \in R_{M\text{-}V}.T.T; \\ R_{M\text{-}V}.pre\text{-}in\text{-}use(\overleftarrow{ru}, t); P_{M\text{-}V}.pre\text{-}exists(p, t) \end{array}$$

$$\boxed{M\text{-}V\text{-}S\text{-}2} \quad R_{M\text{-}V}.in\text{-}use(\overleftarrow{ru}, t) \subseteq P_{M\text{-}V}.exists(p, t)$$

This requires the rule showing that the collection of meetings in the pool is increased by *CREATE*:

$$\begin{array}{l} \overleftarrow{p}, p \in P_{M\text{-}V}.Pool; ts \in P_{M\text{-}V}.T.T\text{-set}; x \in P_{M\text{-}V}.X.X; \\ P_{M\text{-}V}.pre\text{-}CREATE(\overleftarrow{p}, ts, x); P_{M\text{-}V}.post\text{-}CREATE(\overleftarrow{p}, ts, x, p); \\ t \in R_{M\text{-}V}.T.T; \\ P_{M\text{-}V}.pre\text{-}exists(\overleftarrow{p}, t); P_{M\text{-}V}.pre\text{-}exists(p, t) \end{array}$$

$$\boxed{M\text{-}V\text{-}S\text{-}3} \quad P_{M\text{-}V}.exists(\overleftarrow{p}, t) \subseteq P_{M\text{-}V}.exists(p, t)$$

Now from the theory of $P_{M\text{-}V}$, the following similar result holds:

$$\begin{array}{l} \overleftarrow{p}, p \in P_{M\text{-}V}.Pool; ts \in P_{M\text{-}V}.T.T\text{-set}; x \in P_{M\text{-}V}.X.X; \\ P_{M\text{-}V}.pre\text{-}CREATE(\overleftarrow{p}, ts, x); P_{M\text{-}V}.post\text{-}CREATE(\overleftarrow{p}, ts, x, p); \\ t \in P_{M\text{-}V}.T.T; \\ P_{M\text{-}V}.pre\text{-}exists(\overleftarrow{p}, t); P_{M\text{-}V}.pre\text{-}exists(p, t) \end{array}$$

$$\boxed{M\text{-}V\text{-}S\text{-}4} \quad P_{M\text{-}V}.exists(\overleftarrow{p}, t) \subseteq P_{M\text{-}V}.exists(p, t)$$

where the penultimate hypothesis is in terms of $P_{M\text{-}V}.T.T$ rather than $R_{M\text{-}V}.T.T$ as required in $M\text{-}V\text{-}S\text{-}3$. These two types are the same, by the definitions of $P_{M\text{-}V}$ and $R_{M\text{-}V}$, so $M\text{-}V\text{-}S\text{-}4$ yields $M\text{-}V\text{-}S\text{-}3$ as required.

The fact that *pre-exists* is unaffected by *CREATE* is also used:

$$\overleftarrow{p}, p \in P_{M\text{-}V}.Pool;\ ts \in P_{M\text{-}V}.T.T\text{-set};\ x \in P_{M\text{-}V}.X.X;$$
$$P_{M\text{-}V}.post\text{-}CREATE(\overleftarrow{p}, ts, x, p);$$
$$t \in P_{M\text{-}V}.T.T;$$

$$\text{exists-1}\quad \frac{P_{M\text{-}V}.pre\text{-}exists(p, t)}{P_{M\text{-}V}.pre\text{-}exists(\overleftarrow{p}, t)}$$

This allows the application of the invariant in the state prior to the application of *CREATE*.

The proof also uses the "...-def" rules which are axiomatic to the theory of the body of $M\text{-}V$, since they refer to locally-defined constructs.

5 Discussion

5.1 The Structuring Language

How far has the suggested structuring language gone towards meeting its objectives? Certainly a notion of module has been developed, with a separate theory associated with each module: but what of the objectives of restriction, genericity and recorded dependency?

Restriction: The main mechanism for hiding information in a module is the reduct performed at export. It is readily acknowledged that the particular reduct suggested in Section 3.3 represents only one view of the sort of hiding which can be applied. There the reduct allows the publication of rules describing the representations of non-state types. The representations of state types are not revealed. This reflects very closely the interpretation of a flat specification in Meta-IV, prior to implementation using VDM. This approach worked satisfactorily in the example of Section 4, enabling the separate writing of each module without the writer having to be concerned about the form taken by other parts of the system, or even the names given to constructs specified in other modules. This was reflected in the formal reasoning about the contents of modules in that proofs could proceed using only published rules about imported modules.

One criticism which can be levelled at the CAVIAR example is that the reduct helped achieve this separation of concerns precisely because the main modules involved were state-based. A reduct which hides representations of all exported constructs might better insulate one module's contents from others, but for modules which encapsulate relatively simple non-state-based data types, the primitive operators on their representations would have to be explicitly renamed and exported, inflating the interface to the module. Another alternative is to allow the writer of a module to define which exported constructs to hide, and which to reveal. This can be taken further to provide for alternative export clauses in a single module, allowing alternative "views" of the theory due to the module's body.

Genericity: Parameterisation is not higher-order in the formalism described in this paper: arguments may not themselves have parameters. The effect of admitting higher-order parameterisation is a considerable complication to the formal semantics of a structuring language, requiring the apparatus of reflexive domain theory [21], or at least the construction of indexed hierarchies of denotations (e.g. [22], employing a technique dating from [23]). Is the gain from higher-order modules worth this? Jonkers, in [24], points to what is described as the "limited practical applicability" of higher-order modularisation, though facilities for it are included in COLD-K ([19]). Higher-order parameterisation is used extensively in the case studies of [8] and may prove important as a source of future work. However, it is felt that its practical usefulness ought to be established before it is supplied as a facility in the structuring sublanguage developed here. Though many other model-oriented languages (e.g. RSL, VVSL) appear to provide higher-order modules, there is not yet a substantial corpus of realistic case studies justifying its use.

Arguments to modules are restricted only by signatures. It is possible to instantiate a module by any argument modules which supply constructs with the correct names and signatures. This is a weaker form of restriction than that used in many formalisms (e.g. Clear, VVSL, COLD-K and RSL) where the restriction is itself a specification which any argument must be shown to satisfy in order that the instantiation be well-formed. This has the advantage that the permitted class of arguments can be closely specified, but has the disadvantage that conformance of an argument to its restriction cannot be statically checked so that, in general, a proof obligation must be discharged by the specification writer at each instantiation.

Recording dependencies: The distinction between parameterisation and import is important. In some cases where higher-order parameterisation might be used, import provides a more intuitively satisfactory alternative. The user of a module need know nothing about imported modules or their contents. A common example is the interpreter which is parameterised over a notion of stack. Should a user of the interpreter know that it uses a stack? If yes, then the interpreter module must genuinely be higher-order, with the generic stack module as a parameter. This is not the case, and so an alternative mechanism for utilising the stack definition is needed, which shields it from the user of the interpreter module. This is achieved by direct import.

5.2 The Structuring Facilities in Use

The CAVIAR example has illustrated the structuring facilities in use, and an example proof has been conducted in the theory of a module within the structure. As indicated above, the ability to reason separately about the contents of modules has been achieved. The rules used are no different from those which would be used in a proof about an unstructured specification, and the proofs are of the same form. However, the need to manage rules from a collection of theories due to imported modules and parameters complicates the situation. In particular, the highly disciplined approach to naming acquired constructs by qualifying them all with their source seems somewhat inflexible. It would be expected that syntactic "sugaring" could overcome this. However, the origins of constructs must still be recorded, so that the merging of differently-named constructs having the same point of definition can take place. This was exemplified in the case of $M\text{-}V\text{-}S\text{-}4$ and $M\text{-}V\text{-}S\text{-}3$ in Section 4.4.

This is in marked contrast to the [17] version of the specification of CAVIAR in Z. There the schema calculus is used to separate specifications of CAVIAR subsystems. However, schemas are not the same as modules (c.f. [25]). They do not, for example, close the name space. The coincidence of names on which schema extension depends in Z does not accord with the principles of encapsulation and separation of concerns in the approach employed here. For example, the specification in [17] uses the schema calculus to define parameter lists for whole classes of operations at once by defining widely re-used schemas which are quoted by operation-defining schemas. This saves space in the specification but sometimes forces lengthier predicate parts in schemas defining promotions of lower-level operations, where parameter names from different operations must be explicitly equated. In Meta-IV, this is not required, since the parameter names are restated for the promoted operation.

Another distinction between the module-based approach to structuring employed in this paper and that of the Z schema calculus is in the support given to conservative extension ([26]) here. Each module's theory is a new theory, derived from the theories of the imports and arguments. Thus it is possible to derive all the properties of a particular type from the theory of the module in which the type is defined. In Z, however, any schema may extend another by adding a new predicate, for example. It is not therefore possible in general to deduce the properties of a single type by looking at a single schema. The whole specification must be examined. This ability to make non-conservative extensions leads to many useful textual manipulations. For example, the *RES-USR* module above needs a *RESTR* parameter to fix the cardinality of resource-user relationships. This single parameter can take one of only four values. In the [17] specification, four separate schemas are produced – one for each cardinality. This is elegantly done by writing a schema for the *M-M* case and extending it by three separate schemas which impose the appropriate restriction on the relationships. This elegance is paid for by the the loss of the ability to reason about a construct without having to refer to the whole specification, regardless of its structure.

There is certainly a lack of flexibility in the simple approach to modular structuring facilities taken here. The ability to record different "views" of a module in the form of alternative export lists and the ability to partially instantiate parametric modules are just two features which would have their place in a fully-developed specification language with modular structuring. In fairness, it should be remembered that the facilities presented here are primarily a vehicle for experimentation in formal reasoning about structured specifications, rather than a finished system. The facilities have been useful in that they have helped formulate requirements for formal reasoning support in structured specifications and substantial specifications can be structured using these basic facilities alone.

5.3 Implementation and Specifications of Database Systems

This paper has laid most of its stress on the specification of CAVIAR *as a specification*. There are some important points to emerge from a brief consideration of its implementation as a database system.

In [12], a (tentative) modular specification of the NDB database system was given. This paper has further developed the naïve structuring facilities employed in former work by showing how an abstract view of a database application can be given a modular specification. An obvious next step is to consider the process of reification. CAVIAR might easily be implemented in NDB, but could the implementation proceed by formal reification? The specifications of CAVIAR and NDB are modular. The question of how the database system specification is to be instantiated by the differently structured specification of the application is an open one. It may, for example, not be helpful to write a reification of the CAVIAR specification (using NDB) which reflects the structure of the abstract CAVIAR specification. A separate, but relevant area of research [27] is the use of program code, with accompanying specifications, within larger systems.

The problems of reconciling implementation structure with the structure of a modular specification were anticipated in [12], where the view was expressed that the structure of an implementation should not in general be expected to reflect that of its abstract specification. This view has been strengthened by work on algebraic specification ([22], [28]) which carefully distinguishes structured specifications from specifications of structured systems. It is apparent that some specification languages have a semantics which may force reifications to reflect the structure of their abstract specifications (e.g. ACT-ONE [29], [30]). It continues to be the author's view that specification structuring techniques should be regarded primarily as tools for marshalling facts about specifications and should not dictate the structure of an implementation.

6   Concluding Remarks

This paper has given an illustration of "modularity at work". Some modularisation facilities have been introduced and their effects on formal reasoning about a structured specification discussed. Even with the elementary facilities described, it has been shown possible to structure part of the specification of a database application. The relationship between the structure of the specification of an application and its implementation via a specified database system has been discussed as an area of further work. The work described here also suggests further research in a number of other areas. For example, the problems of theory structuring must be addressed by developers of specification and proof support tools (e.g. [10], [11]). The relationship between the notion of theory described here and the operation decomposition aspects of formal development VDM remain to be explored. The augmentation of theories by theorems using Hoare/Jones triples ([31]) may be required.

Acknowledgements   The author is grateful to Cliff Jones for advice and many fruitful discussions. Many colleagues at Manchester University and elsewhere are to be thanked for their influence on this and related work, especially Andrzej Tarlecki, Brian Monahan, Alan Wills, Ian Hayes, Stephen Bear and Tim Clement. The organisers of the 1991 Workshop on Specifications of Database Systems at Glasgow University have also been most helpful. The financial support of the Department of Education for Northern Ireland is acknowledged.

A Module Definitions in Full

This section contains the specifications of the library modules and the defined modules in the CAVIAR document.

A.1 Resource-User Module

$RES\text{-}USR \triangleq$
Parameters T: Type T,
$\qquad\qquad R$: Type R,
$\qquad\qquad U$: Type U,
$\qquad\qquad RESTR$: Value $restr$: $\{1\text{-}1, 1\text{-}M, M\text{-}1, M\text{-}M\}$
State RU
$\quad RU :: ru : T.T \xrightarrow{m} (R.R \times U.U)\text{-set}$
$\quad$ inv $(ru) \triangleq$
$\qquad \forall t \in$ dom $ru \cdot$cases $RESTR.restr$ of
$\qquad\qquad\qquad 1\text{-}1 \to \forall (r_1, u_1), (r_2, u_2) \in ru(t) \cdot r_1 = r_2 \iff u_1 = u_2$
$\qquad\qquad\qquad 1\text{-}M \to \forall (r_1, u_1), (r_2, u_2) \in ru(t) \cdot u_1 = u_2 \implies r_1 = r_2$
$\qquad\qquad\qquad M\text{-}1 \to \forall (r_1, u_1), (r_2, u_2) \in ru(t) \cdot r_1 = r_2 \implies u_1 = u_2$
$\qquad\qquad\qquad$ others true
$\qquad\qquad\qquad$ end

$in\text{-}use : RU \times T.T \to R.R\text{-set}$
$in\text{-}use(ru, t) \triangleq$ Dom $ru(t)$
pre $t \in$ dom ru

$users : RU \times T.T \to U.U\text{-set}$
$users(ru, t) \triangleq$ Rng $ru(t)$
pre $t \in$ dom ru

$ur : RU \times T.T \to (U.U \times R.R)\text{-set}$
$ur(ru, t) \triangleq ru(t)^{-1}$
pre $t \in$ dom ru

$BOOK$ $(ts: T.T\text{-set}, r: R.R, u: U.U)$
ext wr $ru : RU$
pre $\forall t \in ts \cdot t \in$ dom $ru \wedge (r, u) \notin ru(t) \wedge$
$\quad$ inv-$RU(ru \dagger \{t' \mapsto ru(t') \cup \{(r, u)\} \mid t' \in ts\})$
post $\forall t \in ts \cdot ru(t) = \overleftarrow{ru}(t) \cup \{(r, u)\} \wedge ts \triangleleft ru = ts \triangleleft \overleftarrow{ru}$

$CANCEL$ $(ts: T.T\text{-set}, r: R.R, u: U.U)$
ext wr $ru : RU$
pre $\forall t \in ts \cdot t \in$ dom $ru \wedge (r, u) \in ru(t)$
post $\forall t \in ts \cdot ru(t) = \overleftarrow{ru}(t) - \{(r, u)\} \wedge ts \triangleleft ru = ts \triangleleft \overleftarrow{ru}$

DEL-RES (*ts*: *T.T*-set, *r*: *R.R*)
ext wr *ru* : *RU*
pre $\forall t \in ts \cdot t \in \text{dom } ru \land r \in \text{Dom } ru(t)$
post $ru = \overleftarrow{ru} \dagger \{t \mapsto \{r\} \lhd \overleftarrow{ru}(t) \mid t \in ts\}$

DEL-USR (*ts*: *T.T*-set, *r*: *U.U*)
ext wr *ru* : *RU*
pre $\forall t \in ts \cdot t \in \text{dom } ru \land r \in \text{Rng } ru(t)$
post $ru = \overleftarrow{ru} \dagger \{t \mapsto \overleftarrow{ru}(t) \rhd \{r\} \mid t \in ts\}$

Export *RU*, *T.T*, *R.R*, *U.U*, *in-use*, *users*, *ur*,
     BOOK, *CANCEL*, *DEL-RES*, *DEL-USR*

A.2 Pool Module

POOL $\triangleq$
Parameters *T*: Type *T*,
        X: Type *X*
State *Pool*
   Pool :: *pl* : *T.T* $\xrightarrow{m}$ *X.X*-set

   exists : *Pool* × *T.T* → *X.X*-set
   exists(*p*, *t*) $\triangleq$ *pl*(*p*)(*t*)
   pre $t \in \text{dom } pl(p)$

   CREATE (*ts*: *T.T*-set, *x*: *X.X*)
   ext wr *pl* : *T.T* $\xrightarrow{m}$ *X.X*-set
   pre $ts \subseteq \text{dom } pl$
   post $pl = \overleftarrow{pl} \dagger \{t \mapsto \overleftarrow{pl}(t) \cup \{x\} \mid t \in ts\}$

   DESTROY (*ts*: *T.T*-set, *x*: *X.X*)
   ext wr *pl* : *T.T* $\xrightarrow{m}$ *X.X*-set
   pre $ts \subseteq \text{dom } pl$
   post $pl = \overleftarrow{pl} \dagger \{t \mapsto \overleftarrow{pl}(t) - \{x\} \mid t \in ts\}$

Export *Pool*, *X.X*, *T.T*, *exists*, *CREATE*, *DESTROY*

A.3 Meeting-Visitor Module

M-V $\triangleq$
Import $R_{M\text{-}V}$, $P_{M\text{-}V}$
State *M-V-S*

$M\text{-}V\text{-}S :: ru : R_{M\text{-}V}.RU$
$\qquad\quad p : P_{M\text{-}V}.Pool$

$\text{inv}\ (ru, p) \triangleq$
$\quad \forall t \in R_{M\text{-}V}.T.T \cdot (R_{M\text{-}V}.pre\text{-}in\text{-}use(ru, t) \wedge P_{M\text{-}V}.pre\text{-}exists(p, t)) \;\Rightarrow$
$\qquad R_{M\text{-}V}.in\text{-}use(ru, t) \subseteq P_{M\text{-}V}.exists(p, t)$

$exists : M\text{-}V\text{-}S \times P_{M\text{-}V}.T \rightarrow P_{M\text{-}V}.X\text{-set}$

$exists(mvs, t) \quad\triangleq\quad P_{M\text{-}V}.exists(p(mvs), t)$

$\text{pre}\ P_{M\text{-}V}.pre\text{-}exists(p(mvs), t)$

$users : M\text{-}V\text{-}S \times R_{M\text{-}V}.T \rightarrow R_{M\text{-}V}.U\text{-set}$

$users(mvs, t) \quad\triangleq\quad R_{M\text{-}V}.users(ru(mvs), t)$

$\text{pre}\ R_{M\text{-}V}.pre\text{-}users(ru(mvs), t)$

$ADD\text{-}VIS\text{-}TO\text{-}MEETING\ (ts: R_{M\text{-}V}.T.T\text{-set}, r: R_{M\text{-}V}.R.R, u: R_{M\text{-}V}.U.U)$

ext wr $ru : R_{M\text{-}V}.RU$
$\quad$ rd $p\ \ : P_{M\text{-}V}.Pool$

$\text{pre}\ R_{M\text{-}V}.pre\text{-}BOOK(ru, ts, r, u) \wedge$
$\quad \forall t \in ts \cdot P_{M\text{-}V}.pre\text{-}exists(p, t) \wedge r \in P_{M\text{-}V}.exists(p, t)$

$\text{post}\ R_{M\text{-}V}.post\text{-}BOOK(\overleftarrow{ru}, ts, r, u, ru)$

$REM\text{-}VIS\text{-}FROM\text{-}MEETING\ (ts: R_{M\text{-}V}.T.T\text{-set}, r: R_{M\text{-}V}.R.R, u: R_{M\text{-}V}.U.U)$

ext wr $ru : R_{M\text{-}V}.RU$

$\text{pre}\ R_{M\text{-}V}.pre\text{-}CANCEL(ru, ts, r, u)$

$\text{post}\ R_{M\text{-}V}.post\text{-}CANCEL(\overleftarrow{ru}, ts, r, u, ru)$

$CREATE\text{-}MEETING\ (ts: P_{M\text{-}V}.T.T\text{-set}, x: P_{M\text{-}V}.X.X)$

ext wr $p : P_{M\text{-}V}.Pool$

$\text{pre}\ P_{M\text{-}V}.pre\text{-}CREATE(p, ts, x)$

$\text{post}\ P_{M\text{-}V}.post\text{-}CREATE(\overleftarrow{p}, ts, x, p)$

$CANCEL\text{-}MEETING\ (ts: R_{M\text{-}V}.T.T\text{-set}, r: R_{M\text{-}V}.R.R)$

ext wr $ru : R_{M\text{-}V}.RU$
$\quad$ wr $p\ \ : P_{M\text{-}V}.Pool$

$\text{pre}\ R_{M\text{-}V}.pre\text{-}DEL\text{-}RES(ru, ts, r) \wedge P_{M\text{-}V}.pre\text{-}DESTROY(p, ts, r)$

$\text{post}\ R_{M\text{-}V}.post\text{-}DEL\text{-}RES(\overleftarrow{ru}, ts, r, ru) \wedge P_{M\text{-}V}.post\text{-}DESTROY(\overleftarrow{p}, ts, r, p)$

Export $M\text{-}V\text{-}S$, $ADD\text{-}VIS\text{-}TO\text{-}MEETING$, $REM\text{-}VIS\text{-}FROM\text{-}MEETING$,
$\quad CREATE\text{-}MEETING$, $CANCEL\text{-}MEETING$
$\quad R_{M\text{-}V}.T.T, R_{M\text{-}V}.R.R, R_{M\text{-}V}.U.U, P_{M\text{-}V}.T.T, P_{M\text{-}V}.X.X, P_{M\text{-}V}.exists, R_{M\text{-}V}.users$

References

[1] BSI. *VDM Specification Language – Proto-Standard*, March 1991. BSI Working Document: BSI IST/5/50.

[2] United Kingdom Ministry of Defence. *Interim Defence Standard 00-55: Procurement of safety-critical software*, 1991.

[3] F.P. Brooks, Jr. *The Mythical Man-Month*. Addison-Wesley, 1975.

[4] R. M. Burstall and J. A. Goguen. An Informal Introduction to Specifications Using Clear. In R. Boyer and J. Moore, editors, *The Correctness Problem in Computer Science*, pages 185–213. Academic Press, New York, 1981.

[5] J. V. Guttag, J. J. Horning, and J. M. Wing. Larch in Five Easy Pieces. Technical Report 5, DEC Systems Research Center, 1985.

[6] D. Sannella and A. Tarlecki. Extended ML: Past, present and future. In *Proceedings of the 7th. Workshop on Specification of Abstract Data Types, Wusterhausen, Germany*, Lecture Notes in Computer Science. Springer-Verlag, 1991. To Appear.

[7] S. Bear. Structuring for the VDM specification language. In *[32]*, 1988.

[8] C.A. Middelburg. *Syntax and Semantics of VVSL: A Language for Structured VDM Specifications*. PhD thesis, University of Amsterdam, 1990.

[9] K. Havelund. An RSL Tutorial. Technical report, Computer Resources International A/S, August 1990. LACOS/CRI/DOC/1/V1.

[10] C. B. Jones, K. D. Jones, P. A. Lindsay, and R. Moore, editors. *mural: A Formal Development Support System*. Springer-Verlag, 1991.

[11] J. R. Abrial. Abstract Machines (Parts 1-3) & The B Proof Assistant. In *Notes from the B Tutorial, University of Manchester, April 1991*. BCS FACS, 1991.

[12] J.S. Fitzgerald and C.B. Jones. Modularizing the Formal Description of a Database System. In *[33]*, 1990.

[13] L. M. G. Feijs. Norman's Database Modularised in COLD-K. In J. A. Bergstra and L. M. G. Feijs, editors, *Proceedings of the METEOR Mierlo Workshop*, volume 490 of *Lecture Notes in Computer Science*. Springer-Verlag, 1990.

[14] J.S. Fitzgerald. *Modularity in Model-Oriented Formal Specifications and its Interaction with Formal Reasoning*. PhD thesis, Dept. of Computer Science, University of Manchester, UK, 1991.

[15] C. B. Jones. *Systematic Software Development Using VDM*. Prentice Hall International(UK), second edition, 1990.

[16] H. Barringer, J.H. Cheng, and C.B. Jones. A Logic Covering Undefinedness in Program Proofs. *Acta Informatica*, 21:251–269, 1984.

[17] B. Flinn and I. H. Sørensen. CAVIAR: A Case Study in Specification. In *[34]*. 1987.

[18] J. M. Spivey. *Understanding Z: A Specification Language and its Formal Semantics*, volume 3 of *Cambridge Tracts in Theoretical Computer Science*. Cambridge University Press, 1988.

[19] L.M.G. Feijs, H.B.M. Jonkers, C.P.J. Koymans, and G.R. Renardel de Lavalette. Formal Definition of the Design Language COLD-K. METEOR Report t7/PRLE/7, Philips Research Laboratories, April 1987.

[20] R. M. Burstall and J. A. Goguen. The Semantics of Clear, a Specification Language. In *Proceedings of Advanced Course on Abstract Software Specifications*, volume 86 of *Lecture Notes in Computer Science*. Springer-Verlag, 1980.

[21] D. Scott. Data types as lattices. Technical Report PRG-5, Oxford University Programming Research Group, September 1976. Reprinted from the SIAM Journal on Computing, Volume 5, 1976, pp. 522–587.

[22] D. Sannella, S. Sokolowski, and A Tarlecki. Toward formal development of programs from algebraic specifications: parameterisation revisited. Technical Report 6/90, Informatik, Universität Bremen, 1990.

[23] A.J. Blikle and A. Tarlecki. Naïve Denotational Semantics. In R. Mason, editor, *Information Processing '83, Proceedings of IFIP Congress 1983*, pages 345–355, 1983.

[24] H.B.M. Jonkers. An introduction to COLD-K. Technical Report METEOR/t8/PRLE/8, Philips Research Labs, Eindhoven, July 1988.

[25] A. Sampaio and S. Meira. Modular Extensions to Z. In *[33]*, 1990.

[26] W. M. Turski and T. S. E. Maibaum. *The Specification of Computer Programs*. Addison-Wesley, 1987.

[27] A. C. Wills. Capsules and types in Fresco. In P. America, editor, *Proceedings of ECOOP'91*, July 1991. To appear.

[28] D. Sannella and A. Tarlecki. A kernel specification formalism with higher-order parameterisation. In *Proceedings of the 7th. Workshop on Specification of Abstract Data Types, Wusterhausen, Germany*, Lecture Notes in Computer Science. Springer-Verlag, 1991. To Appear.

[29] H. Ehrig and B. Mahr. *Fundamentals of Algebraic Specification 1: Equations and Initial Semantics*, volume 6 of *EATCS Monographs on Theoretical Computer Science*. Springer-Verlag, 1985.

[30] H. Ehrig and B. Mahr. *Fundamentals of Algebraic Specification 2: Module Specifications and Constraints*, volume 21 of *EATCS Monographs on Theoretical Computer Science*. Springer-Verlag, 1990.

[31] J. Coenen, W-P. de Roever, and J. Zwiers. Assertional Data Reification Proofs: Survey and Perspective. In *Proceedings of the Fourth Refinement Workshop, Logica Cambridge*. Logica Cambridge, 1991.

[32] R. Bloomfield, R. B. Jones, and L. S. Marshall, editors. *VDM '88: VDM – The Way Ahead*, volume 328 of *Lecture Notes in Computer Science*. Springer-Verlag, Berlin, 1988.

[33] D. Bjørner, C.A.R. Hoare, and H. Langmaack, editors. *VDM '90: VDM and Z – Formal Methods in Software Development*, volume 428 of *Lecture Notes in Computer Science*. Springer-Verlag, Berlin, 1990.

[34] I. Hayes, editor. *Specification Case Studies*. Prentice-Hall International, 1987.

Object Models and Methodology for Object-Oriented Database Design

Catherine Hamon   Marion Créhange

Centre de Recherche en Informatique de Nancy (CRIN)
URA 262 of CNRS
Campus Scientifique - B.P. 239
54506 Vandoeuvre-Les-Nancy Cédex France

Abstract

Advantages related to object-oriented technology are at present well known. However, when designing, they must be considered as key objectives on equal terms with the description of the semantic and computer requirements of a problem. In this paper, we present a methodology for object-oriented database design that aims at reaching these objectives through stages of different abstraction levels (conceptual, logical, and implementation stages), the use of models and graphical notations. Moreover, since there is no standard object-oriented data model, we propose to construct during the conceptual and logical stages a database representation as complete as possible and independent on a specific OODBMS.

1 Introduction

Editorial-like applications deal with large and structured databases that require document version management, concurrency control, real-time updating, interactive graphical facilities for document part identification, storage and retrieval.

Object-oriented database management systems (OODBMS) represent a very promising way to implement editorial-like applications requirements. This new generation of database management systems (DBMS) [1], [2] is the result of active research and development in two domains, database management and object-oriented programming (OOP). OODBMSs provide both traditional facilities of DBMSs (like data persistence or query language) and expressibility of object-oriented programming. Moreover, they are designed to handle large programs that operate on large and complex data stores. With this in mind, a study of existing OODBMSs is being undertaken both by CRIN and AIS (Advanced Information Systems), a company specializing in editorial engineering located at Neuilly (Paris). A first prototype implementing multi-version documents has been carried out using O2, the OODBMS designed by GIP Altaïr [3], [4].

The aim of this paper is to outline the design effort needed in an object-oriented approach. We present an object-oriented design method that we have defined to handle some difficult points of the design process. This method has been used to design and implement an editorial database.

1.1 Related work on object-oriented design

Until now software development with object-oriented languages (OOL) has received the most attention. However object-oriented technology is more than just a way of programming as it is stressed in [5]: Object-oriented technology "... is a way of thinking abstractly about a problem using real-world concepts, rather than computer concepts". So if an object-oriented development emphasis on object-oriented constructs as models of real things, rather than as techniques for programming, it can address both large software and object database design.

Many data models have been proposed to apply object-oriented techniques to large software developments. A lot of these models combine object-oriented concepts (like class and inheritance) with information modelling concepts (like entities and associations). For example, the entity/relationship (E/R) approach [6], which is the most common approach to information modelling, has been widely reused and extended in various ways [5], [7], [8]. Other models have also been proposed, some of them are based on ADA-oriented works [9], [10] or mainly deal with object behaviour so as not to violate encapsulation of information into classes [11]. However, only a few complete object-oriented methods have been published [5], [7], [8], [9], [10] and a restricted number of methods (mainly those focusing on the static aspects of an application domain) can deal with object-oriented database design.

Object-oriented design methods generally provide reliable modelling rules (often tested by relevant experiences in object-oriented programming) as well as precise notations for a clean design. However, some aspects of the object design process remain hard to control in a rigorous manner. These aspects are mainly concerned with building up inheritance hierarchies. Contrary to the conventional procedural approach, in the object-oriented approach the inheritance hierarchy combines both data structure hierarchy and operation inheritance hierarchy. The construction of such a hierarchy generally demands some revisions and requires much more careful thought. Indeed, this kind of construction is often a matter of judgment and can lead one to misrepresent the semantics of an application. In the long run, it can be prejudicial to a good modularity and reusability of the application.

During the object design of our editorial application we have had to cope with this problem and with others related to the description of both semantic and computer requirements of the application, as well as many revisions of the application model. We have so defined a method which incorporates our ideas for a cleaner design. Section 2 presents the stages of the method. Object-oriented models and graphical notations are defined in Section 4 (to support iterative and successive revisions of the application model) and Section 7 (to give a final representation of the application suitable for implementation on any OODBMS). Sections 5, 6, 8 and 9 give more details on sensitive points of the design process.

2 Object-oriented database design

OODBMSs supply abstractions such as classification and generalization borrowed from semantic models [12], [13], [14], and powerful object-oriented mechanisms like genericity and inheritance [15] that are useful for both modelling and implementation. Thereby the semantic gap between the real-world application domain and its representation with an OODBMS data model is relatively reduced [16]. A new kind of design which consists in prototyping the application domain directly with a specific OODBMS is therefore offered to database designers.

2.1 Prototyping

In addition to their own OOL, most of OODBMSs are provided with a complete graphical programming environment (containing browser for classes and methods, database schema view(s), a debugger, ...) as well as libraries of classes and methods, and tools for building up interactive applications. These facilities make prototyping as easy as it is in object-oriented systems like SMALLTALK [17].

The prototyping phase consists in implementing quickly a simplify schema using the OODBMS data model. The opportunity to rapidly prototype some parts of the application can efficiently help with crucial points of the database design. The purpose of prototyping can be to evaluate particular aspects of an application (such as database interface) or to make the database designer aware of mechanisms that can be used during both design and implementation phases.

However prototyping should be carefully used. As a matter of fact, when prototyping too large parts of an application, it can lead to a "dirty" implementation where the schema suffers from too many useless classes and a bad linkage of data and code to classes. In most cases, an object-oriented design method is essential especially when dealing with large and complex databases.

2.2 Potential benefits of object-oriented technology

As is stressed in Subsection 2.1, prototyping can be of great help during a design process if it is considered as a way of carrying object database design through to a successful conclusion. Moreover, object databases largely benefit from techniques of OOL that have been created to solve software engineering problems such as modularity, extensibility, reusability and maintainability. However these advantages do not just happen when designing an object-oriented database. On the contrary, they must be considered as main key objectives that must be planned by thinking beyond the immediate application.

Also, since the object-oriented approach offers the prospect of reusing design and code and reducing maintenance effort, it is worth making an object-oriented database understandable by widely documenting its structure. This activity is greatly facilitated by the object paradigm which unites data and code.

2.3 A progressive object-oriented design method

When designing, it is important to focus both on the requirements and relevant semantics of an application as well as on the key objectives that have been previously mentioned. We call a database representation that fills all the application requirements and gets full advantage from the object-oriented technology, a canonical representation. The method that we propose aims at building such a representation for any OODBMS data model.

In this respect, we use three main stages to describe a same problem at different levels of abstraction: Conceptual, logical and implementation stages. The final database representation is indeed built up iteratively throughout the entire design process receiving at each step details of different abstraction levels. Database design techniques generally use two models for capturing related but different important aspects of an application: The data model to represent the structural aspects of a system and the dynamic model to represent the temporal and behavioural aspects. In this paper, we only focus on the data and programming structure of the database application. Thereby, the models and the stages that we describe here only deal with the static aspect of databases.

Conceptual stage

At this stage, our aim is to build a high-level representation of the database. To do this, we start from the application analysis and requirements that ensue from it and we use concepts from the Information Analysis (IA) model [18], [19]. This model is a binary relationship model which is concerned with data structuring only and permits object type, fact type (association), sub-type and constraints to be formally graphically represented. To deal with the organizational structure for both data and code, our conceptual model also includes concepts of OOP such as binding operations to object type. The model used is called object model and is presented in Section 4.

The outcome of the conceptual stage is the conceptual schema, a graphical database representation that unites the two parts. The first part deals with the data structure of object types (this is the data part of the application). The second part shows a particular view of the inheritance operation hierarchies (this is the behavioural part) that match those defined in the data part of the conceptual schema. The model and the graphical notations that we use should help to build a conceptual schema understandable by everybody, open to criticism and easily adaptable.

Logical stage

At the logical level, we consider real-world object types rather as computer object types. Extra data structure may then be required to implement the real-world object types defined at the conceptual stage or to create computer object types. This new way of viewing an application domain permits strategies and extra code to be defined for optimization purposes. Moreover, the logical stage, which is supposed to be as independent as possible on features of a specific OODBMS, is divided into two sub-stages: Standard logical step and adapted standard logical step (this idea is also used by the REMORA design method [20]).

The goal of the standard logical step is to build a logical standard schema starting from the conceptual schema and progressively add details into it. The iteration process performed consists in enhancing and adapting the standard schema so as to finally obtain a canonical schema capturing the semantic and computer requirements of the application. The object model and the graphical notations used at this step are the same as those used at the conceptual stage.

Since there is no standard object-oriented data model, we have defined a model including concepts shared by most of the OODBMS data models. The concepts that we have chosen are object-oriented concepts like object, class, attribute (simple or complex), method and generalization. This new model is called the adapted object model and is introduced in Section 7. Our purpose at the adapted standard logical stage is to transform the standard logical schema into another one based on this model and a new graphical notation. This mapping involves decisions on how to implement the relationships of the standard schema. The result is an adapted schema composed of a data view showing classes, attributes (embedded in class definitions) and generalization relationships, and of a behavioural view showing in a classical manner the inheritance operation hierarchies. The adapted standard schema includes all the decisions that have been taken at each step of the design process. Our aim in using a new model and a new graphical notation is to get a database representation which is completely defined and suitable for a rapid mapping to any OODBMS data model.

Implementation

The purpose of this stage is to map the adapted logical schema into a new one in accordance with a specific OODBMS data model. The target OODBMS allows a new schema to be specified and the behaviour of the application to be implemented in an object-oriented programming language.

Before describing more precisely sensitive points of our design method, a short example is given in the next section in order to illustrate some aspects of the presented method.

3 Problem specification of the example

As mentioned in the previous section, we only deal in this paper with the static aspect of a database. So we will focus on the static aspect of the example, which is a short and simplified specification of our editorial database.

Our editorial application deals with large and structured documents that must conform to a particular grammar (AIS is working with the standard SGML [21]). The grammar formalism decomposes a given document into different components that we call units of document (ud). Particular document units (called udc) can be themselves composed of more primitive document units. Other kinds of document units are associated with information which is atomic (we call these atomic document units uda). Furthermore, document units may have attributes called sgml-attributes. We have also to manage document versions (more precisely versions of document units) after each session "edition of a document from the database - updating of the document - restore of the document into the database". We call uda-date the state of an atomic document unit, udc-date the state of a composed document unit at a given date.

4 Object model

When designing a database, decomposition of the problem into objects is a first and crucial phase which should promote understanding of the application domain. In this respect, we propose a model, called object model, suitable for describing the structural aspect of a database application and improving communication between programmers and non-programmers. Natural concepts that can be used in ordinary discourse and graphical notations have therefore been chosen to facilitate revisions of the application model.

Our object model combines concepts of the IA (Information Analysis) model and concepts of OOP. Some important concepts of this model and their graphical notations are described in the next subsections.

4.1 Important concepts

Object instances and object types

The concept of object type is borrowed from the IA model: It allows the entities in the universe of discourse to be classified. The IA model distinguishes between real-world concepts, called non-lexical object types (NOLOT) (like person or document types) and labels used to reference real-world concepts, called lexical object types (LOT) (like the type document-name).

An object type describes a set of potential object instances (objects). A NOLOT instance (a specific person or document) is an entity that is to say "a thing that can be distinctly identified [6]". A LOT instance is a pure data value that is generally called attribute. Since we look at things from an object-oriented approach, a NOLOT is specified by both relationships to other object types (LOT or NOLOT) and behaviour (operations). The set of all possible instances of a NOLOT shares relationships, behaviour and semantics of the NOLOT.

Fact type: Horizontal relationship

Fact types (also called idea types) are IA bidirectional associations between object types. They are only concerned with data structure and permit the overall structure of an application to be readily apparent.

A fact type describes a set of potential fact type instances (facts) with common structure and common semantics in the same way that an object type describes a set of possible object instances.

Fact types are associated with names and roles played by each involved object type. They may be one-to-one, many-to-one, many-to-many: Cardinality constraints specify how many instances of one object type may relate to a single instance of the associated object type.

Operations

Non-lexical object types define the values (LOT instances) carried by each object instance and the operations that each object instance performs or undergoes. When defining an operation, we are particularly interested in the following features:

- The name of the operation that must be carefully defined. This name should represent both the specific behaviour and the semantics of the operation.

- The category of operations to which the operation belongs. To facilitate an inventory of all the operations defined in an application, we have chosen to categorize the operations by grouping the operations that aim at achieving common goals.

- The signature of the operation.

- The visibility of the operation, which is progressively defined: The operation can be used by a restricted number of NOLOTs, in addition to the NOLOT that supports it.

- The status of the operation which permits us to know whether the operation is inherited (that is to say obtained by inheritance), overriden (the operation is obtained by redefining the behaviour and/or the signature of an inherited operation), or specific (neither inherited, nor overriden).

- The actions performed by the operation: These generally trigger network traversals (the network is the graphical representation of the application, see Section 4.2), creation, deletion or updating of object instances and fact instances.

Generalization: Hierarchical relationship

Generalization is widely used in semantic data models. This abstraction is particularly useful to make intellectually manageable large amount of relevant details. Indeed, it organizes them into hierarchies of abstractions [12]: The most general information is at the top of the hierarchy whereas the most specialized is at the leaves.

IA permits the sub-type/super-type definitions among NOLOTs. Generalization can then be used in the same way as it is in semantic data models. However, in our object model, a same hierarchy combines both data structure hierarchy and operation inheritance hierarchy. We therefore use the inheritance mechanism (simple and multiple), supported by the generalization relationship, for the sharing of data and operations. Overriding is also used to redefine data and operations that are inherited, along with strict type conformance rules.

However, these mechanisms often demand careful thought and in the short or long run, some restructuring of the inheritance hierarchies. While building them, it is important to consider "a sub-type as a special case of its super-type that should be compatible with it in every respect [5]" (one can talk about semantic, behaviour, signature compatibilities). These compatibility problems are crucial when using incremental specification, as is the case when building or maintaining inheritance hierarchies.

4.2 Graphical representation

A coherent, precise and simple formalism is needed to express the object model. A schema can be a graphical representation of the database. As said previously, the object model is used at the conceptual stage and at the standard logical stage. Our purposes in constructing a schema based on this model is to facilitate communication between programmers and non-programmers, schema revision during design (and also all through the maintenance phase) and to document the application structure. In these respects, we have divided the schema into two parts. One part describes the data structure of the application with the NIAM (Nijssen Information Analysis Method) graphical language. Since operations are not represented, this part of the schema, which is a network of object types and relationships, looks like any other schema drawn with the NIAM language (see Fig.1).

The other part describes the behaviour of the application and more particularly the operation inheritance hierarchies according to a specific formalism. This formalism aims at making easier restructuring of hierarchies during the conceptual and standard logical stages.

4.2.1 Data views

The NIAM graphical language permits the deep semantic structure of a problem to be precisely and unambiguously represented. We will present here only a restricted number of NIAM graphical facilities.

Graphical notations

In the NIAM graphical representation, NOLOT occurs as circle, LOT as dotted circle. The generalization relationship is represented by an arrow between two NOLOT circles, pointing to the super-type. Fact types are drawn as rectangles divided into two role boxes connected to the object types involved. Cardinality constraints are expressed by uniqueness and totality constraints. Uniqueness constraints are indicated by drawing a line over the box (each one-to-one fact type has two such lines) or over the fact type (an instance of an object type is related to at least one instance of the associated object type). If a fact type concerns all instances of an object type, the corresponding role is said to be total. This totality constraint is indicated with the universal quantifier on the line connecting the object type and the role.

Moreover, roles or fact types concerning one NOLOT may mutually exclude each other. This exclusion constraint is drawn as a line having a small circle with the character "+" and relating roles of fact types concerned to each other. This constraint can also be applied to sub-types.

When drawing the application schema on paper, the schema may not fit on a single sheet. This is especially the case when the application is large and the amount of relevant semantics important. It is then sometimes better to break the data part of the schema down into several complementary sub-schemas. We use sub-schemas for two purposes: Firstly, to provide global views of each aspect of the application model; secondly, to detail global views when necessary.

Global sub-schemas

One particular aspect of an application model can be associated with one or several global sub-schemas. When considering the set of global schemas modelling a given application, each fact type and generalization relationship appear on a single global schema (It is better, when possible, not to scatter generalization relationships belonging to a same hierarchy among several sub-schemas). Only NOLOTs are shared by several global sub-schemas making the sub-schemas interdependent.

For example, Fig.1 focuses on the representation of document unit states (In the figures of this paper, NOLOTs occur as ovals and LOTs as circles. Moreover not all role names have been given for space consideration). One hierarchy deals with states of document units, while another organizes the different types of document units. All associations that are concerned with the state hierarchy are represented. Two particular fact types named states and structure relate the state hierarchy to the document unit hierarchy. So as to keep a readable schema, we have chosen not to precise the way how fact types are inherited (for example, the constraints on the inherited fact types may be stronger). However, detailed sub-schemas are used to refine the existing semantics.

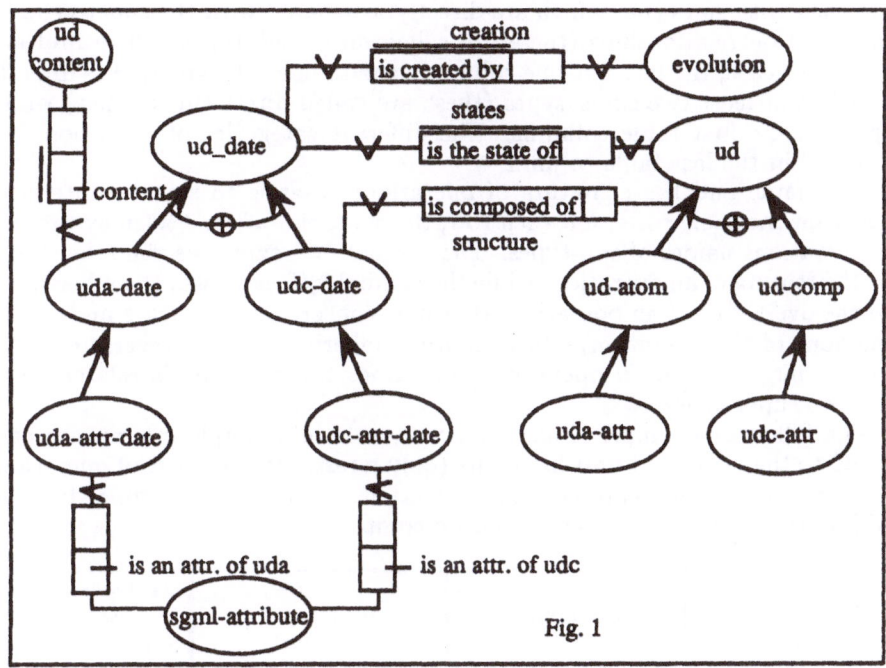

Fig. 1

Detailed sub-schemas

As mentioned previously, it happens that inherited fact types cannot be explicitly represented, although it would be necessary to do so. To avoid this semantic vagueness, we use detailed sub-schemas to zoom in on NOLOTs which semantics need precision. Fig.2 shows a sub-schema that gives semantic details of object type udc-date.

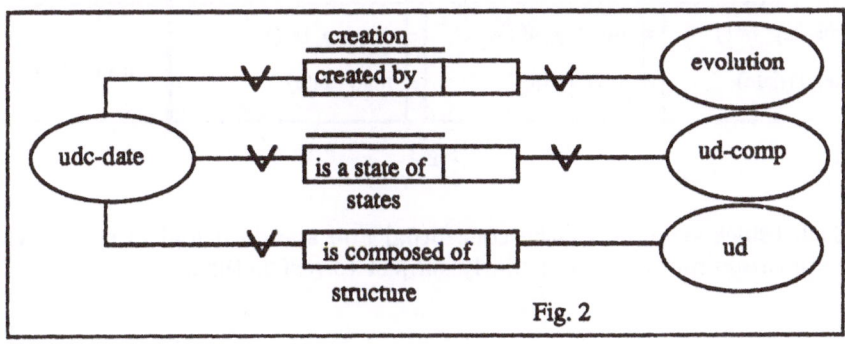

Fig. 2

4.2.2 Behavioural views

We have defined a formalism to express the operation inheritance hierarchies in a way that helps the designer to possibly restructure the hierarchies and that also serves as documentation. The formalism used is the table formalism. Each hierarchy defined in the application model is represented by one or several tables in which specific, inherited, overriden operations explicitly appear (see Subsection 4.1). In a simple inheritance case, the first table column refers to one super-type of a hierarchy. The other columns - except the last one - are concerned with sub-types which are directly associated with the super-type by generalization relationships (these are called direct sub-types). In a multiple inheritance case, the last-but-one column refers to one sub-type that is directly related to at least two super-types (these are called direct super-types) which appear in the first table columns. The different categories of operations are presented in the last table column.

The name and the signature of operations (that is to say the interface) appear on the table rows. On each row, the symbols "=" or "≠" may precede the operations names of sub-types. The symbol "=" expresses the inheritance and the reusing of an operation, while the symbol "≠" expresses the inheritance and the overriding of an operation (that may concern the signature and/or the behaviour of the operation). In a multiple inheritance case, several of these symbols may precede an operation name since the sub-type is related to at least two super-types.

The following example (Fig.3) shows a table in a simple inheritance case related to the document unit hierarchy (only a restricted number of operations is shown). This table represents the operations associated with super-type ud and its direct sub-types ud-atom and ud-comp.

ud	ud-atom	ud-comp	categories of operations
		create-ud (evolution)	ud creation
	new-state (evolution, content)	new_state (evolution) add_inStructure (ud)	ud storage
display_bf () read (date)	= display_bf () ≠ read (date)	= display_bf () ≠ read (date)	ud edition

Fig.3

Such tables are used at the conceptual and standard logical stages where the application model is particularly subject to restructuring.

5 Object modelling at the conceptual stage

Our aim at this stage is to build a conceptual schema that captures interesting semantics of the application domain without including computer details. It is thus important to have a good understanding of the real-world environment and requirements. In this respect, an analysis of the problem statement in natural language (as complete as possible) is helpful to identify the different aspects (static as well as dynamic) of the real-world. Analysis is a starting point for conceptual modelling which will remove redundant information and give a more precise, concise representation of the problem. However, as is the case for each stage of the design process, the conceptual stage is iterative. So the designer can at any moment examine again different results to complete or modify them.

5.1 Analysis

Analysis is a descriptive activity which is valuable to identify relevant objects, relations between objects (facts) and actions (that may be user-dependent or object-dependent). Furthermore, for reusability, it is worth distinguishing between objects needed for a specific application, objects needed for similar kinds of applications and objects needed for any kind of application. For example, while analysing our editorial application, we have distinguished between objects that can be reused by any editorial systems and those that are dependent on the document to be stored. This kind of analysis, which is particularly downplayed in [22], can lead to different libraries of object types.

5.2 Object modelling

To start the object modelling process, we propose to model firstly the data part of the application and then the behavioural part.

Data modelling

The activity that consists in abstracting from facts and objects to obtain fact types and object types may be a highly complex one, especially when certain aspects of the situation to be modeled remain ambiguous. In [18], a methodology based on the IA model is proposed to help the designer during this activity.

Once object types are described (through roles and fact types), generalization and specialization are used to capture similarities and differences among NOLOTs. Sets of NOLOTs are arranged into hierarchies of abstractions: Abstract object types can be defined to only provide inheritance for sub-types (Abstract object types do not generate any instances of an application and, in this respect, are opposed to concrete object types).

This description leads to a first graphical representation of the data part of the application. While building it, the behaviour of NOLOTs is not taken into account. In fact, the data structure hierarchies that are defined serve as skeletons of the inheritance hierarchies which will be constructed by progressively integrating the behaviour of each NOLOT. To better master the construction of such hierarchies, we use the table formalism described in Subsection 4.2.

Behavioural modelling

The data views of an application are suitable supports to define operations that can be associated to each NOLOT, to write a first algorithm of these operations (where only main actions are described) by realizing network traversals and to construct behavioural views (tables) of the conceptual model.

Behavioural views permit the designer to evaluate and to restructure when necessary each inheritance hierarchy. In fact, behavioural similarities and differences among NOLOTs can be easily detected through the formalism that we propose. For example, in a simple inheritance case, operations that appear in the same row in the columns associated with sub-types may be factorized to increase the amount of inheritance. If the factorization is possible, the resulting operation is represented in the column of the direct super-type. The factorization of operations can also lead to the creation of a new super-type (for example, if the sub-types have nothing but the interfaces of the operations in common). Abstract object types may be created in this way.

6 Object modelling at the standard logical stage

At this stage, the conceptual schema is refined and extended with implementation details as well as restructured for optimization purposes (they concern both implementation issues and benefits related to an object-oriented design). The outcome of this stage is a standard logical schema also composed of a data part and a behavioural part (as defined in the previous stage). Before modelling, we worry about how to implement object types defined at the conceptual stage.

6.1 Definition of a computer solution

Choices must be made to adapt the structure for satisfying information needs and for computational efficiency. Strategies are generally defined to control crucial aspects of the database application such as concurrent accesses, version management and interactive interfaces. These strategies are later carried out in the standard logical schema.

So as to let the database act as expected, the operations of the conceptual stage have to be precisely described. The signature and algorithm of complex operations are progressively defined by incorporating strategic details. Complex algorithms generate new simpler operations that have also to be carried out in the application schema.

6.1.1 Object modelling

Adaptations of the conceptual schema may be necessary to integrate strategies and new computer object types. For example, to handle performance issues related to document editing or restore, we have considered how document versions have to be stored. This has led to some adaptations and extensions of the conceptual schema where *sgml* attributes become specialized document units.

Generally, the amount of operations to carry out in the schema is important and the new operations defined in inheritance hierarchies may involve some revisions of the hierarchy structure. To do this, the tables representing operation inheritance hierarchies are helpful for controlling the integration of new operations and rearranging when necessary the inheritance structure.

7 Adapted object model

The adapted object model describes the structural aspect of an application but, by contrast with the object model, it uses purely object-oriented concepts. Indeed, we have chosen concepts that are generally used by most of object-oriented data models. Concepts of the object model can be associated with new equivalent ones defined in the adapted object model, except fact types that can only be simulated by concepts defined in the new model.

The adapted object model gives a final and complete representation of an application suitable for implementation. This representation is semantically less rich and may be more difficult to restructure than the representations based on the object model. However, revisions of the schema should be limited since most of the decisions about a database representation (independent on a specific OODBMS) have been taken at the conceptual and standard logical stages. Some important concepts are described afterwards with their graphical notations.

7.1 Important concepts

Object instances and object classes

We use concepts that are generally supported by computer environments. A NOLOT is associated with the concept of object class which is specified by a set of attributes and a set of methods. An object class can be considered as a template for generations of objects called object instances.

Attributes

Attributes are named fields which form the static part of classes. The value of each attribute characterizes the state of the object instances. An attribute can refer to a single value (for example, an one-to-one LOT reference) or a complex value (for example, a NOLOT reference). An attribute is also defined by its visibility (the designer must decide what attributes should be accessible from outside the class).

Methods

Methods are procedures or functions which form the dynamic part of classes. Methods manipulate the attributes of object instances. A method is defined by its name, signature, visibility and algorithm.

7.2 Graphical representation

Our purpose in constructing a schema based on the adapted object model is to express all the decisions that have been taken from the analysis phase up to the final logical step, independently on a specific OODBMS data model. Like the previous schemas, the adapted logical schema is composed of two parts. The first one describes the data structure of the application with graphical notations associated with the concepts of class, attribute (related to a class by a line) and generalization. The second represents the method inheritance hierarchies in the same way that they are generally specified in OODBMS schemas (this is the reason why we say that this representation is classical).

7.2.1 Data views

As is the case at the conceptual and standard logical stages, global sub-schemas may be required to give global views on different parts of an application. However, detailed sub-schemas are no more useful. As a matter of fact, either extra information is buried in the code or it appears explicitly on the global sub-schemas (as attributes, see Section 8). Fig.4 shows how the global sub-schema of Fig.1, based on the object model and defined at the conceptual stage, has been extended at the standard logical stage (where *sgml* attributes are defined as particular document units) and mapped at the adapted standard logical stage into a new sub-schema. Class udac-date represents the state of an atomic document unit that has *sgml* attributes.

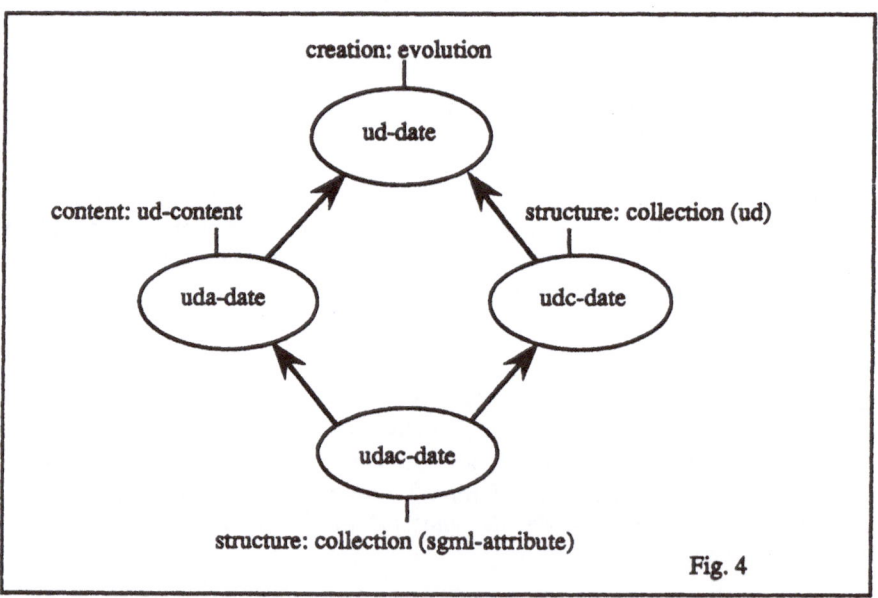

Fig. 4

7.2.2 Behavioural views

To represent graphically method inheritance hierarchies at the adapted standard logical stage, we use the table formalism: New tables are constructed after examining all the tables of the standard logical stage (those showing the most specialized classes are examined first). In simple inheritance cases, only specific and overriden methods are represented (see Subsection 8.2).

8 Object modelling at the adapted standard logical stage

As stressed in Section 7, the main purposes of this stage consist in implementing fact types and mapping the operation hierarchy tables of the previous stage to new tables giving a classical view of these hierarchies. The first activity is concerned with the data part of the standard logical schema whereas the second activity is concerned with the behavioural part of this schema. The outcome of this stage is a new schema suitable for an easy mapping into any OODBMS data model.

8.1 Implementation of fact types

As it is outlined in [5] and [23], relations between object instances are not well supported by OOPL (and OODBMS) although some applications would greatly benefit of such a facility. In fact, these relations can be simulated by creating attributes or relation classes.

For example, constructors can be used to create complex attributes from fact types whose roles are associated with a "many" value. As shown in Fig.5, a collection of objects, instances of class ud, can be related to an object, instance of class udc-date. This collection of objects can be modeled like a complex attribute that is then embedded in the definition of class udc-date. This grouping is realized by means of constructors that will be precisely defined only when a specific OODBMS data model is taken into account. Since two attributes can be created and associated with the corresponding class, the designer is responsible for deciding which attribute to create.

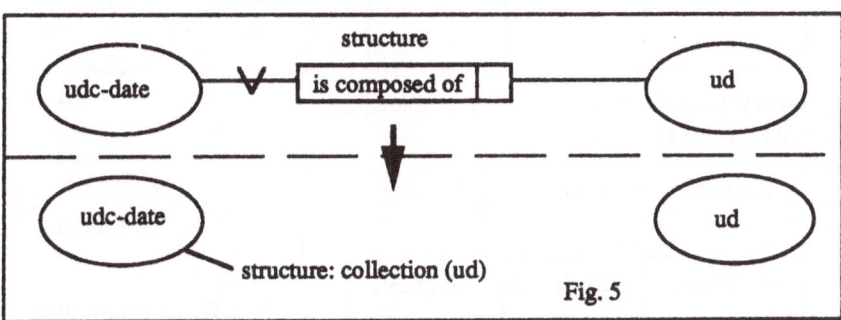

Fig. 5

8.2 Method hierarchy tables

Simple rules can be used to transform a method inheritance hierarchy from a view where all the methods associated with a class explicitly appear by a view where only specific or overriden methods are represented (except in multiple inheritance cases when it is necessary to cope with ambiguities). Moreover, the symbols "=" and "≠" that guide the transformation are removed and can be replaced by explicit information about methods status.

Mapping in a simple inheritance case: "Super-class - sub-classes" scheme

Each row of the tables is transformed into a new row that contains:

- The interface of specific or overriden methods supported by the sub-classes.

- The interface of methods supported by the super-class. More precisely, if the super-class does not own itself super-classes, then the methods that appear are specific to this super-class. Else, methods are considered as being inherited until the table where the super-class is viewed as a sub-class has been examined. When all the tables have been transformed, only specific or overriden methods are represented.

The example given next (Fig. 6) deals with a simple inheritance case. It shows how tables (table (1)) constructed during the conceptual and standard logical stages can be transformed into new tables (table (2)) giving a classical view of method inheritance hierarchies. In this simple example, only the names of methods (m1, m2, m3) are given. Also, the last table column associated with the different categories of methods is not represented.

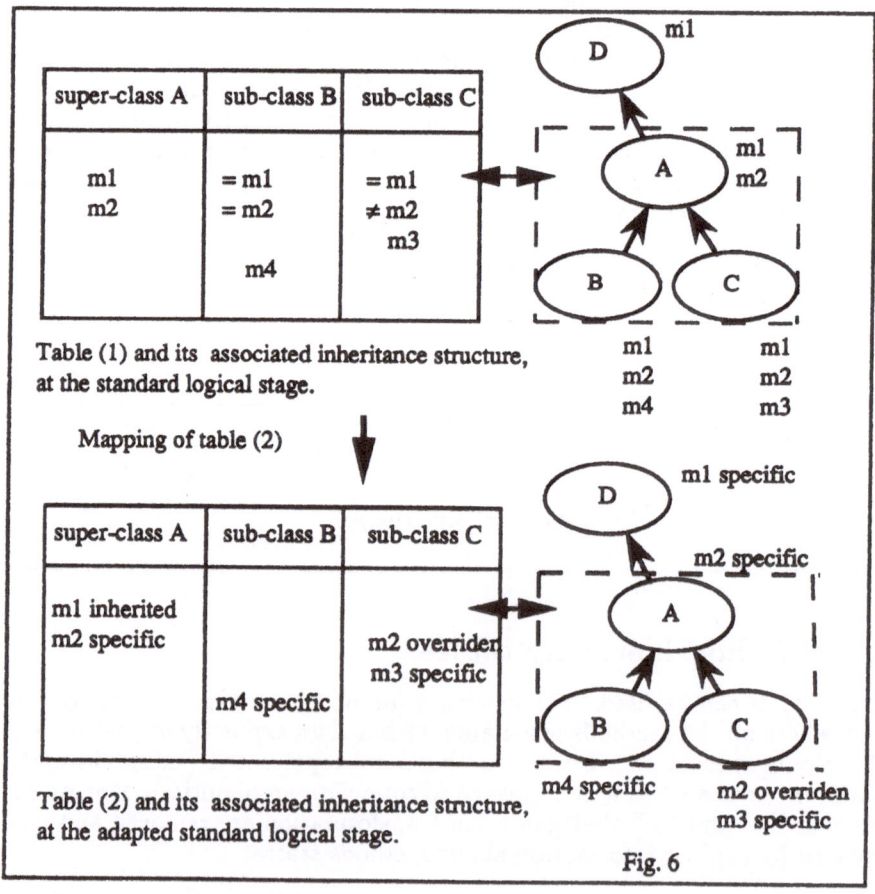

Fig. 6

Mapping in a multiple inheritance case : "Super-classes - sub-class" scheme

The aim is to fully specify the methods of the sub-class. As opposed to simple inheritance, possible ambiguities may arise when a method name is defined in two or more super-classes. In such cases, if a method is obtained by inheritance without being overriden, the designer should precise the inheritance path with the aid of the symbols "=" and "≠".

9   Implementation stage

The data model concepts of a target OODBMS are compared with those defined in the adapted object model. This may lead to some adaptations and refinements. In fact, each OODBMS supplies various predefined types, constructors, classes that can be used as intelligently as possible when mapping the adapted standard logical schema into a new one in accordance with the OODBMS data model.

10   Conclusion and perspectives

Advantages related to object-oriented technology are currently well known. However, in design they must be considered as key objectives on an equal footing with the description of the semantic and computer requirements of a problem. We aim at reaching these objectives through the presented method by focusing on the following points:

- First express in a schema all the semantic information and requirements of the database application (at the conceptual stage). Then (at the logical stage), to adress the implementation of objects described in the conceptual stage without considering features of a specific OODBMS.

- Give equal importance to the graphical representations of the data structure and the programming structure. We propose therefore two complementary views of a same application: a view which is only concerned with the data structure and another one which describes the programming structure.

- Start the conceptual modelling by representing first the data structure of an application as is the case when modelling databases with standard semantic data models.

- Allow schema revisions during the design process. In this respect, we use an object model containing high-level concepts borrowed from semantic data models. Furthermore, we represent discriminating and shared behaviour of each object in behavioural views of the application so as to better handle inheritance hierarchy restructuring.

We are currently studying the way of integrating document browsing techniques with graphical interfaces, allowing different kinds of users to consulte the database or to update stored parts of document according to their own way of thinking. Such realizations require all the capacities of the object approach in which objects will play the role of active objects. These topics will enable us to enrich the models and the associated methodology .

References

[1] F. Bancilhon, Object-oriented database systems, Proceedings 7th ACM SIGART/SIGMOD/SIGACT Symposium on Principles of Database Systems, Austin, Texas, March 1988

[2] W. Kim, Architectural issues in object-oriented databases, Journal of Object-Oriented Programming, March/Avril 1990, pp 29-38

[3] F. Velez, G. Bernard, V. Darnis, The O2 object manager: an overview, Proceedings of the fifteenth International Conference on Very Large Data Bases, Amsterdam, 1989

[4] C. Lécluse, P. Richard, The O2 Database Programming Language, Proceedings of the fifteenth International Conference on Very Large Data Bases, Amsterdam, 1989

[5] J. Rumbaugh, M. Blaha, W. Premerlany et al, Object-oriented modeling and design, Prentice Hall, 1991

[6] P.P. Chen, The Entity-Relationship model - Toward a unified view of data, ACM Transactions on Database Systems, vol 1, $n^{o}1$, March 1976, pp 9-36

[7] H. Nguyen, J. Thrasher, OODDM: an object-oriented database design model, Proceedings of Technology of Object-Oriented Languages and Systems, Paris 1990, pp 335-345

[8] P. Desfray, A method for object oriented programming: the Class-Relationship method, Proceedings of Technology of Object-Oriented Languages and Systems, Paris 1990, pp 121-131

[9] M. Lai, HyperHood ++: an object oriented design tool for developments in object oriented programming languages, Proceedings of Technology of Object-Oriented Languages and Systems, Paris 1989, pp 295-308

[10] G. Booch, Object-oriented design with application, The Benjamin Cummings Publishing Company, Inc., 1991

[11] R. Wirfs-Brock, B. Wilkerson, Object-oriented design: a responsibility-driven approach, Proceedings of Object-Oriented Programming: Systems, Languages and Applications, 1989, pp 71-75

[12] J.M. Smith, CP. Smith, Database abstractions: aggregation and generalization, ACM Transactions on Database Systems, vol 2, n° 2, June 1977, pp 105-133

[13] R.Hull, R. King, Semantic Database Modeling: Survey, Applications, and Research Issues, ACM Computing Surveys, vol 19, $n^{o}3$, Sept. 1987, pp 201-260

[14] M.L. Brodie, J. Mylopoulos, JW. Schmidt, On conceptual modeling, Springer-Verlag, New-York, 1984

[15] B. Meyer, Object Oriented Software Construction, Prentice Hall International series in Computer Science, 1988

[16] K.R. Dittrich, Object-oriented Database Systems: the notion and the issues, ACM/IEEE, International Workshop on Object-Oriented Database Systems, 1986, pp 2-4

[17] A. Goldberg, Robson, Smalltalk-80: the language and its implementation, Adison Wesley, 1983

[18] D. Vermeir, GM. Nijssen, A procedure to define the object type structure of a conceptual schema, Information Systems, vol 7, $n^{\underline{o}}4$, 1982, pp 329-336

[19] H. Habrias, Le modèle relationnel binaire, la méthode NIAM, Eyrolles, 1988

[20] C. Rolland, O. Foucaut, G. Benci, Conception des systèmes d'information: la méthode REMORA, Eyrolles, 1988

[21] ISO 8879 Information processing; text and office systems; Standard Generalized Markup Language (SGML)

[22] J.G.M. van den Goor, A practical approach to object-oriented software engineering, Proceedings of Technology of Object-Oriented Languages and Systems, Paris 1990, pp 285-298

[23] G.C. Murphy, Genericity, inheritance and relations: a practical perspective, Proceedings of Technology of Object-Oriented Languages and Systems, Paris 1990, pp 381-392

A Formal Model for Databases with Applications to Schema Merging *

Anthony S. Kosky

Department of Computer and Information Sciences

University of Pennsylvania

Philadelphia, PA 19104-6389

kosky@saul.cis.upenn.edu

August 2, 1991

Abstract

In this paper we present a simple and general model for database schemas
and their instances. The model is sufficiently expressive to represent complex,
higher order data structures and incorporates representations for specialisation relations and object identity. It is general enough to encode data structures arising from many other semantic data models in a natural way, though
we do not attempt to model some of the more sophisticated constraints that
occur in other models.

We claim that using a formal mathematical model can help us to understand and deal with various problems arising from database systems, and, to
demonstrate this, we present some work on the problem of schema merging
that has been carried out using our model.

1   Introduction

In this paper we will develop a new, formal model for database structures and use
it to investigate the problem of schema merging. In particular we will concentrate
on providing a general model for database schemas which will be similar to the
functional data model ([1]), and will support specialisation relationships. Wherever
possible we try to minimise the number of different concepts involved in modelling
both schemas and database instances, in order to get as simple and uniform a model

---

*This research was supported in part by ARO DAAL03-89-C-0031PRIME, ARO DAAL03-89-
C-0031SUB5 and NSF IRI 8610617

as possible. We construct a representation of *database instances* which supports object identity, and define what it means for an instance to *satisfy* a database schema. Despite its simplicity, our model is very general and expressive so that database schemas and instances arising from a number of other data models can be translated into it.

We will go on to look at *schema merging*: a problem about which much has been written (see [2]) though the author believes that the formal semantics of such merging processes has not been properly explored or understood. The problem of merging database schemas arises when two or more databases, originating from different sources and possibly containing overlapping information, are combined to form a federated database system (see, for example, [3], [4]), and also in the initial design of a database system, when forming a global database schema from a number of user views of the database. The problem is to find a common view of a number of distinct databases, that is a database schema that, in some sense, *supersedes* the schemas of the databases being merged.

The use of a simple and flexible formal model, such as the one established here, gives us a new insight into the problems of schema merging: we attempt to define an ordering on schemas representing their informational content and define the merge of a collection of schemas to be the least schema which contains all the information of the schemas being merged. However we establish that one cannot, in general, find a meaningful binary merging operator which is associative, though we would clearly require this of any such operator. We rectify this situation by relaxing our definition of schemas, defining a class of *weak schemas* over which we can construct a satisfactory concept of merges. Further we define a method of constructing a *canonical* proper schema with the same informational content as a weak schema whenever possible, thus giving us an adequate definition of the merge of a collection of proper schemas whenever such a merge exists. In addition we show that, if the schemas we are merging are translations from some other data model, our merging process "respects" the original data model. Due to limited space we will only summarise these results here: a more detailed coverage is given in [5].

2   A Model for Database Structures

In this section we will describe a model for databases with complex data structures and object identity. The model will provide a means for representing specialisation, or "is-a" relationships between data structures. It will not attempt to take account of such things as generalisation relationships (see [6]) or various kinds of dependencies, partly due to lack of space and partly because we wish to keep our model sufficiently simple in order for the following sections to be as comprehensible as possible. However the author does not believe that adding such extensions to the model or extending the following theory to take account of them should be overly difficult.

We will describe the model's features in terms of ER-structures ([7]) since they provide a well known basis for explanations and examples, though the model can be used equally well to represent other semantic models for databases (for a survey of such models see [1]). In addition to allowing higher order relations (that is relations amongst relations) the model can represent circular definitions of entities and relations, a phenomenon that occurs in some object oriented database systems. Consequently, despite its apparent simplicity, the model is, in some sense, more general and expressive than most semantic models for databases.

2.1   Database Schemas

Digraphs

We will make use of *directed graphs* (*digraphs*) in our representations of both database schemas and instances. We must first give a definition of digraphs which is tailored to the needs of this paper, and consequently may differ a little from definitions that the reader has come across elsewhere. In particular our digraphs will have both their edges and their vertices labelled with labels from two disjoint, countable sets.

Suppose $\mathcal{V}$ and $\mathcal{L}$ are disjoint, countable sets, which we will call the set of *vertex labels* and the set of *arrow labels* respectively. A **digraph** over $\mathcal{V}$ and $\mathcal{L}$ is a pair of sets, $G = (V, E)$, such that

$$V \subseteq \mathcal{V}$$
$$E \subseteq V \times \mathcal{L} \times V$$

If $G = (V, E)$ is a digraph and $p, q \in V$, $a \in \mathcal{L}$ are such that $(p, a, q) \in E$ then we write $p \xrightarrow{a}_G q$, and we may omit the subscript G where the relevant digraph is clear from context.

We will represent database schemas by triples of sets, the first two sets forming a digraph, and the third set representing specialisation relationships between data structures. Before giving a formal definition of database schemas we will explain how we represent a system of data structures (ignoring specialisations) by a digraph.

Representing data structures

Suppose we have a finite set, $\mathcal{N}$, of **class names** and a finite set, $\mathcal{L}$, of **attributes** or **arrow labels**. Then we can represent a system of data structures by a digraph $(\mathcal{C}, \mathcal{E})$ over $\mathcal{N}$ and $\mathcal{L}$ satisfying the following condition:

$$\textbf{A1}\ \ p \xrightarrow{a} q \wedge p \xrightarrow{a} r \text{ implies } r \equiv q$$

That is, for any class name $p \in C$ and any arrow label $a \in \mathcal{L}$, there is at most one class $q \in C$ such that $p \xrightarrow{a} q$.

If $p, q \in C$ and $a \in \mathcal{L}$ are such that $p \xrightarrow{a} q$ (that is, $(p, a, q) \in \mathcal{E}$) then we say that p *has an a-arrow of class q*.

The intuition here, in terms of ER-structures, is that classes, which are the vertices of the digraph, correspond to entity sets, relations and base types, and arrows correspond to the attributes of entities and the *roles* of entities in relations. The concepts of relations/entities/base types and of attributes/roles are therefore unified into two concepts: classes and arrow labels. For example the ER-diagram shown in Figure 1 would be represented by the digraph in Figure 2.

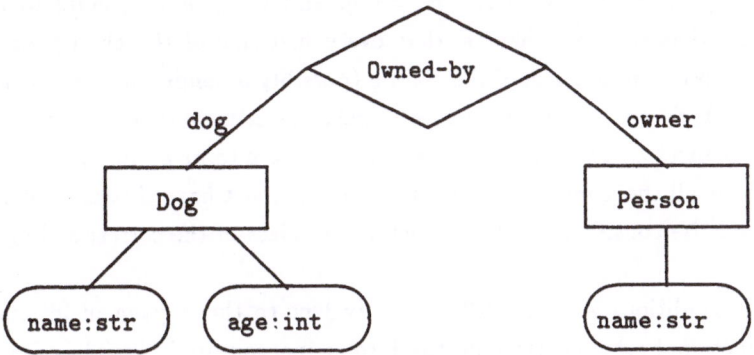

Figure 1: An ER-Diagram

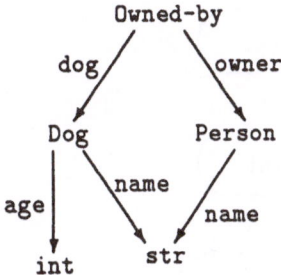

Figure 2: A database schema

Database schemas with specialisation

With the explanation of the use of digraphs given above in mind, we should now be in a position to make sense of our formal definition of database schemas.

Suppose we have a finite set of class names, $\mathcal{N}$, and a finite set of arrow labels, $\mathcal{L}$. Then a **database schema** over $\mathcal{N}$ and $\mathcal{L}$ is a triple of sets, $\mathcal{G} = (\mathcal{C}, \mathcal{E}, \mathcal{S})$, where $(\mathcal{C}, \mathcal{E})$ forms a digraph over $\mathcal{N}$ and $\mathcal{L}$ satisfying the axiom **A1** above, and $\mathcal{S}$ is a partial ordering on $\mathcal{C}$ (that is, it is transitive, reflexive and antisymmetric), such that $\mathcal{S}$ satisfies:

A2 $\forall p, q, r \in \mathcal{C} \cdot \forall a \in \mathcal{A} \cdot (p, q) \in \mathcal{S} \land q \xrightarrow{a} r$ implies
$$(\exists s \in \mathcal{C} \cdot p \xrightarrow{a} s \land (s, r) \in \mathcal{S})$$

That is, for every pair $(p, q) \in \mathcal{S}$, if q has an a-arrow of class r, then p also has an a-arrow with some class s where $(s, r) \in \mathcal{S}$. (Note that we write $p \xrightarrow{a}_{\mathcal{G}} q$ to mean $(p, a, q) \in \mathcal{E}$ and we omit the subscript $\mathcal{G}$ when it is obvious from the context).

If $(p, q) \in \mathcal{S}$ then we write $p \Longrightarrow q$, and say p is a **specialisation** of q. Intuitively what we mean here is that every instance of the class p can also be considered to be an instance of the class q (possibly extended with some additional information). So our axiom, given above, makes sense if we consider it to mean that, in order for us to be able to consider an instance of p to be an instance of q, p must at least have all the arrows of q, and these arrows must have classes for which every instance can be considered to be an instance of class of the corresponding arrow of q.

The conditions **A1** and **A2** are equivalent to those given in [8] and also in [9] for functional schemas (though the former incorporated specialisation relations between arrows, while the later used unlabelled arrows).

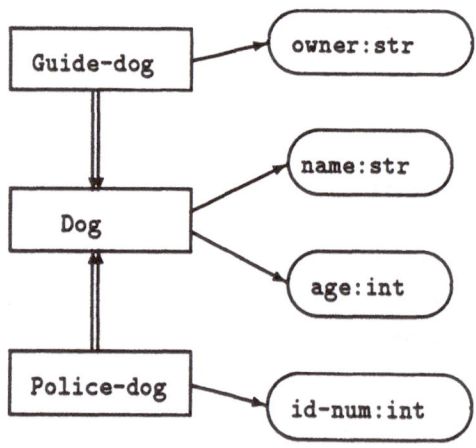

Figure 3: An ER-diagram with "isa" relations

For example the ER-diagram shown in figure 3, where specialisation relationships are marked by double arrows, corresponds to the database schema shown in figure 4, where single arrows are used to indicate edges in $\mathcal{E}$ and double arrows are used to represent pairs in $\mathcal{S}$.

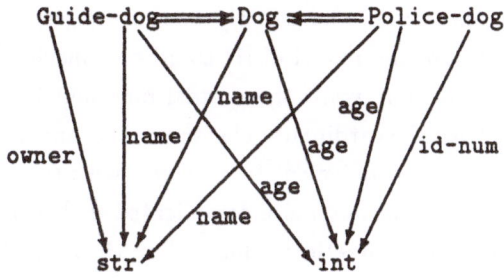

Figure 4: A database schema with "isa" relations

By putting suitable restrictions on the schemas of our model, we can use them to interpret the schemas of a variety of other data models: relational, entity-relationship, functional, object-oriented, and so on. For example, in order to interpret a relational database schema, we can stratify C into two sets of classes, C_R and C_A, corresponding to relations and attribute domains respectively, dissallow specialization edges, and restrict arrows so that they may only go from classes in C_R to classes in C_A. Similarly, in order to interpret ER-schemas, we stratify C into three sets (attribute domains, entity sets and relationships), and again place certain restrictions on arrows and specialization relations. Such restrictions on schemas can be though of as *meta-schemas* which the schemas must satisfy. In [5] we define a representation for such meta-schemas and use them to show that the merging process described in Section 3 respects such restrictions.

In an unconstrained form, our schemas are similar to those of the *functional data model* ([8, 10]), though they are not sophisticated enough to interpret data models such as those proposed in [1] or [11], which incorporate constructors for variants. As we develop our data model, we will incorporate the idea of *object identity*, thus making it suitable for modeling the *object oriented databases* described in [12].

Extending schemas with cardinality constraints

If one of our schemas asserts that a class p has an a-arrow of class q, we interpret this as meaning that, for any instance of the schema, if an object of class p has an a-arrow going to some other object, then that object will have class q. However the schema does not tell us whether all objects of class p have a-arrows, or *how many* a-arrows they may have. To include this kind of information, which is common in many database models, we need to assign *cardinality constraints* to arrows.

We will limit ourselves to considering only four different possible **cardinality constraints**, 0-m, 1-m, 0-1 and 1-1, meaning any number of arrows, at least one arrow, at most one arrow, and exactly one arrow respectively. For example the set-valued functions of the model of [1] could be considered to be arrows with the cardinality constraint 0-m, while the normal functions in that model would be equivalent to arrows with the cardinality constraint 1-1, and a function which could take on null values would be equivalent to an arrow with the cardinality constraint 0-1. It would be possible to have a more complicated and specific set of cardinality constraints, but there is little practical value and no theoretical interest in doing so.

We assume an ordering, $\leq$, on cardinality constraints, forming the lattice shown in figure 5. So $\leq$ represents the idea of one cardinality constraint being more specific than or implying another.

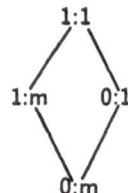

Figure 5: The lattice of cardinality constraints

We extend our schemas with a mapping $\mathcal{K}$ assigning cardinality constraints to arrows. That is

$$\mathcal{K} : \mathcal{E} \rightarrow \{0\text{-m},\ 1\text{-m},\ 0\text{-1},\ 1\text{-1}\}$$

and add the additional axiom

> **A3** $\forall p, q, r, s \in \mathcal{C} \cdot \forall a \in \mathcal{L} \cdot p \xrightarrow{a} q \wedge r \xrightarrow{a} s \wedge r \Longrightarrow p \wedge s \Longrightarrow q$
> implies $\mathcal{K}(p \xrightarrow{a} q) \leq \mathcal{K}(r \xrightarrow{a} s)$

This means that, if r is a specialisation of p and p has an a-arrow of class q, then the corresponding a-arrow of r has a cardinality constraint at least as specific as the one from p to q.

2.2 A Model for Database Instances

In this section we will describe a representation for *instances* of databases, and define what it means for an instance to *satisfy* a database schema.

An **instance**, $\mathcal{M}$, over class names $\mathcal{N}$ and arrow labels $\mathcal{L}$, is a triple, $(\mathcal{O}, \mathcal{R}, \mathcal{I})$, where $\mathcal{O}$ is a countable set of **object identities**, $\mathcal{R} \subseteq \mathcal{O} \times \mathcal{L} \times \mathcal{O}$ is such that $(\mathcal{O}, \mathcal{R})$ forms a digraph over $\mathcal{O}$ and $\mathcal{L}$, and $\mathcal{I} : \mathcal{O} \rightarrow \mathcal{N}$ (that is $\mathcal{I}$ maps object identities to class names) is said to be the **interpretation** of the object identifiers. (Once again we will use notation $o \xrightarrow{a}_{\mathcal{M}} o'$ to mean $(o, a, o') \in \mathcal{R}$, where $\mathcal{M} = (\mathcal{O}, \mathcal{R}, \mathcal{I})$.)

The idea here is that object identifiers correspond to the real world objects represented in the database, and the relation $\mathcal{R}$ represents how these objects are related by the attributes in $\mathcal{L}$. The interpretation, $\mathcal{I}$, shows the least class (under the ordering $\mathcal{S}$) to which a particular object belongs. An object can also be considered as belonging to any superclasses of this class, so that, for the schema shown in Figure 4, every object belonging to the class police_dog also belongs to the class dog.

A database model, $\mathcal{M} = (\mathcal{O}, \mathcal{R}, \mathcal{I})$, is said to **satisfy** a database schema $\mathcal{G} = (\mathcal{C}, \mathcal{E}, \mathcal{S}, \mathcal{K})$ iff

S1 $\forall o, o' \in \mathcal{O} \cdot \forall p, q \in \mathcal{C} \cdot \forall a \in \mathcal{L} \cdot$
$$p = \mathcal{I}(o) \wedge p \xrightarrow{a}_{\mathcal{G}} q \wedge o \xrightarrow{a}_{\mathcal{M}} o' \text{ implies } \mathcal{I}(o') \Longrightarrow q$$

S2 $\forall o \in \mathcal{O} \cdot \forall p, q \in \mathcal{C} \cdot \forall a \in \mathcal{L} \cdot \quad p = \mathcal{I}(o) \wedge p \xrightarrow{a}_{\mathcal{G}} q \wedge 1\text{-m} \leq \mathcal{K}(p \xrightarrow{a} q)$
$$\text{implies } (\exists o' \in \mathcal{O} \cdot o \xrightarrow{a}_{\mathcal{M}} o')$$

S3 $\forall o, o', o'' \in \mathcal{O} \cdot \forall p, q \in \mathcal{C} \cdot \forall a \in \mathcal{L} \cdot$
$$p = \mathcal{I}(o) \wedge p \xrightarrow{a}_{\mathcal{G}} q \wedge o \xrightarrow{a}_{\mathcal{M}} o' \wedge o \xrightarrow{a}_{\mathcal{M}} o'' \wedge 0\text{-1} \leq \mathcal{K}(p \xrightarrow{a} q)$$
$$\text{implies } o' = o''$$

The first condition says that, if a schema specifies an a-arrow of some class p, and an object of class p has an a-arrow then the object connected to it by the a-arrow must belong to the class specified by the schema. For example, again for the schema in Figure 4, if a dog has a name and an age recorded in the database, then these must belong to the classes str and int respectively.

The second and third conditions mean that, if class p has an a-arrow of class q, then if the arrow has associated cardinality constraint 1-m or 1-1, then for every object of class p must have an a-arrow going to an object of class q, while, if the arrow has a cardinality constraint of 0-1 or 1-1, then any object of class p can have at most one a-arrow.

A simple example

In order to clarify our idea of models we will give a brief example. We will start with the schema shown in figure 6 (certain implicit edges, namely those induced on the class Police_dog by its specialisation relationship to the class Dog have been omitted). In this diagram cardinality constraints have been marked in small type at the ends of the arrows.

We consider the following set of object identities:

$$\mathcal{O} = \{\text{Fido, Bonzo, Rover, Humphrey, George,}$$
$$\text{Poodle, German-Shepherd, Old-English-Sheepdog,}$$
$$\text{Rover-id}\}$$

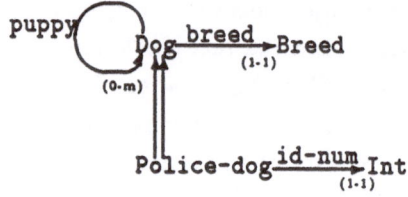

Figure 6: A simple example

The classes of these object identities are given by:

$\mathcal{I}(\text{Fido}) = \mathcal{I}(\text{Bonzo}) = \mathcal{I}(\text{Humphrey}) = \mathcal{I}(\text{George}) = \text{Dog}$
$\mathcal{I}(\text{Rover}) = \text{Police-dog}$
$\mathcal{I}(\text{Poodle}) = \mathcal{I}(\text{German-Shepherd}) = \mathcal{I}(\text{Old-English-Sheepdog}) = \text{Breed}$
$\mathcal{I}(\text{Rover-id}) = \text{Int}$

and our attribute relations are

$\mathcal{R} = \{$ Fido $\xrightarrow{\text{breed}}$ Poodle, Bonzo $\xrightarrow{\text{breed}}$ Poodle, Rover $\xrightarrow{\text{breed}}$ German-Shepherd,
Humphrey $\xrightarrow{\text{breed}}$ Old-English-Sheepdog, George $\xrightarrow{\text{breed}}$ Poodle,
Fido $\xrightarrow{\text{puppy}}$ Bonzo, Fido $\xrightarrow{\text{puppy}}$ George, Rover $\xrightarrow{\text{id-num}}$ Rover-id, $\}$

Note that the cardinality constraints are satisfied: each dog has exactly one breed, and each police dog has exactly one id number.

3 An Application to Schema Merging

Having developed a flexible, formal model for database systems, we can now go on to use it to interpret and express various phenomenon which occur when studying or working with databases. Giving a mathematical formulation of such phenomenon helps us to clarify the problem and, in addition, can help bring to light various complexities and problems which might remain unnoticed if we studied the phenomenon in an informal way. Two such applications of the model were studied in detail in [5], and considerable insights into the problems were gained. First the model was extended by associating *printable values* to objects, and a theory of the *observable behaviour* of databases was developed and discussed. Also the problem of merging database schemas was investigated and a mathematically precise definition of the merge of a set of database schemas was constructed. In this section we will summarise the results on schema merging given in that paper.

3.1 Merging Database Schemas

Much has been written on the subject of merging database schemas (see [2] for a survey) and a number of tools and methodologies have been developed. These range from sets of tools for manipulating schemas into some form of consistency, [9, 3], to algorithms which take two schemas, together with some constraints, and produce a merged schema [13]. However, to the best of our knowledge, the question of what meaning or semantics this merging process should have has not been adequately explored. Indeed, several of the techniques that have been developed are *heuristics*: there is no independent characterisation of what the merge should be.

The first problem to be resolved in forming such a common schema is deciding on the correspondences between the classes of the various databases. This problem is inherently *ad hoc* in nature, and is dependent on the real-world interpretations of the databases, so that such information must be provided by the designer of the system.

In the study of merging in [5], the only correspondences between classes considered are equivalence, where classes from two separate database schemas represent the same class of real world objects, and subclass correspondences, where a class from one schema is included in a class from another. The interpretation that the merging process places on names is that if two classes in different schemas have the same name, then they are the same class, regardless of the fact that they may have different arrow edges. Subclass correspondences are represented by adding an extra *correspondence* schema to the set of schemas being merged which encodes such correspondences as specialisations between the classes. The designer of the system is, therefore, called upon to resolve naming conflicts, whether homonyms or synonyms, by renaming classes and arrows where appropriate. For example, if one schema has a class *Dog* with arrow edges *License#*, *Owner* and *Breed*, and another schema has a class *Dog* with arrow edges *Name*, *Age* and *Breed*, then the merging process will collapse them into one class with name *Dog* and arrow edges *License#*, *Owner*, *Name*, *Age*, and *Breed*, with the potential result that null values are introduced[1]. However, if the user intends them to be separate classes, the classes must be renamed (for example, *Dog1* and *Dog2*), and, if the user intends *Dog1* to be a subclass of *Dog2* then he/she should include the classes *Dog1* and *Dog2* and a specialisation relation between *Dog1* and *Dog2* in the correspondence schema.

What we want to find is a schema that presents all the information of the schemas being merged, but no additional information. Hence we want the *"least upper bound"* of the database schemas under some sort of information ordering. Recall that, in addition to defining a view of a database, a database schema expresses

---

[1]This contrasts with [3], which states that entities *should* be renamed, and specialization edges introduced to *avoid* introducing null values

certain requirements on the structure of the information stored in the database. When we say that one database schema presents more information than another, we mean that any instance of the first schema could be considered to be an instance of the second one. The first schema must, therefore, dictate that any database instances must contain at least all the information necessary in order to be an instance of the second schema.

Our approach is to first find a way to describe the merge of exactly two database schemas. This can be thought of as providing a binary operator on database schemas, which, provided it is associative and commutative, can then be extended to a function on finite sets of database schemas in the obvious manner. Such a binary merge is defined as the join (least upper bound) of two schemas under some suitable information ordering.

Some problems with finding merges of schemas

Having developed some intuitive idea of what the merge of two databases should be, we must then go on to find some formal definition of an information ordering on schemas and hence of merges of schemas. We proceed via a series of experiments and examples, in order to try to get a better idea of what the ordering should be. However it soon becomes apparent that things are more complicated than we might have hoped at first.

One of the first problems we notice is that the merge of two schemas may contain extra *implicit* classes in addition to the classes of the schemas being merged. For example figure 7 shows two schemas being merged. The first schema asserts that the class Guide-dog is a subclass of both the classes Dog and Working-animal. The second schema asserts that the classes Dog and Working-Animal both have name-arrows of classes Dog-Name and Animal-Name respectively. Combining this information, as we must when forming the merge, we conclude that Guide-Dog must also have a name-arrow and that this arrow must be of both the class Dog-name and Animal-Name. Consequently, due to the restrictions in our definition of database schemas in Section 2.1, the name-arrow of the class Guide-Dog must have a class which is a specialisation of both Dog-Name and Animal-Name and so we must introduce such a class into our merged schema.

When we consider these implicit classes further we find that it not sufficient merely to introduce extra classes into a schema with arbitrary names: the implicit classes must in fact be treated differently from normal classes. Firstly, if we were to give them the same status as ordinary classes we would find that binary merges are not associative. This is because, having introduced a implicit class into the merge of two schemas, merging with a third schema may cause additional implicit classes to be introduced which are specialisations of the first class. Consequently the order in which schemas are chosen for merging affects the order in which implicit classes

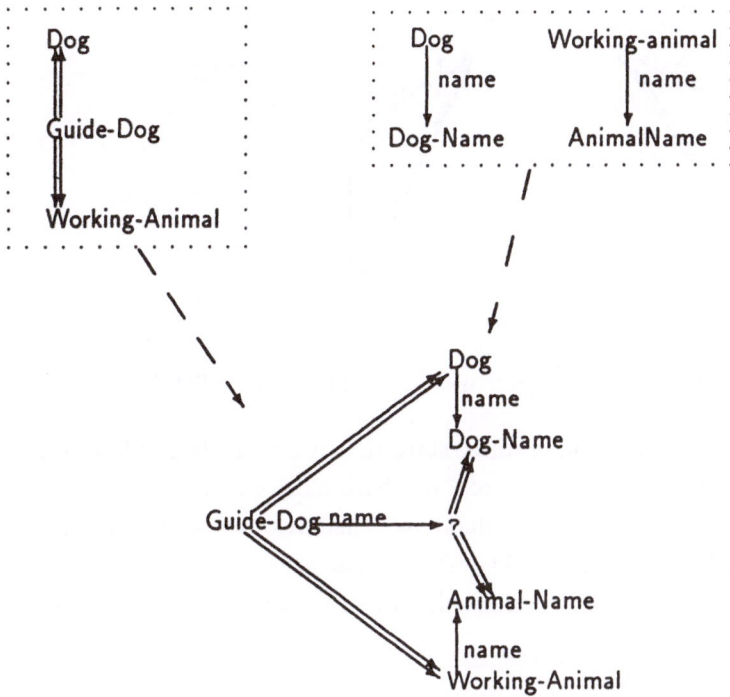

Figure 7: Schema merging involving implicit classes

are introduced and how they are related to one another.

Another problem is that, in our as yet hypothetical information ordering on schemas, it is possible for one schema to present more information than another without containing as many implicit classes.   It is clear that for one schema to

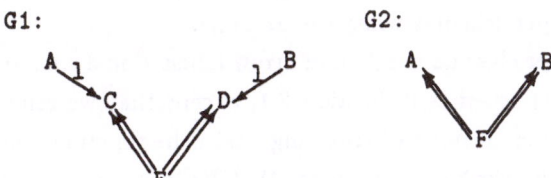

Figure 8: Yet more schemas

present all the information of another (plus additional information) it must have, at least, all the normal classes of the other. However let us consider the two schemas shown in figure 8. We would like to assert that the schema G3 shown in figure 9 is the merge of the two schemas, G1 and G2. However the schema G4 also presents all the information of G1 and G2, and in addition contains fewer classes than G3. The point is that G4 asserts that the 1-arrow of F has class E, which may impose

G3:   G4:

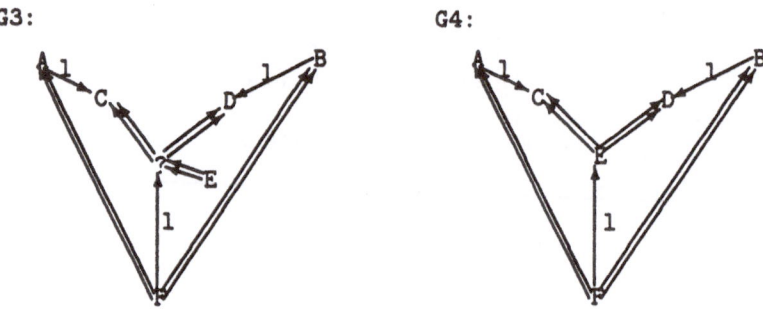

Figure 9: Possible candidates for the merges of the schemas

restrictions on it in addition to those which state that it's a subclass of both C and D, while G3 only states that the 1-arrow of F has both classes C and D.

We could extend our definition of database schemas to allow special implicit classes, and then try to find an ordering which takes account of them. However such a treatment would be very complicated, and so we adopt a slightly different approach.

3.2   Weak Schemas

In order to avoid the complexities of introducing implicit classes, what we do is first weaken our definition of database schemas so that these classes become unnecessary (they are indeed *implicit*). We then define an information ordering on these *weak schemas*, such that binary joins exist and are associative; and finally we present a method of converting a weak schema into a proper schema by introducing additional "implicit" classes. The idea is that we can do all our merging using weak schemas, and then convert the results to proper schemas when we are done.

We define a **weak schema** over class names $\mathcal{N}$ and arrow labels $\mathcal{L}$ in a similar manner to our definition of (*proper*) schemas in Section 2.1, except that we relax the axiom **A1** in the following manner: instead of requiring that $\mathcal{E}$ be functional in its first two arguments, we adopt the weaker requirement that for any class p and arrow label a, and any two distinct classes q and r, if $p \xrightarrow{a} q$ and $p \xrightarrow{a} r$ then q and r may not be specialisations of one-another. Hence, for any $p \in C$ and any $a \in \mathcal{L}$, the set $\{q \mid p \xrightarrow{a} q\}$ is a *co-chain* under the ordering $\mathcal{S}$.

Note that any proper database schema, according to the definitions in section 2.1, is also a weak schema according to this definition.

We define an ordering $\sqsubseteq$ on weak schemas, such that $\mathcal{G}_1 \sqsubseteq \mathcal{G}_2$ iff all the classes of $\mathcal{G}_1$ are also classes of $\mathcal{G}_2$, each specialisation edge in $\mathcal{G}_1$ is also in $\mathcal{G}_2$, and for each class p in $\mathcal{G}_1$, if p has an a-arrow of class q in $\mathcal{G}_1$, then p has a corresponding a-arrow in $\mathcal{G}_2$ which is at least as specific: that is, which has at least as specific a cardinality constraint and which has a class which is a specialisation of q in $\mathcal{G}_2$.

It can be shown that $\sqsubseteq$ is a partial ordering on weak schemas, and, further, that if $\mathcal{G}_1 \sqsubseteq \mathcal{G}_2$, then every instance of $\mathcal{G}_1$ can also be considered to be an instance of $\mathcal{G}_2$ via a natural projection.

In [5] it is proven that the ordering $\sqsubseteq$ on weak schemas is bounded complete. That is, for any weak schemas $\mathcal{G}_1$ and $\mathcal{G}_2$, if there exists a weak schema $\mathcal{G}'$ such that $\mathcal{G}_1 \sqsubseteq \mathcal{G}'$ and $\mathcal{G}_2 \sqsubseteq \mathcal{G}'$ then there is a least such weak schema $\mathcal{G}_1 \sqcup \mathcal{G}_2$. Further the proof is constructive so that it can be used as an algorithm to construct $\mathcal{G}_1 \sqcup \mathcal{G}_2$ from $\mathcal{G}_1$ and $\mathcal{G}_2$. Since $\sqsubseteq$ is a partial order, the operator $\sqcup$ is associative, commutative and idempotent, and so can be repeatedly applied in order to find the least upper bound of any collection of weak schemas whenever it exists.

It is shown that the least upper bound of a collection of weak schemas exists whenever their specialisation relations satisfy some *compatibility constraints*, and such a collection of weak schemas is said to be **compatible**. Consequently we have a way of formulating a weak schema which contains all the information contained in any compatible collection of schemas but no additional information, and can therefore be considered to be the **weak schema merge** of the collection of schemas. For example the two schemas, G1 and G2, shown in figure 9 are compatible and their

G1 ⊔ G2

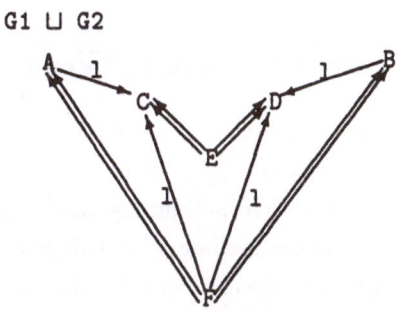

Figure 10: The least upper bound of two schemas

least upper bound is the weak schema shown in figure 10.

Having found the weak schema merge of a collection of schemas, we must then introduce the necessary implicit classes into the weak schema in order to make it into a proper schema according to the definition in section 2.1. An algorithm for doing this is presented in detail in [5]. Basically we start by recursively finding all the sets of classes, X, such that, for some class p and series of arrow labels $a_1, \ldots, a_n$, we have $p \xrightarrow{a_1} \ldots \xrightarrow{a_n} q$ for every class q in X. For each such set X we check to see if it has a unique minimal element, and, if not, we introduce an implicit class which is a specialisation of all the classes in X and make this class inherit the arrows of all the classes in X. Finally we rearrange the arrows of the resulting weak schema so that, if some class u has several a-arrows then we replace them with a single a-arrow to the implicit class which is a specialisation of the classes of all the original a-arrows.

If $\overline{\mathcal{G}}$ is the schema built from $\mathcal{G}$ using this algorithm, then we show that $\overline{\mathcal{G}}$ is indeed a proper schema, that $\mathcal{G} \sqsubseteq \overline{\mathcal{G}}$, and claim that, in some sense, $\overline{\mathcal{G}}$ is the least such proper schema (except for the possible inclusion certain unnecessary but inconsequential specialisation edges). Consequently, given a collection of compatible proper schemas, we define their **merge** to be the proper schema constructed from their weak schema merge in this manner.

Finally, in [5], we define *meta-schemas* to represent the restrictions imposed on the structure of schemas by various data models. A meta-schema divides the class names into a number of disjoint sets, such as entity-sets, relationships and attribute domains, and then imposes restrictions on which arrows may go from classes in each set to classes in each other set. We show that our merging process respects meta-schemas: that is, given a compatible collection of schemas satisfying some meta-schema, their merge will also satisfy the meta-schema. We conclude that we can apply our definition of merging to the schemas of other, established data models by first translating them into our model, then merging them, and then translating the result back into the original data model.

4 Conclusions and Further Work

While the model for database schemas and their instances presented in this paper is both simple and extremely general, there are a number of concepts in the literature for database systems which are potentially useful but which have not been incorporated in this model. These include such things as generalisation relationships, functional dependencies, existence dependencies and so on. The model does incorporate representations for specialisation relations and cardinality constraints, and the author believes that representations for these other concepts would be no more difficult to add. However we have chosen to keep the model relatively simple so as to make it as easy to reason about formally as possible.

By weakening the definition of schemas, we have been able to define the merge of a collection of *weak schemas* as their least upper bound under an information ordering. We can then form a *proper schema* from a weak schema by introducing additional *implicit classes* as necessary, thus giving us a way of defining the merge of a collection of proper schemas. Although the number of implicit classes introduced in the examples we have looked at so far have been small, we have not investigated how many might be introduced in general. It may be possible to construct pathological examples where the number of implicit classes required is huge, though the author believes that such examples are unlikely to arise in practice.

There may well be equally valid, alternative interpretations of what the merge of a collection of schemas should be, though we believe that, in order for some concept of a schema merge to be useful, it should have a similar, simple and intuitive definition in terms of a formal data model such as the one presented here. Consequently we believe that the methods used in this paper should be equally applicable to other such concepts of merging databases. In general we feel that this paper illustrates the potential benefits of using mathematical techniques and uniform, well-defined models in investigating the underlying theory of database systems.

Finally the author has noticed a number of similarities between the various levels of information considered (instances, schemas, meta-schemas, etc.) and their relationships to one another, and would like to investigate the possibility of forming a still more uniform and general model capable of spanning these various information levels.

Acknowledgements: I would like to thank Peter Buneman for his original ideas and advice, and also Susan Davidson for numerous comments, help and advice.

5 Bibliography

References

[1] R. Hull and R. King. Semantic database modelling: survey, applications and research issues. *ACM Computing Surveys*, 19(3):201–260, September 1987.

[2] C. Batini, M. Lenzerini, and S. Navathe. A comparative analysis of methodolgies for database schema integration. *ACM Computing Surveys*, 18(4):323–364, December 1986.

[3] J. Smith, P. Bernstein, U. Dayal, N. Goodman, T. Landers, K. Lin, and E. Wong. Multibase– Integrating Heterogeneous Distributed Database Systems. In *Proceedings of AFIPS*, pages 487–499, 1981.

[4] A. Sheth and J. Larson. Federated database systems for managing distributed heterogeneous and autonomous databases. *ACM Computing Surveys*, 22(3):183–236, September 1990.

[5] A. Kosky. *Modeling and Merging Database Schemas*. Technical Report, University of Pennsylvania, 1991.

[6] John Miles Smith and Diane C.P. Smith. Database abstractions: aggregation and generalisation. *ACM Transactions on Database Systems*, 2(2):105–133, June 1977.

[7] Peter Pin-Shan Chen. The entity-relationship model — toward a unified view of data. *ACM Trans. on Database Systems*, 1(1):9–36, March 1976.

[8] U. Dayal and H. Hwang. View definition and generalisation for database integration in multibase. *IEEE Transactions on Software Engineering*, SE–10(6):628–644, November 1984.

[9] A. Motro. Superviews: virtual integration of multiple databases. *IEEE Transactions on Software Engineering*, Vol. SE-13(7):785–798, July 1987.

[10] D. Shipman. The Functional Data Model and the Data Language DAPLEX. *ACM Transactions on Database Systems*, 6(1):140–173, March 1981.

[11] A. Ohori. Semantics of Types for Database Objects. *Theoretical Computer Science*, 76:53–91, 1990.

[12] F. Bancilon. Object-oriented database systems. In *Principles of Database Systems*, pages 152–162, 1988.

[13] A. Sheth, J. Larson, J. Cornellio, and S. Navethe. A tool for integrating conceptual schemas and user views. In *Proceedings of 4th International Conference on Data Engineering*, pages 176–183, 1988.

Specifying a Database System to Itself

David Maier

Dept. of Computer Science & Engineering
Oregon Graduate Institute
Beaverton 97007
USA

Abstract

Query processors have long been monolithic pieces of software that re-
sist extension. Query capabilities are needed in many applications of
persistent object bases, but object models and storage managers are
evolving so rapidly that matching a monolithic query processor to each
of them is infeasible. The EREQ project seeks to structure object query
processors into well-defined software components that can be independently modified, extended and exchanged. This paper sets forth our
initial ideas on what the major components will be and how we will
specify the interfaces to each.

1   Introduction

The EREQ Project[1] is a recently launched effort to devise a common internal architecture
for query processing in persistent object bases. A goal of the work is to specify the interfaces to the query optimizer component precisely enough that we can interchange query
optimizers between query processing systems. We are conducting our investigations in
an object-oriented database setting, but expect them to apply to other models having user-
defined database types with complex state. We expect to test our results through reconciling the internal architectures of the ENCORE, Revelation and EXODUS query processor
prototypes [1-3].

Some of the interfaces to a query optimizer are obvious, such as an object algebra for
input expressions and a query plan language for its output to the query evaluating layer.
There are other less obvious or less direct interfaces. There are connections to one or
more programming languages, if the query language is embedded in a host programming
language or an algebra expression can contain calls to programming language functions.
An optimizer needs information from a schema manager on type definitions and name
bindings. Statistics and selectivity information on instances, as well as existence of auxiliary access paths must be available. Other possible inputs are physical properties of the
underlying computer system and search heuristics. At each of these interfaces, there is a
question of how much of the semantics of the entities crossing the boundary the optimizer

---

[1]EREQ stands for "Encore-Revelation-Exodus Query System." It is a joint project of Stanley
Zdonik at Brown University, David DeWitt and Michael Carey at University of Wisconsin at Madison,
David Maier of Oregon Graduate institute, and Goetz Graefe of University of Colorado at Boulder.

needs to understand. At the object algebra interface, it may not need "full" semantics (the denotational meaning of operators). It needs to know about algebraic identities involving the operators, but it does not necessarily need to know how to evaluate a particular operator. At the query plan interface, the optimizer needs to know more than what logical function an operator procedure computes. For reasonable cost estimation, it must know how an algorithm affects physical properties of the data, such as sort order.

Another facet of query optimization is the stability of the information. Information that is stable for the one-shot execution of an ad hoc query may be variable over the life of a query embedded in an application program. Depending on how the validity of query plans is tracked, the optimizer may have to differentiate information that is stable between compilations of the database system from information that is stable between schema changes from information that is only valid until the next database update.

The mind of the questioning reader may still be back at the first paragraph, asking "Why?" That is, what is so important or useful about the ability to change query optimizers in a query processing system? There is some utility in the research setting, being able to compare the efficiency and efficacy of different query optimization strategies in the same environment. One might also speculate on being able to upgrade the query optimizer module of an installed database system, say with a module from a third-party vendor. What we are really after with this exercise in interchangeability is discovering good formalisms or notations with which to describe the various interfaces. The goal is not so much defining a particular query processing architecture as in having a *meta-architecture* in which changes to interfaces resulting from extensions and evolution can be captured. A meta-architecture is a system in which to define particular architectures. The demands of applications for data modeling features, the sophistication of access methods and hardware platform capabilities all increase steadily. Monolithic query processing engines are proving unmanageable to maintain in the face of such changes. A more modular architecture demands a precise means to describe evolving module boundaries, so that work can proceed on different parts of a query processing system in parallel.

A secondary issue is what does "interchangeable" mean in this context? How much rebinding is allowed when exchanging optimizers? Is it simply a matter of relinking code, or are there configuration tables and other supporting data structures the optimizer uses that must be modified? Other possibilities are that the optimizer is generated by an optimizer generator, and must be regenerated in the new environment, or that the optimizer is extensible and requires certain additions in order to conform. Simple relinking is probably too much to expect, but we hope the process can be done automatically—by running tools rather than necessitating any hand-coding.

This project is scarcely begun, so it is generous to even call the ideas here preliminary. This paper marks a trailhead, rather than a point of progress down any path.

2 A Reference Architecture

In this section we describe a generic architecture for query processing, in order to give an overview of the major components involved and their interactions. Figure 1 depicts the architecture.

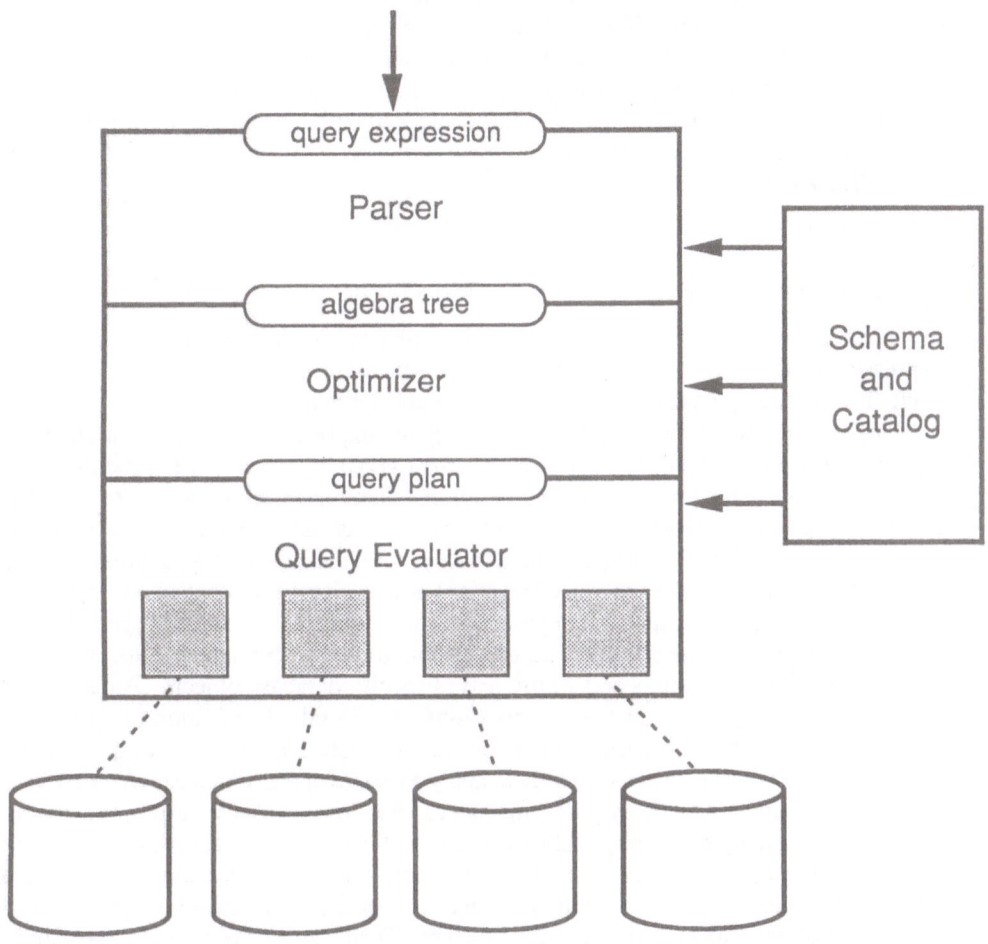

Figure 1. Sample Query Processing Architecture.

Query expressions, either from ad hoc queries or extracted from programs, are parsed into expression trees over a logical object algebra. The optimizer transforms these expressions into query plans for immediate or later evaluation by a query evaluation layer. The schema manager and catalog provide logical and physical information on types and instances to the other three layers. The source form of queries does not concern us much. It might be an SQL-like syntax, an iterator construct in a persistent language, or some form of comprehension notation. In any case, scanning and parsing the source is straightforward.

The logical algebra will be a generalization of the relational algebra. However, rather than dealing with simply sets of records over base types, the values are formed by free composition of a variety of constructors, such as tuple, set (or bag), array and reference. Algebraic expressions can also operate on instances of user-defined abstract types, through the interfaces of those types. An algebra expression might also contain embedded code segments from some programming language. The operations in the algebra will include arithmetic or calculi on the base types (such as addition and Boolean negation), selectors and accessors on some of the constructed types (field selector, array indexing, dereference) and bulk operations on other types (selection, unnest, map, and so forth).

It is the job of the optimizer both to create choices and to make choices. It creates choices by developing algebraic expressions equivalent to the input expression and by exploring alternative query plans. It makes choices by selecting among the algebraic expressions on the basis of heuristics, and among query plans on the basis of cost estimates. The alternative algebra expressions come from identities such as

```
join(R, S) = join(S, R)
```

```
select(select(R, P), Q) = select(R, and(P, Q))
```

In general the number of equivalent expressions that can be developed for a given input expression can be large or even infinite. Hence the optimizer needs to employ search heuristics and strategies to limit the amount of search space it examines.

The alternative query plans for a given algebra expression arise through choosing among different physical operator procedures for a given logical operation, such as hash-join or merge-join for the logical join operation. There need not be a direct match between each physical algorithm and a single logical operation. A join procedure at the query plan level might perform a combination of join and selection as expressed at the logical level. A single physical procedure might also implement more than one logical algebra operation. For example, a join procedure can be used for intersection, generally.

Query plans are typically directed expression graphs whose internal nodes specify physical operator procedures and whose leaves specify database objects. A query plan might not be a tree if common subexpressions are shared. In addition to specifying which physical procedures are applied in which order, a query plan might contain scheduling information, such as whether to apply a certain operator in a demand-driven or data-driven manner. The query plan language can be viewed as a physical, or more concrete, algebra. Many of the physical procedures will have direct counterparts among the logical algebra operations, as far as function goes. Such procedures might also have physical parameters, specifying options such as sort orders or duplicate information that are not part of the semantics of the logical algebra. There can also be physical procedures that are no-ops at the logical level. Such an operator is inserted to affect physical properties of intermediate results, such as partitioning and placement in the memory hierarchy, or to modify the processing of the query plan, such as to use parallelism.

A query plan may be executed immediately or catalogued away for later use. The query evaluation layer might interpret plans directly, or compile them into some lower level operations. Execution of plans can take place in data-driven rather than demand driven mode. Also, physical operator procedures might evaluate in "batch" rather than stream mode, constructing the entire result relation of an operation at once, rather than a record at a time. (The possibilities here must also be known by the query optimizer, whether it is making the decision on evaluation mechanism, or it is given that information from without.) In Figure 1, the query evaluation layer comprises the physical operator procedures, buffer and file management routines, access methods, data structure realizations, and connections to the concurrency and recovery services of the DBMS. In general, the evaluator will have parallel processing capabilities. By data structure realizations, we mean that a given type constructor, such as tuple or set, might have more than one physical implementation. For example, small sets might be implemented with single records, while large sets might use files of records or B-trees.

The schema and catalog contain type definitions, type implementations and declarations of persistent variables. It is the persistent variables that are the starting points for queries. We posit that the persistent variables reside in some sort of name space, where constraints on and between the variables can be declared. The schema and catalog also must be able to provide physical information on individual instances, such as sizes, ranges of values and existence of indices. One feature that sets query optimization off from programming language optimization is recognizing that instances of the same type may have widely different physical properties.

2.1 An Example of Query Processing

We illustrate this process with a relational database example. Consider relations

```
issued(Album, Group, RecordedOn, DateOfIssue)
belong(Group, Member, Instrument, From, To)
```

Where issue gives the dates that a musical group recorded and issued an album, and belong gives the range of dates a particular musician played a given instrument with a specific group. Consider a query to find an album with a vibraphone player on it, plus the player. Such a query might appear in a relational calculus language as

```
{[i.Album, b.Member]|i from issued, b from belong,
        i.Group = b.Group, b.Instrument = "vibes",
        between(b.From, i.RecordedOn, b.To)}
```

This form of the query can be parsed and expressed in the logical algebra as follows. (Attributes have been abbreviated to a single letter here.)

```
                    project(AM)
                        |
    select(((I="vibes") and (F <= R) and (R <= T))
                        |
                      join
                      / \
                    /     \
              issued     belong
```

On the basis of a general heuristic or a cost estimate, this logical algebra expression can be transformed by moving a portion of the selection condition below the join:

```
                    project(AM)
                        |
        select((F <= R) and (R <= T))
                        |
                      join
                      / \
                    /     \
              issued     select(I = "vibes")
                                |
                              belong
```

The query plan phase then selects particular physical algorithms for each logical operator, filling in the appropriate arguments, and binding identifiers to files or offsets based on catalog information on the location and physical layout of relations. The choices are based on statistics kept for the relations and cost estimates for the physical procedures:

```
                        dup-elim
                           |
            filter[7,LE,3; 3,LE,8; 1,4]
                           |
                  merge-join[2, 1]
                     / \
                    /    \
    sort[2, string]   filescan[3,EQ,"vibes"](file55)
            |
    filescan(file196)
```

Here we assume the evaluation strategy is demand driven, with each physical algorithm providing a stream of records as input to the algorithm above it. There are a couple points to note here. One is that the correspondence between logical operators and physical algorithms is not necessarily one-to-one. For example, the filescan on the right branch of the join implements both access to the belong relation (located in file55) and a select. Also, the top select-project pair is realized with a filter procedure, which passes records selectively and removes fields, followed by a procedure for eliminating duplicate record values. The second point is that certain procedures may be sensitive to physical properties of the data and additional operations may be inserted to achieve the requisite properties. For example, merge-join requires its input streams to be sorted on the join attributes, hence the need for the sort procedure. Here we assume that file55 is already in the desired order. Note that the sort procedure is a no-op at the logical level, since relations are treated as unordered sets of tuples at that level.

3 Interface Specification Issues

Evidently, the logical algebra and query plan expressions represent two key interfaces in our reference architecture. There are also one or more interfaces to the schema and catalog component. Less obvious interfaces include the one between an application programming language and the query subsystem, both for invoking queries and returning results. Another is from the query processor to information about the capabilities of the underlying computing platform: available memory, scratch space on disk, number of processors, processor loads, and so forth.

In the rest of this paper, we discuss these interfaces, with particular attention to the parser-optimizer interface and the optimizer-query evaluator interface. Clearly, in specifying the interfaces between the layers, there is at a minimum a need for an operational fit. That is, the values passed down by one layer must be expected by the layer below. But there is much to decide about the interface beyond the format of their values. The main issue for is now is what notation or formalism to use to describe each interface. That choice, in turn, depends on what needs to be described.

A word on terminology. We use the adjective "logical" to refer to the object algebra and the software layers around it. We use "physical" to indicate operator procedures and other parts of the query evaluator layer.

4 The Parser-Optimizer Interface: The Logical Algebra

In our reference architecture, it is quite clear what passes from the parser to the optimizer: expressions from a logical object algebra. A data algebra is characterized by a collection of base types and data structures, with their associated operators. The relational algebra of the relational data model is probably the best formalized aspect of database systems. (Still, definitions of relational algebra [4-6] exhibit variations in several areas: typed or untyped domains, the particular choice of base types and associated operators, labelled or positional column notation, provision for constant relations, and so forth. Also, even though the operators can be precisely specified, typing systems that handle highly poly-morphic operators such as join are non-trivial [7].) The relational algebra has one data structuring construct, the relation, which cannot be applied iteratively. We expect an object algebra will contain several constructors, such as set, tuple, and array, that may be composed freely. We also expect it to incorporate object identity and the ability to operate on user-defined types through messages. There have been numerous proposals for object algebras, such as those of Beeri and Kornatsky [8] and Osborn [9]. We expect that ours will resemble those of Vance [10] and Vandenberg [11].

It might seem, then, that specifying the parser-optimizer interface is a matter of selecting a semantic formalism, such as set theory, equational specifications or denotational semantics, and giving a definition to each operator in the algebra. However, from the point of view of the optimizer architecture, that approach might be both too much and too little. Yes, the optimizer does receive algebra expressions as input, but it does not necessarily need to know their precise meaning to do its job. The optimizer is concerned with what are valid transformations on algebra expressions; it does not necessarily need to know enough about the algebra to evaluate those expressions. For example, the equivalence

```
intersect(union(Q, R), S) =
        union(intersect(Q, S), intersect(R, S))
```

holds whether Q, R and S are sets or multisets (where intersection and union take the minimum and maximum of element cardinalities, respectively). For transforming expressions, the precise meaning of `intersect` and `union` does not matter, as long as the appropriate algebraic properties hold. (Of course, there may be other operations where sets and multisets differ.) On the other hand, given the formal semantics of the algebra operators, deducing useful equivalences automatically may be non-trivial. Hence, it seems that an optimizer needs not so much the formal definition of the operators as the legal transformations that hold on them.

Positing that expression transformations are the description the optimizer needs for the object algebra, what system do we use for capturing them? A legal transform might be captured simply as a chunk of code. Given an input expression, the code uses arbitrary means to reformulate it to a transformed output expression. Such a solution seems less than satisfactory. Captured as a chunk of code, transformations would not be easily manipulable, say to recognize commonalities in patterns for efficient search or to combine transformations that are used together frequently. A better starting point is likely a term-rewriting system. Many algebraic equivalences are easily captured with rewrite rules, such as commutativity of join:

```
join(R, S) --> join(S, R)
```

and the relationship between nested selections and logical conjunctions:

```
select(select(R, P), Q) --> select(R, and(P, Q))
```

4.1 Complications

While we believe term-rewriting is a promising approach, we foresee a number of challenges in extending it to a fully expressive system for all the kinds of transforms we anticipate. We enumerate some of the potential problem areas below, which we illustrate for the most part with examples from relational algebra.

4.1.1 Conditional Transforms

Some transforms may only apply if certain relationships hold among the arguments. Consider pushing selection through projection:

```
project(select(R, P), X) -->
         select(project(R, X), P)
```

This transform is only valid when the predicate P is "over" the attributes in X. We will either need an expressive pattern-matching mechanism or the ability to attach conditions to transforms to treat such cases.

4.1.2 Complex Transforms

The exact details of a transformation can get quite complicated, particularly for the auxiliary arguments to operators. Consider the following basic schema for pushing selection through join:

```
select(join(R, S), P) -->
         select(join(select(R, P1), select(S, P2)), P3)
```

It is not a simple matter to describe the decomposition of P into the conjunction of P1, P2 and P3 so that each mentions the appropriate attributes.

4.1.3 Approximate Transforms

There are transforms that give approximate but not exact equivalence, such as associativity of floating-point addition. In some cases exact numerical equivalence may not be required. However, it is difficult to imagine distinguishing permissible cases without the use of programmer-defined directives [12]. Other kinds of approximation come up in substituting value equality for identity, and vice versa [13].

4.1.4 Variadic Operations

To cut down on the size of the search space for optimization, it is useful to group multiple applications of a binary operator into a single application of a multiway operator. For example, for choosing join orders, one might want to collapse a group of adjacent joins to a single pseudo-operation

```
join(join(R1, R2), join(join(R3, R4), R5)) -->
         multijoin(R1, R2, R3, R4, R5)
```

and then proceed to partition the argument set back to binary joins in another order. One could possibly use list notation for arguments

```
join(R, multijoin(L)) --> multijoin(cons(R, L))
```

but that still leaves the problem of providing transforms to change list orderings. Some work on transforms in object algebras with variadic operators already exists [14].

4.1.5 Non-Local Transforms

Some transforms seem to have a non-local character that is not easily expressed with term rewriting [15]. Here, relief might come from transformation grammar techniques used in natural language processing for specifying non-local transforms on sentential forms [16].

4.1.6 Exploiting Similarities

We expect that our object algebra will contain multiple bulk types, and it may well be that these bulk types have some similar operations (such as selection) with similar legal transforms. Having "duplicated" transforms in several bulk types probably is not a problem in increasing the size of the search space—the result type of an expression node will limit the choice to the instance of the transform for that type. However, if special heuristics or strategies are provided in the optimizer, those tactics might get repeated for each of several similar operations. For example, there might be a strategy that attempts to split predicates in selection conditions so one part can be pushed through the operation below the selection. That strategy likely applies equally well for a selection on bags, sets and lists, and we would rather not have to specify it three times.

An approach to explore here is to organize the bulk types into a "subalgebra" hierarchy [17], with abstractions of bulk types at the top, and concrete bulk types at the bottom, such as illustrated below:

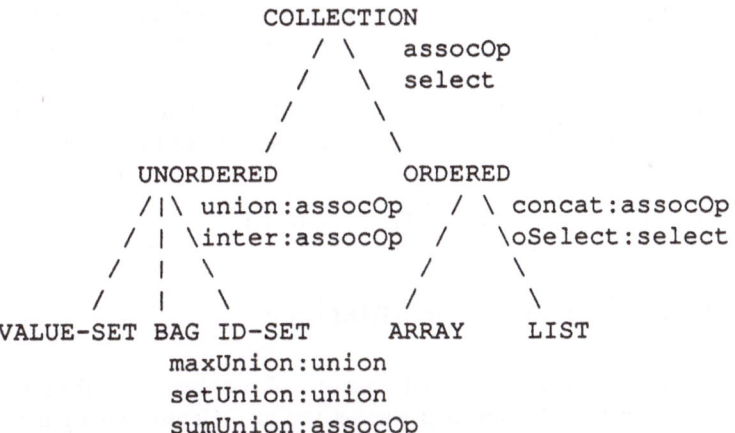

The more abstract types could define operations and transforms that have one or more specializations at the lower levels. Heuristics or strategies can then be expressed in terms of the abstracted operators and applied to the concrete versions of those. Note that having transforms on the abstract operations does not prevent having additional transforms on the specialized versions. We think the work on comprehensions of bulk types [18, 19] is an excellent start on such an organization. It seems to capture the essence of some common operations on bulk types at an abstract level, though we expect some extensions will be needed for types such as multidimensional arrays.

Such an organization for bulk types could also accommodate user-defined bulk types. By inserting such a type at the appropriate point in the hierarchy, the query optimizer would be able to apply transforms to operations on that type.

4.2 Instance Parameters

We touch upon one final area in terms of specifying the logical algebra to the optimizer, and it is related to the specificity of the typing system for the data types in the algebra. There are tradeoffs in how specific the types are, between the amount of information one can develop statically about an expression versus how generically an expression will operate. For example, for multidimensional arrays, one might specify the ranges of the dimensions (`Array[50, 100]`), just the dimensionality (`Array[*, *]`) or just have a single type for all dimensions of arrays. In the context of database processing, given a particular type system, it is important to observe that the typing for an expression must hold over all executions of that expression, whereas there may be more detail that can be articulated on a specific execution. Consider an expression that aggregates a three-dimensional array across two of its dimensions:

```
reduce(+, reduce(+, M))
```

In a type system that captures dimensionality but not ranges of dimensions, the best that the type information can tell us is that the result is one-dimensional. However, for a particular execution of the expression where M has shape 800 by 120 by 200, the optimizer may want to know that the inner expression produces an 800 by 120 matrix and the result has size 800. (It would be unusual to analyze a single execution of an expression in the programming language setting, since it is doubtful the cost of the analysis would ever be recovered. However, in a database environment, the sizes of the arguments might be large and there could be a payoff from optimizing a single execution.)

We refer to the kinds of information that can describe data values beyond their types as *instance parameters*. The optimizer needs to know how to calculate the instance parameters of the results of algebraic expressions, given the values of those parameters on the inputs. We think abstract interpretation [20, 21] of the algebraic operators will be a good mechanism to capture this information. For example, abstracting lists to their lengths, the abstract interpretation of concatenation could be expressed by

```
LEN[concat(M, N)] = LEN[M] + LEN[N].
```

5   The Optimizer-Evaluator Interface

The query plan that the optimizer passes to the query evaluator represents the same function as the object algebra expression that was passed to the optimizer by the parser. However, the query plan embodies choices on particular physical procedures to implement each logical operator, on evaluation order of subexpressions and on additions of special procedures to modify physical properties of data. The principal information that the optimizer needs about this interface is the correspondence between logical algebra operators and the procedures in the evaluator that implement them. It also needs to know cost estimates for executing those procedures to use in the planning process. Good cost estimates in turn derive from knowing physical properties of procedure inputs.

5.1   The Logical-to-Physical Correspondence

Capturing the logical-operator-to-physical-procedure correspondence seems well handled by term-rewriting rules, even in the non-one-to-one case. For instance, one of the translations used in the example of Section 2.1 was

```
project(select(R, P), X) -->
        dup-elim(filter(R, P; X)).
```

The only unusual case is physical operators, such as `sort`, that are logical no-ops. The optimizer needs to know that they can be introduced into a plan at arbitrary points.

Again, the optimizer does not need to know precisely what function a physical procedure computes. It only needs to now how it relates to the logical algebra operators. (Of course, for a correctly functioning query processor, the physical procedures must conform to the definitions of the algebra operators.)

5.2 Cost Modeling and Physical Properties

In translating an algebra expression to a query plan, the query optimizer is attempting to minimize some costs, such as total CPU usage, elapsed time, memory usage or a combination of those. The basic input to the cost estimation process is statistics and layout information on the data objects at the leaves of the query plan. That information is obtained from the schema and catalog manager, which is treated in the next section. The rest of the process involves propagating this information through the procedures in the query plan to calculate the cost contribution of each. What we need is a behavioral model of each procedure that captures its costs as a function of properties of its inputs. To continue the process, we also need to compute or estimate properties for the output of the procedure. There is also the possibility that some procedures expect or require certain physical properties to hold on their inputs, and those requirements must be checked in producing a valid query plan. An example is the `merge-join` procedure in the query plan of Section 2.1. Thus, it is useful to classify procedures as to whether they preserve, enforce, require or destroy physical properties. Examples of such information are that selection preserves duplicates (or the absence thereof) and hash join destroys sort order.

One approach to capturing the behavior of physical procedures that we plan to investigate is to model the various costs and physical properties as abstract interpretations of the physical procedures. For example, suppose we have the following plan using nested-loops join:

```
nl-join(R(AB), S(AC))
```

where R is the outer relation and S is the inner relation. If R is sorted on A and S is sorted on C, then the resulting relation will be lexicographically sorted on AC.

To express how various operations interact with sort order as an abstract interpretation, we need a domain of sort orders and an interpretation function. Assume we are in the relational case, where sort orders can be described as sequences of attributes. Let SO[P] mean the sort-order interpretation of a plan P. The creator of new physical procedures would then be responsible for extending the abstract interpretation to that procedure. Consider

```
SO[nl-join[X, Y, Z](R(XY), S(YZ))] ==
        concat(SO[R], restrict(SO[S], X, Z))
```

Here the `restrict` operator computes what ordering exists on Z-values in S for tuples with equal X-values. To express that stream selection (as opposed to indexed selection) preserves sort order, we have

```
SO[stream-select(S, P)] == SO[S].
```

Some operators will destroy any sort order on their operands:

```
SO[hash-project(R, X)] == null-order
```

The abstract interpretation can then be used as input to cost functions on procedures and to express input requirements for procedures, for instance

```
merge-join[X, Y, Z](R(XY), R(XZ)) requires
        restrict(SO[R], empty, X) =
                restrict(SO[S], empty, X) and
        covers(SO[R], X)
```

which says that the sort order of R and S must imply equal sort orders on the attributes in X and they must be sorted on all those attributes.

As with using term rewriting for algebraic transforms, there are challenges in adapting abstract interpretation to cost and physical property modeling. We mention some of the problems here.

5.2.1 Defining the Domain for Interpretation

The basis of an abstract interpretation is a domain of interpretation. In some cases the domain will be simple, such as integers or Booleans for time cost or presence of duplicates. In other cases, such as describing the clustering of an object or sort orders on collections with complex objects, the domains need to be quite complex. Can the domain be general enough to capture user-defined values, such as a special sort ordering on a type. In addition, one may need to define new functions on the domain, such as restrict above, to express the behavior of a certain procedure. A final question is how abstract to make the domain for a particular property. For example, if we are interested in the distribution of values in a collection, we might capture that information as a max-median-min triple, as a histogram or even as a count of all values present. In making this choice it is important to remember that many of these interpretations are approximations, and there is no point in extending the precision of the domain much past the accuracy of the estimate.

5.2.2 Relationships on the Domain

In looking to satisfy physical requirements of a procedure in a query plan, the optimizer needs to know implications between domain values. For example, if some procedure on relations needs its input sorted on AB, then the optimizer should be able to conclude an ABC-sorted relation fulfills this requirement.

5.2.3 Interdependence of Properties

In traditional usage in programming languages and compilers, abstract interpretations are defined independently, for such purposes as typing and strictness analysis. For our purposes, some of the interpretations will depend on the value of others. For example, result size estimates might take into account the presence of duplicates, as might an interpretation on distribution of values.

5.2.4 Properties Versus Realizations

As we mentioned earlier, we anticipate multiple physical realizations of a given data structure. It may be that a given physical property does not apply to all realizations. For example, sort order might not apply for a set realized as a bit vector.

5.2.5 Parameter and Procedure Selection

The scenario we have sketched so far in conjunction with property computation and cost estimation is too simplistic. It is not always a case of generating a candidate query plan and then making various abstract interpretations of it. In order to limit search in the optimizer, it is useful to turn the situation around and ask if there is a particular combination of procedure and parameters that achieves a given cost or satisfies a given property. For example, a sort-based projection can accommodate a variety of output orderings based on a sort-order parameter to it. Different input orderings for merge join give different output orderings. The optimizer would like to ask about which parameter choices and input properties could produce a given output property, and in that way guide the generation of query plans for consideration. Going a step further in that direction, the optimizer might want to know whether any of the physical procedures corresponding to the logical join operator can deliver its result in a particular sort order. We have not yet decided on how to encode this information. It might be as search pragmas, as separate "property forcing" functions associated with the abstract interpretations, or as ancillary rules connected with each physical procedure.

6 Optimizer Interfaces to the Schema and Catalog

Unlike the interfaces discussed in Sections 4 and 5, which were internal to the query processor, the schema and catalog interface is an external interface to another module in the persistent object base. We should probably be writing in terms of multiple interfaces for the parser, optimizer and evaluator layers, but we have only begun to articulate the different information requirements of these levels. Here we mainly categorize the kinds of information that the query processor needs from the schema or catalog.

6.1 Definitions

We expect the schema to maintain definitions of user-defined types and implementations for those types. A type will be described in terms of the signatures of its operations. An implementation of a type will be expressed in terms of an internal representation of the instances of the type and methods for the operations of the type. In general, we wish to allow multiple implementations for a single type. It may be the schema manager's job as well to provide information about subtype relationships between types.

6.2 Bindings

We assume that part of the database schema is a name space where persistent identifiers reside. (In a relational database system, this name space holds the identifiers (names) of relations and view definitions.) For a given identifier, various kinds of information may be bound to it, such as a type, integrity constraints, an implementation, an object identifier, instance parameters and state. The query processor needs to inquire about these bindings for identifiers that show up in expressions it is processing.

    A catalog or data directory might have further information on location and layout of data objects, as well as keep track of auxiliary access paths that exist. The query processor will ask about the existence of access paths, and needs a notation that expresses what each path is good for. Most auxiliary access paths in existing database systems are indexes or hash tables. However, we imagine that researchers will discover new kinds of structures, and the notation must be general enough to describe the utility of these. As an example of such a path, consider a collection Albums of record album objects, where every record algorithm has a distributor. Suppose the distributors are company objects drawn from a collection Companies. There is no explicit collection of just those companies that distribute record albums in this model. It might be useful to maintain such a collection, however, for processing queries on Albums. That is, we want to maintain an auxiliary structure Distributors, defined as

```
{c in Companies|a in Albums, distributor(a) = c}
```

Then, for instance, given a query for all albums distributed by Canadian companies, the query processor could choose to iterate over Distributors rather than the likely much larger collections Albums and Companies.

6.3 Statistics

Another kind of information we expect the schema or catalog to contain is statistics on objects. A statistic in this context is usually a count or a value distribution, formed by aggregation or reduction of the data object. In the persistent object base setting, other useful abstractions of data may suggest themselves, such as the average fan-in or fan-out when objects reference other objects.

A key problem here is that statistics are derived from object instances, where the expression that the optimizer receives contains object names. If the name space treats identifiers as variables that may be reassigned arbitrarily, it will be hard for the query processor to obtain appropriate statistics at query optimization time. Note that in relational systems this problem usually does not arise, because each relation name is statically bound to a particular relation instance (though the contents of that instance can change).

6.4 Stability of Information

The kinds of information we discussed in Sections 4 and 5 that the optimizer needs about the object algebra and query plan language is relatively static. We anticipate that information being constant across many databases and over time within a given database system. On the other hand, the information that the query processor obtains from the schema or catalog is likely to change over the life of an application (and hence during the lifetime of some queries). The query processor and schema manager need some way to communicate about the stability of information. The optimizer either must avoid using information that might change during the lifetime of a query plan, or some service must record the appropriate dependencies so a plan can be marked out of date when information it incorporates has changed.

We are thinking about classifying schema and catalog information in terms of the kind of change that can invalidate it. The most volatile information changes because of a database update, such as modifying the state of an object, creating a new object or assigning to a persistent variable. Less volatile is information about physical organizations, which can change because of adding or deleting indexes, reclustering objects and computing new statistics, and so forth. Schema changes probably happen less frequently, with modifications such as adding an implementation or a type and changing a type interface.

One way of viewing the problem is to treat obtaining information from the schema and catalog as partial evaluation of an expression, and classify database changes as to how they affect the environment in which that evaluation takes place.

7   Other Interfaces

We briefly mention two other interfaces for which we have done much less analysis. One is the connection of the query processor to a host programming language. There might be little difficulty if the persistent object base is actually a persistent programming language with a type system matching that of the object algebra. In other cases the host language will be non-persistent or not support bulk types directly. The most challenging situation is where some mapping of type systems and values must take place between the query processor and the programming language. We would then need notation to specify the target formats of values in the programming language. IDL [22] is a possible starting point here. If a query can contain embedded fragments from the host language, what is needed to make the linkage to execute such code during query evaluation? Is the source code translated into a form that can execute directly on the database format of objects or will the database make "up-calls" to the application? In the latter case, must the database reformat objects into the form expected by the programming language (for example, changing object IDs to memory addresses or converting strings from start-offset format to self-delimiting format) before passing them up as arguments?

The other interface is to the status of computational capabilities of the environment in which the query processor is running. Some of those factors may be fairly constant, such as the number of processors and communications bandwidth. Others may change more frequently, such as memory available for buffers, processor loads and unused data space. We need a mechanism for describing resources and a methodology for factoring information about those resources into the cost model for query plans.

8   Remarks and Future Work

We have presented our ideas on how to articulate various internal and external interfaces for a query processor in a persistent object system. It is perhaps important to mention two interfaces that we do not intend to specify right away, namely the external query language and the interface to the underlying persistent object store. Our reasons are twofold. One is that we do not see as much similarity at those boundaries among the prototypes of the participating groups, and we think the parser and evaluator can insulate the query optimizer from them in any case. The second reason is that we do not want to preempt other ongoing efforts to gain consensus on module boundaries in persistent object systems [23].

Most of the ideas presented herein are as yet unsullied by the realities of implementation attempts. In the coming year we will make our initial essay at defining the interfaces of the query processor, and then try to adapt the prototype query processors of the various participants in the EREQ project to those interfaces. We will then be able to attempt an optimizer transplant. In all likelihood the heart will reject the body, but we should have enough feedback to refine our interfaces so that the next attempt at the operation is successful.

9   Acknowledgements

Most of these ideas grew out of many discussions with other members of the Revelation group—Scott Daniels, Goetz Graefe, Tom Keller and Bennet Vance—and have been influenced by the work of other members of the EREQ project—Mike Carey, Dave DeWitt, Gail Mitchell, Scott Vandenberg and Stan Zdonik. This work was partially supported by NSF grant IRI 8920642.

References

[1]   Zdonik, SB and Mitchell, G.   ENCORE: An object-oriented approach to database modeling and querying. *Data Engineering* 14(2), June 1991.

[2]   Daniels, S, Graefe, G, Keller, T, et al. Query optimization in Revelation, an overview. *Data Engineering* 14(2), June 1991.

[3]   Vandenberg, SL and DeWitt, DJ. Algebraic query processing in EXTRA/ EXCESS. *Data Engineering* 14(2), June 1991.

[4]   Elmasri, R and Navathe, SB. *Fundamentals of Database Systems*, Benjamin/ Cummings, 1989.

[5]   Maier, D. *The Theory of Relational Databases*, Computer Science Press, 1983.

[6]   Ullman, JD. *Principles of Database and Knowledge-Base Systems*, volume 1. Computer Science Press, 1988.

[7]   Buneman, OP. Data types for database programming. Proc. of the Appin Conf. on Data Types and Persistence: 295-308, Dept. of Computing Science report PPRR 16, Univ. of Glasgow, August 1985.

[8]   Beeri, C and Kornatsky, Y. Algebraic optimization of object-oriented query languages. *Proc. Third Intl. Conf. on Database Theory*:72-88, Springer-Verlag LNCS 470, Paris, December 1990.

[9]   Osborn, SL. Identity, equality and query optimization. *Advances in Object-Oriented Database Systems:*346-351, Springer-Verlag LNCS 334, October 1988.

[10]   Vance, B. Toward an object-oriented query algebra. Computer Science & Engineering report 91-08, Oregon Graduate Inst., May 1991.

[11]   Vandenberg, SL and DeWitt, DJ. Algebraic support for complex objects with arrays, identity and inheritance. *Proc. 1991 ACM SIGMOD Intl. Conf. on Management of Data:*158-167, Denver, May 1991.

[12]   Lieuwen, DF and DeWitt, DJ. Optimizing loops in database programming languages. To appear, *Proc. of the Third Intl. Workshop on Database Programming Languages*, Morgan Kaufmann, 1991.

[13]   Shaw, GM and Zdonik, SB. Object-oriented queries: Equivalence and optimization. In *Deductive and Object-Oriented Databases:*264-278, Elsevier Science Publishers, 1990.

[14]   Straube, DD and Özsu, MT. Queries and query processing in object-oriented database systems. *ACM Trans. on Information Systems* 8(4):387-430, October 1990.

[15]   Mitchell, G, Zdonik, SB and Dayal, U. An architecture for query processing in persistent object stores. Dept. of Computer Science report 91-38, Brown Univ., June 1991.

[16]   Winograd, T. *Language as a Cognitive Process, volume 1: Syntax*, Addison-Wesley, 1983.

[17]   Wegner, P and Zdonik, SB. Models of Inheritance. In *Database Programming Languages: Proceedings of the Second Intl. Workshop*, Morgan Kaufmann, 1989.

[18]   Trinder, P. Comprehensions, a query notation for DBPLs. To appear, *Proc. of the Third Intl. Workshop on Database Programming Languages*, Morgan Kaufmann, 1991.

[19]   Wadler, PL. Comprehending monads. *Proc. ACM Conf. on Lisp and Functional Programming*:61-78, Nice, France, June 1990.

[20]   Abramsky, S and Hankin, C (eds.). *Abstract Interpretation of Declarative Languages*, Ellis Horwood, 1987.

[21]   Mycroft, A. *Abstract Interpretation and Optimizing Transformations for Applicative Programs*, PhD Thesis, Univ. of Edinburgh, 1981.

[22]   Snodgrass, R. *The Interface Description Language: Definition and Use*, Computer Science Press, 1989.

[23]   Thatte, SM. A modular and open object-oriented database system. *SIGMOD Record* 20(1):47-52, March 1991.

VVSL Specification of a Transaction-oriented Access Handler

C.A. Middelburg*

Dept. of Computer Science, PTT Research

Leidschendam, The Netherlands

Abstract

VVSL is a mathematically well-defined VDM-like specification language with features for (1) modular structuring and (2) specifying operations which interfere through a partially shared state. This paper gives an short overview of these features. Thereafter, the VVSL specification of an access handler interface given in [1] is outlined. The purpose is to clarify the extent to which the description of interfaces to software systems can be improved by the special features of VVSL. This issue is further discussed. The access handler interface concerned is a hypothetical interface which is meant to provide for a way of looking at transaction management.

1   Introduction

In [1], the author presents a definition of the syntax and semantics of VVSL, a language for modularly structured specifications which combines a VDM specification language and a language of temporal logic. VVSL (VIP VDM Specification Language) is a specification language designed in the ESPRIT project VIP (VDM for Interfaces of the PCTE) [2, 3]. That project was concerned with describing in a mathematically precise manner the interfaces of the PCTE (Portable Common Tool Environment) [4], using the notation offered by the software development method VDM (Vienna Development Method) [5] as far as possible.

Important differences between VVSL and the main VDM specification languages are:

1. operations which interfere through a partially shared state (hereafter called non-atomic operations) can be implicitly specified in a VDM-like style with the use of inter-conditions — which are formulae from a language of temporal logic — in addition to the usual pre- and post-conditions;

2. large state-based specifications can be modularly structured by means of modularization and parameterization mechanisms which permit two modules to have parts of their state in common, including hidden parts, and allow requirements to be put on the modules to which a parameterized module may be applied.

---

*Correspondence to C.A. Middelburg, PTT Research, Dr. Neher Laboratories, P.O. Box 421, 2260 AK Leidschendam, The Netherlands; e-mail: CA_Middelburg@pttrnl.nl.

The main examples of the use of VSSL are the formal specification of the PCTE interfaces in the project VIP [6, 7][1] and the formal specification of an air traffic control system by Praxis Systems plc (Bath, England). Some experiences with the formal specification of the PCTE interfaces are mentioned in [10]. In [1], VVSL has also been used to formalize many of the underlying concepts of relational database management systems and two abstract interfaces for such systems. Relational database management systems are sufficiently familiar to most people involved in the construction of software systems to allow them to concentrate on the formalizations rather than on the examples used for the formalizations. Both interfaces are complex enough to demonstrate the usefulness of the modularization and parameterization mechanisms provided by VVSL. Besides, the specification of the second interface illustrates the use of inter-conditions.

The second interface is a hypothetical internal interface of relational database management systems which handles concurrent access to stored relations by multiple transactions. Its specification in [1] can serve as a starting-point for further formalization in the areas of transaction management. An outline of that specification is given in this paper. It is meant to clarify the extent to which the description of interfaces to software systems can be improved by the mechanisms provided by VVSL for modular structuring and inter-conditions (in addition to pre- and postconditions) for specifying interference of operations. It is also meant to show how the special features of VVSL are used.

A short overview of modular structuring in VVSL and specifying interfering operations with inter-conditions is given in Sections 2 and 3. Section 4 summarizes in brief what is formalized, using VVSL, in [1] and describes the scope of the formalization of the access handler interface. The specification of this interface is outlined in Section 5. Its main module is treated in more detail in Section 6. In Section 7, the need for specifications like this one and the usefulness of the special features of VVSL are discussed.

2   Modular structuring in VVSL

In this section, a short overview of modular structuring in VVSL is given. VVSL can be considered to be a language for flat VDM specifications extended for non-atomic operations together with a language for modularization and parameterization that is put on top of it, both syntactically and semantically.

The modularization and parameterization constructs of VVSL are like those of COLD-K (Common Object-oriented Language of Design, K stands for Kernel) [11] and have the same semantic basis. Description Algebra, an algebraic model of specification modules introduced by Jonkers in [12], is used as the semantic foundation of the modularization constructs. $\lambda\pi$-calculus, a variant of classical lambda calculus introduced by Feijs in [13], is used as the semantic foundation of the parameterization constructs.

[1] VVSL has been improved in the course of the work on the formal specification of the PCTE interfaces based on the feedback by the specifiers about their actual needs. This led to various preliminary versions of VVSL. They were also developed by the author. It is worth mentioning that the preliminary version of VVSL described by the author in [8] and the language described under the name EVDM by Oliver in [9] are the very same.

2.1 Features for modular structuring

In VVSL, modules can be adapted and combined by means of *renaming*, *importing*, and *exporting*. The basic modularization concepts of decomposition and information hiding are supported by importing and exporting, respectively. Renaming provides for control of name clashes in the composition of modules. The usual flat VDM specifications are used as the basic building blocks. Like any module, they are essentially interpreted as presentations of logical theories. For these flat VDM specifications, the models of the logical theory coincide with the models according to the original interpretation. Modules can also be parameterized over modules, by means of *abstraction*, and these parameterized modules can be instantiated for given modules, by means of *application*. The concept of reusability is primarily supported by abstraction and application.

VVSL is a language for model-oriented, state-based specification. Effective separation of concerns often motivates the hiding of state variables from a module (access to state variables is permitted only via exported operations), in particular where a suitable modular structuring of the specification requires that the same state variables are accessed from several modules. For the adequacy of a modularization mechanism for the modular structuring of specifications of many existing software systems, it is indispensable that it permits two or more modules to have hidden state variables in common. The modularization mechanism provided by VVSL permits such common hidden state variables.

Defining types in a VDM-like style introduces subtype relationships with accompanying implicit conversions. If a type is defined as a subtype of another type, then the introduced subtype relationship is pragmatically a relationship between an "abstract data type" and its "representation". A modularization mechanism that does not hide such representations is not very useful. The modularization mechanism provided by VVSL hides representations.

For the adequacy of a parameterization mechanism for practical applications, it is highly desirable that it makes it possible to put requirements on the modules to which a parameterized module may be applied. The parameterization mechanism provided by VVSL allows such requirements to be put.

The modularization and parameterization constructs of VVSL are:

module $\mathcal{D}$ end: The basic module construct. Its visible names are the names introduced by the definitions $\mathcal{D}$. Its formulae represent the properties characterizing the types, state variables, functions and operations which may be associated with these names according to the definitions. If this construct occurs as an importing module, then the visible names from the imported module, that are used but not introduced in it, are treated as if they are introduced.

rename R in M: The renaming construct has the same meaning as the module M, except that the names have been changed according to the renaming R.

import M_1 into M_2: The import construct combines the two modules M_1 and M_2. Its visible names are the visible names of both modules. The formulae representing the properties characterizing what is denoted by these names (as well as hidden ones, if present) are also combined.

export S **from** M: The export construct restricts the visible names of module M to those which are also in the signature S, leaving all other names hidden. The formulae remain the same.

abstract $m_1: M_1, \ldots, m_n: M_n$ **of** M: The abstraction construct parameterizes the module M. Usually, the module names $m_1, \ldots, m_n$ occur in M. The visible names and formulae of the abstraction module depend upon what these module names stand for. That is, $m_1, \ldots, m_n$ act as formal parameters. What the actual parameters may be is restricted by the parameter restriction modules $M_1, \ldots, M_n$. The visible names of the actual parameter corresponding to m_i must include the visible names of the parameter restriction module M_i. Likewise the properties represented by its formulae must include those represented by the formulae of M_i.

apply M **to** $M_1, \ldots, M_n$: The application construct instantiates the parameterized module M. The modules $M_1, \ldots, M_n$ act as actual parameters. This means that the meaning of the application module is the meaning of M when its formal parameters stand for $M_1, \ldots, M_n$. If some actual parameter does not satisfy the parameter restriction associated with the corresponding formal parameter, then the meaning is undefined.

The definitions of the basic module construct may be free. A free definition is a definition in which the keyword free occurs following its header. A free definition introduces a free name and a non-free definition introduces a defined name. A free name is a name which is supposed to be defined elsewhere. This means that, in case of a free name, the body of the definition (empty if a type name or a state variable name) must be considered to describe assumptions about the function or operation denoted by the name.

In case of name clashes, the union of the formulae of the imported module and the importing module of the import construct may lead to undesirable changes in the properties represented by the formulae. Therefore, a restriction applies to visible names. Visible names are allowed to clash, provided that the name can always be traced back to at most one non-free definition. Name clashes of hidden names can be regarded as being avoided by automatic renamings, in case the name can be traced back to more than one non-free definition. Otherwise they are not avoided. This makes it possible for two modules to have hidden state variables in common.

For another presentation of modular structuring in VVSL, see [14]. That paper gives an overview of the structuring sublanguage of VVSL and a concise description of its semantic foundations. It also presents a variation on a "challenge problem" of Fitzgerald and Jones [15] as an example of the use of VVSL's structuring sublanguage.

2.2 Example of modular structuring in VVSL

In this subsection, the formalization of the underlying concepts of relational database systems given in [1] is outlined. The outline of the formalization comprises a skeleton of its modular structure and a very brief informal explanation of the modelling in each module. The skeleton has been obtained from the specification by replacing the collection of definitions in each basic module construct and the signature in each export construct by "···".

In the definitions concerned, relation names, attributes, and values are regarded as primitive concepts about which a few assumptions have to be made. The modules **RELATION_NM**, **ATTRIBUTE** and **VALUE** contain the assumptions concerned. Relation names and attributes have no a priori properties. For values, it is assumed that any finite set of values constitutes a domain.

Finite sets of attributes, one-to-one maps between these attribute sets, etc. are repeatedly used (e.g. as arguments of functions on tuples, relations, tuple structures and so on). The supplementary type and function definitions, which are closely connected, are collected in one module, viz. **ATTR_SUPPL**.

In the module **TUPLE**, tuples are defined as maps from attributes to values. Tuple predicates are defined as maps from tuples to truth values. A tuple predicate is used to select tuples from some relation.

In the module **RELATION**, relations are defined as sets of tuples. All tuples from a relation must have the same attributes (i.e. they must have the same domain).

In the module **DATABASE**, databases are defined as maps from relation names to relations.

In the module **TUPLE_STRUCTURE**, tuple structures are defined as maps from attributes to domains. A tuple structure is used to present structural constraints on all tuples from some relation.

In the module **RELATION_SCHEMA**, relation schemas are defined as composite values with a tuple structure and a set, whereof the elements are called keys, as components. A relation schema is used to present intra-relational constraints on some named relation. Each key presents a uniqueness constraint on the relation concerned.

In the module **DATABASE_SCHEMA**, database schemas are defined as composite values with a map from relation names to relation schemas and a set, whereof the elements are called inclusions, as components. A database schema is used to present intra-relational constraints on the named relations of some database as well as inter-relational constraints on the database. Each inclusion presents a referential constraint between two named relations in the database concerned.

RELATION_NM is
   module ··· end
and

ATTRIBUTE is
   module ··· end
and

VALUE is
   module ··· end
and

ATTR_SUPPL is
   abstract X: **ATTRIBUTE** of
   import X into
   module ··· end
and

TUPLE is
  abstract **X: ATTRIBUTE, Y: VALUE** of
  import apply **ATTR_SUPPL** to **X** , **Y** into
  module $\cdots$ end
and

RELATION is
  abstract **X: ATTRIBUTE, Y: VALUE** of
  import apply **TUPLE** to **X, Y** into
  module $\cdots$ end
and

DATABASE is
  abstract **X: RELATION_NM, Y: ATTRIBUTE, Z: VALUE** of
  import **X** , apply **RELATION** to **Y, Z** into
  module $\cdots$ end
and

TUPLE_STRUCTURE is
  abstract **X: ATTRIBUTE, Y: VALUE** of
  import apply **ATTR_SUPPL** to **X** , **Y** into
  module $\cdots$ end
and

RELATION_SCHEMA is
  abstract **X: ATTRIBUTE, Y: VALUE** of
  import
    apply **RELATION** to **X, Y** , apply **TUPLE_STRUCTURE** to **X, Y**
  into
  module $\cdots$ end
and

DATABASE_SCHEMA is
  abstract **X: RELATION_NM, Y: ATTRIBUTE, Z: VALUE** of
  import
    apply **DATABASE** to **X, Y, Z** , apply **RELATION_SCHEMA** to **Y, Z**
  into
  module $\cdots$ end

The definitions in the basic modules that occur as importing modules, are in terms of concepts defined in the imported modules concerned. For example, relations and functions on relations are defined in terms of tuples and functions on tuples. So **TUPLE** is imported into the basic module concerned.

The export construct is not used. This means that everything is visible — nothing is hidden. The reason is that none of the concepts defined in the above modules is regarded as an auxiliary concept.

3   Specifying interfering operations in VVSL

In this section, a short overview of specifying interfering operations with inter-conditions is given. VVSL can be considered to be an extension of a VDM specification language wherein operations which interfere through a partially shared state, can be specified while maintaining the VDM style of specification where possible. This is mainly accomplished by adding an inter-condition to the body of the usual operation definition — which consists of an external clause, a pre-condition, and a post-condition.

The inter-condition is a formula from a temporal language. This language has been inspired by a temporal logic from Lichtenstein, Pnueli and Zuck that includes operators referring to the past [16], a temporal logic from Moszkowski that includes the "chop" operator [17], a temporal logic from Barringer and Kuiper that includes "transition propositions" [18] and a temporal logic from Fisher with models in which "finite stuttering" cannot be recognized [19]. The operators referring to the past, the chop operator and the transition propositions obviate the need to introduce auxiliary state variables acting as history variables, control variables and scheduling variables, respectively.

3.1 Specifying interference with inter-conditions

An operation is implicitly specified by an operation definition. The definition consists of a header and a body. The header introduces a name for the specified operation and defines the types of its arguments and results. The header also introduces names for the argument values and result values to be used within the body. The body consists an external clause, a pre-condition, a post-condition, and an inter-condition. The *external clause* indicates which state variables are of concern to the behaviour of the operation and also indicates which of those state variables may be modified by the operation. The *pre-condition* defines the inputs (combinations of initial state and argument values) for which the operation possibly terminates (see below). The *post-condition* defines the possible outputs (combinations of final state and result values) from each of these inputs. The *inter-condition* defines the possible computations of the operation from each of these inputs.

These computations represent the successions of state changes that can be generated by the operation concerned working interleaved with an interfering environment, distinguishing between state changes effected by the operation itself and state changes effected by its interfering environment. The state changes of the former kind are called *internal steps*, those of the latter kind are called *external steps*.

The pre-condition of an operation only defines the inputs for which the operation possibly terminates, i.e. for which its possible computations include finite ones. This allows that the operation only terminates due to certain interference of concurrently executed operations. Moreover, the post-condition of an operation will be rather weak in case of sensitivity to interference, for inputs must often be related to many outputs which should only occur due to certain interference of concurrently executed operations. The inter-condition is mainly used to describe which interference is required for termination and/or the occurrence of such outputs.

The inter-condition is a formula from the temporal language outlined in the next subsection. It can be used to express that the operation is atomic — computations of atomic operations have at most one internal step and no external steps. However, this may also be indicated by leaving out the inter-condition. This means that atomic operations can be implicitly specified as in other VDM specification languages. Besides, for atomic operations, the new interpretation is equivalent to the original VDM interpretation.

The operation definition

$$op(x_1 : T_1, \ldots, x_i : T_i)\, x_{i+1} : T_{i+1}, \ldots, x_n : T_n$$
$$\text{ext rd } v_1 : T'_1, \ldots, \text{rd } v_j : T'_j, \text{wr } v_{j+1} : T'_{j+1}, \ldots, \text{wr } v_m : T'_m$$
$$\text{pre } E_{pre}$$
$$\text{post } E_{post}$$
$$\text{inter } \varphi_{inter}$$

introduces the name op for an operation from argument types $T_1, \ldots, T_i$ to result types $T_{i+1}, \ldots, T_n$. It defines op as an operation such that, for all values $x_1, \ldots, x_n$ belonging to types $T_1, \ldots, T_n$, respectively:

1. if c is a computation of the operation op for arguments $x_1, \ldots, x_i$ that yields results $x_{i+1}, \ldots, x_n$, then no step of c leaves all of the state variables $v_1, \ldots, v_m$ unmodified (unless this will last forever), but internal steps leave state variables other than $v_{j+1}, \ldots, v_m$ unmodified;

2. if evaluation of the logical expression E_{pre} yields true in some state s, then the operation op has a terminating computation with initial state s for arguments $x_1, \ldots, x_i$;

3. if evaluation of the logical expression E_{pre} yields true in some state s, c is a terminating computation with initial state s of the operation op for arguments $x_1, \ldots, x_i$ that yields results $x_{i+1}, \ldots, x_n$, and t is the final state of computation c, then evaluation of the logical expression E_{post} yields true in the states $\langle s, t \rangle$;

4. if evaluation of the logical expression E_{pre} yields true in some state s and c is a computation with initial state s of the operation op for arguments $x_1, \ldots, x_i$ that yields results $x_{i+1}, \ldots, x_n$, then evaluation of the temporal formula φ_{inter} yields true at the first position in computation c.

An example will be given following the next subsection.

For another presentation of the specification of interfering operations based on inter-conditions, see [20]. That paper explains the role of inter-conditions in the specification of interfering operations. It also deals with the formal aspects of combining a VDM specification language with a temporal language.

3.2 The temporal language

The evaluation of a temporal formula yields *true*, *false* or *neither-true-nor-false*. The meaning of the logical connectives and quantifiers is as in LPF [21]. They distinguish between false and neither-true-nor-false. The temporal operators identify false and neither-true-nor-false. So the three-valuedness can be safely ignored when only the temporal operators are considered. The meaning of the temporal operators is explained by the following informal evaluation rules:

is-I: Evaluation yields true if there is an internal step from the current position in the computation.

is-E: Evaluation yields true if there is an external step from the current position in the computation.

$\varphi_1; \varphi_2$: Evaluation yields true if it is possible to divide the computation at some future position into two subcomputations such that evaluation of φ_1 yields true at the current position in the first subcomputation and the evaluation of φ_2 yields true at the first position in the second subcomputation, or the computation is infinite and evaluation of φ_1 yields true at the current position in the computation.

$\bigcirc \varphi$: Evaluation yields true if there is a next position in the computation and evaluation of the temporal formula φ yields true at that position.

$\varphi_1\ \mathcal{U}\ \varphi_2$: Evaluation yields true if evaluation of the temporal formula φ_2 yields true at the current or some future position in the computation and evaluation of the temporal formula φ_1 yields true at all positions until that one.

$\ominus \varphi$: Evaluation yields true if there is a previous position in the computation and evaluation of the temporal formula φ yields true at that position.

$\varphi_1\ \mathcal{S}\ \varphi_2$: Evaluation yields true if evaluation of the temporal formula φ_2 yields true at the current or some past position in the computation and evaluation of the temporal formula φ_1 yields true at all positions since that one.

$\bigcirc \tau$: Evaluation yields the value that is yielded by evaluation of the temporal term τ at the next position in the computation. In case there is no next position, evaluation is undefined.

$\ominus \tau$: Evaluation yields the value that is yielded by evaluation of the temporal term τ at the previous position in the computation. In case there is no previous position, evaluation is undefined.

The notations $\Diamond \varphi$ (meaning "eventually φ"), $\Box \varphi$ (meaning "henceforth φ") and their counterparts for the past can be defined as abbreviations:

$$\Diamond \varphi := \textbf{true}\ \mathcal{U}\ \varphi, \qquad\qquad \diamondsuit \varphi := \textbf{true}\ \mathcal{S}\ \varphi,$$
$$\Box \varphi := \neg(\Diamond \neg\varphi), \qquad\qquad \boxdot \varphi := \neg(\diamondsuit \neg\varphi).$$

3.3 Example of specification with inter-condition

The use of inter-conditions for specifying interference is illustrated below, using an interruptable "wait-and-lock" command as an example.

The state variable *locked* is used to indicate which objects are currently locked. The state variable *signal* is used for interruption of commands. In the external clause is expressed that the state variables *locked* and *signal* are relevant for the behaviour of *WLOCK*, but that it can only change *locked*. In the pre-condition is expressed that *WLOCK(obj)* should possibly terminate for any initial state (i.e. it should terminate in at least one environment). In the post-condition is expressed that, if it terminates, finally *obj* is locked or *signal* is up. In the inter-condition is expressed that one of the following occurs:

- Eventually it will lock *obj* at a point in time that *obj* is not locked and it will terminate immediately thereafter. Until then all steps have to be external.

- It will terminate at a point in time that *signal* is up. Until then all steps have to be external.

$WLOCK(obj: Object)$
   ext rd $signal$: **B** ,
      wr $locked$: $Object\text{-}set$
   pre true
   post $obj \in locked \vee signal$
   inter is-E $\mathcal{U}$ ($obj \notin locked \wedge$ is-I $\wedge \bigcirc(obj \in locked \wedge \neg \bigcirc$ true)) $\vee$
      is-E $\mathcal{U}$ ($signal \wedge \neg \bigcirc$ true)

Note that the inter-condition excludes non-termination of $WLOCK(obj)$: it normally waits until the object to be locked is not locked, but it will be interrupted if it would otherwise be waiting forever.

4   Interfaces for database management systems

This section is an introduction to the outline of the VVSL specification of an access handler interface given in Sections 5 and 6. A brief summery of what is formalized, using VVSL, in [1] is given and the scope of the formalization of the access handler interface is described.

4.1   Formalizations in VVSL

In [1], the author presents VVSL specifications of two interfaces for relational database management systems (RDBMS's).

One interface comprises commands for data manipulation and data definition according to the concepts of the relational data model (RDM). It should be regarded as an external interface: the commands are made available directly to the users of the RDBMS. It is abstract in the sense that it does not deal with details of actual interfaces like concrete syntax of commands, their embedding in a host language, concrete representation of the data objects yielded by query commands, etc.

Its specification covers many of the basic RDM concepts, including the ones which are considered fundamental in [22]. The modular structure of the specification isolates the formalization of the RDM concepts from the formalization of the external RDBMS interface. This means that large parts of the specification can be re-used in specifications of other possible external RDBMS interfaces and even various internal RDBMS interfaces.

In formalizing the RDM concepts, relations are viewed as sets of maps. Originally, relations were viewed as sets of sequences [23]. The consequences of choosing one view over the other are illustrated in [24]. In the set-of-maps view of a relation, its tuples are maps from attributes to values (all with the same domain). Restriction to a finite universe of values for the attributes of tuples allows extensive use of maps in formalizing RDM concepts.

The other interface comprises commands for handling concurrent access to stored relations by multiple transactions. This interface should be regarded as an internal interface: the commands are not made available directly to the users of the RDBMS. In any existing RDBMS, the execution of the high-level data manipulation commands of its external interface (either by interpretation or via compilation) gives rise to the issue of lower-level access handling commands of an internal interface which is comparable to the specified internal interface.

Its specification covers concepts associated with concurrency control for databases and in-progress transaction backup. It does not cover the concepts that are needed for solving concurrency control and transaction backup problems (e.g. locking protocols and log protocols are not formalized). However, it can serve as a starting-point for further formalization in this area.

The specified external interface does not deal with concurrency at all. This is in accordance with the view that it should appear to any user of the RDBMS as if each command is executed in isolation. The specified internal interface deals with concurrency. The Access Handler (AH), which supports this internal interface, allows that access handling commands issued on behalf of various data manipulation commands are executed in an interleaved way. Moreover, according to the specification, it provides for an interleaving by which it appears as if each of the data manipulation commands is executed in isolation. Thus, the AH can be used for a correct implementation of the RDBMS with concurrent execution of data manipulation commands in a multi-user environment.

4.2   Scope of the formalization of an AH interface

The formalization of an access handler interface in [1] deals with a hypothetical internal interface of an RDBMS. This hypothetical interface is meant to provide for a way of looking at transaction management. It may be regarded as an idealization of comparable internal interfaces of existing RDBMS's, but naturally it reflects the taste and biases of the author.

The formalization covers concepts associated with the following facets of transaction management in database systems: concurrency control for databases [25, 26] and in-progress transaction backup [27, 28]. Some formalized concepts are precisely defined instances of concepts, which are widely used in this area but which are usually only vaguely described. Even nameless concepts described by expressions like "the dynamic syntactic information about the transactions issuing access requests" had to be formalized. Other formalized concepts are generalizations of concepts, which are mostly used in theoretical work on transaction management but which are often not pertinent for practice. For example, many concepts are based on assumptions that preclude dynamic creation of transactions. However, in existing systems, AH interfaces provide for dynamic transaction creation. Some formalized concepts are abstractions of concepts which are used in this area, since the original concepts were too concrete to underlie the intended interface. The points made in this paragraph are relevant to the discussion in Section 7.1.

Concerning concurrency control, the view has been taken that the AH interface should completely hide the mechanism used for scheduling of the access requests issued on behalf of various transactions. For example, the AH interface should not include commands for locking. A main reason for this choice is that it leads to an interface which reflects the essential characteristics of concurrency control for databases instead of the details of a particular mechanism supporting it. Such an interface seems more suitable to provide for a way of looking at transaction management. Another reason for this choice is that it gives rise to an interface which, as far as concurrency control is concerned, can be defined in terms of a small collection of underlying concepts that are relatively simple and general.

One usually distinguishes two purposes of transaction-oriented database recovery: in-progress transaction backup and crash recovery (see e.g. [27]). In-progress transaction backup is wanted to be able to undo the updates of the database made by a particular transaction in the event that the transaction cannot complete due to an error which allows its abortion in a controlled manner. Crash recovery is wanted to be able to undo the updates made by any transaction that was incomplete at the time of a crash — an error which does not allow its abortion in a controlled manner — and to redo the updates made by any completed transaction whose effects were lost due to the crash. A choice has been made not to take crash recovery into account. A useful treatment of crash recovery would require a multitude of low-level concepts to be formalized.

An access handler for access to a relational database may handle access to either single tuples of stored relations, subsets of stored relations or entire stored relations. For the formalization of an abstract AH interface a choice from these "units of access" has been made in favour of subsets of stored relations. The main reason for this choice is that access to subsets of stored relations is a generalization of the other cases. Moreover, the distinction between access to single tuples and access to subsets of stored relations is blurred in comparable internal interfaces of existing RDBMS's by the provision of "scans" (also called cursors; see e.g. [27]).

The above-mentioned choices highly determine the scope of the formalization. For example, concepts underlying particular concurrency control mechanisms and concepts underlying crash recovery are not covered. Besides, this formalization builds on the formalization of RDM concepts. It means that the definitions are couched in terms of the RDM. This restricts the scope of the formalization slightly.

5 Specification of the AH interface

In this section, the specification of the AH interface given in [1] is outlined. The ideas, which are elaborated in that specification, were mainly developed by abstraction and combination of many useful ideas that have been developed in the area of transaction management. Concerning concurrency control, the latter ideas are usually associated with particular (kinds of) concurrency control mechanisms. Amongst the ideas that have been most influential are the ideas of "two-phase" locking and "predicate locks" which are introduced in [25], the ideas of "strict" and "superstrict" concurrency control which are introduced in [29], and the idea of "optimal schedulers" (for availabe information) which is introduced in [26]. Influential ideas with respect to transaction backup are mainly the ideas described in [27].

The specification is modularly structured. The modules concerning concepts of the relational data model, concurrency control and transaction backup only contain definitions of types and functions. The modules concerning access handling only contain definitions of state variables and operations; except the definition of the type *Status* which is used to return an indication of success or failure by most operations. The part of the specification concerning concepts of the RDM is outlined in Section 2.2. Outlines of the other parts are given following the overview of the AH interface in the next subsection.

5.1 Overview of the AH interface

The formalized abstract interface comprises commands for starting and stopping a transaction, commands for accessing a subset of one of the stored relations to read it or to overwrite it, and commands for creating and destroying stored relations. The main constituents of the commands are simple propositional formulae for stating properties of tuples.

Most of the commands which constitute this interface can be regarded as requests on behalf of some transaction to perform an action on a subset of a stored relation. In this section, this view is implicit in the introduction of the concepts concerned. Transactions are introduced as the units of consistency. It is assumed that each action which is performed on behalf of a transaction may violate database consistency, but that each transaction, when executed alone, preserves database consistency. The AH, which supports the specified interface, provides for interleaved performance of actions requested by several transactions in such a manner that each transaction sees a consistent database and produces a consistent database. In this case, it is said that the requests are granted in a consistency preserving order. The AH does so on the ground of the above-mentioned assumption; it does not know what the consistency requirements are.

When a transaction issues a request, it is never made to wait forever for the grant of the request. Deadlock is one possible reason why a transaction might wait forever. The AH will reject an issued request immediately, if the request would cause deadlock. Other reasons, e.g. livelock, are prevented from occurring by the way of granting requests. If a request is rejected, then the transaction concerned usually has to stop after undoing all changes made to the database so far. The AH also provides for this rollback of transactions.

5.2 Outline of the specification: concurrency control

In the definitions concerned, value constants and transaction names are regarded as primitive concepts about which a few assumptions have to be made. The modules **VALUE_CONSTANT** and **TRANSACTION_NM** contain the assumptions concerned.

In the module **SIMPLE_FORMULA**, simple formulae are defined. They can be viewed as expressions denoting tuple predicates. Their well-formedness and evaluation are also defined.

In the module **ACCESS**, accesses are defined in terms of relation names and simple formulae. They can be viewed as abstractions of requests to perform a read action or a write action on a subset of some stored relation. An access is used to present syntactic properties of an access request issued by some transaction. It contains all the details of the request that can be used to grant this request amongst requests issued by other transactions in a consistency preserving order. One access is in conflict with another one if the effects of the requested actions possibly interfere according to their syntactic properties. This concept is also formalized.

In the module **ACCESS_TABLE**, access tables are defined in terms of transaction names and accesses. They can be viewed as abstractions of states of a collection of transactions whose actions are performed in an interleaved fashion. An access table is used to present, for each active transaction, the syntactic properties of its previously granted requests and its currently waiting request (only when it is currently waiting). It contains all the details of the active transactions that can be used to grant their waiting and coming requests in a consistency preserving order. For a given transaction, an access is in conflict with an access table if the effect of the requested action possibly interferes with the effect of one of the actions that were previously requested by another active transaction. A conflicting request is not granted immediately. Either it becomes a waiting request which eventually will be granted or it is rejected. The latter will happen when it would otherwise be waiting for itself indirectly. In that case the access is called liable for deadlock. The concepts of being in conflict and being liable for deadlock are also formalized.

```
VALUE_CONSTANT is
  abstract X: VALUE of
  import X into
  module ··· end
and

TRANSACTION_NM is
  module ··· end
and

SIMPLE_FORMULA is
  abstract X: ATTRIBUTE, Y: VALUE, Z: VALUE_CONSTANT of
  export ··· from
  import
    apply TUPLE to X, Y ,
    apply TUPLE_STRUCTURE to X, Y ,
    apply Z to Y
  into
  module ··· end
and

ACCESS is
  abstract
    X: RELATION_NM,
    Y: ATTRIBUTE,
    Z: VALUE,
    U: VALUE_CONSTANT
  of
  import
    apply RELATION to Y, Z ,
    apply DATABASE_SCHEMA to X, Y, Z ,
    apply SIMPLE_FORMULA to Y, Z, U
  into
  module ··· end
and
```

ACCESS_TABLE is
  abstract
    X: RELATION_NM,
    Y: ATTRIBUTE,
    Z: VALUE,
    U: VALUE_CONSTANT,
    V: TRANSACTION_NM
  of
  import apply **ACCESS** to X, Y, Z, U , V into
  module ··· end

5.3 Outline of the specification: transaction backup

In the module **TRANSITION_RECORD**, transition records are defined. A transition record reflects the effect of a write action on some stored relation.

In the module **TRANSITION_LOG**, transition logs are defined in terms of transition records. They can be viewed as histories of changes to stored relations.

In the module **LOG_TABLE**, log tables are defined in terms of transaction names and transition logs. They can be viewed as collections of transaction histories corresponding to collections of transactions whose actions are performed in an interleaved fashion. A log table is used to record the effects of all write actions on stored relations which have been performed on request of active transactions, in the order in which they have taken place and aggregated by transaction. The log table provides all the details that are required to abort any of the active transactions. Such abortion of transactions, called rollback, is also defined.

TRANSITION_RECORD is
  abstract X: RELATION_NM, Y: ATTRIBUTE, Z: VALUE of
  import apply **RELATION** to Y, Z , apply **DATABASE** to X, Y, Z into
  module ··· end
and

TRANSITION_LOG is
  abstract X: RELATION_NM, Y: ATTRIBUTE, Z: VALUE of
  import apply **TRANSITION_RECORD** to X, Y, Z into
  module ··· end
and

LOG_TABLE is
  abstract
    X: RELATION_NM,
    Y: ATTRIBUTE,
    Z: VALUE,
    U: TRANSACTION_NM
  of
  import apply **TRANSITION_LOG** to X, Y, Z , U into
  module ··· end

5.4 Outline of the specification: access handling

In the module **AH_STATE**, a varying database, a varying database schema, a varying access table and a varying log table are defined as state variables. They can be viewed as taking at any point in time the current database value, the current database schema value, the current access table value and the current log table value, respectively. Together, they constitute the changing state of the access handler.

In the module **ACCESS_HANDLING**, the commands which constitute the AH interface are defined as operations. The definition of these commands is rather straightforward but far from concise. A large part is related to the characterization of all possible ways in which they may be scheduled.

In the system module, the relevant definitions from the previous modules are combined and it is specified what from the defined concepts constitutes the abstract AH interface by making only the names of these concepts visible.

> **AH_STATE** is
>   abstract
>   X: RELATION_NM,
>   Y: ATTRIBUTE,
>   Z: VALUE,
>   U: VALUE_CONSTANT,
>   V: TRANSACTION_NM
>   of
>   export ⋯ from
>   import
>   apply **DATABASE** to X, Y, Z ,
>   apply **DATABASE_SCHEMA** to X, Y, Z ,
>   apply **ACCESS_TABLE** to X, Y, Z, U, V ,
>   apply **LOG_TABLE** to X, Y, Z, V
>   into
>   module ⋯ end
> and
>
> **ACCESS_HANDLING** is
>   abstract
>   X: RELATION_NM,
>   Y: ATTRIBUTE,
>   Z: VALUE,
>   U: VALUE_CONSTANT,
>   V: TRANSACTION_NM
>   of
>   export ⋯ from

```
import
  apply DATABASE to X, Y, Z ,
  apply DATABASE_SCHEMA to X, Y, Z ,
  apply ACCESS_TABLE to X, Y, Z, U, V ,
  apply LOG_TABLE to X, Y, Z, V ,
  apply SIMPLE_FORMULA to Y, Z, U ,
  apply AH_STATE to X, Y, Z, U, V
into
  module · · · end
and
system is
  abstract
    X: RELATION_NM,
    Y: ATTRIBUTE,
    Z: VALUE,
    U: VALUE_CONSTANT,
    V: TRANSACTION_NM
  of
  export · · · from
  import
    apply SIMPLE_FORMULA to Y, Z, U ,
    apply ACCESS_HANDLING to X, Y, Z, U, V
  into
  module end
```

6 Details of the access handling module

In this section, one of the modules from the specification outlined in the previous section, viz. the module **ACCESS_HANDLING**, is treated in more detail. A detailed skeleton of the module is presented and explained; there are only the bodies of the operation definitions missing. Furthermore, one of the operation definitions is presented and explained.

6.1 Detailed outline of the module ACCESS_HANDLING

In the module **ACCESS_HANDLING** a command for *starting* a transaction, commands for stopping a transaction by *commitment* and *abortion*, and commands for accessing a subset of one of the stored relations (for reading or overwriting it) by *selection*, *insertion*, *deletion* and *replacement*, and commands for *creating* and *destroying* stored relations, are formalized with operations. Together they constitute the AH interface of a database management system.

The module **ACCESS_HANDLING** is based on assumptions with respect to relation names, attributes, values, value constants and transaction names and on definitions regarding databases, database schemas, access tables, log tables, simple formulae and states of the access handler.

The collection of access handling operations defined in this module, reflects roughly what is offered in the AH's of existing RDBMS's. Only these access handling operations are exported. The idea is that consulting or modifying the state variables should only be done by means of the operations made available by the access handler.

ACCESS_HANDLING is
   abstract
     X: **RELATION_NM**,
     Y: **ATTRIBUTE**,
     Z: **VALUE**,
     U: **VALUE_CONSTANT**,
     V: **TRANSACTION_NM**
   of
   export
     $START: \Rightarrow Transaction\_nm$,
     $COMMIT: Transaction\_nm \Rightarrow$,
     $ABORT: Transaction\_nm \Rightarrow$,
     $SELECT$:
       $Transaction\_nm \times Relation\_nm \times Simple\_formula \Rightarrow Relation \times Status$,
     $INSERT: Transaction\_nm \times Relation\_nm \times Simple\_formula \Rightarrow Status$,
     $DELETE: Transaction\_nm \times Relation\_nm \times Simple\_formula \Rightarrow Status$,
     $REPLACE$:
       $Transaction\_nm \times Relation\_nm \times Simple\_formula \times Simple\_formula \Rightarrow$
       $Status$,
     $CREATE: Transaction\_nm \times Relation\_nm \Rightarrow Status$,
     $DESTROY: Transaction\_nm \times Relation\_nm \Rightarrow Status$
   from
   import
     apply **DATABASE** to X, Y, Z ,
     apply **DATABASE_SCHEMA** to X, Y, Z ,
     apply **ACCESS_TABLE** to X, Y, Z, U, V ,
     apply **LOG_TABLE** to X, Y, Z, V ,
     apply **SIMPLE_FORMULA** to Y, Z, U ,
     apply **AH_STATE** to X, Y, Z, U, V
   into
   module
     types
       $Status = \{GRANTED, REJECTED\}$
     operations
       $START()tnm: Transaction\_nm$
         $\ldots$

       $COMMIT(tnm: Transaction\_nm)$
         $\ldots$

       $ABORT(tnm: Transaction\_nm)$
         $\ldots$

       $SELECT(tnm: Transaction\_nm, rnm: Relation\_nm, sf: Simple\_formula)$
               $r: Relation, st: Status$
         $\ldots$

$$INSERT(tnm: Transaction\_nm, rnm: Relation\_nm, sf: Simple\_formula)$$
$$st: Status$$

...

$$DELETE(tnm: Transaction\_nm, rnm: Relation\_nm, sf: Simple\_formula)$$
$$st: Status$$

...

$$REPLACE(tnm: Transaction\_nm, rnm: Relation\_nm,$$
$$sf_1: Simple\_formula, sf_2: Simple\_formula)st: Status$$

...

$$CREATE(tnm: Transaction\_nm, rnm: Relation\_nm)st: Status$$

...

$$DESTROY(tnm: Transaction\_nm, rnm: Relation\_nm)st: Status$$

...

end

6.2 Specification of the operation *SELECT*

A command for accessing a subset of one of the stored relations for reading it, is formalized with the non-atomic operation *SELECT*.

The operation will normally produce a relation and a status as results and it will normally change the state. Only the current access table may be modified by this operation, but the current database and the current database schema are also relevant for the behaviour of *SELECT*. *SELECT*(tnm, rnm, sf) should possibly terminate for a transaction name tnm that is in use according to the current access table, a relation name rnm that is in use according to the current database, and a simple formula sf that is well-formed with respect to the structure of the rnm relation schema from the current database schema. Finally, if it terminates and yields GRANTED as status, then it must yield as relation the selection of the rnm relation from the current database filtered through the predicate denoted by sf. It yields GRANTED as status iff the appropriate access is granted to tnm according to the current access table. *SELECT* is a non-atomic operation. During execution, one of the following occurs:

1   a. Eventually the read access requested by tnm will not conflict with the granted and waiting accesses of other transactions according to the current access table, the next state is the final state and is reached by an internal step which changes the current access table by adding the requested access to the granted accesses of tnm. In this case, granted will be the status.

   b. Until then all steps were external, except the initial step which only changes (if it is not also the final step) the current access table by adding the requested access to the waiting accesses of tnm.

2. Initially the read access requested by tnm is liable for deadlock according to the current access table and the initial state is also the final state (i.e. nothing is changed). In this case, rejected will be the status.

So *SELECT* waits until the requested access does not conflict with granted and waiting accesses of other transactions or rejects it immediately. A requested access is rejected if it would otherwise be waiting for itself indirectly.

In the inter-condition given for *SELECT*, the first disjunct corresponds to 1 and the second disjunct corresponds to 2. In the first disjunct, the second argument of the temporal operator $\mathcal{U}$ corresponds to 1a and the first one corresponds to 1b.

$SELECT(tnm: Transaction\_nm, rnm: Relation\_nm, sf: Simple\_formula)$
$\qquad\qquad r: Relation, st: Status$
$\quad$ ext rd $curr\_dbschema: Database\_schema$,
$\qquad$ rd $curr\_database: Database$,
$\qquad$ wr $curr\_acctable: Access\_table$
$\quad$ pre $in\text{-}use(curr\_acctable, tnm) \wedge in\_use(curr\_database, rnm) \wedge$
$\qquad is\_wf(sf, structure(curr\_dbschema, rnm))$
$\quad$ post let $acc: Access \triangleq mk\text{-}Access(READ, rnm, sf)$ and
$\qquad\qquad r'': Relation \triangleq relation(curr\_database, rnm)$ and
$\qquad\qquad tp: Tuple\_predicate \triangleq predicate(sf, structure(curr\_dbschema, rnm))$ in
$\qquad (st = GRANTED \Rightarrow r = selection(r'', tp)) \wedge$
$\qquad (st = GRANTED \Leftrightarrow granted(tnm, acc, curr\_acctable))$
$\quad$ inter let $acc: Access \triangleq mk\text{-}Access(READ, rnm, sf)$ in
$\qquad ((\neg\ominus true \Rightarrow$
$\qquad\quad \text{is-I} \wedge \bigcirc(curr\_acctable = add\_to\_waits(\ominus curr\_acctable, tnm, acc))) \wedge$
$\qquad\quad (\ominus true \Rightarrow \text{is-E})) \, \mathcal{U}$
$\qquad\qquad (\neg conflicts(tnm, acc, curr\_acctable, curr\_dbschema) \wedge \text{is-I} \wedge$
$\qquad\qquad\quad \bigcirc(curr\_acctable = add\_to\_grants(\ominus curr\_acctable, tnm, acc) \wedge$
$\qquad\qquad\qquad st = GRANTED \wedge \neg\bigcirc true)) \vee$
$\qquad\quad (deadlock\_liable(tnm, acc, curr\_acctable, curr\_dbschema) \wedge$
$\qquad\quad st = REJECTED \wedge \neg\bigcirc true)$

One of the design objectives for the temporal sublanguage of VVSL was the objective to obviate the need to introduce auxiliary state variables acting as history variables, control variables or scheduling variables. The state variable *curr_acctable* appears to be an auxiliary one acting as history variable, but cannot be dispensed with. This is not a weakness of the temporal language. The necessity of such a state variable has its origin in the fact that the low-level commands which constitute the AH interface support concurrent execution of several higher-level commands, i.e. transactions, in a consistency preserving way (see Section 5.1). This brings about that the history relevant to an individual low-level command execution goes beyond its starting state.

7 Discussion

In this section, it is argued that there is a need for specifications like the one outlined in this paper. The usefulness of modular structuring of specifications and specifying interference is also discussed.

208

7.1 Formal specifications of hypothetical interfaces for database systems

First of all, VVSL is a language for writing formal specifications, that is mathematically precise specifications. First some salient aspects of formal specifications concerning development of software systems are dwelled upon. A mathematically precise specification of what is required of a software system that is to be developed provides a reference point against which the correctness of the ultimate software system can be established, and not forgetting, guided by which it can be constructed. This is regarded as the most important aspect of software specification by most theoreticians and practitioners. For the time being, (professional) practitioners will mainly establish correctness by precise informal arguments, whereas theoreticians are usually exploring formal proofs of correctness. It should not be overlooked that a precise specification also makes it possible to analyze a software system before its development is undertaken. This opens up a way to increase the confidence that the specified system conforms to the requirements for it. For the actual practice of software engineering, all this means that a precise specification is the right starting-point for the development of a satisfactory software system.

In the author's opinion, this carries over to theoretical development of solutions for idealizations of common problems in software systems of a certain kind — such as locking protocols for concurrency control problems in database systems. Here, a formal specification of the idealization of such a problem provides a reference point against which the correctness of the proposed solutions can be established and the confidence in the pertinence of the idealization to the actual problems can be increased. The usual absence of such specifications in the area of transaction management in database systems — as well as in many other areas — is reflected by the difficulties to relate the different solutions to seemingly the same problem. A specification like the one outlined in this paper was already needed before the early work concerning locking protocols for solving database concurrency control problems and log protocols for solving transaction backup problems (such as the work presented in [25, 30, 27]) was carried out. Actually, the outlined specification was largely acquired by seeking the unmentioned assumptions about the problem(s) to be solved in the presentations of that work (which are often informal too, as briefly described in Section 4.2).

7.2 Modular structuring of specifications

In [15], Fitzgerald and Jones emphasize one aspect of modular structuring of specifications: the ability to develop theories about separate modules. This emphasis originates partly from the issue of formal proofs to establish the correctness of design steps, but also from the issue of module reusability. In order to clarify the concepts described in a module, a theory about the module is very useful. This means that in general the potential reusability of a module is enhanced by the availability of an accompanying theory. However, there are more aspects of modular structuring of specifications.

The roles of a mathematically precise specification, which are mentioned in the previous subsection, give rise to an aspect of modular structuring of specifications which is the primary one in practice: the potentialities to aid comprehension of specifications. The comprehensibility of a whole specification partly depends on the comprehensibility of its separate modules. Enhancing comprehensibility of a module does not always imply reducing the complexity of a theory about the module (and vice versa). Should the case arise, reducing complexity in the above sense should be weighted against the desirability to aid comprehension. It may be important to take into account whether or not the reusability of the separate modules is actually considered to be an intended side-effect of the development of the specified system. Of course, there are still other aspects of modular structuring of specifications which are in practice more important than the ability to develop theories about separate modules, e.g. the possibility to control changes in specifications.

It is difficult to assess whether a different modularization could make the specification outlined in this paper more comprehensible. In any case, it is clear that the chosen modularization aids a global understanding. In the outlined specification, the formalization of the RDM concepts from the specification of an external RDBMS interface (mentioned in Section 4) is re-used. The modular structure of that specification isolates the formalization of the RDM concepts. Each of the modules that constitute the formalization of the RDM concepts describes concepts of great generality and wide applicability (see also Section 2.2). Moreover, it must be relatively easy to develop theories about most of the modules concerned (but it has not been done yet).

7.3 Specifying interference

What matters to the users (persons, programs or whatever) of a software system are the commands that the system can execute and the observable effects of their execution. A software system may provide for concurrent execution of multiple commands in a multi-user environment or it may not. If the system provides for concurrent execution, then it may arise that some of its commands are intentionally made sensitive to interference by concurrently executed commands. The execution of such a command terminates in a state and/or yields a result that depends on intermediate state changes effected by the concurrent execution of other commands. Its execution may even be suspended to wait for an appropriate state change. It is also possible that certain intermediate external state changes causes non-termination. Most commands of the outlined access handler interface are of this kind and so are some commands of the PCTE interfaces [6, 7].

If a command that is sensitive to interference is specified by means of a pre- and post-condition only, then it is not described which interference is required for the occurrence of many final states and/or yielded results. For example, the specification of *SELECT* (given in Section 6) without the inter-condition permits that nothing happens but the return of the status REJECTED (unless the requested access was previously granted to the transaction concerned). Rely- and guarantee-condition pairs, as proposed by Jones in [31] for specifying interference, can be regarded as as abbreviations of simple inter-conditions. Their main limitation is the inadequacy in case synchronization with concurrently executed commands is required. Synchronization is required for most commands of the access handler interface (including *SELECT*). Stølen adds in [32] a wait-condition to the rely- and guarantee-condition pairs to make it possible to deal with synchronization. It appears that this recent addition permits that the access handler commands are adequately specified, but it is certain that auxiliary state variables must be employed. Because internal steps and external steps can only be related via the auxiliary state variables, the specifications concerned will fail to mirror the intuition behind the commands.

Specifying interference with inter-conditions can be done close to the way it is naturally discussed. Moreover, anything that can be specified with rely-, guarantee- and wait-conditions (with or without auxiliary state variables) can also be specified with inter-conditions. It is argued in [32] that it is less intricate to reason about shared-state interference with rely-, guarantee- and wait-conditions. The examples show that the intricacy is still present, but it has been shoved away by relying on the judicious use of auxiliary state variables.

Acknowledgements

This paper simplifies material from my Ph.D. thesis [1]. It is a pleasure to be able to acknowledge here the help that I have received from Jan Bergstra and Cliff Jones, my supervisors, with the creation of the thesis. Furthermore, I wish to thank both referees for their suggestions which have contributed to improvements of the presentation of this paper.

References

[1] C.A. Middelburg. *Syntax and Semantics of VVSL — A Language for Structured VDM Specifications.* PhD thesis, University of Amsterdam, September 1990. Available from PTT Research, Dr. Neher Laboratories.

[2] C.A. Middelburg. The VIP VDM specification language. In R. Bloomfield, L. Marshall, and R. Jones, editors, *VDM '88*, pages 187–201. Springer Verlag, LNCS 328, September 1988.

[3] C.A. Middelburg. VVSL: A language for structured VDM specifications. *Formal Aspects of Computing*, 1(1):115–135, 1989.

[4] ESPRIT. *PCTE Functional Specifications*, 4th edition, June 1986.

[5] C.B. Jones. *Systematic Software Development Using VDM*. Prentice-Hall, second edition, 1990.

[6] VIP Project Team. Kernel interface: Final specification. Report VIP.T.E.8.2, VIP, December 1988. Available from PTT Research.

[7] VIP Project Team. Man machine interface: Final specification. Report VIP.T.E.8.3, VIP, December 1988. Available from PTT Research.

[8] VIP Project Team. VDM extensions: Initial report. Report VIP.T.E.4.1, VIP, December 1987.

[9] H.E. Oliver. *Formal Specification Methods for Reusable Software Components*. PhD thesis, University College of Wales, Aberystwyth, 1988.

[10] C.A. Middelburg. Experiences with combining formalisms in VVSL. In J.A. Bergstra and L.M.G. Feijs, editors, *Algebraic Methods II: Theory, Tools and Applications*, pages 83–103. Springer Verlag, LNCS 490, 1991.

[11] H.B.M. Jonkers. An introduction to COLD-K. In M. Wirsing and J.A. Bergstra, editors, *Algebraic Methods: Theory, Tools and Applications*, pages 139–205. Springer Verlag, LNCS 394, 1989.

[12] H.B.M. Jonkers. Description algebra. In M. Wirsing and J.A. Bergstra, editors, *Algebraic Methods: Theory, Tools and Applications*, pages 283–305. Springer Verlag, LNCS 394, 1989.

[13] L.M.G. Feijs. The calculus $\lambda\pi$. In M. Wirsing and J.A. Bergstra, editors, *Algebraic Methods: Theory, Tools and Applications*, pages 307–328. Springer Verlag, LNCS 394, 1989.

[14] C.A. Middelburg. Modular structuring of VDM specifications in VVSL. Pub. 288/91, PTT Research, March 1991. To appear in Formal Aspects of Computing, 4(1), 1992.

[15] J.S. Fitzgerald and C.B. Jones. Modularizing the formal description of a database system. In D. Bjørner, C.A.R. Hoare, and H. Langmaack, editors, *VDM '90*, pages 189–210. Springer Verlag, LNCS 428, 1990.

[16] O. Lichtenstein, A. Pnueli, and L. Zuck. The glory of the past. In R. Parikh, editor, *Proceedings Logics of Programs 1985*, pages 196–218. Springer Verlag, LNCS 193, 1985.

[17] R. Hale and B. Moskowski. Parallel programming in temporal logic. In J.W. de Bakker, A.J. Nijman, and P.C. Treleaven, editors, *Proceedings PARLE, Volume II*, pages 277–296. Springer Verlag, LNCS 259, 1987.

[18] H. Barringer and R. Kuiper. Hierarchical development of concurrent systems in a temporal logic framework. In S.D. Brookes, A.W. Roscoe, and G. Winskel, editors, *Seminar on Concurrency*, pages 35–61. Springer Verlag, LNCS 197, 1985.

[19] M.D. Fisher. Temporal logics for abstract semantics. Technical Report UMCS-87-12-4, University of Manchester, Department of Computer Science, 1987.

[20] C.A. Middelburg. Specification of interfering programs based on inter-conditions. Pub. 166/91, PTT Research, March 1991.

[21] H. Barringer, H. Cheng, and C.B. Jones. A logic covering undefinedness in program proofs. *Acta Informatica*, 21:251–269, 1984.

[22] M.L. Brodie and J.W. Schmidt. *Final Report of the ANSI/X3/SPARC DBS-SG Relational Database Task Group*. Doc. No. SPARC-81-690, 1981.

[23] E.F. Codd. A relational model for large shared data banks. *Communications of the ACM*, 13(6):377–387, 1970.

[24] D. Bjørner. Formalization of data models. In D. Bjørner and C.B. Jones, editors, *Formal Specification and Software Development*, chapter 12. Prentice-Hall, 1982.

[25] K.P. Eswaran, J.N. Gray, R.A. Lorie, and I.L. Traiger. The notion of consistency and predicate locks in a database system. *Communications of the ACM*, 19(11):624–633, 1976.

[26] H.T. Kung and C.H. Papadimitriou. An optimality theory of concurrency control for databases. *Acta Informatica*, 19:1–11, 1983.

[27] J.N. Gray. Notes on database operating systems. In R. Bayer, R.M. Graham, and G. Seegmüller, editors, *Operating Systems: An Advanced Course*, pages 393–481. Springer-Verlag, LNCS 60, 1978.

[28] T. Haerder and A. Reuter. Principles of transaction-oriented database recovery. *ACM Computing Surveys*, 15(4):287–317, 1983.

[29] D.J. Rosenkrantz, R.E. Stearns, and P.M. Lewis II. System level concurrency control for distributed database systems. *ACM Transactions on Database Systems*, 3(2):178–198, 1978.

[30] J.N. Gray, R.A. Lorie, G.R. Putzolu, and I.L. Traiger. Granularity of locks and degrees of consistency in a shared data base. In G.M. Nijssen, editor, *Modelling in Data Base Management Systems*, pages 365–394. North Holland, 1976.

[31] C.B. Jones. Specification and design of (parallel) programs. In R.E.A. Mason, editor, *IFIP '83*, pages 321–332. North-Holland, 1983.

[32] K. Stølen. Development of parallel programs on shared data-structures. Technical Report UMCS-91-1-1, University of Manchester, Department of Computer Science, 1991.

A Specification of an Object-Oriented Data Model with Relations

Moira C. Norrie

Department of Computing Science,
University of Glasgow,
17 Lilybank Gardens, Glasgow G12 8QQ, Scotland, U.K.

Abstract

A system specification may consist of a formal specification along with an informal textual description. In this paper, we focus on an intermediate level of specification which is semi-formal and describes the overall structure of the system. Here we demonstrate the use of this intermediate level of specification by presenting a meta-circular description of the structural part of a data model and indicating how this may then be transformed into a formal specification in the Z language. This intermediate level of specification serves both as an important stage in the design process and also as a useful part of the documentation of the model. The data model, BROOM, combines features of the object-oriented, entity-relationship, semantic and relational data models.

1 Introduction

A complete specification of a data model will usually consist of an informal textual description along with a formal specification. The informal textual description will provide an overview of the model and identify its main features. The formal specification should be a complete and precise definition of the semantics and is the basis for the implementation of the model. Somewhere between these two forms of specification is the semi-formal specification: it is a description of the overall structure of the model and may possibly be presented using a graphical notation. We classify it as semi-formal since it may be incomplete; for example, it may be the case that not all constraints can be expressed in the graphical notation. Further, the semi-formal specification may describe only some aspects of the model, e.g. structure rather than behaviour, and would be accompanied by some explanatory text.

Here, we want to emphasise this intermediate level of specification. In particular, we employ a meta-circular description [1] of the data model for this purpose. By a meta-circular description we mean that we describe the data model in terms of itself.

Those familiar with data modelling will be aware of the benefits to be gained by a graphical description of the overall structure of an application domain. Such a graphical description is beneficial in terms of documentation as it provides the reader with an insight into the structure of the system and hence enables them to grasp the detailed specification more quickly. Further, it represents an important stage in the design process in providing an abstract overview of the system which will then be refined into a detailed formal specification. Thus, it provides an initial structuring of the specification.

214

This is could be likened to the use of entity-relationship models in database design [2]. The entity-relationship model identifies the entities of interest in the application domain - and the relationships between these entities. The resulting entity-relationship schema may then be transformed into an equivalent relational database schema which may undergo transformations into a form suitable for implementation. The entity-relationship model plays an important role in establishing a structure of the relational schema which is then enhanced with implementation and operational details. Further, the entity-relationship model of the application will be an important part of the system documentation.

Similarly, we believe that data modelling concepts may play an important role in providing an intermediate, semi-formal specification of any application system and thereby determining the initial structure of a formal specification of that system. In particular, we discuss in this paper the use of a description of a data model in terms of itself as an intermediate level of specification. This meta-circular description is an extremely valuable part of the documentation of the model and provides a basis for the structuring of the formal specification. It is also a useful test of the modelling capabilities of the data model.

Further, the meta-circular description can be used to develop a database system which supports a uniform treatment of metadata and data. Thus, browsers and query processors can be used to retrieve both schema information and data.

The data model we have used in this context is an object-oriented model into which the notion of relations has been introduced to provide support for the direct representation of relationships between entities. It turns out that these relations provide an important basis for the initial structuring of the formal specification in the language Z [4]. This data model, BROOM (Binary Relational Object Oriented Model), was developed within the Comandos project.

Comandos [5] is an Esprit project concerned with the construction and management of distributed open systems. The data management services of the Comandos system is provided through a library of generic collection types which support the BROOM model [6].

Here, we present a specification of the structural part of the BROOM model in three sections with each section corresponding to a level of the specification. Thus, section 2 discusses the philosophy of the model design and gives an informal description of the general features of the model. Section 3 presents the meta-circular definition of the model in which BROOM is described in terms of itself. Section 4 indicates how the meta-circular description of section 3 could be transformed into a formal specification of the BROOM model in the language Z. Some concluding remarks are given in section 5.

2 An Overview of the BROOM Data Model

Four varieties of data model have gained wide popularity in recent years - the relational data model, the entity-relationship models, the semantic data models and object-oriented models.

The success of the relational model was due to its simplicity, uniformity and high-level query languages: these stemmed from its introduction of the single generic data collection type - the relation. The basis for its high-level query languages was an algebra of operations on these collections as opposed to the notion of operations on individual data records that had underpinned the network and hierarchical data models.

At the same time, the entity-relationship models were being adopted for the high-level data modelling of applications: originally they were proposed for database design and although some implementations ensued none of these were widely used. The semantic data models [7] might be considered as developments of the entity-relationship models that support classification structures based on ISA relationships between entity sets.

The recent trend has been towards object-oriented data models: the claim made is that, unlike the other three varieties, they can model both the dynamic and static properties of data and further that they also capture the high-level semantics of applications. Thus, they were considered by many as surpassing the relational, entity-relationship and semantic data model approaches. However, the lack of direct representation for relationships is now recognised as a major deficiency of object-oriented models. This can be seen to have a number of disadvantages as described by Rumbaugh in [8]. Since relationships between objects are represented by methods of these objects and therefore are effectively buried within objects, the overall structure of the application domain is not readily apparent. By decomposing relationships in this way, we cannot handle a relationship as a single logical unit. As Rumbaugh states: "it is not possible to separate the abstraction from the implementation with the same clarity as the relational model". Further, in the design of large systems, relationships have been shown to be a useful abstraction mechanism for partitioning systems into subsystems and we shall see later how these are used to structure the Z specification. Recently, there have been a number of proposals for some form of extension to object-oriented models to support relationships as first-class objects [6], [8], [9], [10], [11],[12] and [13].

Although there have been some proposals for an algebra which operates on collections of objects, e.g. [14], a number of systems seem to have lost the advances of the relational model in terms of high-level query processing by using single object at a time processing.

The BROOM data model combines the favourable features of these four varieties of model, i.e.

a) It is object-oriented with multiple kinds of collections such as sets, sequences and bags.

b) It has direct support for the representation of relationships.

c) It has rich classification structures.

d) It has a collection algebra.

In the BROOM model, objects are classified through membership of unary collections. A unary collection may be regarded as a grouping of object identifiers and may have the properties of a set, bag or sequence depending on whether it can have duplicates and maintains some specified ordering on its elements. The kind of a unary collection and the type of its members are specified in the type declaration associated with that collection. For example, given a collection type declaration of *PersonSet* as

type PersonSet = **set** [person]

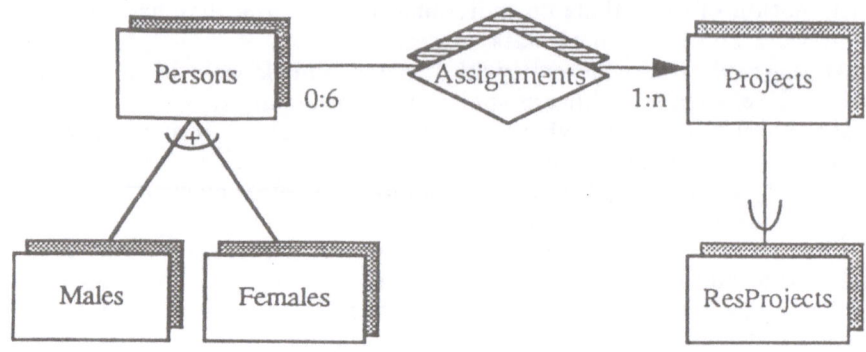

Figure 1: A BROOM Example

then for a collection *Persons* of type *PersonSet*, the members of *Persons* must be of type *person* and *Persons* will have the properties of a set i.e. unordered and no duplicates. Note that a collection type may have any number of instances.

Relationships between objects are represented by binary collections. A binary collection is a grouping of pairs of object identifiers. A binary collection will have associated target and source collections to which belong the first and second member of the pair, respectively. Just as unary collections may exhibit set, bag or sequence properties - so may binary collections. For example, given a collection type declaration of *AssignmentSeq* as

type AssignmentSeq = seq [person,project]

then an instance *Assignments* of type *AssignmentSeq* will be a binary collection with each member being a pair of object identifiers. Since the collection is declared to be of kind seq, the pairs will have an ordering imposed: this ordering will be based on order of insertion unless some other ordering is specified. Clearly, there must be some restrictions on the object identifiers that can appear in the member pairs of *Assignments*. The type declaration specifies that the first element of a pair must be of type *person* and that the second element be of type *project*. Further, any instance of a binary collection will represent relationships between the members of two specific collections. Thus, if a binary collection contains the pair (x, y) then x must belong to a specified source collection and y to a specified target collection. For example, if we let *Projects* be a unary set collection of *project* objects, then we might specify the source of *Assignments* to be *Persons* and the target to be *Projects*. This is represented diagrammatically in figure 1.

Unary collections are represented by a shaded rectangle and binary collections by a shaded rhombus. Different shadings are used to indicate whether a collection has set, sequence or bag properties. A "dot" shading indicates set properties: a "lined" shading indicates sequence properties and a "basketweave" shading indicates bag properties. (Note that none of the examples in this paper involve a collection with bag properties.)

Optionally, the type of the member elements of a collection may be written adjacent to the collection symbol.

The arcs connecting a binary collection to its source and target collections are labelled with cardinality constraints. A directed arc is used to indicate which collection is the target collection. The constraint '0:6' on the source *Persons* specifies that each member of *Persons* may be assigned to up to six members of *Projects*. The constraint '1:n' on the target *Projects* specifies that each member of *Projects* must be assigned to at least one member of *Persons* but there is no maximum number of assignments in which a member of *Projects* may be involved.

These cardinality constraints permit one to specify that a relation is functional, total, one-to-one etc. It is important to emphasise that specification does not correspond to implementation: thus, a binary collection which has cardinality constraints that specify it to be functional may have a different representation from one that is specified to be many-to-many.

The example in figure 1 also illustrates the forms of classification structures supported in the model. *Projects* has a subcollection *ResProjects* and *Persons* has two subcollections *Males* and *Females*. The '+' indicates that the two subcollections form a cover of *Persons* i.e. that each member of *Persons* must belong to at least one of the collections *Males* and *Females*. The '⌣' specifies that the two subcollections are disjoint i.e. no person object can be both a member of *Males* and a member of *Females*. If the members of a set of subcollections are mutually disjoint then we say that they form a partition of the parent collection: if they form a cover and a partition, then they form a strict partition of the parent collection. These classification structures can be applied to any collections: thus, it is possible for example to have a partition of a binary collection into a set of subcollections. In addition, a collection can have more than one classification structure associated with it. For example, *Persons* could have an additional strict partition into subcollections *Staff* and *Students*: these classification structures may be considered as providing alternative classification views of *Persons*.

In the above discussion, the unary collections represent groupings of objects and the elements of a unary collection are object identifiers. In fact, unary collections can have any kind of values as members (according to the type declaration) - where values may be object identifiers, records or base values such as integers. Correspondingly, the elements of a binary collection can be pairs of values of any kind.

It should be stressed that a binary collection is not equivalent to a unary collection of a record representation of pairs because of the inherent dependency constraints involving a binary collection and the two collections that it relates.

A further generalisation to note is that the source and target collections of a binary collection may be any collections: thus, it is possible to have a binary collection which relates a binary collection to a unary collection. These generalisations allow us to model n-ary relationships and also attributes of relationships.

Associated with the BROOM model there is an algebra of collections, AQL. The operations of the algebra may be considered as generalisations of the operations of the relational algebra to the kinds of collections supported in BROOM. There are also operations to support conversions between the various kinds of collections. Since this paper only deals with the structural part of BROOM, we give no further details of AQL here.

3   A Meta-Circular Description of BROOM

Once the general features of the BROOM model had been established, the task of producing a meta-circular description of the model was undertaken. This intermediate level of specification focussed on the structural part of the model. Before refining our notions of a collection algebra, it was necessary to establish clearly the forms of collections to be supported.

A collection is an object which represents a grouping of values and is itself a value. (Note that here we use the term "value" to refer to both objects and non-objects. Others have used the term "value" to refer to non-objects and here we refer to these as "base values".) In figure 2, we give a graphical BROOM description of the collection structures in BROOM.

A value may be either a pair with a value as first and second element - or an atomic value. An atomic value may be either an object or a base value such as an integer or a string: other base values such as Boolean values and indeed composite record values are possible but we have omitted them here for the sake of brevity.

Every collection is an object as indicated by the subcollection arc between *Objects* and *Collections*.

Collections has two classification views. On the one hand, we strictly partition *Collections* into *Sets*, *Sequences* and *Bags* while, on other hand, we strictly partition *Collections* into *UnaryCollections* and *BinaryCollections*. Thus, each collection has set, sequence or bag properties and is either unary or binary. This ability to support multiple classification views in BROOM is a very powerful and flexible modelling device - and it avoids the often complex structures with multiple "mixins" [15] that would be required to describe the same thing in other object-oriented models.

Each member of *BinaryCollections* is related to a target collection and a source collection.

The *Members* binary collection represents the relationship between a collection and its member values. Note that *Members* is specialised by a strict partition into *BinaryMembers* which relates *BinaryCollections* to *PairValues*, and, *UnaryCollections* which relates *UnaryCollections* to *AtomicValues*.

A value in BROOM is associated with one or more types. For example, an integer value is of type INTEGER. An object value which is an instance of type male will also be an instance of all supertypes of type male. All types in BROOM - including collection types - may have any number of instances. Thus, there is a many-to-many relationship between types and values.

We have not included a diagram of the BROOM description of BROOM types since essentially it has the same structures as that of figure 2. These two structures are related by the binary collection *Instances* as indicated in figure 3.

The *Instances* binary collection will be specialised over the structure to ensure that there is consistency between the form of a type and its value. For

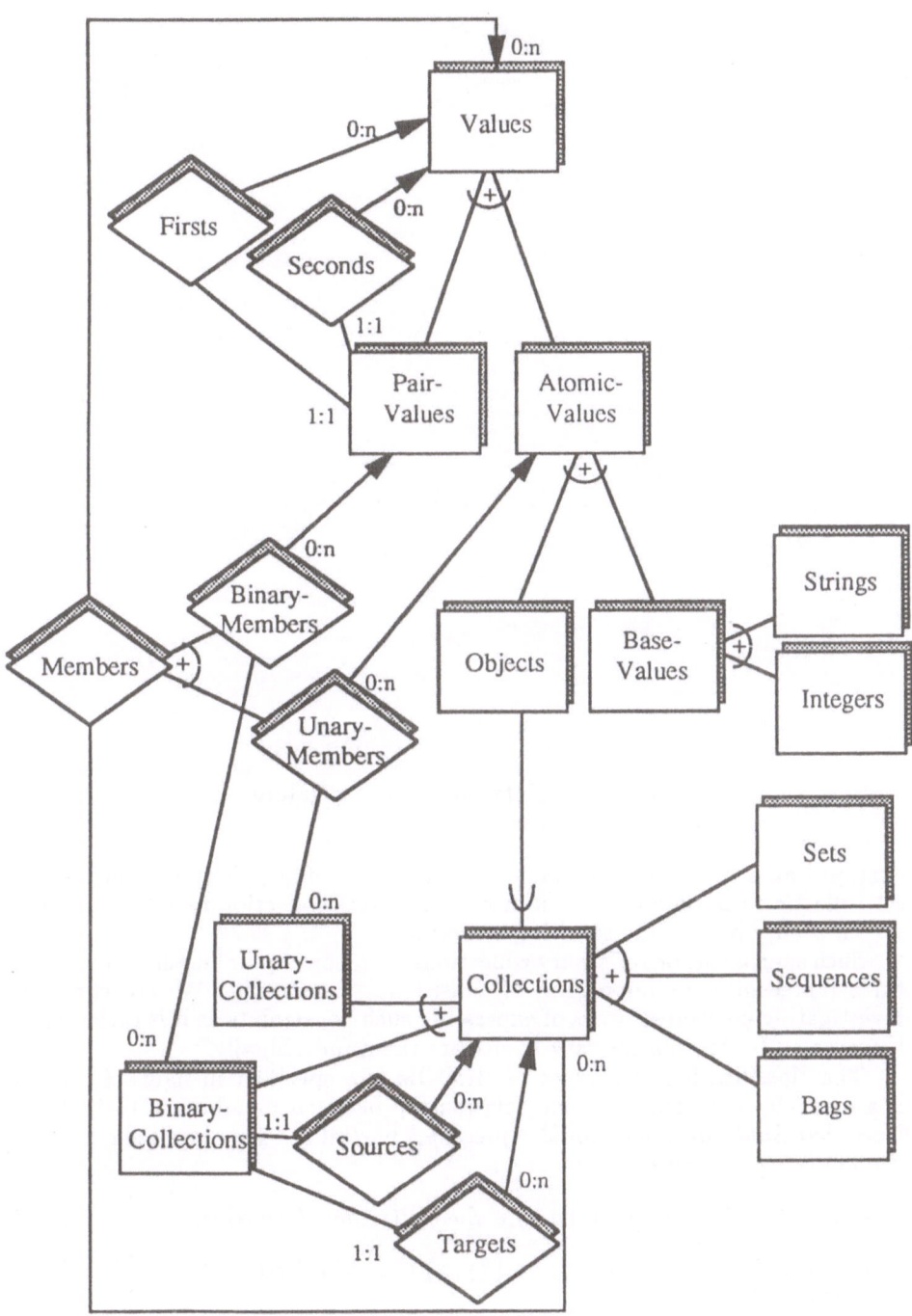

Figure 2: Value Structures in BROOM

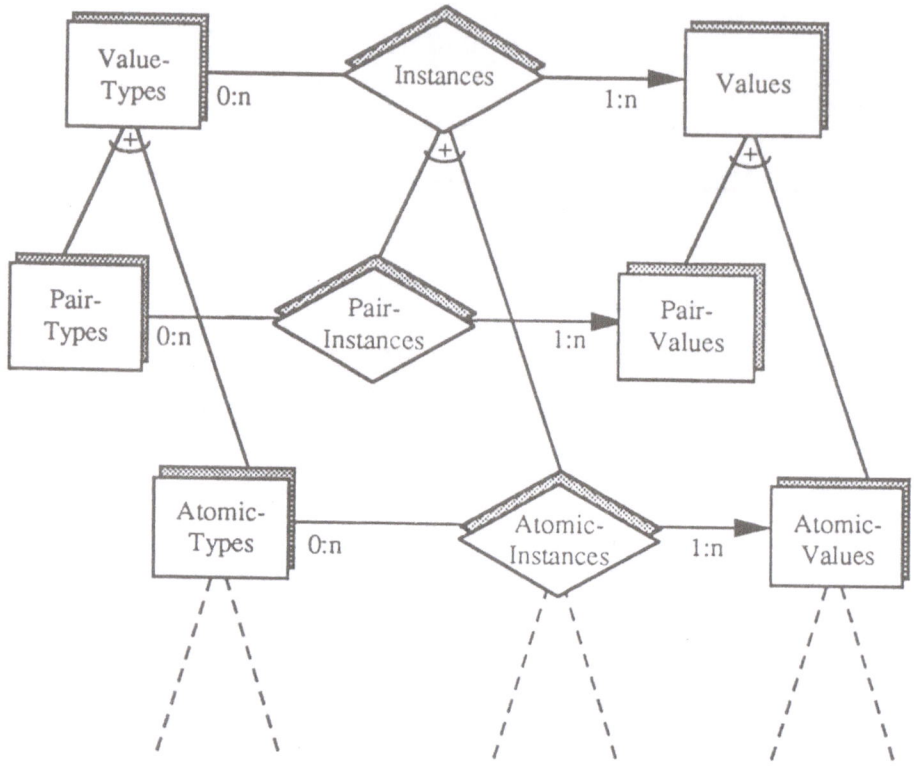

Figure 3: Relating Types to Values

example, an atomic value can only be an instance of atomic types and a unary
set collection can only be an instance of unary set collection types. In figure 3,
we show only part of the resulting structure.

Such specialisations of binary collections over isomorphic classification structures represent a common form of consistency constraint. We are currently
investigating convenient ways of expressing such constraints as it is rather cum-
bersome and often unnecessary to declare them individually.

The classification structures of BROOM are specified in figure 4. There
is a many-to-many subcollection relationship between members of *Collections*.
Note that *SubCollections* should represent a partial ordering i.e. it should have
the following properties

a) if $c \in$ *Collections* then $(c, c) \in$ *SubCollections* (reflexive)

b) if $(x, y) \in$ *SubCollections* and $(y, x) \in$ *SubCollections* then $x = y$ (antisymmetric)

c) if $(x, y) \in$ *SubCollections* and $(y, z) \in$ *SubCollections* then $(x, z) \in$ *Sub-
Collections* (transitive).

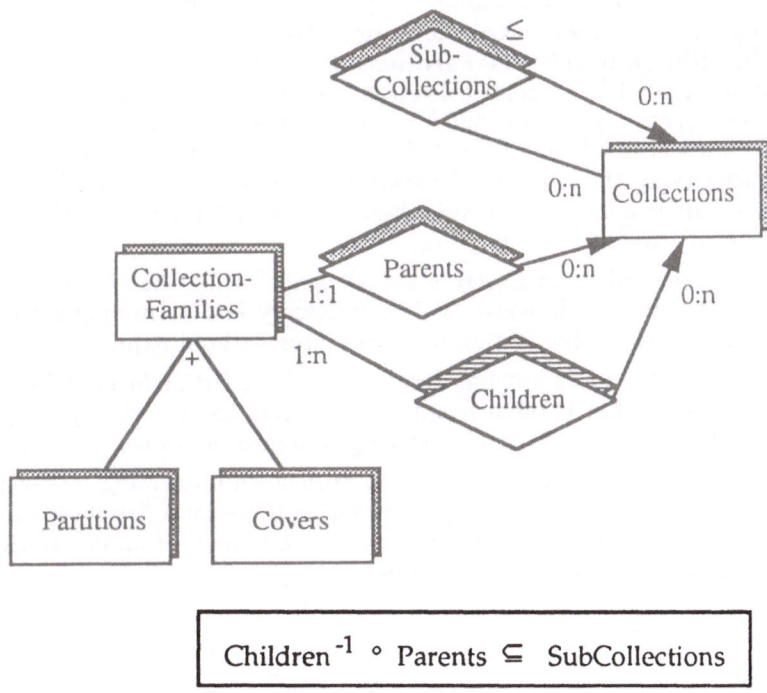

$$\text{Children}^{-1} \circ \text{Parents} \subseteq \text{SubCollections}$$

Figure 4: BROOM Classification Structures

Such properties of relations are important properties of homogeneous binary collections for which the source and target collections are not necessarily disjoint, i.e. the member types of the source and target collections have a common supertype. A homogeneous binary collection may be labelled with one of the following properties:

$=$	reflexive
$\neq$	irreflexive
$\equiv$	equivalence
$\leq$	partial order
$<$	total order
$<^+$	irreflexive transitive closure

The last of these specifies that a homogeneous binary collection is non-circular.

Interestingly, some of these properties can be considered as constraints to be checked when elements are inserted while others may be considered as a form of derived information. For example, if we state that a binary collection is reflexive, then there is no need to store entries such as (x, x) in the collection.

A member of *CollectionFamilies* represents a set of collections that forms a partition or cover of some other collection. Each member of *CollectionFamilies* must be either a member of *Partitions* or *Covers* - and possibly both. Each collection family has a parent collection and one or more child collections. The "children" form a partition and/or cover of the "parent" and therefore each "child" must be a subcollection of the "parent". We augment the diagram with a box specifying this additional constraint: the inverse of *Children* composed with *Parents* is contained in *Subcollections*. Note that a collection may be a "child" of many collection families.

The binary collection *Children* is a sequence rather than a set in order that the subcollections are indexed. This is necessary in determining corresponding subcollections in related isomorphic structures without explicit declaration.

Producing the meta-circular description of the BROOM model was an iterative process in that it often resulted in changes to our original proposals for the model. These changes tended to be generalisations of some of the concepts.

Such meta-circular descriptions also present an interesting test of the modelling capability of the model: it provides a fairly complex "application domain" and it is of course useful to test a model on a variety of applications and not just on the standard database examples.

4   Specification of BROOM in Z

In this section, we present general guidelines for the translation of a BROOM description into a Z specification. The description of value structures given in figure 2 will be used to illustrate the methodology.

First of all we have to provide a Z construct for each of the basic concepts of the BROOM model such as the forms of collections and structural constraints on collections. These concepts may be provided either as some basic construct of Z or as a generic constant. For example, for figure 2, the concepts of unary set, sequence and bag collections; binary set collections; partitions and covers; functionality constraints on binary collections and non-circularity constraints on homogeneous binary collections are all required. The unary set, sequence and bag collections, and, the binary set collections can be represented by the sets, sequences, bags and relations of the Z language, respectively. A binary set collection with a cardinality constraint that specifies the relation to be functional can be represented by the functions of Z. Generic constants can be used to specify partitions, covers and non-circular homogeneous binary collections.

A general library of generic constants for BROOM would be provided, but here we shall give only those required for figure 2.

Generic constants for the notions of disjointness and partitions with respect to sequences of sets are usually included as part of Z (as given in [4]). However, note that the usual Z partition corresponds to our strict partition in that it specifies that the sequence of sets must be not only disjoint but also a cover of the parent set. We therefore define our own generic constants for covers, partitions and strict partitions.

$$\begin{array}{|l}
\hline\!\!\!= [I, X]\!\!=\!\!=\!\!=\!\!=\!\!=\!\!=\!\!=\!\!=\\
\quad \text{\_covers\_}, \text{\_partitions\_}, \text{\_strictlypartitions\_} : (I \nrightarrow \mathbf{P}\,X) \leftrightarrow \mathbf{P}\,X\\
\hline
\quad \forall S : I \nrightarrow \mathbf{P}\,X;\; T : \mathbf{P}\,X \bullet\\
\quad (S \text{ covers } T \Leftrightarrow \bigcup\{n : \text{dom}\,S \bullet S\,n\} = T) \wedge\\
\quad (S \text{ partitions } T \Leftrightarrow \text{ disjoint } S \wedge \bigcup\{n : \text{dom}\,S \bullet S\,n\} \subseteq T) \wedge\\
\quad (S \text{ strictlypartitions } T \Leftrightarrow S \text{ covers } T \wedge S \text{ partitions } T)\\
\hline
\end{array}$$

In addition, we should define generic constants for the properties of homogeneous binary collections given in the previous section, i.e. reflexive, non-circular etc. As an example, we specify the set of all non-circular relations as follows:

$$\begin{array}{|l}
\hline\!\!\!= [X]\!\!=\!\!=\!\!=\!\!=\!\!=\!\!=\!\!=\\
\quad \text{noncircular} : \mathbf{P}(X \leftrightarrow X)\\
\hline
\quad \forall R : X \leftrightarrow X \bullet\\
\quad R \in \text{noncircular} \Leftrightarrow \neg\; \exists x : X \bullet (x, x) \in R^{+})\\
\hline
\end{array}$$

The general approach we adopt for transforming a BROOM description into a Z specification is to produce a Z specification for each classification structure and then combine these into a specification for the entire BROOM description. Generally, a classification structure is an acyclic directed graph that describes a collection and all its subcollections. We define a Z schema for each collection family in a classification structure and combine these into a schema for the whole classification structure.

Different classification structures describe fundamentally different sorts of entities. For example, one classification structure might describe various collections of person entities whereas another classification structure might describe various collections of project entities. If these two classification structures were associated by means of a binary collection *Assignments*, then a schema would be produced that included the schemas describing the classification structures for persons and projects and a specification of the *Assignments* relation.

Note that there are two forms of binary collections : some are homogenous in that they relate a collection either to itself or to one of its subcollections while others relate collections that belong to different classification structures. For example, *Sources* and *Targets* of figure 2 are homogeneous whereas *Instances* of figure 3 is not. The homogeneous binary collections are included as part of the schema of the classification structure of the source and target collections. Binary collections which are non-homogeneous link different classification structures and correspondingly we introduce a schema for a binary collection which incorporates the schemas for the classification structures of its source and target collections.

Hopefully, this general approach will become clear as we develop the Z specification for figure 2.

In figure 2 and the related discussion we gave no mention to the types of the collections involved. What, for example, is the type of the members of collection Objects? We equate an object with its object identifier and hence Objects would be a set of object identifiers. We therefore introduce a basic type definition OBJID which is the set of all object identifiers.

[OBJID]

Then we can define a schema for the Collection Family which classifies collections into the kinds set, sequence or bag.

```
┌─ COLLECTIONKINDS ─────────────────────────────────
│ Collections, Sets, Sequences, Bags : P OBJID
├───────────────────────────────────────────────────
│ ⟨Sets, Sequences, Bags⟩ strictlypartitions Collections
└───────────────────────────────────────────────────
```

We now introduce a schema COLLECTIONFORMS for the other classification of collections into one of the forms unary and binary.

```
┌─ COLLECTIONFORMS ─────────────────────────────────
│ Collections, UnaryCollections, BinaryCollections : P OBJID
│ Sources, Targets : OBJID → OBJID
├───────────────────────────────────────────────────
│ dom Sources = BinaryCollections
│ ran Sources = Collections
│ Sources ∈ noncircular[OBJID]
│ dom Targets = BinaryCollections
│ ran Targets = Collections
│ Targets ∈ noncircular[OBJID]
│ ⟨UnaryCollections, BinaryCollections⟩ strictlypartitions Collections
└───────────────────────────────────────────────────
```

Note that the binary collections *Sources* and *Targets* are declared to be total functions. In general, the cardinality constraints on binary collections can specify a relation to be a partial function, total function, surjection etc. and this will be captured in the associated schema.

These two schemas can be combined into a single schema for COLLECTIONS as follows:

$$COLLECTIONS \cong COLLECTIONKINDS \wedge COLLECTIONFORMS$$

If we were to work "up" the classification structure for values, we would next introduce a schema for OBJECTS as follows:

```
┌─ OBJECTS ─────────────────────────────────────────
│ COLLECTIONS
│ Objects : P OBJID
├───────────────────────────────────────────────────
│ Collections ⊆ Objects
└───────────────────────────────────────────────────
```

So far we have only dealt with collections that have the member type OBJID. The other type definitions that we require for the value specification are the set of all strings, STRING and the given set of all integers **Z**.

[*STRING*]

The remaining unary collections of figure 2 have members of different types. These can be strings, integers, object identifiers or pairs of values. All of these sets of values are disjoint and we introduce the following union types to correspond to the collections in figure 2.

$$BASEVALUE == STRING \cup \mathbb{Z}$$

$$ATOMICVALUE == BASEVALUE \cup OBJID$$

$$VALUE == ATOMICVALUE \cup VALUE \times VALUE$$

A schema for the *Values* collection can now be introduced. This schema incorporates the specification of the binary collection *Members*. The elements of *Members* are pairs of elements - the first an element of OBJID and the second an element of VALUE. *Members*, *BinaryMembers* and *UnaryMembers* are all introduced as homogenous relations on the set VALUE.

```
┌─ VALUES ──────────────────────────────────────────────
│ COLLECTIONS
│ Values : P VALUE
│ Members, UnaryMembers, BinaryMembers : VALUE ↔ VALUE
├───────────────────────────────────────────────────────
│ dom Members ⊆ Collections
│ ran Members ⊆ Values
│ Members ∈ noncircular[VALUE]
│ dom UnaryMembers ⊆ UnaryCollections
│ ran UnaryMembers ⊆ ATOMICVALUE
│ dom BinaryMembers ⊆ BinaryCollections
│ ran BinaryMembers ∩ ATOMICVALUE = ∅
│ ⟨UnaryMembers, BinaryMembers⟩ strictlypartitions Members
└───────────────────────────────────────────────────────
```

The predicate part restricts the domain of *Members* to be a value of type OBJID which belongs to the set *Collections*. The domains and ranges of the relations *UnaryMembers* and *BinaryMembers* are restricted to the appropriate sets of values.

Members is specified to be a non-circular relation on VALUE; this ensures that no collection is a member of itself.

Having specified the BROOM description of figure 2 in the schema VALUES, we could similarly specify the BROOM description of the type structure in a schema TYPES. The *Types* collection is a set of names and we introduce another base type definition NAME which is the set of all names.

$$[NAME]$$

Given the schemas VALUES and TYPES, we could then construct the schema INSTANCES which defines the *Instances* binary collection and includes VALUES and TYPES.

```
┌─ INSTANCES ────────────────────────────
│ VALUES
│ TYPES
│ Instances : NAME ↔ VALUE
├────────────────────────────────────────
│ dom Instances ⊆ Types
│ ran Instances ⊆ Values
└────────────────────────────────────────
```

The above discussion is intended to outline the general approach of transforming BROOM descriptions into Z schemas. One could make better use of generics to specify commonly occurring structures - whether these are structures of the BROOM model or isomorphic structures within a BROOM description.

Having determined the Z specification for the structural part of the BROOM model, the operations of the collection algebra could then be specified.

5 Conclusion

We have presented a meta-circular description of the BROOM data model which was used as an intermediate stage in the development of the model. Such a specification lies somewhere between an informal, textual description and a complete formal specification. The process of producing the meta-circular description was an important stage in the refinement and clarification of our ideas and in itself proved a useful test of the modelling capabilities of the model. The final stage of development was to transform the meta-circular description into a Z specification of the structural part of the model. Having completed this, the operational part of the model could be specified.

The production of the meta-circular description was also useful in providing documentation of the model. Further, it provides a direct path into an implementation of the model in terms of itself: this allows the uniform treatment of metadata and data.

As stated in the paper, we feel that the use of BROOM descriptions as an intermediate level of specification could be of more general use in producing formal specifications of systems. We are currently investigating its use in this respect.

Acknowledgements

This work is part of the ESPRIT Project 2071 Comandos (Construction and Management of Distributed Open Systems). Special thanks are due to David Harper who was also responsible for the design of the BROOM data model and made many useful comments on this paper. The other members of the Glasgow Comandos ODMS group were a source of many stimulating discussions on this work: they are Steve Blott, Jack Campin, Daniel Chan, David Kerr and Andrew Walker. In addition, I thank Roberto Barros for his comments on the paper.

References

[1] J. C. Reynolds, Definitional Interpreters for Higher-Order Programming Languages, In Proceedings of the ACM Conference, 1972.

[2] P. P. Chen, The entity-relationship model: Toward a unified view of data, ACM Transactions on Database Systems, Vol. 1, No. 1, pp 9-36, 1976.

[3] D. R. Howe, Data Analysis for Data Base Design, pub. Edward Arnold, 1983.

[4]   J. M. Spivey, The Z Notation, pub. Prentice Hall, 1989.

[5]   Comandos Consortium, The Comandos Guide, Esprit Project 2071, 1991.

[6]   D. J. Harper and M. C. Norrie, Data Management for Object-Oriented Systems, In Aspects of Databases, pub. Butterworth-Heinemann, 1991.

[7]   R. Hull and R. King, Semantic Data Modelling: Survey, Applications and Research Issues, ACM Computing Surveys, Vol. 19, No. 3, pp 201-260, 1987.

[8]   J. Rumbaugh, Relations as Semantic Constructs in an Object-Oriented Language, In Proceedings OOPSLA 1987, pp 466-481, 1987.

[9]   A. Albano, G. Ghelli and R. Orsini, A Relationship Mechanism for A Strongly Typed Object-Oriented Database Programming Language, to appear In Proceedings of VLDB 91, 1991.

[10] S. E. Bratsberg, FOOD: Supporting explicit relations in a Fully Object-Oriented Database, In Proceedings IFIP TC2 Conference on Object Oriented Databases, Windermere, U.K., 1990.

[11] O. Diaz and P. M. D. Gray, Semantic-rich User-defined Relationship as a Main Constructor in Object Oriented Databases, In Proceedings IFIP TC2 Conference on Object Oriented Databases, Windermere, U.K., 1990.

[12] T. Harder, K. Meyer-Wegener, B. Mitschang and A. Sikeler, PRIMA - a DBMS Prototype Supporting Engineering Applications, In Proceedings 13th VLDB Conference, Brighton, U.K., 1987.

[13] R. Nassif, Y. Qiu and J. Zhu, Extending the Object-Oriented Paradigm to Support Relationships and Constraints, In Proceedings IFIP TC2 Conference on Object Oriented Databases, Windermere, U.K., 1990.

[14] S. Cluet, C. Delobel, C. Lecluse and P. Richard, RELOOP, an algebra based query language for an object-oriented database system, Data and Knowledge Engineering, 5, pp 333-352, 1990.

[15] G. Booch, Object Oriented Design with Applications, pub. Benjamin/Cummings, 1991.

Specification of Database Applications in the TROLL Language*

Gunter Saake & Ralf Jungclaus

Abt. Datenbanken, Techn. Universität Braunschweig

Postfach 3329, 3300 Braunschweig, FRG

Abstract

In the area of large database applications, i.e. complex interactive software systems with persistently stored information, suitable formalisms for specification are almost not present. Traditionally, the description of a database application consists of two parts, the database schema and a more or less formal description of the application functions. We present an object-oriented approach to integrate both aspects. A formal model is described that models objects as processes that can be observed through attributes. Based on this model, the language TROLL is introduced. It is a logical language for the abstract object-oriented description of information systems. Finally, we propose mechanisms for defining external views and for queries that fit in the framework.

1 Introduction

The use of formal specification techniques is a way to reach higher reliability of software systems and is now commonly used especially for critical software parts. The area of large database applications, i.e. complex interactive software systems with persistently stored information, lacks, however, suitable formalisms for specification. Information analysis usually leads to different kinds of *knowledge* about the database application [1, 2]:

- Information structures for the static aspects,
- functions or activities for the dynamic aspects and
- assertions for possible states and behavior.

Following the established design approaches, the description of a database application consists of two, often uncorrelated, parts :

- The *database schema* describes merely the static aspects of structuring the database storage. The description is done in terms of a so-called data model like the relational one or semantic data models, which usually have a formal semantics for single database states but do not cover the dynamic evolution of the persistent information.

*This work was partially supported by CEC under ESPRIT BRA WG 3023 IS-CORE (Information Systems – COrrectness and REusability) and by Deutsche Forschungsgemeinschaft under grant no. Sa 465/1-1.

- *Application functions* cover the functional aspects of a database application and are described in a more or less formal way for example using specification mechanisms for software functions.

The problem is to integrate both description aspects because the database schema component usually lacks of a formal semantics for dynamic aspects. To have an integrated specification mechanism for database applications, we have to develop a method allowing to specify static aspects (i.e., the structure of database information) and the application dynamics both on an appropriate modelling level.

Some proposals for conceptual modeling languages allow the separate description of static and dynamic aspects in a uniform language (e.g. RML [3], Taxis [4] or TDL [5]). On a lower level of abstraction, database applications may be developed using *database programming languages* like DBPL [6] or Galileo [7].

A recent approach to solve the mismatch in the description of structure and behaviour is the *object-oriented paradigm* [8, 9]. Data and functions *local* to an object are integrated in object descriptions [10]. Thus, the relevant aspects of the database application are structured in objects. Objects integrate the structural and behavioral aspects of 'entities' into inseparable design units. An object has an encapsulated internal state which can be observed and manipulated solely through an object interface. Objects communicate with each other to provide the overall services of the system. Objects are classified, i.e. we have classes of objects that share the same characteristics. Objects and classes are embedded into a class hierarchy with inheritance, which may either be syntactical (i.e. code reuse) or semantical (i.e. components). For database applications, an important feature of object-oriented approaches is the composition of complex objects from objects. The composition has to preserve structure and behavior of the component objects.

We propose to use an *object-oriented specification language* for database applications. The basic idea is to regard the *Universe of Discourse* (UoD) of a database application as a *collection of interacting objects*. In such objects, the description of structure (by means of properties) and dynamics (by means of processes over abstract events) is encapsulated. Collections of objects are structured using specialization, generalization, aggregation, and classification. System dynamics are described by interactions between dynamic objects.

In this paper, we will introduce the specification language TROLL developed in the IS-CORE project. The language TROLL evolved from language features presented in [11] for the Oblog model for abstract objects. A preliminary version of this language was called **Oblog+** [12, 13]. For theoretical fundamentals of object-oriented specification approaches see [11, 14, 15, 16]. The language TROLL is presented in more detail in [17, 18].

2 Requirements for Specifying Database Applications

Database applications are complex software systems having some properties which make them difficult to handle using established specification mechanisms :

1. The central database of such an application consists of a lot of information carrying objects, which must be structured and classified using enhanced data modelling techniques. These objects are persistent, i.e. they survive application sessions. The notion of persistency is unfamiliar to most of the established software specification techniques concentrating merely on computation functions.

2. Database applications may be interactive, distributed and multi-user applications. Therefore, we need a process description facility as part of our formalism.

3. A database may be used by several applications and / or user groups having different views on the database schema. A mechanism for defining and handling of external views is a necessary feature for specifying database applications.

4. Set-oriented, descriptive data retrieval is state of the art for database management systems. It must be formalized, too, and integrated with the more oprational mechanisms of up-to-date database manipulation facilities.

These requirements make the formal specification of database applications a difficult task. To describe all aspects of a datbase application in a coherent framework, a variety of different specification formalisms is necessary, among them specification of abstract data types, temporal logics, process description techniques etc. [19]. In the following sections, we will discuss how these requirements can be satisfied using object-oriented specification techniques.

3   A Formal Model for Objects

We use a two-tired approach to define the formal semantics of object bases. The first layer defines the domains of *values* in the abstract data type sense, i.e. we do not regard values as objects but as values of a data type algebra. In our approach, objects are dynamic entities having a temporal existence interval which is not the case for values. The domains of values are specified as abstract data types using one of the established formalisms (OBJ, ACT ONE, CLEAR, etc.). These domains serve as codomains for object properties (attributes), as object identifiers and as parameter types for events.

The semantics of *objects* are *observable communicating processes*. An object is in a certain state at any moment in time. A state transition corresponds to an occurrence of an *event* (which is an abstraction of a method). A set of events may occur simultaneously, which is said to be a snapshot. A sequence of events starting from creating the object (*birth event*) and either ending with deleting the object (*death event*) or going on "forever" is called a *life cycle*. The possible behavior of an object thus is modeled by a set of admissible life cycles which is called a *process*. The object's state may be observed using *attributes* that represent relevant properties of an object. The values of the attributes (an *observation*) depend on the object's state which is fully determined by the object's history, i.e. it depends on the sequence of state transitions occurred so far. The history is a finite prefix of an admissible life cycle.

Let us now sketch the formalization of these characteristics. Let X be a set of events including at least one birth event. Let $\mathcal{L}_X$ be the set of all life cycles over X, i.e. those sequences of snapshots that start with a snapshot including at least one birth event and (in case they are finite) that end with a snapshot including at least one death event plus the empty sequence denoted by ϵ.

Definition 3.1 *A* PROCESS *P is a pair (X, Λ) where X is a set of events and $\Lambda \subseteq \mathcal{L}_X$ is the set of permitted life cycles over X such that $\epsilon \in \Lambda$.* ∎

Such a process is the behavioral component of an object model, determining it's implicit state. The empty life cycle ϵ describes the fact that the object has not been created. We now formalize how a process determines the observations. Let A be a set of attributes. Associated with each attribute $a \in A$ is a data type **type**(a) that determines the range of the attribute. Let $\Pi(\Lambda)$ be the set of all finite, non-empty prefixes of life cycles in Λ.

Definition 3.2 *An* OBSERVATION STRUCTURE *V over a process P is a pair (A, α) where A is a set of attributes and α is an observation mapping $\alpha: \Pi(\Lambda) \to obs(A) \subseteq \{(a, d) \mid a \in A, d \in \textbf{type}(a)\}$. A given prefix $\pi \in \Pi(\lambda)$ is called (possible) state of an object.* ∎

Note that by definition we allow for non-deterministic observations.

An object model is defined by putting together a process and an observation structure over that process yielding a complete description of possible behavior and evolution through time.

Definition 3.3 *An* OBJECT MODEL *$ob = (P, V)$ is composed of a process P and an observation structure V over P.* ∎

Thus, an object is an *observed process*. As a notational convention, the sequence of observations during the execution of a life cycle $\lambda \in \Lambda$ is denoted by $\omega \in \Omega$, the set of all possible sequences of observations.

Recall that a system is represented by a collection of interacting objects. Thus, we need a mechanism to relate object models. This mechanism is an *object morphism*. A special case of object morphism is the *object embedding morphism*. It describes an embedding of an object ob_2 as an encapsulated entity into another object ob_1. Thus, both component morphisms h_P and h_V are inclusions. This implies that the set of life cycles of ob_2 must be preserved and ob_1-events must employ ob_2-events to alter ob_2's state. The latter requirement is captured by the concept of *calling*. If an event e_1 calls an event e_2, then whenever e_1 occurs, e_2 occurs simultaneously. Events may also call processes, i.e. the occurrence of an event may imply the occurrence of a sequence of events (*process calling*). The process being called is treated as a transaction, i.e. it is regarded to be an atomic event. Process calling is essential when it comes to implementing abstract objects over base objects as described in [20].

Let us now define an object embedding morphism.

Definition 3.4 *Let $ob_1 = (P_1, V_1)$ and $ob_2 = (P_2, V_2)$ be object models. Then ob_2 is* EMBEDDED INTO *ob_1, $ob_2 \hookrightarrow ob_1$, iff*

$$X_2 \subseteq X_1$$

$$\forall \lambda_1 \in \Lambda_1 \exists \lambda_2 \in \Lambda_2 \colon \lambda_1 \downarrow\downarrow X_2 = \lambda_2$$

$$A_2 \subseteq A_1$$

$$\forall \tau_1 \in \Pi(\Lambda_1) \colon \alpha_1(\tau_1) \downarrow A_2 = \alpha_2(\tau_1 \downarrow\downarrow X_2)$$

∎

$\lambda_1 \downarrow\downarrow X_2$ denotes life cycle restriction. All events that are not in X_2 are eliminated from the snapshots in λ_1 and only the sequence of non-empty snapshots is taken into account. A single arrow on observations like in $\alpha_1 \downarrow A_2$ only takes into account those attributes that are in A_2.

Embedding is the basic mechanism for constructing complex objects from components (part_of relationship). Through restriction, we may also express IS_A relationships.

Usually, objects models are classified. For this purpose, we introduce the notion of a class type.

Definition 3.5 *A* CLASS TYPE *$ct = (I, ob)$ consists of a set I of object identifiers and a (prototype) object model ob.* ∎

The set I is the carrier set of an arbitrary abstract data type. Following this definition, each object of a class has the same object model as structure definition. This definition can be generalized to heterogeneous classes as proposed in [11].

Object classes in our setting are sets of objects of a certain type fixed by the corresponding class type. Thus, with each object class we associate one corresponding class type. A class type describes possible extensions of a class definition in terms of object sets identified by identifier values $i \in I$. Therefore, possible class populations are subsets of $\{\langle i, ob \rangle \mid i \in ct.I \land ob = ct.ob\}$. Usually, the term *object class* is conneceted with the current state of a class variable, i.e. a concrete current object population with current states for included objects.

Definition 3.6 *A state of an* OBJECT CLASS *$oc = (ct, O)$ consists of an class type ct and a set of instances O. Instances $\langle i, ob, \pi \rangle \in O$ are described by an object identifier i, an object model $ob = ct.ob$ and a current state $\pi \in \Pi(ob.\Lambda)$. The identifier i identifies instances in O uniquely.* ∎

In this way, an object class definition is extensional. Note that we use the "dot notation" to refer to components of structures. Analogously to single objects, we can define *class life cycles* as sequences of object class states induced by event sequences. A class model following this idea would consist of class life cycles and (possibly) observable class attributes — the semantic model of a class following this idea is the model of one complex and aggregated object again.

Taking object models as objects and object morphisms as arrows, a category of objects is established. Models representing the system to be developed can be constructed using category-theoretic operations. For details see [16].

4 The Specification Language TROLL

In this section we present the language TROLL to specify a model of the system to be developed of which the characteristics have been described in the previous section. That is, the intended models of TROLL-specifications are societies of object models that are connected by object morphisms.

Let us first consider the specification of single isolated objects. The structure and behavior of an object is specified in a *template* which is not the object itself. As an example, we want to specify a template describing an object representing a book:

```
template Book
    data types nat, string, |PERSON|, list(|PERSON|);
    attributes
        Authors: list(|PERSON|);
        Publisher: string;
        Edition: nat;
        Year: nat;
        derived no_authors: nat;
    events
        birth published;
    constraints
        static
            Year > 1500;
        derivation rules
            no_authors = length(Authors);
```

In the **data types** section, the signatures of the data types being used in the template specification are imported. The data types may either be chosen from a set of predefined types (like 'nat' or 'string') or from a set of user-defined data types that were specified using a specification language for abstract data types. Since object identifiers are values of a certain data type (cf. section 3), these data types may also be imported and are denoted by |OC| for an object class OC.

Attributes and events make up the *local signature* of a template. The signature of a template includes the data type signatures, the signatures of embedded objects and the local signature defined for the template and is the alphabet underlying the specification of objects.

In the Book-template, there are attributes Authors, Publisher, Edition, Year and no_authors which represent the relevant observable properties of books. Note that the codomain type of the attribute Authors is list(|PERSON|), i.e. lists of identifiers of instances of class PERSON. The attribute no_authors is a derived attribute, i.e. its value depends on the values of other attributes.

The only event in the Book-template is the event published, which is the birth-event for objects being described by the Book-template, i.e. an occurrence of published brings such an object into existence. The initialization of the attribute values is made by supplying the values as parameters of the birth-event.

In the constraint section, static and dynamic integrity constraints may be given. Static integrity constraints are formulae given in first-order logic that

234

specify the permitted observations. For books, we state that the year of publication must always be greater than 1500 (which means we are not interested in older books). Dynamic integrity constraints state how the values of attributes may evolve over time. A popular dynamic integrity constraint (for employees) e.g. states that their salary may not decrease in the future. Dynamic integrity constraints are formulae given in linear temporal logic [21, 22].

We may use the **Book**-template to specify objects and object classes. Single objects have a proper name and an associated template:

```
object Gone_with_the_wind
    template Book
end object Gone_with_the_Wind;
```

The class of books is specified by the following specification:

```
object class BOOK
    identification
        data types string, |PERSON|;
            Title: string;
            FirstAuthor: |PERSON|;
    template Book
end object class BOOK;
```

Note that we implicitly specify the class type **BOOK** with the specification of the object class **BOOK**. Similar to template specifications, we may specify class types in isolation, too. We may then use pre-specified class types to define several object classes. An class type is defined by a template along with a set of identifiers which is the carrier set of a data type. As a convention, we may define identification types as sets of (nested) tuples using a notation similar to the attribute specification. Thus, the data type associated with the type **BOOK** is the following:

$$|BOOK| := \textbf{tuple}(\texttt{Title: string, FirstAuthor: |PERSON|}).$$

Let us now look at a specification of objects that evolve through time. Consider the object class **COPY** that models copies of books being in the library. Copies are identified by document numbers. The constant **of** denotes the identification of the book of which a particular instance is a copy.

```
object class COPY
    identification
        data types nat, |BOOK|;
            doc_no: nat;
    constants
            of: |BOOK|;
    template
        data types bool, date, |USER|, list(|USER|), nat;
        attributes
            On_loan: bool;
            Due: date;
            Borrowers: list(|USER|);
```

```
events
    birth get_copy;
    death throw_away;
    check_out(|USER|,date,nat);
    return;
valuation
    variables U:|USER|, d:date, n:nat;
    [ get_copy ] On_loan = false;
    [ get_copy ] Borrowers = emptylist();
    [ check_out(U,d,n) ] On_loan = true;
    [ check_out(U,d,n) ] Due = add_days_to_date(d,n);
    [ check_out(U,d,n) ] Borrowers = append(U,Borrowers);
    [ return ] On_loan = false;
safety
    variables U:|USER|, d:date, n:nat;
    { On_loan = false } check_out(U,d,n);
    { ((exists U:|USER|, d:date, n:nat)
       sometime(after(check_out(U,d,n)))
          since last(after(return))) } return;
obligations
    { ((exists U:|USER|, d:date, n:nat) after(check_out(U,d,n))) }
          ⇒ return;
end object class COPY;
```

The attributes of the object class COPY are the boolean attribute On_loan which indicates whether a copy has been borrowed, the return date Due, and the list of borrowers up to now (Borrowers). The events represent the acquisition of a copy (get_copy), the lending and returning of a copy (check_out and return, respectively) and the removal of copies from the library (throw_away). The check_out-event has parameters for the borrower, the date the lending takes place, and the number of days the user is allowed to keep the copy. Event parameters allow for data to be exchanged during communication between objects and to define the effects of events on attribute values.

These effects are specified using valuation rules after the keyword **valuation**. The rules are implicitly universally quantified and invariant. A valuation rule has the following form (here simplified):

[event] attribute = data term;

Such a rule denotes that the attribute **attribute** after the occurrence of the event **event** will have the value of the term **data term**. The data term is evaluated in the state *before* the occurrence of the event and thus corresponds to an assignment in imperative programming languages. Note that we use an implicit frame rule stating that attribute values not being set by a valuation rule remain unchanged after an event has occurred.

The following rule computes the return date after a book has been borrowed using a function of the data type 'date':

valuation

```
    variables U:|USER|, d:date, n:nat;
    [ check_out(U,d,n) ] Due = add_days_to_date(d,n);
```

The set of possible life cycles Λ may be specified using several different formalisms. This is due to the fact that objects may represent a wide variety of UoD concepts which include typical passive objects like books and active objects like a calendar as well as abstract user interface objects and even objects performing query evaluation [23].

Currently, TROLL supports the following formalisms for process specification:

- *Safety rules* state preconditions for the occurrence of events.

- *Obligations* state completeness conditions for life cycles, i.e. events which are obliged to occur if a certain condition holds.

- A process can be specified explicitly using a CSP-like notation. We will not consider this further in this paper.

In the COPY-template we state two safety rules. The first rule simply states that a copy can only be borrowed if it is not on loan currently:

```
safety
    variables U:|USER|, d:date, n:nat;
    { On_loan = false } check_out(U,d,n);
```

The second rule states that a book can only be returned if it has been lend sometime in the past and has not been returned already:

```
{ ((exists U:|USER|, d:date, n:nat)
    sometime(after(check_out(U,d,n)))
        since last(after(return))) } return;
```

Note that we refer to the history of an object. In safety rules, we thus may use a temporal logic in the past with operators like **always in the past** or **sometime ... since last ...**, which can be defined analogously to the known operators in temporal logics for the future (cf. [21, 22]). The predicate **after** holds in each state after the occurrence of the particular event.

In obligations, requirements for complete life cycles are stated. The requirements must be fulfilled before an object can be deleted. Simple obligations require events to occur, maybe depending on the current state. For copies of books we state that they have to be returned sometime after having been checked out:

```
obligations
    { ((exists U:|USER|, d:date, n:nat) after(check_out(U,d,n))) }
            ⇒ return;
```

Objects in a system may be related to each other in various ways – they may interact, they may be components of complex objects, and there may be generalization hierarchies of objects and object classes. We refer to [13, 18] for further details.

5   Integration of Database-Specific Concepts

Two main concepts of database methodology are the definition of *external views* and the possibility of set-oriented *data retrieval*. External views are restricted access interfaces on object populations used for access control and schema structuring. This restricted access concerns data retrieval as well as object property update and must therefore be defined on the level of dynamic objects.

Set-oriented data retrieval using some database query formalism on the other hand is a read-only access on the current values of object properties seen as an extension of a data model and can be handled on the level of data values, i.e. in an abstract data type framework. *Query evaluation*, however, is a very dynamic task and must be realized using active objects [23].

5.1   Query Facility

The role of *ad hoc* queries (in contrast to manipulations) in database systems is the retrieval of information, i.e. of data (!), out of the stored database. Typically, the retrieved information is structured according to a data model offering concepts like relations or tuples as query results. Even if these data modeling concepts can also be used to structure the *database contents*, the result of a query is information *about the database contents* and should in our opinion not be confused with persistent objects stored in the database. It is possible, however, to *use* the result of queries to create new persistent objects – but that is a completely different task.

In our approach, object queries interpret the structural part of the current object population as a state of a value-oriented data model. In general, all query formalisms known from value-oriented data models can be used, for example query algebras or SQL dialects for complex objects [24, 25] or even deductive database query languages. We will discuss only facets of a query algebra QUAL for objects [26]. Our query algebra QUAL is *many-sorted*, because many-sorted algebras are already part of the Oblog semantics framework and it can therefore be defined as a direct extension of the data type part of the formal semantics. Furthermore, a pure set-theoretic approach like in classical relational algebra is not powerful enough to handle the variety of data type constructors used already in our framework for example as attribute domains.

To give an impression of the query algebra QUAL, consider the following example for queries using QUAL:

> *Deliver the set of tuples describing the borrowers of the copy no. 12345.*

The corresponding QUAL expression is:

$$\text{materialize}(\text{apply}_{\text{Borrowers}}(\text{select}_{\text{SELF.Doc\_no}=12345}([\text{COPY}])))$$

After having selected the tuple representing the copy **12345**, we project on the **Borrowers**-attribute and yield a set of object identifiers that identify all past borrowers of the copy. The database relation [COPY] contains the current state information of all **COPY** objects, i.e., it is a set of tuples built from the current attribute values. The **materialize**-operator applies to a set of identifiers and yields the set of tuples representing the objects identified by the input operand.

The formal semantics of query algebra expressions can be defined like in ordinary value-oriented data models. We propose an algebraic construction of query result domains leading to a strongly-typed query algebra. This construction is outlined in detail in [26]. We have to define an algebra containing the basic data types as subalgebras and containing all instantiations of data type constructors like **set of** or **relation** possibly being the result type of a query. Please note that we have the usual polymorphism of query algebras concerning data type constructors.

The basic idea for defining the formal semantics of our object algebra can be described as follows:

- *The current global state of the object society is expressed by variables taking values from sorts of the universe $\mathcal{U}$.*

- *The added object algebra operators define (a family of) new operators for $\mathcal{U}$.*

Following this idea, the denotational semantics of query algebra terms is defined using a layered construction of an algebra for a given object society where the semantics of each QUAL term is fixed by an associated algebra function. The semantics construction is presented in detail in [26]. As an overview, the layered construction is done in five steps as follows :

1. We start with a many-sorted base algebra $\mathcal{B}$ containing the basic data types **integer**, **boolean**, **point**, etc.

2. The identification data types of object types are added to $\mathcal{B}$ leading to the algebra $\mathcal{B}^+$ by instantiations of the used data type constructors and renaming of the resulting types. An example for such a identification type is the data type |BOOK| for the object class BOOK. For database objects, the identification data types define the possible values for object identifiers [27].

3. The data universe $\mathcal{U}$ is constructed by building the closure of the instantiation of type constructors over $\mathcal{B}^+$. An example for a type constructor is the **set** constructor. The constructed universe is state-independent.

4. A database state S is constructed by adding constants for each observable database object. These constants serve as global variables containing the current database state. A state S is an extension of a value-oriented data model.

5. We denote each query algebra operator by a familiy of functions added to S. Hereby, each different non-data parameter of the query operator causes a different function in the semantic domain. This is only a technical point to avoid function-valued parameters not being included in the classical algebraic framework.

The first four steps can be done using the known algebraic specification techniques, for example using equational specification of abstract data types [28]. We will present the definition of the **select** operator as an example for the fifth step.

The **select** operator has a boolean formula p as a non-data parameter. In order to use the algebraic framework, we have to introduce for each non-data parameter p a different function $[\![\textbf{select}_p]\!]$ in the semantic domain. The **select** operator is defined for arbitrary sets as input including the concept of **relation** as special case. The semantics of the **select** operator is given by the following recursive definitions:

Variables: e: **elemtype**, s: **set(elemtype)**

$$[\![\textbf{select}_p]\!](\textbf{insert}(e, s)) = \textbf{if } [\![p_{\text{SELF}\leftarrow e}]\!] = \textbf{true}$$
$$\textbf{then insert}(e, [\![\textbf{select}_p]\!](s))$$
$$\textbf{else } [\![\textbf{select}_p]\!](s)$$

$$[\![\textbf{select}_p]\!](\textbf{empty}) = \textbf{empty}$$

The operators **insert** and **empty** are operations of the data type constructor **set**. The notation $[\![p_{\text{SELF}\leftarrow e}]\!]$ denotes the value of the boolean term p after substituting the variable **SELF** by the value e.

Transformation rules for algebraic optimization can be extracted from the algebraic specification of the type constructors and the definitions of the query operators.

We also made an attempt to specify *query evaluation* in the TROLL-language. Briefly, a *query object* is associated with each operation in a QUAL-expression. Query objects then perform the operation they represent and produce a(n intermediate) result. For details see [23].

5.2   Definition of (External) Views

An *object (class) interface* is mainly a mechanism for controlling access to objects in an object base. Access control for a single object is achieved by defining a restricted interface for the object, e.g. by performing a projection on the attributes and events of the object. Furthermore, we allow a restricted form of deriving new attribute values and events. This projection can be defined for single objects as well as for all instances of an object class. The following examples show the principles of defining object class interfaces.

The first example defines an external view COPY_STATISTICS on COPies used for statistical use only showing the On_loan state and the return date of all copies. This interface definition encapsulates attributes of the class COPY and corresponds to a projection view of a relational database.

interface class COPY_STATISTICS
encapsulating COPY
    attributes
        On_loan: bool;
        Due: date;
end interface class COPY_STATISTICS;

The semantics of this interface definition is a restriction of the *access* to COPY objects as it is done in relational databases by a projection view. Technically, a projection view is defined by a signature restriction for accessing COPY objects. Analogously to relational views, we can add a selection predicate to filter the instances of a class being visible in the view. As an example we have a modified statistics view showing only the return days of currently loaned copies :

interface class LOANED_COPY_STATISTICS
encapsulating COPY
selection where On_loan = true;
  attributes
    Due: date;
end interface class LOANED_COPY_STATISTICS;

This object class interface allow the selection of a subpopulation of the object class **COPY**. In the formal semantics, it is defined by an object class specialization followed by a projection view. To define a selection filter, we allow arbitrary QUAL terms of sort **boolean** evaluated locally to the encapsulated object (class).

Please note that a projection view definition for dynamic objects has not only to restrict the observation of attributes but also the possible modification events being offered to the view users. Additionally, this kind of projection can be used to restrict the access to complex object components, too. As an example for an encapsulation of the update behavior, we have the interface class **LIB_USERS_COPY** where only the update events **check_out** and **return_copy** are presented to library users (users are not allowed to **throw_away** copies ...).

interface class LIB_USERS_COPY
encapsulating COPY
  attributes
    doc_no: nat;
    On_loan: bool;
    Due: date;
  events
    check_out(|USER|,date,nat);
    return_copy;
end interface class LIB_USERS_COPY;

The object's external keys (for **COP**ies the value of **doc_no**) are not generally preserved by an interface definition, but the internal object identity is preserved since we do not derive new objects. This implies that we in general do not have a set of tuples representing instances but a multiset as for example in the **COPY_STATISTICS** interface class.

In general, we do not only want to encapsulate attributes and events in an interface definition, but even present derived attributes and events to the view users. As an example for an interface with *derived attributes* consider the interface class **COPY_ON_LOAN** where the attribute **Who** is derived from the value of the attribute **Borrowers**.

interface class COPY_ON_LOAN
encapsulating COPY
  attributes
    doc_no: nat;
    Due: date;
    Who: |USER|;

derivation
    derivation rules
        Who=first(Borrowers)
end interface class COPY_ON_LOAN;

The derivation part is usually hidden to the users. Technically, such an interface consists of a formal object implementation [15] and an projection view. For the derivation of attribute values we have the full power of the QUAL algebra. QUAL terms are evaluated locally to the encapsulated object. The derivation of events is done using *event or process calling*. The following example shows a restricted interface for students which are allowed to check out copies for seven days only. Therefore, a special event **student_check_out** restricts the access to the general **check_out** event using event calling. This example additionally shows the possibility to apply interface definitions to already defined interfaces.

interface class STUDENT_USERS_COPY
encapsulating LIB_USERS_COPY
    attributes
        doc_no: nat;
        On_loan: bool;
        Due: date;
    events
        student_check_out(|USER|,date);
        return_copy;
derivation
    calling
        variables U: |USER|, d: date;
        student_check_out(U,d) >> check_out(U,d,7);
end interface class STUDENT_USERS_COPY;

For the derivation of events we can use arbitrary *process calling* [15] as needed also for arbitrary object implementation. Thus, the derived event may be evaluated by a finite process defined over the local events of the encapsulated object. Examples and syntax of process calling can be found in [18].

Interface views can be defined to encapsulate object aggregations, too. This resembles the concept of join views known from relational databases. If there are name clashes, we can use class names or explicit class name variables to solve ambiguities. Explicit class name variables are needed for example in the case of a join of a class with itself. As an example we have the join view BORROWER_LIST, where we list the book-Titles of currently loaned books together with their current Borrower. In the example, we introduce the object class variable C for presentation reasons only — its use is not necessary in this example because the source class of all attributes can be uniquely determined. The same holds for the explicit derivation of the Title attribute.

interface class BORROWER_LIST
encapsulating COPY as C, BOOK
selection where C.of = BOOK.identification;
    attributes
        Title: string;
        Borrower: |USER|;

```
derivation
    derivation rules
        Borrower = first(C.Borrowers);
        Title = BOOK.Title;
end interface class BORROWER_LIST;
```

The semantics of interfaces is in principle only an *authorization for object manipulation* and *attribute value retrieval*. It has nothing to do with object copies — it is only a restricted view on existing objects rather than an object-manipulating operation. We can regard interface definitions as a mechanism to select objects for manipulation. The manipulations themselves are encapsulated within the objects, therefore we do not have to describe new concrete manipulations but the restrictions for using them correctly.

6   Conclusions

In this paper we have presented a formal framework for the specification of database applications. Database applications are characterized by a (large) database storing persistent objects in a structures way, by interactive (multi-user) functions over the database and by access through external views and set-oriented queries. The framework is suitable for uniform modeling of structure, functionality, and dynamics of database applications in an object-oriented way. We presented a formal model for objects and the formal specification language TROLL. The framework also allows for the smooth integration of queries and views.

In contrast to object-oriented data models (see e.g. [24, 29, 30]), our approach addresses the early phases of system design and puts special emphasis on the dynamics of objects over time. TROLL is a logical language with a fair amount of syntactic sugar. Thus, a specification is formal and makes reasoning about it possible. We are currently in the process of defining a suitable logic. Similar languages we are aware of are following an object-centered rather than an object-oriented paradigm in that they do not integrate the dynamics of the system into objects but into activities which are separated from objects. The advantage of our approach is that we achieve higher levels of modularity because static properties and dynamic behavior are encapsulated in objects. Thus, we support modifiability of specifications (since changes are local to objects and do not affect other parts of the specification) and allow for reasoning about objects in isolation (since all structuring mechanisms preserve the properties of objects).

Currently, we are investigating the formal implementation of specifications. The model-theoretic approach to implement objects over objects has been examined in [20]. Our goal is to follow a transformational approach towards the implementation of objects by objects specified in a kernel language which can be executed or interpreted.

Acknowledgements

We are very grateful to Cristina Sernadas who participated significantly in the development of the TROLL language. Thanks also to all other IS-CORE colleagues, who contributed to the definition of the TROLL specification language. In particular, Hans-Dieter Ehrich and Amílcar Sernadas developed basic ideas of objects and object descriptions. Special thanks to David Harper for calling our attention to a missleading definition in the workshop version of this paper. Thanks also to Thorsten Hartmann for reading and commenting the final version.

References

[1] M. L. Brodie and J. Mylopoulos, editors. *On Knowledge Management Systems*. Springer-Verlag, Berlin, 1986.

[2] J. W. Schmidt and C. Thanos, editors. *Foundations of Knowledge Base Management*. Springer-Verlag, Berlin, 1989.

[3] S. Greenspan, A. T. Borgida, and J. Mylopoulos. A Requirements Modelling Language and its Logic. In M. L. Brodie and J. Mylopoulos, editors, *On Knowledge Base Management Systems*, pages 471–502. Springer-Verlag, Berlin, 1986.

[4] J. Mylopoulos, P. A. Bernstein, and H. K. T. Wong. A Language Facility for Designing Interactive Database-Intensive Applications. *ACM Transactions on Database Systems*, 5(2):185–207, 1980.

[5] A. Borgida, E. Meirlaen, J. Mylopoulos, and J.W. Schmidt. Report on the Taxis Design Language. ESPRIT 892 (DAIDA), FORTH-CRC, Iraklion, Greece, 1989.

[6] J.W. Schmidt and F. Matthes. DBPL Language Report and User Manual. ESPRIT 892 (DAIDA), Universität Hamburg, FRG, 1990.

[7] A. Albano, L. Cardelli, and R. Orsini. Galileo: A Strongly Typed Interactive Conceptual Language. *ACM Transactions on Database Systems*, 10:230–260, 1985.

[8] G. Booch. *Object-Oriented Design*. Benjamin/Cummings, Menlo Park, CA, 1990.

[9] J. Rumbaugh, M. Blaha, W. Premerlani, F. Eddy, and W. Lorensen. *Object-Oriented Modeling and Design*. Prentice-Hall, Englewood Cliffs, NJ, 1990.

[10] P. Wegner. Concepts and Paradigms of Object-Oriented Programming. *ACM SIGPLAN OOP Messenger*, 1(1):7–87, 1990.

[11] A. Sernadas, C. Sernadas, and H.-D. Ehrich. Object-Oriented Specification of Databases: An Algebraic Approach. In P. Hammerslay, editor, *Proc. 13th Int. Conf. on Very Large Databases VLDB'87*, pages 107–116, Brighton (GB), 1987. Morgan-Kaufmann, Palo Alto, 1987.

[12] G. Saake and R. Jungclaus. Konzeptionelle Modellierung von Objektgesellschaften. In H.-J. Appelrath, editor, *Proc. Datenbanksysteme für Büro, Technik und Wissenschaft BTW'91*. pages 327–343, IFB 270, Springer-Verlag, Berlin, 1991.

[13] R. Jungclaus, G. Saake, and C. Sernadas. Formal Specification of Object Systems. In S. Abramsky and T. Maibaum, editors, *Proc. TAPSOFT'91*, pages 60–82, Brighton (UK), 1991. LNCS 494, Springer-Verlag, Berlin.

[14] J. Fiadeiro, C. Sernadas, T. Maibaum, and G. Saake. Proof-Theoretic Semantics of Object-Oriented Specification Constructs. In R. Meersman and W. Kent, editors, *Object-Oriented Databases: Analysis, Design and Construction (Proc. 4th IFIP WG 2.6 Working Conference DS-4)*, Windermere (UK), 1990. North-Holland, Amsterdam. *In print*.

[15] A. Sernadas and H.-D. Ehrich. What Is an Object, After All? In R. Meersman and W. Kent, editors, *Object-Oriented Databases: Analysis, Design and Construction (Proc. 4th IFIP WG 2.6 Working Conference DS-4)*, Windermere (UK), 1990. North-Holland, Amsterdam.

[16] H.-D. Ehrich, J. A. Goguen, and A. Sernadas. A Categorial Theory of Objects as Observed Processes. In J.W. de Bakker, W.P. de Roever and G. Rozenberg, editors, *Foundations of Object-Oriented Languages (Proc. REX School/Workshop 1990*, pages 203–228, LNCS 489, Springer-Verlag 1991.

[17] R. Jungclaus, G. Saake, and T. Hartmann. Language Features for Object-Oriented Conceptual Modeling. In T. Teory, editor, *Proc. 10th Int. Conf. on the ER-Approach*, San Mateo (CA), 1991. To appear.

[18] R. Jungclaus, G. Saake, and C. Sernadas. Object-Oriented Specification of Information Systems: The TROLL-Language. Informatik-Bericht, TU Braunschweig, 1991. *To appear*.

[19] G Saake. Conceptual Modeling of Database Applications. In D. Karagiannis, editor, *Proc. 1st Workshop Information Systems and Artificial Intelligence : Integration Aspects. Ulm 1990)*, pages 213–232, LNCS 474, Springer-Verlag, Berlin 1991.

[20] H.-D. Ehrich and A. Sernadas. Algebraic Implementation of Objects over Objects. In W. deRoever, editor, *Stepwise Refinement of Distributed Systems: Models, Formalisms, Correctness (Proc. REX'89)*, pages 239–266, Mood (NL), 1989. LNCS 394, Springer Verlag, Berlin, 1989.

[21] A. Sernadas. Temporal Aspects of Logical Procedure Definition. *Information Systems*, 5:167–187, 1980.

[22] G. Saake. Descriptive Specification of Database Object Behaviour. *Data & Knowledge Engineering*, 6(1):47–74, 1991.

[23] R. Jungclaus, G. Saake, and C. Sernadas. Using Active Objects for Query Processing. In R. Meersman and W. Kent, editors, *Object-Oriented Databases: Analysis, Design and Construction (Proc. 4th IFIP WG 2.6 Working Conference DS-4)*, Windermere (UK), 1990. North-Holland, Amsterdam. *In print*.

[24] C. Beeri. A Formal Approach to Object Oriented Databases. *Data & Knowledge Engineering*, 5(4):353–382, 1990.

[25] A. Heuer and M.H. Scholl. Principles of Object-Oriented Query Languages. In H.-J. Appelrath, editor, *Proc. Datenbanksysteme für Büro, Technik und Wissenschaft BTW'91*, pages 178–197, Kaiserslautern, 1991. Springer-Verlag, Berlin.

[26] G. Saake, R. Jungclaus, and C. Sernadas. Abstract Data Type Semantics for Many-Sorted Object Query Algebras. In B. Thalheim, J. Demetrovics and H.-D. Gerhardt, editors, *Proc. 3rd Symp. on Mathematical Fundamentals of Database and Knowledge Base Systems MFDBS-91*, pages 291–307, Rostock, FRG, 1991. LNCS 495, Springer-Verlag, Berlin, 1991.

[27] S.N. Khoshafian and G.P. Copeland. Object identity. In *Proc. OOPSLA Conference*, pages 406–416, Portland, OR, 1986. ACM, New York, 1986. (Special Issue of SIGPLAN Notices, Vol. 21, No. 11, November 1986).

[28] H. Ehrig and B. Mahr. *Fundamentals of Algebraic Specification I: Equations and Initial Semantics*. Springer-Verlag, Berlin, 1985.

[29] W. Kim. Object-Oriented Databases: Definition and Research Directions. *IEEE Transactions on Knowledge and Data Engineering*, 2(3):327–341, 1990.

[30] S. B. Zdonik and D. Maier, editors. *Readings in Object-Oriented Database Systems*. Morgan-Kaufmann, Palo Alto, CA, 1989.

Algebraic Specification of Databases — A Survey from a Database Perspective

W B Samson and A W Wakelin

Department of Mathematical and Computer Sciences,
Dundee Institute of Technology,
Bell Street,
Dundee. DD1 1HG. Scotland.

Abstract

Algebraic specification of databases is critically reviewed in terms of its applicability to database implementation. A number of key issues of database design are identified and the bearing of algebraic specification on these issues is discussed. Attention is drawn to those aspects of database design which have been neglected by the algebraic specification community. Strengths and weaknesses in other aspects of algebraic specifications of databases are highlighted.

1 Background

In the search for a formal definition of the relational model that could be used as a vehicle for exploring novel database languages and provide a basis for an implementation, the authors were surprised to find no specification which completely met their needs. This led to an attempt to construct a specification/prototype in terms of Standard ML **abstypes** and a subsequent implementation in an object-oriented environment (LINGO on a Rekursiv [1]).

Many authors have introduced the ideas of algebraic specification to the application area of databases, with the relational model being particularly well represented. Some have taken the view that algebraic techniques are well exemplified by database issues, while others have been more interested in what they can learn about databases and their properties by algebraically specifying them and then reasoning about the specifications. The innate concept of *state* which is central to the idea of a database has encouraged authors to introduce state explicitly into their algebraic specifications(— where state is usually considered to be a "foreign" concept as in a referentially transparent functional programming language). Non-classical logics are also considered by a number of authors; particularly temporal logics, because the state of a database depends largely on its transaction history. These, and other issues are discussed in the following sections of this paper.

This paper reviews published work in algebraic specification in the light of the authors' requirements for a generally applicable model of a relational database that could be used as a basis for an implementation.

1.1 Algebraic Specification

First-order algebraic specification is based on the concept of a data type, or family of data types which is viewed as a collection of (named) sets with a collection of (named) operations between the sets. For example, the sets **integer** and **Boolean**, with operations 0, +, -, **true, false,** =, >=, <=, >, <, **and, or** and **not**.

A collection of named sets and operations between them is a *many-sorted algebra*. Such algebras are well understood and certain ideas from category theory can be exploited in dealing with data types.

More formally, an *S-sorted Σ-algebra*, A, consists of a set S of *sorts* (the names of the sets — Boolean and integer in the above example —) together with an (S* × S)-indexed set of operations (— for example +:integer × integer → integer; >:integer × integer → Boolean).

$$\Sigma =< \Sigma_{w,s} \mid w \in S^*, s \in S >$$

For each $s \in S$ there is given a set A_s and for each $\sigma \in \Sigma_{w,s}$ there is given a function

$$\sigma_A : A^w \rightarrow A_s$$

where, if $w = s_1 \dots s_n$ then

$$A^w = A_{s_1} \times \dots \times A_{s_n}$$

This formal definition provides us with a basis for reasoning about algebras. In particular, the idea of the *initiality* of an algebra (from category theory [2]) provides the basis for correctness proofs.

One great attraction of algebraic specification is that programming languages have been developed which are based on the ideas of abstract data types and so prototypes in the form of executable specifications can be generated; for example OBJ [2], which was originally intended to be a specification language, but is now considered to be a functional programming language; and functional programming languages such as Standard ML [3]. Not all functional programs should, however, be considered to be executable algebraic specifications since higher-order functions are permitted by most functional programming languages but are, typically, not to be found in algebraic specifications.

2 Specification of Databases

Key issues in the specification of databases are listed in the table below. These are issues which we believe are of direct interest to database implementors and researchers. The numbers along the top of the table are references to the publications listed at the end of this paper.

Topic	4	5	7	8	9	10	11	12	16	17	18	19	20	21	22	23	26	27	28	29	30	31	32	33
Relational Model as ADT	x			x								x								x				
Schemata	x											x				x					x	x		
Domains				x								x					x				x			
Attributes	x			x								x									x			
Tuples	x			x								x				x								
Values	x			x																				
Naming																								
Keys											x				x							x		
Relational Algebra	x	x		x								x			x				x					
Integrity (Static and Dynamic)				x							x							x			x	x		
Transactions	x			x									x	x	x						x		x	
Concurrency										x			x											
Physical DB — Reification																								
Representation of State			x	x	x	x	x	x										x						
Views																x								
Application Specific			x	x					x					x				x		x				x
Data Dependencies																		x			x			
Non Classical Logics							x	x										x				x		x
Object oriented concepts							x		x	x											x	x		

There are some surprises (for the authors, at any rate) in the above list. These are mostly concerned with issues which seem to have been ignored, or "swept under the carpet" by the algebraic specification community. Some of these are now considered.

2.1 The relational model as an abstract data type

The vast majority of the papers reviewed have been based on the relational database model. Some features of databases have been well explored — for example transactions and state. Several of the papers referenced have concerned themselves with specific applications with pre-defined relations, rather than with the more general relational model. Only one of these application-specific papers [16] defines general relational algebra operations — the others, inasmuch as queries are considered, deal with the definition of specific queries rather than a more general query language. It is surprising that so few authors have attempted to define the relational model in terms of constructor operators as a basis for their specification. For example, the constructor

makepair: scheme × tupleset → relation

will build a relation from a scheme and a tuple set, both of which are abstract data types defined in terms of their own constructors.

Many of the papers consider database issues in relative isolation from each other — so it is difficult to see whether these issues could be integrated to form a coherent and consistent model.

2.2 Domains

In the few cases where the concept of a domain, the set from which the values of a specific attribute are drawn, has been considered, there is a lack of generality in the model and domains are application- specific. The correspondence between domains and data types is surely of great importance to database workers who wish to apply their databases to problems involving complex objects - particularly non-normal form relations. This is discussed further, below.

2.3 Naming

Naming conventions are extremely important when relational views are defined. For example, when the union of two union-compatible relations, A and B, takes place the names given to the attributes of the result relation may be those of A or of B, or may be explicitly specified by the user. Ideally, the DBMS will supply names that are independent of the order of the relations in the union so that union is truly commutative. Whichever way it is done, a number of interesting problems arise. There is clearly a gap in the literature on this issue.

2.4 Relational Algebra

Few ideas can be more familiar to the database community than the operators of the relational algebra. The authors have, with one exception [4], been unable to find a single consistent and complete specification of these in the literature. The five fundamental operators are

- select

- project

- cartesian product

- union

- difference

The most problematic of these is **select**. Most authors have provided a limited operator that will not permit general conditions on tuples to be specified. For example, the authors are aware of only one [4] specification of select which will permit conditions such as "select those employees whose age is less than twice their years of service". In this case **age** and **years of service** are assumed to be two different, but comparable attributes of an employee relation. Hayes has achieved this using only first-order logic but it is very awkward without recourse to higher-order functions [5] and requires a good deal of supporting parameterised specification. The signature of a higher-order select is:

select: relation × (tuple → boolean) → relation

Unfortunately, the theory of higher-order functions in an algebraic specification is far from straightforward [6, 5] and their use greatly increases the difficulty of fulfilling proof obligations; thereby removing one of the great advantages of algebraic specification at a stroke. Higher-order functions can be avoided by using parameterised specifications as Hayes has done, but this results in longer specifications. There would therefore seem to be a trade-off between the elegance and generality of a specification and its mathematical tractability. This is discussed further below when algebraic specification and functional programming are compared.

A more general difficulty encountered by specifiers is the confusion that surrounds the definitions of the operators — for example "select" and "restrict". It would seem that an agreed standard is required before further progress can be made.

2.5 Reification

It is interesting to note that, despite the much-vaunted ideas of reification of algebraic specifications and the relative simplicity of the resulting proof obligations, we can find no author who addresses the problem of reifying the abstract database towards a physical implementation. The mapping of an abstract specification onto an implementation in terms of, say, a more concrete model for B-trees, must surely be of great interest to implementors. It seems likely that such an abstraction function would open up possibilities of performance studies at an early stage in the specification of a DBMS.

2.6 State

The question of state is a vexed one when databases are being specified algebraically. As has been mentioned, algebraic specification techniques draw much of their power from the absence of a state — leading to referentially transparent expressions which are simple to manipulate. There have been a number of different approaches to the representation of state in algebraic specifications. One straightforward approach, considered by Wagner [7] is to explicitly represent state as an additional argument of every operator that requires it. As he points out, this leads to a combinatorial explosion of the number of required axioms. He uses categorical arguments to show that the introduction of finite sets of integers to generate indexed data types (like arrays, for example) avoids the complexity of a more general state while retaining the advantages of algebraic specification.

Furtado and Maibaum [8] advocate **traces** which record the transaction history of the database which led to its present state. They discuss the significance of the ordering of transactions in a trace. Maibaum [9] develops a rather different approach with explicit database **instances** in his specification.

Trinder [10], while not explicitly working in the area of algebraic specification, argues that non-destructive updates are feasible on today's hardware and so state and referential transparency are not incompatible concepts.

Other authors adopt different approaches [11, 12] and the matter of representing state in an algebraic system is not really settled, yet.

3   Reflexive vs. non-reflexive typing

The representation of **domains** has not been fully explored. A domain is a set of values that may be taken by attributes belonging to that domain. This is not really very different from the idea of a data type or **sort** which defines a **carrier** of legal values which may be assumed by values of that sort. The main difficulty faced by specifiers of domains is that domains require to be manipulated (at least in a limited way) in order to check that the values held in a tuple belong to the domains specified in the relational scheme. A scheme is composed of an ordered collection of attribute names and their domains. This is not possible in current algebraic specification systems, presumably since the underlying theory of treating types as values is difficult and would therefore make reasoning about the specification intractable. On the other hand, the specification could itself be made simpler and more general if type manipulation were permitted. Exciting possibilities of introducing highly complex domains could also be more fully explored.

Burstall and Lampson [13] proposed a functional programming language, "Pebble", which has a *reflexive* type system where values may be of type **type** thus allowing type manipulation. (A similar concept, though less well defined, forms one of the major strengths of the *class* system of object-oriented languages like Smalltalk.) This is in contrast to the majority of strongly typed functional languages where the type system is not accessible to the programmer [14] and are said to be non-reflexively typed.

4   When is a functional program an algebraic specification?

We have identified two instances, higher-order functions and reflexive type systems, where concepts which are available in functional programming languages would, if permitted in algebraic specifications, make the specification of a relational database a much simpler matter and would, in addition, contribute to more flexible and general specifications. The authors, and probably many other database researchers and implementors, feel frustrated by this problem which, in one sense at least, stifles the full potential of the relational model. Nevertheless, in many cases the specification/prototype is used primarily as a tool for exploring and clarifying ideas and there is no reason to suppress expressiveness simply because it is mathematically awkward.

Functional programming is of great interest as a potential database manipulation and query language, mainly because of its expressiveness [15, 10, 16]. The ideas of functional programming tie in very naturally with the algebraic specification of a database, giving the user a very clear mental picture of the operations he/she is performing.

5   Conclusions

Many authors have tackled the problems of algebraically specifying database systems, or aspects of them. In some cases the database application area has been chosen to display the usefulness of algebraic specification and (dare one say it?) the mathematical virtuosity of the authors. In some of these cases the results are of more interest to the algebraic specification community than to the database community. In other cases, however, the work has clearly been motivated by a desire to clarify problems of database models, by attempting to formalise them. This has, indeed, had some success in — for example — showing that certain database concepts such as integrity and updating constraints have developed in an *ad hoc* way and the underlying theory is, to say the least, very shaky. Databases have, on the other hand, pointed up a number of limitations to the usefulness of algebraic specification. For example the idea of *state* is far from settled and the specification of ideas which can be expressed very naturally in terms of higher-order concepts is made clumsy and awkward by restrictions demanded to make specifications mathematically tractable.

Two issues have been identified which are, undoubtedly, ripe for investigation using algebraic techniques. These are the issues of naming conventions and data reification. The choice of names for attributes has no consensus in the database community, and it is possible that mathematically modelling the process could help justify the selection of one paradigm in preference to others. The avoidance of data reification in the literature suggests that the problem is not a straightforward one and this must raise questions about the practical usefulness of algebraic specification in this context.

References

[1] L.D. Natanson, W.B. Samson and A.W. Wakelin *Object-oriented Implementations from a Functional Specification*, Proc. Software Quality Workshop, Dundee, 1990.

[2] J. A. Goguen, J. W. Thatcher, E. G. Wagner, *An initial algebra approach to the specification, correctness and implementation of abstract data types* in Current Trends in Programming Methodology, vol IV, R. Yeh ed., Prentice Hall, 1978.

[3] R. Harper, D. Macqueen, R. Milner *Standard ML*, Edinburgh University Internal Report ECS-LFCS-86-2, 1986.

[4] F. Hayes *A relational algebra specification using AXIS*, Hewlett Packard technical memo HPL-ISC-TM-88-019, 1988

[5] W. B. Samson, S. M. Deen, A. W. Wakelin, R. Sadeghi *Formalising the Relational Algebra — Some specifications, observations, problems and suggestions*, presented at Formal Methods Workshop, Teesside Polytechnic, 1987.

[6] A. Poigne *On specifications, theories and models with higher types*, Information and Control, vol 68, pp 1-46, 1986

[7] Eric G. Wagner *Categorical semantics, or extending data types to include memory*, Recent Trends in Data Type Specification - 3rd Workshop on theory and applications of abstract data types, ed H.-J. Kreowski, Springer-Verlag, pp 1-21, 1985.

[8] A. L. Furtado, T. S. E. Maibaum, *An informal approach to formal (algebraic) specifications*, Computer Journal, vol. 28, no. 1, pp 59-67, 1985.

[9] T. S. E. Maibaum, *Database instances, abstract data types and database specification*, Computer Journal, vol 28, no. 2, pp 154-61, 1985.

[10] P. W. Trinder *Referentially transparent database languages*, in Functional Programming, Springer Workshops in Computing, Glasgow, 1990.

[11] H.-D. Ehrich *Algebraic (?) specification of conceptual database schemata*, Recent Trends in Data Type Specification - 3rd Workshop on theory and applications of abstract data types, ed H.-J. Kreowski, Springer-Verlag, pp 22-27, 1985.

[12] S. Khosla, T. Maibaum, M. Sadler *Database specification* 1985

[13] R. Burstall, B. Lampson *A kernel language for modules and abstract data types*, Semantics of Data Types, LNCS 173, Springer-Verlag, 1984.

[14] E. Dennis-Jones and David Rydeheard *Categorical ML - Category-Theoretic Modular Programming* University of Manchester Technical Report UMCS-89-8-3, 1989.

[15] W. B. Samson, A. W. Wakelin, *PEARL — a database query language for the integration of data and knowledge bases*, Proc. Int. Conf. on AI in industry and government, Hyderabad, India, ed P. Balagurusamy, Macmillan 1989

[16] A. Bossi, C. Chezzi, *Using FP as a query language for relational databases*, Computer Languages, vol 9, no. 1, pp25-37, 1984.

[17] R. Wieringa, R. van der Riet, *Algebraic specification of object dynamics in knowledge base domains*, Artificial intelligence in databases and information systems, ed. by R. A. Meersman and Shi Zhonggzhi, North Holland, pp 411-36 1990.

[18] H.-D. Ehrich, *Key extensions of abstract data types, final algebras and database semantics*, Category theory and computer programming, ed. by D. Pitt, S. Abramsky, A. Poigne, D. Rydeheard, Springer-Verlag , pp 412-33, 1986.

[19] E. Y. Wong, W. B. Samson *The specification of a relational database (PRECI) and its realisation in HOPE*, Computer Journal, vol 29, no 3, pp261-268, 1986.

[20] H. Ehrig, A. Habel, B. K. Rosen, *Concurrent transformations of relational structures*, Fundamenta Informaticae, vol 9 pp 13-50, 1986.

[21] H. Ehrig, H.-J. Kreowski, H. Weber, *Algebraic specification schemes for data base systems* HMI-B 266, Hahn-Meitner-Institut fur Kernforschung Berlin GMBH, 1978.

[22] M. A. Melkanoff, M. Zamfir, *The axiomatisation of data base conceptual models by abstract data types*, UCLA-ENG-7785, University of California, Los Angeles, 1978.

[23] P. C. Lockemann, H. C. Mayr, W. H. Weil, W. H Wohlleber, *Data abstractions for database systems*, ACM ToDS, vol 4, no 1, pp 60-75, 1979.

[24] H.-J. Kreowski (ed.) *Recent trends in data type specification*, Springer-Verlag, 1985.

[25] K. Benecke, *On dependencies in hierarchical data structures*, Tanulmanyok Magy. Tud. Akad. Szamtastech. & Autom. Kut. Intez. (Hungary) no. 185, pp 113-20, 1986.

[26] B. G. Claybrook, A. M. Claybrook, J. Williams, *Defining database views as data abstractions*, IEEE Transactions in Software Engineering, vol SE-11, no.1, pp3-14, 1985.

[27] A. L. Furtado, E. J. Neuhold, *Formal Techniques for Database Design*, Springer Verlag, 1985

[28] W. Dosch, G. Mascari, M. Wirsing, *On the algebraic specification of databases*, Proc. VLDB, pp370-385, 1982.

[29] F. W. Tompa *A practical example of the specification of abstract data types*, Acta Informatica, vol 13, no 3, pp 205-24, 1980.

[30] S. Abiteboul, V. Vianu *A transaction-based approach to relational database specification*, J.A.C.M. vol 36 no 4, pp758-89, 1989.

[31] H.-D. Ehrich, K. Drosten, M. Gogolla, *Towards an algebraic semantics for database specification*, Data and Knowledge (DS-2). Proc. Second IFIP 2.6 working Conf. on database semantics. pp 119-35, North Holland 1988.

[32] P. A. S. Veloso, A. L. Furtado *Stepwise construction of algebraic specifications (databases)*, in H. Gallaire, J. Minker, J. M. Nicolas (eds), Advances in Database Theory vol. 2, pp 321-352, Plenum, 1984.

[33] F. Golshani, T. S. E. Maibaum, M. R. Sadler, *A modal system of algebras for database specification and query/update language support*, Proc 9th VLDB Conf., Florence, 1983

Towards a Structured Specification Language for Database Applications*

Klaus-Dieter Schewe
Ingrid Wetzel
Joachim W. Schmidt
Fachbereich Informatik, Universität Hamburg
Schlüterstr. 70, D-2000 Hamburg 13, FRG

Abstract

Database application programs may be considered as good candidates for the application of formal specification methods, because much of the database and transaction semantics can be captured in terms of integrity constraints as well as pre- and postconditions. Furthermore, the use of current transaction models as units of database state transitions favours the use of Dijkstra's substitutions.

Traditional DBMS solutions guarantee database integrity by expensive tests at transaction commit time. In the DAIDA project a different approach was taken interpreting database constraints as parts of formal specifications and by extracting correct database programs from such specifications. Database and transaction constraints are captured by an expressive semantic data model in the style of TAXIS, transformed into Abstract Machines and finally refined into AM versions that are equivalent to programs written in the strongly-typed database programming language DBPL.

The work reported in this paper evaluates the DAIDA experience and addresses the shortcomings of DAIDA. A new formal specification language SAMT is proposed that essentially allows to structure and modularize specifications and to capture particular classes of constraints by its type system. Moreover, SAMT is considered as a framework for both the specification of database applications as well as the refinement of specifications into executable programs, thus eliminating some of the complexity issues found in the multi-language approach of DAIDA.

1 Introduction

Formal specification and verification methods are gaining increasing interest in the area of database applications, where it is necessary to guarantee the consistency of long-lived, highly interrelated data. Unfortunately database applications were not yet the focal point of the formal specification community. The well-founded algebraic specifications [9,19] follow more or less the line of abstract data types. The same applies for model-based specifications like VDM [3,11], Z [17] and more recently the Abstract Machines [2].

---

*This work has been supported in part by research grants from the E.E.C. Basic Research Action 3070 FIDE: "Formally Integrated Data Environments".

The formalism of Abstract Machines has been used in the DAIDA ESPRIT project [5] to establish a mapping from conceptual design in the semantic data and transaction model TDL [4] down to an implementation in the database programming language DBPL [15]. It was the explicit specification of state spaces and invariants on them and the possibility of stepwise refinement within the same language that made the Abstract Machine approach a natural choice for the specification of database applications. The main difference between Abstract Machines and their forerunners VDM and Z is the style, in which operations are specified. Abstract Machines are based on Dijkstra's calculus of substitutions [7,10,8], whereas VDM and Z use a predicative style, mostly known as pre-post-specifications (see also [16]). The predicative style seems to be more elegant, since it looks a little more declarative. However, it can be shown that both specification styles are equivalent. Since transactions in TDL use a predicative style, whereas database programming languages like DBPL include – besides other things – imperative constructs, the equivalence of the two styles gave a reasonable basis for the refinement task.

Our current work is built upon the DAIDA experience preserving the style of transaction specifications. All our changes and extensions to the basic work of J. R. Abrial will lead us to a new specification language SAMT (Structured Abstract Module Types).

The organization of the paper is as follows. In the remaining section of this introduction we summarize the requirements of formal specifications that arise from database application systems and illustrate our experiences from the DAIDA project. Section 2 gives a brief and informal introduction to the SAMT data type discipline. Section 3 introduces persistent and non-persistent modules and discusses their semantics as well as the notion of consistency. In section 4 we focus on the two structuring principles mentioned above. Moreover, we redefine operational refinement and show, how data refinement could be defined, if we followed the line of "standard" refinement theory. Instead of this we explain, why we decided to deviate from this theory. We conclude with a short summary and conclusion in section 5. Throughout the paper we try to illustrate our ideas with small examples, and we add short remarks on formal semantics issues, whereas the full formal semantics is postponed to future work.

1.1 Requirements for Formal Database Design

In a database we store long-lived, shared data, i.e. data that is used by different application programs over a long period. During lifetime the programs that access these data may even change, whereas the data itself is still used by other programs. Hence the following problems:

- We must be able to distinguish in the specification language persistent data, i.e. the data that is to reside in the database, from those data that are used only for a short time in a program.

- Specification refinement on persistent data may not change the semantics of the data.

- Operations on persistent data must obey the serializibility constraint of transactions. This imposes the strong requirement to keep track of concurrent transactions, at least as the formal semantics of the specification language is concerned.

Persistent data in a database may have complex structure. The most familiar complex data types, called bulk data types, are relations [15]. A formal specification language that is suitable for database applications should provide the possibility to specify such bulk data types in such a way that verification using these data types is still possible.

The data that reside in a database normally are highly interrelated. This is expressed by the use of integrity constraints which are either static or dynamic.

- **Static integrity constraints** impose restrictions on the data that may be stored. Requirements include e.g. referential integrity, i.e. that some attribute of a stored data object must always refer to some other data object, key constraints and inclusion constraints.

- **Dynamic integrity constraints** impose restrictions on the history of data, e.g. that certain values may never decrease, others may never be deleted, etc.

A formal specification language for database applications must be able to specify both kinds of integrity constraints. Moreover, verification must be able to show that these constraints are never violated by the specified operations.

As to the kind of operations, database transactions allow for set-oriented queries and updates of persistent data. Thus, the formal specification of a database application must be at least as declarative as the expected database program will be.

In addition, several kinds of modules appear very often, espacially in case of object-oriented design [14], where most modules come along with a class definition, a standard treatment of object-identity and with standard operations on classes such as update-, insert- and delete-operations. Moreover, even the handling of IsA-relationships between classes leads to standard modules. For these reasons it is necessary to allow generic specifications — in our sense: parameterized specifications and higher-order type concepts — to be built.

Moreover, one of the important issues of database programming is the optimization of queries. This is in fact nothing more than some special kind of refinement intended to achieve higher performance. We need to extend considerations in this direction to address problems of performance optimization and distribution during refinement. Having this in mind, we should also be able to introduce or to remove modularization during refinement in order to minimize the efforts for concurrency control of nested transactions.

1.2   The DAIDA Approach

In DAIDA we used the original version of Abstract Machines as defined by J. R. Abrial [2]. In an Abstract Machine we glue together a specification of a state space and a specification of state transitions. The state space is given by a set of state variables and an invariant predicate $\mathcal{I}$ defined in a first-order sorted language $\mathcal{L}$, such that the state variables are the free variables in $\mathcal{I}$ [13].

State transitions in Abstract Machines are called operations. Among them there must always be one initialization operation assigning initial values to all state variables. All operations are specified by so-called **substitutions**. Substitutions are comparable to imperative programming language constructs allowing non-determinism. We shall come back to the language of substitutions in the section on the dynamic part of SAMT modules.

According to Dijkstra [8] the semantics of substitutions is given by means of two specific predicate transformers called the **weakest liberal precondition** and the **weakest precondition** respectively denoted *wlp* and *wp*. We shall come back to predicate transformers later.

State variables in Abstract Machines belong to certain basic sets. These sets are either predefined or they have to be defined in a context. Within an Abstract Machine we have to specify the contexts seen by a machine. This includes all the contexts seen by one of the specified contexts. Besides the definition of basic sets, a context is the place for the declaration of constants and the definition of their properties.

The invariant component of an Abstract Machine states properties that partition the state space into two distinguished subspaces. States not satisfying the invariant predicate should never be reached. Therefore, it is necessary to check that the operations defined in the Abstract Machine always preserve the invariant. Abstract Machines offer a formal proof obligation for the preservation of static invariants. We shall come back to the formal definition of consistency later.

1.3   Some Lessons Learnt from DAIDA

In Abstract Machines the specification of state spaces is given through a many-sorted first-order language $\mathcal{L}$ with "built-in" sorts and sort-constructors. Each state variable is the member of a unique **basic set** declared in a **context** visible to the machine [18]. The purpose of such a **context** is to define:

- a list of sorts of the language $\mathcal{L}$, called **basic sets**,

- a list of **constant names** that are constants in $\mathcal{L}$,

- a list of formulas over the language $\mathcal{L}$ called **properties**. Properties may not contain state variables.

In a context four different kinds of basic set specifications are allowed:

- A basic set may be completely abstract, i.e. any denumerable set.

- A basic set may be given by enumeration of its elements.

- A basic set may be defined in terms of seen constants, similar to subrange types.

- A basic set may be defined in terms of other basic sets.

A context being a loose collection of basic sets, constants, this is a little bit similar to algebraic specifications [9], but there is no need to add axioms (properties) in order to define precisely what a function does. Therefore we decided to add a strong typing discipline to Abstract Machines. The idea is to replace contexts by data type declarations on the basis of algebraic specifications with higher-order constructs similar, but not identical to [6].

Another problem concerns the missing use of the predicate transformer $wlp(S)$ in Abrial's work. We believe that it is necessary to close this gap. As a consequence we introduce new stronger definitions for consistency and operational refinement. The advantage of the new definitions is the complete orthogonality of properties concerning termination, consistency and refinement.

In addition, we decided to deviate from "standard" refinement theory [12] in another central point. We dispense with miraculous substitutions, i.e. with partially defined operations, since we still do not see their necessity. The new definitions for consistency and refinement are also senseful in case of partial operations. However, they require the weakest liberal preconditions to be defined for the underlying substitution language. In [14] we give detailed arguments, why we changed the definitions and why we dispense with miracles.

Structuring in Abstract Machines is too weak. Hence the idea to regard a machine as the specification of a module and to extend the language allowing the im- and export of operations. But then the problem arises to distinguish different kinds of modules:

- Ordinary **modules** – just as in MODULA II – only live for short time. Whenever there is a call to a procedure or a function in such a module, a fresh copy of the module will be used.

- **Database Modules** pertain long-lived shared data. Whenever a transaction in such a module is called, the one and only module will be used. This imposes the well-known concurrency problems for transactions, for which we assume a serializibility semantics. In target languages like DBPL transactions are handled by the run-time system.

This leads to the distinction at specification time between persistent and non-persistent modules.

Import- and Export-constructs on these modules are similar to those in MODULA-II. They are also related to an extension of Abstract Machines suggested by J. R. Abrial in the late months of the DAIDA project. However, he allows only complete machines to be imported and only during refinement. We do not want structuring to be coupled with refinement, nor do we restrict the IMPORT-/EXPORT-concept to complete machines. Modularization requires the language of substitutions to be extended by calls.

Moreover, we felt that we should be able to support object-oriented specifications and their refinement down to database programming languages, but also to object-oriented databases. In order to do this, we introduce an inheritance relation between modules as a second structuring principle. The main problem that arises is the specialization of the operations. J. R. Abrial also suggested an extension of Abstract Machines introducing a USES-clause that allows machines to be extended and glued together with respect to some constraints. However, our approach differs from his, because we use a more general notion of inheritance including the specialization of operations. It can be shown that our definition of operational specialization is again equivalent to the one given for pre-post-specifications [16].

2 Invariants and Data Types

In Abstract Machines the only way to specify static constraints were the invariants, e.g. specifying that a state variable belongs to some basic set had to be done by an invariant. However, this specific class of invariants can be captured more easily by data types. Therefore, we want to adopt a slight modification of algebraic data type specifications [9] extended by higher-order constructions similar to [6] in order to structure the value space and to restrict operations on values. In SAMT the approach to data consists in

- defining a type as a set using a Coxeter approach by generators and relations,

- defining algebraic operations on types by functions and axioms, and

- defining functions between different types together with defining axioms.

Hence, in general a type is given by a triplet $T = (S, F, Ax)$, where S denotes the structure of the type T, i.e. the generators of T as a set, F denotes the functions on T including algebraic operations, and Ax is a collection of axioms on S and F.

This approach is similar to algebraic specifications [9]. The main difference is the emphasize on generator functions, which we call **constructors**.

The definition of a type T may depend on other already defined types $T_1, \ldots, T_n$. These types may occur on the left hand sides of constructor declarations. Moreover, each type T_i occurring with multiplicity m on the left hand side of a constructor declaration may give rise to m selector functions of the form $S : T \to T_i$. Functions defined on $T_1, \ldots, T_n$ can be used in the axioms of T but they are not functions defined on T.

Another difference to pure algebraic specifications is the absence of a sort declaration. A type in SAMT always defines only one sort, i.e. the type. Other sorts only come into play via the BASEDON-declaration. Semantically this avoids introducing many-sorted algebras, which are in fact the disjoint union of their sorts with operations partially defined on the sorts. Instead, in SAMT we get structures of generalized topological algebras with continuous algebraic operations and continuous functions between different algebras.

Moreover, the SAMT approach does not explicitly introduce subsorts, but we allow the images of constructor functions to be used as sort expressions in the definition of other constructors.

In SAMT we have a very general notion of subtyping given via functions taking the subtype to its supertype. Syntactically, simple inclusion functions may be omitted. Functions and axioms defined on the supertype, are inherited and restricted by the subtype via the specified subtyping function. If in addition we want to make an algebraic operation also an operation of the subtype — this includes defining subalgebras — me may overwrite the signature of the inherited function in the function declaration of the subtype in a limited way. Semantically this says that restriction to subtypes implies the restriction of the range. An interesting consequence of this kind of subtyping in SAMT is that the number of models of a type may be restricted via the existence of subtypes.

As a last characteristic of data types in SAMT we allow them to be parameterized. Semantically this gives rise to functors on the category of SAMT-algebras.

Let us now give a small example of a type constructor FSETS(α) denoting the type of finite subsets of the type α. In SAMT this type constructor can be defined as a parameterized type.

Example 1 *Let the type BOOL be defined elsewhere. Then FSETS(α) is defined as follows:*
FSETS(α) ==
    BasedOn *BOOL ;*
    Constructors *emptyset : $\rightarrow$ FSETS(α) ;*
        singleton : $\alpha \rightarrow$ FSETS(α) ;
        union : FSETS(α) $\times$ FSETS(α) $\rightarrow$ FSETS(α) ;
    Functions *member : $\alpha \times$ FSETS(α) $\rightarrow$ BOOL ;*
    Axioms *With A :: FSETS(α) :*
        union(emptyset,A) = A ;
        With A,B :: FSETS(α) :
        union(A,B) = union(B,A) ;
        With A,B,C :: FSETS(α) :
        union(A,union(B,C)) = union(union(A,B),C) ;
        With A :: FSETS(α) :
        union(A,A) = A ;
        ...
End *FSETS*

More details can be found in [14].

3 Modules as Structuring Primitives

In SAMT we distinguish two different kinds of abstract module types. Persistent Modules are used to structure persistent data and to maintain these data through their lifetime. They may be regarded as abstract structured databases. Non-persistent modules may be regarded as abstract collections of operations and types. Syntactically these two different kinds of modules are distinguished by the preceding keyword "PERSISTENT", which is missing for non-persistent modules. Semantically a persistent module denotes a set of state sequences, and a non-persistent module denotes a collection of generalized functions. A **module** in general consists of several parts:

- A declaration, whether the module is **persistent** or not.

- A specification of its interface, i.e. to give the modules it **inherits**, the types, operations and constants it **imports** from other modules, the types, operations and constants that it **exports** and a declaration, whether this module is a **refinement** of another one. The parts on modularization, inheritance and refinement will be stressed in section 4.

- A specification of the **module statics** by the declaration of **types, constants, state variables, view variables** and **static invariants**.

- A specification of the **module dynamics** by a declaration of **dynamic invariants**, the **initialization** of the state space and **operations** on the state space. In case of persistent modules these operations are called

transactions, otherwise **procedures**. Operations and the initialization are specified using a slight extension of Dijkstra's substitution calculus.

3.1 The Static Part of a Module

All types that are used in a module must be either declared, inherited from a supermodule or imported from any other module. The cartesian product of their corresponding type is called the **local type** of the module. Constants are declared in the form < constant-name > :: < type-name > := < expression > , where <expression> is a term of the corresponding type without variables. State variables are declared in the form <variable-name> :: <type-name>.

We add **view variables** that are derived from the state variables via an expression, which is a term of that type containing the state variables as the only variables. Syntactically view variables are introduced in the form <variable-name> :: <type-name> := <expression>, where <expression> is a term of the corresponding type including the state variables as the only allowed variables. Intentionally the update of state variables triggers the update of view variables.

Static invariants are used to distinguish legal states from others. They are modelled by predicates, i.e. by functions from the local type of the module to BOOL. These functions are built from the primitive predicates on the types in question, from equality and the usual operations on BOOL.

Let us now give a small example for static invariants denoting a key constraint and an inclusion dependency. Clearly *PersonClass* and *StudentClass* are state variables and *PersonIdentityNo* is a selector on the type *PERSON*. The rest of the example should be self-explaining.

Example 2
INVARIANT
  STATIC *With* P_1, P_2 :: *PERSON* :
    $member(P_1, range(PersonClass)) = true$
    $\wedge\ member(P_2, range(PersonClass)) = true$
    $\wedge\ PersonIdentityNo(P_1) = PersonIdentityNo(P_2) \Rightarrow P_1 = P_2$;
  With n ::*NAT* :
    $member(n, domain(StudentClass)) \Rightarrow member(n, domain(PersonClass))$
    $\wedge\ stud\_isa\_person(StudentClass(n)) = PersonClass(n)$;

Semantically, the state space of a module is given through its local type. Each value in $T_1, \ldots, T_n$ gives rise to a **state**. Invariants distinguish between legal states and others. Therefore we introduced the notion of local type.

3.2 The Dynamic Part of a Module

The dynamics of a module is given by an initialization of the state space, state transitions and dynamic invariants:

- **Transition invariants** restrict the possible changes to state variables. They are given by predicates on the state variables before and after the operation, i.e. by functions of type $T \times T \to BOOL$, where T denotes the local type of the module.

- The **initialization** assigns initial values to each of the state variables. **State transitions** update the state space. The initialization and the state transitions are specified by substitutions on the local type of the module.

For each state variable x we introduce another variable x' of the same type. The intention behind this notation is taken from pre-post-specifications as in [16,17]. The unprimed variable denotes the value of the state variable before the execution of the transition, the primed variable denotes its value afterwards. Transition integrity constraints can be expressed as predicates on these (primed and unprimed) variables.

In the following self-explaining example we express the constraint that professors may never become students:

Example 3
INVARIANT
    TRANSITION With n :: *NAT* :
      member(n,domain(*ProfessorClass*)) $\Rightarrow$
        $\neg$ member(n,domain(*StudentClass'*)) ;

Our language of substitutions is similar to the one given by J. R. Abrial [2] with the main difference that we do not want to allow miracles. We use the substitutions stemming from Dijkstra [7,8] with the only extension of an unbounded choice (@-substitution). For details of the used substitution language refer to [13,14].

These substitutions are all parameter-free and define the type $SUBST_0(\gamma)$, where γ is the local type of the module in question. It is also called the local type of the substitution type without input- and output-parameters. In order to extend this language of substitutions allowing parameterized substitutions, recursion and calls, we add the two following definitions. For the momoment let all substitutions be defined in one module. Thus we always have the same local type. We shall indicate how this can be extended in the section on modularization.

- $o_1, \ldots o_m \longleftarrow S'(c_1, \ldots, c_n) = S$ denotes a substitution named S' with input-parameters $c_1, \ldots, c_n$, output-parameters $o_1, \ldots, o_m$ and body S, where the formal parameters $o_1, \ldots, o_m$ and $c_1, \ldots, c_n$ are not state variables. The informal meaning is that whenever S' is called with actual input-parameters, say $p_1, \ldots, p_n$, and actual output-parameters, say $d_1, \ldots, d_m$, then each c_i in S is replaced by p_i and $d_1, \ldots, d_m$ will be set to the value of $o_1, \ldots, o_m$ after the execution of S.

- $S' = d_1, \ldots, d_m \longleftarrow T[p_1, \ldots, p_n]$

  denotes a "call" of the substitution T with formal input-parameters $c_1, \ldots, c_n$ and formal output-parameters $o_1, \ldots, o_m$, actual input $p_1, \ldots, p_n$ and actual output $d_1, \ldots, d_m$. The intended meaning is that each c_i will be substituted by p_i and d_i will be set to the output o_i of the "call". This requires the p_i to be expressions of the correct type, whereas the d_i musy be variables of the corresponding type.

For sake of brevity we shall use c instead of $c_1, \ldots, c_n$, o instead of $o_1, \ldots, o_m$, d instead of $d_1, \ldots, d_m$, and p instead of $p_1, \ldots, p_n$.

Parameterized substitutions S' with input-parameter c of type α and output parameter o of type β form the type $SUBST(\alpha, \beta, \gamma)$, where γ still denotes the local type. The semantics of substitutions S can be given by means of two specific predicate transformers $wlp(S)$ and $wp(S)$, which satisfy the *pairing condition*, i.e. for all predicates $\mathcal{R}$

$$wp(S)(\mathcal{R}) \equiv wlp(S)(\mathcal{R}) \wedge wp(S)(true)$$

and the *conjunctivity condition*, which states for any family $(R_i)_{i \in I}$ of predicates

$$wlp(S)(\forall i \in I. R_i) \equiv \forall i \in I. wlp(S)(R_i) .$$

These conditions imply the conjunctivity of $wp(S)$ over non-empty families of predicates. As usual $wlp(S)(R)$ will be called the **weakest liberal precondition** of R under S, and $wp(S)(R)$ will be called the **weakest precondition** of R under S. The notation f^*, which we shall use later, denotes the **conjugate predicate transformer** of f. It is defined by

$$f^*(\mathcal{R}) \equiv \neg f(\neg \mathcal{R}) .$$

The definitions of $wlp(S)$ and $wp(S)$ for all parameter-free substitutions that we allow are given in [8] or can be easily derived from there. As to parameterized substitutions refer to [14].

Note that our substitutions satisfy Dijkstra's **Law of Excluded Miracles** [8]:

$$wp(S)(false) \equiv false .$$

The following gives a simple example of a substitution for an insert operation:

Example 4
TRANSACTIONS
   create_Student(S :: STUDENT) =
      @ n :: *NAT*
      ($\neg$ *member*$(n, domain(PersonClass)$ $\longrightarrow$
        StudentClass := union(singleton(Pair(n,S)),*StudentClass* ;
        PersonClass := union(singleton(Pair(n,stud_isa_person(S))),*PersonClass*
)

3.3 Consistency of Operations

The static invariant component of an abstract module states properties that partition the state space into two distinguished subspaces. States not satisfying the invariant predicate should never be reached. Therefore, it is necessary to check that the operations defined in the module always preserve the invariant.

In the following, $\mathcal{I}$ denotes a static invariant and S denotes a substitution. The predicate $wp(S)(\mathcal{I})$ characterizes the initial states for which any computation of S terminates in a state satisfying the invariant $\mathcal{I}$. Thus the natural proof requirement for invariant preservation is $\mathcal{I} \Rightarrow wp(S)(\mathcal{I})$. This proof obligation intuitively means that whenever the substitution gets started from an initial state satisfying the invariant $\mathcal{I}$, then it must terminate again in a state satisfying $\mathcal{I}$. This is obviously the right requirement for sufficiently refined substitutions. In general, however, this is a too strong requirement, since it requires already at early design stages all operations to be always terminating.

As we know, in database application systems there are a lot of exceptions that require a special treatment in the transactions, but not all these exceptions are apparent for the very first design. Therefore we decided that the consistency definition with respect to static invariant should be orthogonal to the goals of refinement in the following sense:

- If S is a transition operation, it should be sufficient to require each terminating execution starting from a state satisfying $\mathcal{I}$ to result also in a state satisfying $\mathcal{I}$. As to initialization S_0, we should require that any computation should result in a state satisfying $\mathcal{I}$ no matter which was the initial state.

Since refinement will never destroy this property (see section 4.3), the elimination of non-terminating branches may be left to refinement. Moreover, if refinement succeeds to eliminate all non-terminating branches, then the required strong consistency property will finally be reached. Hence the following formal definition.

Definition 3.1 (Static Consistency) *Let M be a module with static invariant $\mathcal{I}$. Then we define:*

(i) *A substitution S in M is* consistent *with respect to the invariant $\mathcal{I}$ iff*

$$\mathcal{I} \Rightarrow wlp(S)(\mathcal{I}) \, .$$

(ii) *M is* statically consistent *iff all transistion operations S in M are consistent with respect to all static invariants $\mathcal{I}$ and the initialization operation S_0 satisfies $wp(S_0)(\mathcal{I})$ for all these $\mathcal{I}$.*

As to transition constraints, they are defined by predicates with primed and unprimed variables. Due to a weak equivalence between substitutions and pre-post-specifications [13] such a predicate can be regarded as a general non-deterministic substition, hence satisfying such an invariant should be equivalent to each substitution specializing the substitution associated with the transition constraint.

In [13] we associated a substitution

$$S_{\mathcal{J}} = @x' \bullet (\mathcal{J} \rightarrow x := x')$$

to each predicate $\mathcal{J}$ involving the state variable x and the primed variable x' associated with x. Here x is used as an abbreviation for the bunch $x_1, \ldots, x_n$ of state variables. Hence a substitution S satisfies a transition invariant $\mathcal{J}$ iff it specializes $S_{\mathcal{J}}$, which gives the following definition (compare section 4):

Definition 3.2 (Transition Consistency) *Let M be a module with transition invariant $\mathcal{J}$. Then we define:*

(i) *A substitution S in M is consistent with respect to the invariant J iff for all predicates $\mathcal{R}$:*

$$wlp(S_J)(\mathcal{R}) \;\Rightarrow\; wlp(S)(\mathcal{R})\,.$$

(ii) *M is **dynamically consistent** iff all transistion operations S in M are consistent with respect to all transition invariants J.*

Clearly, modules being both statically and dynamically consistent, will simply be called **consistent**.

3.4 On the Semantics of Abstract Modules

The semantics of substitutions can be given by sets of state pairs together with a set of states allowing non-terminating branches of the substitution. On this basis, the semantics of Abstract Machines could be given by sets of finite and infinite traces on the state space. For the semantics of abstract modules we proceed in a similar way.

If γ is the local type of a module, then for each state $\tau :: \gamma$ we may define a predicate $P_\tau :: \gamma \to BOOL$ by $\sigma \mapsto \delta_{\sigma,\tau}$, where $\delta_{\sigma,\tau}$ denotes a Kronecker-symbol on states. Then each substitution $S :: SUBST_0(\gamma)$ without input- and output-parameters gives rise to a set of state pairs

$$\Delta(S) \;=\; \cdot\, \{(\sigma,\tau) \mid wlp(S)^*(P_\tau)(\sigma) \equiv true\}$$

and a set of states

$$\Sigma_0 \;=\; \{\sigma \mid wp(S)^*(false)\}$$

with the meaning stated above.

As to non-persistent modules the situation is now quite easy, since they simply denote a set of substitutions with a trivial local type given by the semantics of $S_0; S$, where S_0 is the initialization of that module.

For persistent modules we may regard the definition of the semantics of a substitution S as given by a set of lists of states of length one or two. The informal meaning of a unary list was to give an initial state, such that there is a non-terminating execution of S in this state. The informal meaning of a binary list in that set was to give a pair (σ,τ) of states such that there is an execution of S starting in σ and ending in τ.

In a persistent module we have more than one substitution, all working on the same (persistent) state space. Hence the natural idea to define the semantics of a persistent module by lists of states of arbitrary length, including infinite lists.

More formally we get:

Definition 3.3 (Traces) *A **trace** on γ is a non-trivial finite or infinite sequence $\sigma_0,\ \sigma_1,\ \ldots$ of states $\sigma_i \in \gamma$.*

If a trace t is finite, say $t = (\sigma_0, \ldots, \sigma_n)$, then we call $l(t) = n + 1$ the **length** of t. In case of an infinite trace, we write $l(n) = \infty$. Let $Trace(\gamma)$ denote the set of all traces on γ.

Now define the traces given by the substitutions of a persistent module. Let γ be the local type of a persistent module M and let $\mathcal{S}$ denote the substitutions of M. Then M defines a set of traces $T'(M)$. If $t \in Trace(\Sigma)$, then $t \in T'(M)$ iff the following conditions hold:

(i) for all $\sigma_{-1} \in \Sigma$ we have $(\sigma_{-1}, \sigma_0) \in \Delta(S_0)$,

(ii) if $l(t) = n + 1 < \infty$, then there is some $S \in \mathcal{S}$ such that $\sigma_n \in \Sigma_0(S)$ and

(iii) if $l(t) > 1$, then for each $i < l(t)$ there must exist some $S \in \mathcal{S}$ such that $(\sigma_{i-1}, \sigma_i) \in \Delta(S)$.

Having done this, we can define the semantics of a machine M simply by $T'(M)$. In general, however, we would like to extend this result in replacing γ by $\gamma \times BOOL$ in order to distinguish between legal states, i.e. those satisfying the static invariant, and others. This will not be done in this paper.

4   Module Interfaces and Relationships

So far, we only looked at one module without any regard to module interfaces and combinations. However, database application tends to require large specifications [1]. Therefore, we need language construct that allow for structured specifications consisting of more than just one module with clearly defined interfaces between these modules.

In this section, we define two such structuring principles: inheritance and modularization. Moreover, we give a first impression of a refinement relation between modules. The difference between the two structuring principles and refinement is that refinement is used as a means to transform a given specification into a form closer to the implementation.

4.1   Inheritance and Specialization

SAMT introduces **Inherits** as a language construct. Each module may inherit one or more other modules. The intended meaning is to inherit all the types, constants, variables and substitutions declared in the supermodules, to allow them to be overwritten in the submodule and to allow extensions to be added. If there is a name clash between some operations inherited from different supermodules, then these are regarded to be different unless they have been inherited from a common supermodule, in which case they must be overwritten by the same operation in the submodule. We shall see that this can be done in a concise way, if overwriting is restricted to "specialization".

The kind of inheritance introduced so far, defines the semantics of a module with an inherits-clause by copying parts of the semantics of its supermodules. However, arbitrary overwriting allows the "submodule" not to share too much with its supermodules, which would reduce inheritance simply to copying. This is not the intention of inheritance as it is used in most semantic data models for specification (see e.g. [4]). Therefore, we want to forbid arbitrary rewriting and

268

force submodules to be "specializations". Hence the definition of **inheritance consistency** below.

Let us first focus on operational specialization. The intuition behind the definition is that whenever an execution of the specialized operation T establishes some post-predicate $\mathcal{R}$, then this execution should already be one of the general substitution S. The necessary extension for miraculous substitutions are discussed in [14]. Hence the following formal definition:

Definition 4.1 *Let S and T be substitutions on the same state variable x. Then T specializes S iff for all predicates $\mathcal{R}$ we have:*

$$wlp(S)(\mathcal{R}) \Rightarrow wlp(T)(\mathcal{R}) .$$

It can be shown that this definition is equivalent to the one given by Schuman and Pitt for predicative specifications [16]. Note that it allows the specialized operation to terminate in fewer cases the the more general one. This is intended and does not lead to any severe problem, if we restrict the set of legal states by additional invariants. In general inheritance will extend the state space. Let N be some module that inherits the module M. Then the set of variables, types, substitutions, etc. of N should form a superset of M's variables, types, etc., but overwriting should be restricted to specialization. Hence the following definition of inheritance consistency.

Definition 4.2 *Let N be a module inheriting M. Then N satisfies **inheritance consistency** with respect to M iff the following holds:*

(i) *The type of each variable of N inherited from M must be a subtype of the type associated with that variable in M.*

(ii) *For each view variable of N inherited from M the expression associated with it in N must be the restriction of the expression associated with that variable in M via the subtype function taking the local type of N to the local type of M — this subtype function can be canonically derived from the subtype functions associated with inherited state variables and projection.*

(iii) *The type of each substitution of N inherited from M must be a subtype of the type associated with that substitution in M [14].*

(iv) *Each substitution T in N overwriting an inherited operation S in M (including the initialization) must specialize S in the sense of the definition given above.*

As to consistency, it is rather obvious that in case of inheritance consistency each inherited — and specialized — substitution remains consistent with respect to the inherited invariant, which facilitates consistency proofs. However, for additional operations we have to prove consistency without any additional presupposition.

The definition of inheritance consistency may be used to define a more general notion of specialization on modules that could be the basis of inference procedures that infer an inherits relation between two given abstract modules.

Definition 4.3 *An abstract module N is a specialization of M iff:*

(i) the local type of N is a subtype of the local type of M,

(ii) the invariant of N implies the invariant of M and

(iii) for each operation S in M there exists an operation T in N specializing S.

4.2   Import and Export

The goal of modularization is to break specifications down into small pieces in a concise way. Moreover, suitable languages for database applications usually have modules or objects that are interconnected via synchronous or asynchronous procedure calls. In order to be able to map a specification via refinement down to an implementation in one such language without leaving the important task of modularization we should be able to write already modularized specifications.

Therefore, same as for types SAMT allows types, constants and substitutions of other modules to be used. This must be declared by the **IMPORT**-construct. However, this is only allowed, if the imported declarations have been declared to be visible, i.e. they must occur in the **EXPORT**-declaration. IMPORT and EXPORT model a strong hiding principle and they permit modularization.

Imported substitutions may be used in the body of transactions and procedures via the call-substitution. This gives a direct extension of the used substitution language. Although the formal definition of the predicate transformers needs not to be changed, we should mention that each substitution S in a module M that uses a substitution T imported from a module N depends on the local type of N [14].

Modularization has a strong impact on the semantics of modules. The impact of an IMPORT is more indirectly given via the call-semantics, whereas the impact of an EXPORT is direct, since only exported substitutions should contribute to the traces of the module or to the set of generalized functions in case of non-persistence. This implies that substitutions that are neither exported nor used via a call of another substitution in the same module do not contribute anything to the semantics of that module. However, they could be exported (or used) in a submodule, in which case they can not simply be omitted. Moreover, the traces of two persistent modules M and N linked via IMPORT/EXPORT depend on each other. The global semantics of the two modules together is given by pairs (t_M, t_N) of traces such that for each subsequence $(\sigma_{i_1}, \sigma_{i_2}, \ldots)$ in t_M with $i_1 < i_2 < \ldots$ involving on σ_{i_k} the application of a call to some substitution T_{i_k} in N there must exist a subsequence $(\sigma_{j_1}, \sigma_{j_2}, \ldots)$ in t_N with $j_1 < j_2 < \ldots$ involving on σ_{j_k} the application of T_{i_k}.

In [12] the call has been introduced to model call-by-value and call-by-result. However, in our context we can also model call-by-variable as it is used in the implementation language DBPL [15, section 12]. This can be done by allowing some input-parameter c_i to coincide with some output-parameter o_j, in which case the call is restricted to replacing c_i and o_j by the same variable, since each variable of a given type is also an expression of that type.

There is no additional proof obligation for modules involving IMPORT-and EXPORT-clauses. We only use the definition of predicate transformers for the imported substitutions, wherever they are used, e.g. in proving static, transition or inheritance consistency. However, according to the impact on semantics, we need only verify the consistency of exported substitutions [14].

One open problem with modularization is the consistency with respect to integrity constraints that are not expressible by the invariant of only one module. This is a facet of the general problem of how to combine modularization with consistency in the database field. This problem is postponed to future work.

4.3 Operational Refinement

Refinement is used as a means for the stepwise transformation of specifications down to implementations. This includes refining the operations as well as transforming the state space into a more suitable form. We shall address operational refinement and then state some results concerning a normal form proof obligation.

The intention behind refinement of an operation S is to eliminate step by step all non-terminating computations under control of S thereby reducing non-termination and to cancel some of the non-deterministic executions. In the area of database application systems, there is a need to remove non-determinism. We shall see that this does not effect the definition of refinement, but only the goals of the refinement process. However, it should not be possible to throw away just the already terminating computations of S. Moreover, the remaining computations of S should establish at least the same final states.

These considerations lead to the following informal requirements for an operation T to be a refinement of S:

(i) If there exists a terminating execution for S, then there must also exist some for T.

(ii) If there exists a terminating execution for S and all terminating executions lead to a final state characterized by the predicate R, then all terminating executions of T must also establish R.

(iii) If all executions of S terminate and establish the predicate R, then all executions of T must do so, too.

More formally we define:

Definition 4.4 (Operational Refinement) *Let S and T be two substitutions on the same state variables. Then T **refines** S iff the following three conditions hold for all predicates R:*

(i) $wlp(S)^*(true) \Longrightarrow wlp(T)^*(true)$

(ii) $wlp(S)^*(true) \wedge wlp(S)(R) \Rightarrow wlp(T)(R)$

(iii) $wp(S)(R) \Longrightarrow wp(T)(R)$

Note that "standard" refinement theory [1,12] only requires property (iii), which again avoids the use of the weakest liberal preconditions, but neglects all terminating branches that have already been defined by S. This implies that during refinement some already existing terminating branches can be completely redefined. To the authors' point of view this overloads refinement, since it allows designs not only to be extended, more determined and transformed into other representations — taking into account considerations normally associated with the implementation such as efficiency, modular structure and distribution — but to handle real changes to the design.

Moreover, miracles are never removed via refinement (for a more detailed discussion on refinement in case of miracles see [14]), which to the authors' point of view this does not make too much sense.

We are now able to discuss the preservation of consistency. In principle we have to show the consistency of each of its operations, but we can show that this may be reduced to very few cases.

Proposition 4.1 (preservation of static consistency) *Let S be a consistent substitution with respect to the static invariant $\mathcal{I}$ and let T be a refinement of S satisfying the following condition:*

$$wlp(S)(false) \wedge \mathcal{I} \implies wlp(T)(\mathcal{I})$$

Then T is statically consistent with respect to $\mathcal{I}$.

A similar result holds for transition invariants. This can also be extended to the case of miracles [14].

Proposition 4.2 (preservation of transition consistency)
Let S be a consistent substitution with respect to the transition invariant $\mathcal{J}$ and let T be a refinement of S satisfying the following condition for all predicates $\mathcal{R}$:

$$wlp(S)(false) \wedge wlp(S_{\mathcal{J}})(\mathcal{R}) \implies wlp(T)(\mathcal{R})$$

Then T is dynamically consistent with respect to $\mathcal{J}$.

The definition of operational refinement involves assertions of the form *for all predicates $\mathcal{R}$ we have* .... We shall give another form of these proof obligations that do not require a universal quantification over predicates.

Proposition 4.3 (Normal Form Proof Obligation) *Let S and T be substitutions. Then S refines T iff:*

(i) $(z = x) \wedge wlp(S)^*(true) \implies wlp(T)^*(true) \wedge wlp(\{x/z\}.T)(wlp(S)^*(z = x))$ *and*

(ii) $(z = x) \wedge wp(S)(true) \implies wp(T)(true)$

Note that this can be regarded as a trivial form of data refinement by simple renaming the state variables. If we replace $x = z$ by a predicate $\mathcal{A}$ on x and z, then we get a glimpse of how data refinement combined with operational refinement could look like. The definition would be as follows:

Definition 4.5 *Let M, N be modules with mutually different state variables x and z. Let $\mathcal{A}$ be some predicate on x and z. Then N* **refines** *M iff there is a bijection σ from the operations of M to those of N such that for all pairs S, $T = \sigma(S)$ of operations we have:*

(i) $\mathcal{A} \wedge wlp(S)^*(true) \Longrightarrow wlp(T)^*(true) \wedge wlp(T)(wlp(S)^*(\mathcal{A}))$ and

(ii) $\mathcal{A} \wedge wp(S)(true) \Longrightarrow wp(T)(true)$.

However, we are not satisfied with such a definition because of the arbitrariness of $\mathcal{A}$, which is too general for database applications, where the data exist for their own indepently from the current operations on them, whereas allowing any arbitrary change to the representation of the data focusses only on the input-output-relation of the operations.

Having done some technicalities of refinement, let us now consider what are the targets of (operational) refinement.

As a first goal, we want to remove all non-terminating branches at least in those initial states satisfying the static invariant of the underlying module. Dealing only with consistent modules, states not satisfying the invariant are negligible due to the fact that they are not reachable. Note that removing non-termination forces us to prove consistency, since nothing carries over from the refined operation (see proposition 4.1).

Having reached this goal, we are in a situation that all executions of the operation will always terminate unless the initial state does not satisfy the static invariant of the underlying module. Hence the first goal of (operational) refinement is formally expressible as:

- $\mathcal{I} \Longrightarrow wp(S)(true)$,

where $\mathcal{I}$ denotes the static invariant of the module.

The next goal concerns non-determinism. If we want our final operation to be deterministic as it is the case in database application systems, then we must **remove all non-determinism** at least for those initial states satisfying the invariant. This is formally expressed by:

- $\mathcal{I} \wedge wlp(S)^*(\mathcal{R}) \Longrightarrow wp(S)(\mathcal{R})$ for all predicates $\mathcal{R}$

5   Conclusion

In this paper we presented the first results on our continued work on formal specifications and refinements for data-intensive applications. This work is based on the experience we made in the DAIDA project with Abstract Machines as a means for a mapping of designs to implementations. We kept some ground ideas of the Abstract Machine approach as there are:

- the explicit specification of state spaces and static invariant and their combination in modules replacing Abrial's machines,

- the specification of state transitions by substitutions in the style of E. W. Dijkstra, and

- the idea of J. R. Abrial to introduce structured specifications — which first came up at the end of DAIDA and was not used in that project.

However, several open problems and several deficiencies in the approach led to the decision to rework the foundations of the approach. This has been done in [13]. The first decision was to restrict the substitution language to non-miraculous substitutions. The main reason for this were the unnnecessity of miracles and the problems that arose as a consequence from them. Moreover, we discovered that without introducing Dijkstra's second predicate transformer, the weakest liberal precondition, some outstanding problems concerning the set-theoretic semantics of substitutions could not be solved. Based on these decisions we were able to give enhanced definitions for the notions of consistency and operational refinement. We discussed in detail the relation between our definition and the "standard" ones. Moreover, we showed what must be done in order to cope in addition with miracles.

Database application systems require to handle persistence in an adequate way. Therefore, we introduced a distinction between persistent and non-persistent modules already at design time and outlined — although not in complete formal beauty — the differences concerning their semantics.

We introduced modularization and inheritance as two structuring principles on modules. This enables us to cope with large specifications, to break them down into smaller modules linked via IMPORT- and EXPORT-clauses. Furthermore, we now have two different hierarchies, the specialization hierarchy — as also in object-oriented approaches — and the refinement hierarchy.

The last deviation from DAIDA concerned the introduction of types. The new specification language is strongly typed. We outlined the current status of the SAMT type system.

However, all the material presented in this paper is a matter of ongoing research concerning the completion of the SAMT language design and its formal semantics and the work on remaining open problems, e.g. the missing notions of data and type refinement.

References

[1] J.R. Abrial: *A Formal Approach to Large Software Construction*, in J.L.A. van de Snepscheut (Ed.): *Mathematics of Program Construction*, Proc. Int. Conf. Groningen, The Netherlands, June 89, LNCS 375, Springer-Verlag, 1989

[2] J.R. Abrial: *Abstract Machines*, Parts 1 - 3, Technical Reports, January 90

[3] D. Bjørner: *The Vienna Development Method VDM: The Meta Language*, Springer LNCS 61, 1978

[4] A. Borgida, J. Mylopoulos, J. W. Schmidt: *Final Version on TDL Design*, DAIDA deliverable

[5] A. Borgida, J. Mylopoulos, J. W. Schmidt, I. Wetzel: *Support for Data-Intensive Applications: Conceptual Design and Software Development*, in

Proceedings of the 2nd Workshop on Database Programming Languages, Salishan Lodge, Oregon, June 1989

[6] M. Broy: *Equational Specification of Partial Higher Order Algebras*, in F. L. Bauer et al. (Eds.): Logic of Programming and Calculi of Discrete Design, Springer, NATO ASI Series F, vol. 36, 1986, pp. 185 -242

[7] E.W. Dijkstra: *A Discipline of Programming*, Prentice Hall, 1976

[8] E.W. Dijkstra, C.S. Scholten: *Predicate Calculus and Program Semantics*, Springer-Verlag, 1989

[9] H. Ehrig, B. Mahr: *Fundamentals of Algebraic Specification*, vol.1, Springer 1985

[10] E.C.R. Hehner: *The Logic of Programming*, Prentice Hall, 1984

[11] C.B. Jones: *Systematic Software Development using VDM*, Prentice-Hall International, London 1986.

[12] C. Morgan, K. Robinson, P. Gardiner: *On the Refinement Calculus*, Technical Monograph PRG-70, Oxford University Computing Labaratory, Oktober 1988

[13] K.-D. Schewe, J. W. Schmidt, I. Wetzel, N. Bidoit, D. Castelli, C. Meghini: *Abstract machines revisited*, FIDE technical report 1991/11

[14] K.-D. Schewe, B. Thalheim, I. Wetzel, J. W. Schmidt: *Formal Database Specifications Using Structured Persistent Modules*, DBIS memo 062-91

[15] J. W. Schmidt, H. Eckhardt, F. Matthes: *DBPL Report*, DBPL-Memo 111-88, University of Frankfurt, 1988

[16] S.A. Schuman, D.H. Pitt: *Object–Oriented Subsystem Specification*, in L. Meertens, (Ed.): *Program Specifiation and Transformation, The IFIP TC2/WG2.1 Working Conference, Bad Tölz, FRG, April 15-17, 1986*, North Holland Publishing Co, Amsterdam, 1987

[17] J.M. Spivey: *Understanding Z, A Specification language and its Formal Semantics*, Cambridge University Press, 1988

[18] I. Wetzel, Klaus-Dieter Schewe, J. W. Schmidt: *Specification and Refinement in an Integrated Database Application Environment*, to appear in Proc. VDM 91, Noordwijkerhout, October 1991

[19] M. Wirsing: *Structured Algebraic Specifications – A Kernel Language*, Passau University Reports, MIP 8511, 1985

The Reification Dimension in Object-oriented Data Base Design

Cristina Sernadas
Paula Gouveia
João Gouveia
Amílcar Sernadas
Pedro Resende

Secção de Ciência da Computação, Departamento de Matemática,
Instituto Superior Técnico, Av. Rovisco Pais, P-1096 Lisboa Codex
email: css@inesc.uucp

Abstract

The reification of an (abstract) object base schema over another (ground) object base schema is discussed. The concepts of reification object base schema, incorporation (inheritance), derived attribute and transaction are identified as basic. The reification object base schema includes the object classes of the abstract and the ground bases as well as a reification object class for each object class to be reified. The attributes of the abstract object classes under reification are defined as derived attributes and events are introduced as transactions. A brief outline of the semantics is also discussed.

1 Introduction

Object-oriented data base design is nowadays under intensive research [1,2, 3,4] leading to the so called *object bases*. The relationship between object-oriented data bases and other data base paradigms is also a concern [5]. An object base is a collection of objects either passive or active. Thus, the task of differentiating between records and programs does not appear at the conceptual level. The concern for the two kinds of objects puts a stronger emphasis on dynamic aspects. The importance of dynamic aspects is already recognized and has deserved a lot of attention in pure data base contexts [6,7,8,9,10,11,12,13].

Common concepts in object-orientation are those of class, type, inheritance and object identity [14]. The encapsulation principle of object-orientation imposes that objects are independent entities [15,16]. Hence another important issue is to indicate explicitly how objects in an object base *interact* with each other (an issue outside the data base field). Inheritance can then be seen as a strong form of interaction between objects.

Most of the approaches recognize the *object base schema* as a collection of object classes. An object class aggregates a collection of instances (objects) that have the same characteristics as well as the same identification mechanism [17,18]. Hence, the granule of description of object base schemata is the object class. *Inheritance* [19] can also be defined at the schema level by stating which instances are inherited into other instances. Several approaches to object oriented data base design can be found in the literature. The most significant differences of the approaches are in the detailed definition of each class as well as in the specific inheritance mechanisms.

As it is well known, reification (implementation) has always been an important issue in the data base area. Namely, the mapping between the conceptual data base schema onto the logical data base schema [20,21] and the mapping between the logical data base schema onto the physical data base schema were and still are a concern of data base researchers. The reification issue has been almost outside the object-oriented approach to data bases. We think that the latter can be formulated in two ways. On one hand, we may understand reification of object bases over traditional data base systems, e.g., relational data base systems. On the other hand, we can discuss the reification of an object base on top of another object base. Some results about the reification of object communities on top of other object communities can be found in [22].

In this paper, we aim to contribute to the problem of object base schema reification of an *abstract* object base schema on top of a *ground* (more concrete) object base schema adopting a constructive perspective (as understood in the abstract data type area [23]) adopting the object-oriented approach introduced in [24,25,26,27,28]. An object class has an *identification mechanism* for the instances and a *template*. The template includes the common characteristics of the instances, described by *attributes* and *events* (the latter being actions that can happen during the life of an instance). Also part of the template description is the definition of the effects of the events on the attributes as well as precedence relationships between events.

The simpler mechanism for interaction between objects is *event calling* [29,30,25] (that is to say the granule is the event). Stronger forms of interaction are inheritance or *incorporation* and *abstraction*.

In the constructive approach, a partial description of the abstract object base schema (partial because, besides the identification mechanism, we only have to indicate the events and the attributes) and a complete description of the ground object base schema (completed namely with effects of events on attributes and precedence relationships between events) are given. The remaining aspects of the abstract object base schema are defined on top of the ground object base schema using the concepts of *inheritance*, *derived attribute* and *transaction*.

We briefly outline the semantics of reification as a functor between two categories. This functor results from giving the semantics of an object as the category generated by a graph. For more details of this semantics see [31].

In section 2, we present the basic concepts of the object-oriented approach that we follow, trying to relate the concepts to well known data base concepts. Also in this section we include a brief outline of a graph semantics of templates and incorporation. In section 3, we discuss the reification of object bases on top of object bases along with a brief discussion of the semantics.

2   Object bases

An *object base* is a collection of objects, either passive or active. The basic difference between an object base and a data base is that the latter only includes passive objects. The concern for having passive and active objects puts a stronger emphasis upon the description of both structural and dynamic aspects.

Object base schemata are composed by object classes. An *object class* allows the definition of a collection of potential instances, objects, that have a specific identification mechanism and the same characteristics — *attributes*, *events* (an *event* is an atomic action that may have an effect upon the attributes of an object) and *behavior*. We call the common characteristics of an object class the *template*. In many situations we have a unique template for each object class. Hence the granule for introducing schemata is the object class.

As an example we consider a simplified stock management application.The object base schema orders includes the object classes PRODUCT, DEPOT, STOCK, CLIENT, ORDER and ARRIVED_ORDER. We can assume that all instances (objects) of the object class STOCK are active whereas all objects of object class PRODUCT are passive. For instance, the object class PRODUCT allows us to say how products are identified and which are the common aspects of all products.

An object base is composed by the current *objects* that we have at a certain moment. Hence current objects in an object base play the same role as tuples in data bases.

An essential aspect that is not present in traditional data base theory is to say how objects can *interact* because dynamic aspects are left out. In an object-oriented perspective, if not stated otherwise, the objects in an object base do not interact with each other. Interaction means that although objects can be independent they can be synchronized with each other at particular points. An essential step is to identify the basic granule for interaction. We consider this granule to be provided by the event, meaning that the more basic form of interaction is through events. Interaction is generally expressed between object classes stating how the instances of classes interact with each other.

For instance, we can consider an event in STOCK which may lead to the decrease of the quantity on hand. On the other hand, we can assume that instances of object classes ORDER and STOCK interact, namely because the satisfaction of an order (an event of the object class ORDER) corresponds to the emission of an invoice for the target stock of the order.

Objects can interact in a stronger way, namely by incorporation (inheritance). For clarification purposes assume that we call the object that is incorporated the *argument* of the incorporation and *target* of the incorporation the object that incorporates the other. Incorporation is a "code reuse" operation in the sense that all events and attributes of the argument object are events and attributes of the target. It is common in the data base field to consider inheritance as being code reuse in the sense just described.

We consider that incorporation imposes a stronger synchronization between the argument and the target objects namely because we want the argument object to be totally synchronized with the target object but not the other way around. Hence we want all the events of the argument object to be "seen" by the target object.

For instance, we may consider that the instances of the object class PRODUCT are incorporated into the instances of the object class ORDER in the intuitive sense that we want an order to incorporate the product involved in the order, assuming that there is only one. In this way we express that a particular product is totally synchronized with the orders that involve that product. However, we may assume that there are events in the order that are not "seen" by the product involved.

There are several kinds of incorporations related to possible restrictions of the events of the argument object in the target object and to possible updates of attributes of the argument object in the target object. For example, in a *safe incorporation* we may further restrict the occurrence of an event of the argument object in the target object but we do not want to update the values of the attributes of the argument object with events of the target object. That is to say we do not want side effects. In a *liberal incorporation* the latter restriction does not apply.

In data bases the view concept is of utmost importance. In our approach the *abstraction* concept plays the role of a view. We call the object from which we make the abstraction the *argument* and the object that we get after the abstraction the *result* object. For performing an abstraction we must indicate the events and the attributes of the argument that we want to retain in the result. However, in our case, we also have a synchronization between the argument and the result objects. Namely the result "sees" every event of the argument that was retained in it.

For example, we can consider ARRIVED_ORDER as an abstraction of ORDER. We only retain the aspects related to the arrival of the orders and skip such things as satisfaction or pending of orders.

We use a diagrammatic notation for describing object base schemata. The description of an object base schema includes the following diagrams: the *surrogate diagram*, the *template diagrams* for each object class and the *interaction diagrams* for each pair of object classes. The surrogate diagram includes the description of the identification mechanisms for all object classes. The template diagrams include the *matrix diagram* where attributes and events are declared, as well as possible constraints upon the attributes; the *behavior diagram* indicates the relationships between events; the *attribute initialization diagram* and the *attribute updating diagram* state the effects of events upon the attributes. In the attribute initialization diagram we express the effects of the birth events upon the attributes. The effects of update events are indicated in the attribute update diagrams. *Interaction diagrams* indicate how objects interact with each other.

2.1 Surrogate diagram

In the surrogate diagram we introduce the object classes of an object base schema along with the description of their identification mechanisms. These mechanisms provide a unique identification of each instance of an object class using special kinds of attributes, which we call *key attributes*. Key attributes do not change during the life of an instance. Moreover, *constant attributes* are also introduced in the surrogate diagram.

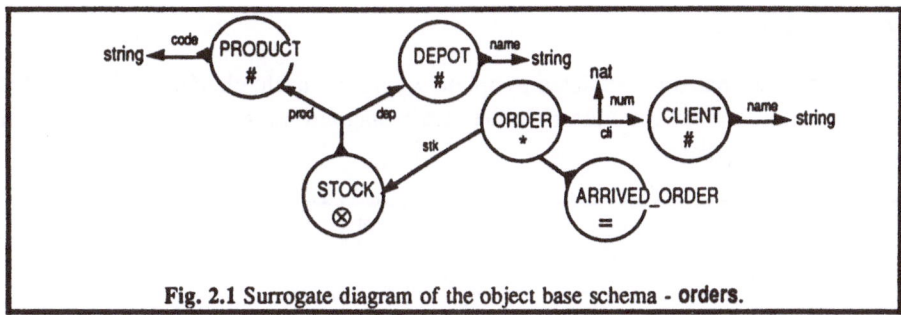

Fig. 2.1 Surrogate diagram of the object base schema - **orders**.

Values of constant attributes are established when the instance is created and cannot change during the life of the instance. They are different from key attributes because they are not part of the identification mechanism.

Fig. 2.1 presents the surrogate diagram for the object base schema orders. The relevant object classes are PRODUCT, DEPOT, STOCK, CLIENT, ORDER and ARRIVED_ORDER.

Object classes are represented by circles. The circle includes the name of the class as well as a character indicating the identification mechanism: #, *, ⊗, = stand for *foundation*, *replication*, *product* and *duplication*, respectively. Key attributes are represented by labeled arrows starting in black triangles and pointing to the corresponding codomain. The other arrows, not originating in black triangles, stand for constant attributes.

A foundation is a class whose instances are identified by data types. CLIENT is a foundation whose key attribute name has values of the data type string. Hence, for every possible string we may have a potencial instance of CLIENT.

One to many relationships are represented by the replication construct. ORDER is a replication of CLIENT, meaning that for each instance of CLIENT there may exist several instances of ORDER related to it. A particular instance of ORDER, for a given instance of CLIENT, is identified by a natural number. Two key attributes are needed for indicating, for a particular order, the client and the number of that order.

Many to many relationships are represented by the product construct. STOCK is a binary product of PRODUCT and DEPOT. In this way, a particular product can be related to different depots and different products can exist in the same depot, if the corresponding instances of STOCK exist. Given a particular product and a particular depot we can have at most one stock. For a binary product we need two key attributes, as expected.

The object class ARRIVED_ORDER is a duplication from the identification point of view. That is to say, we want to have potentially as many instances of ARRIVED_ORDER as instances of ORDER, and identified exactly in the same way. Hence, no new key attributes have to be introduced for duplications.

Stk is a constant attribute. Thus a particular order is always related to the same particular stock until deleted. This stock is assigned when the order is created.

As a synthesis we can say that we have different ways of identifying instances of classes: foundations are identified only by data types, products are identified only by instances of object classes and replications are identified by both an instance of an object class and a data type value.

2.2   Matrices

Each object class has an associated template where the basic characteristics of all the instances of the class are introduced. In the matrix diagram we indicate the events and the attributes of the template.

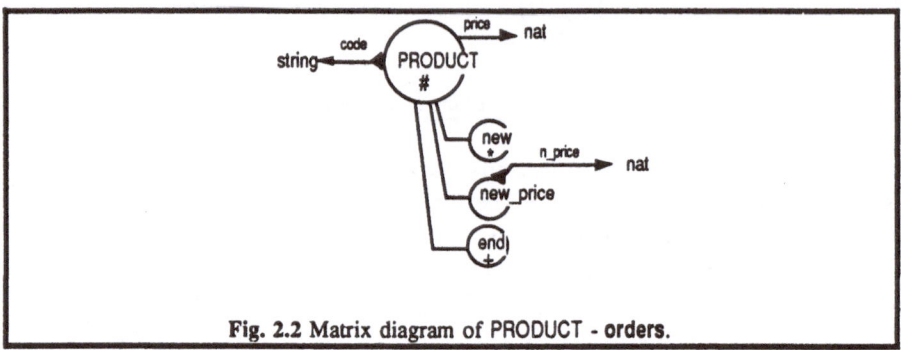

Fig. 2.2 Matrix diagram of PRODUCT - **orders**.

Events are atomic actions that may change the values of the attributes. We can have single events and event spaces. An event space allows the introduction of a collection of possible events with similar characteristics. Key attributes are then introduced for indicating the "parameters" of a particular event. Events are represented by small circles and belong to one of three possible categories —*birth*, *death* and *update*. Birth and death events are the way of starting and ending the life of an object. The indication of a birth event is compulsory but that is not the case with death events. In the matrix diagram birth and death events are labeled with * and +, respectively.

Consider the matrix diagram of the object class PRODUCT in fig. 2.2; new is a birth event and it is a single one; end is also a single event and it is a death event; new_price is an update event space. We can have as many events in this space as natural numbers. The key attribute n_price indicates for each event the respective natural number.

The matrix diagram also introduces the attributes. Besides the key and the constant attributes we also have the state dependent attributes whose value may change when certain events occur.

For instance, price is a state dependent attribute. However, it is not in the matrix diagram that we indicate what are the events responsible for the changes and what are the changes themselves.

As another example consider the matrix diagram of STOCK as introduced in fig. 2.3. The class STOCK is described as having two state attributes: quantity_on_hand, indicating the quantity of the product in stock, and order_queue, keeping the queue of orders waiting to be fulfilled. Note that the values of the attribute order_queue are of a queue data type whose parameter is the surrogate space of ORDER. Besides the birth we have events like arrival, of orders, replenishment, of the stock, decrease and invoice, related to the delivery of pending orders. No death events are declared.

The two object classes described above have different statuses from the activity/passivity point of view. A product is typically passive, whereas we can assume that a stock presents some kind of activity: pending orders are fulfilled as soon as possible. So, the events decrease and invoice of STOCK have self initiative, i.e., a particular stock is always trying to fulfill the pending orders. Events of self initiative are labeled by the symbol "!".

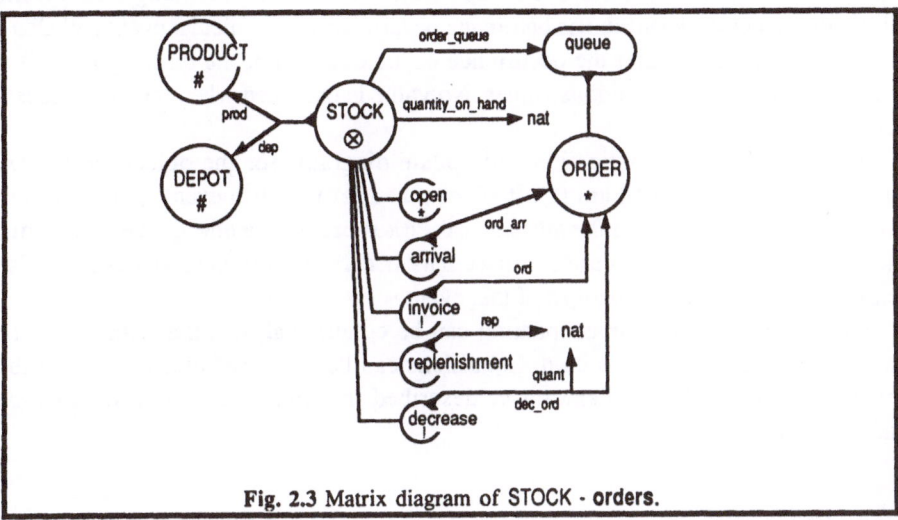

Fig. 2.3 Matrix diagram of STOCK - **orders**.

Constraints on the values of the attributes can be introduced in the matrix diagram, although no example appears above.

2.3 Attribute initialization/updating

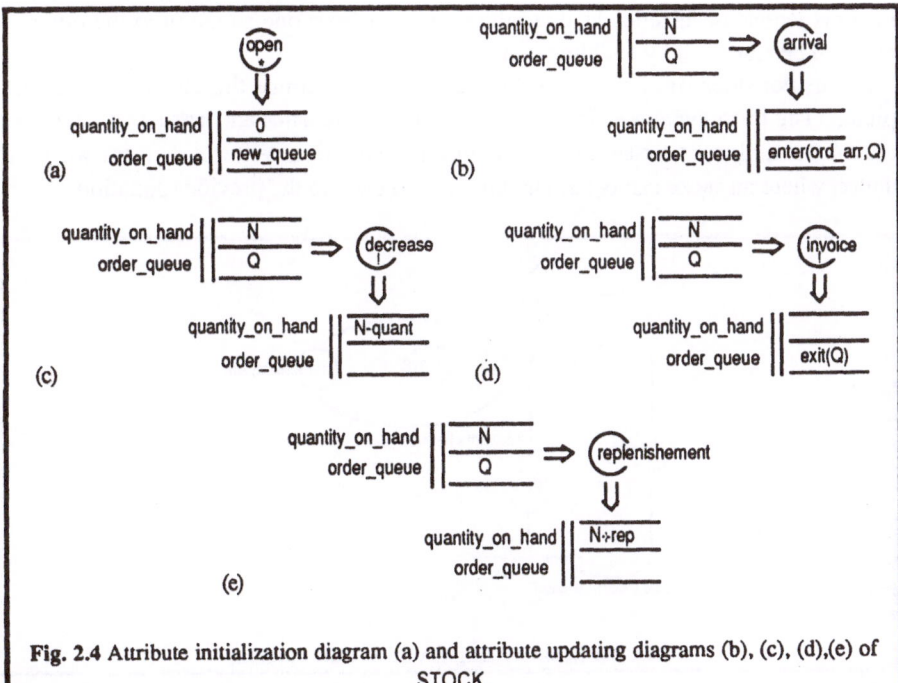

Fig. 2.4 Attribute initialization diagram (a) and attribute updating diagrams (b), (c), (d),(e) of STOCK.

As mentioned in the previous section it is necessary to state how the events change the values of the attributes. For this purpose we use attribute initialization diagrams to define the values of the attributes immediately after birth and attribute updating diagrams to define the effects of non birth events upon their values. In such diagrams we must indicate the values of the attributes before the occurrence of a particular event and also the values of the attributes after the occurrence of the events. For the birth events it is not necessary to indicate the previous values. No value is indicated when the event does not affect a particular attribute.

Fig. 2.4 includes initialization and update diagrams for the object class STOCK. Consider, for instance, diagram (a). It states that after the birth event open the value of quantity_on_hand becomes 0 and the attribute order_queue becomes a new queue. Diagram (b) states that when an event of the event space arrival occurs the attribute order_queue is updated according to the key attribute ord_arr of that event.

Some of the initializations/updating can be conditional, i.e., the effects only take place when certain conditions hold. Conditions can be expressed either in the attribute initialization and updating diagrams or described in (*value*) *binding diagrams*, to be detailed below.

2.4 Behavior

The behavior of an instance of an object class is characterized by the sequences of events that can occur during its lifetime. Allowed sequences are represented diagrammatically in behavior diagrams. Behavior diagrams introduce a collection of situations (horizontal bars) plus a set of transitions (arrows with event circles in the middle). Obviously, there is no situation before a birth event or after a death event. The circles in transitions indicate the events whose occurrence leads to the transition from one situation to the other. The events can be restricted by enabling conditions.

Let us consider fig. 2.5, where the behavior diagram of the object class STOCK is depicted. The birth event open leads to a situation where arrival and replenishment events can occur. Arrival and replenishment do not change the situation. After a decrease we go to a situation where an invoice can occur and then we go back to the previous situation.

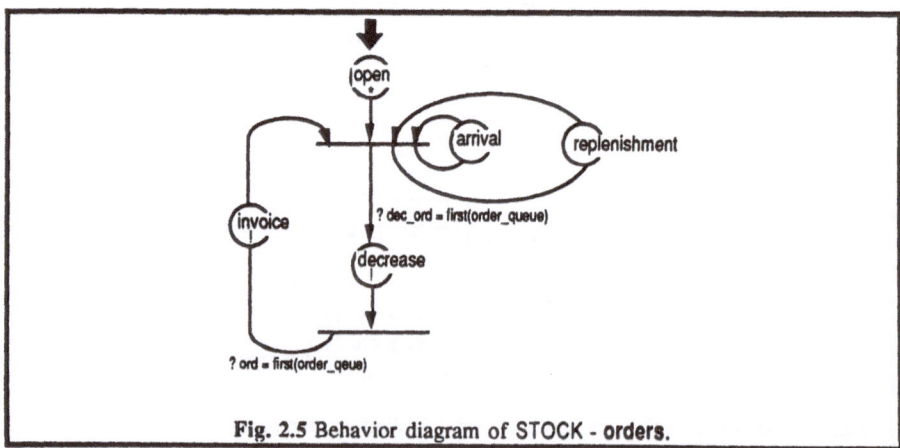

Fig. 2.5 Behavior diagram of STOCK - orders.

The event decrease is constrained by an enabling condition indicated by the symbol "?" labeling the arrow between the situation and the event. The condition states that the decrease can only occur when the corresponding order, indicated by dec_ord, is the first in order_queue. As said before we can express constraints using binding diagrams.

2.5 Semantics of templates

The template of a generic instance @C of an object class C is a triple $\mathcal{T}$@C= ($\mathcal{M}$@C,$\mathcal{V}$@C,$\mathcal{B}$@C) where $\mathcal{M}$@C is the matrix diagram, $\mathcal{V}$@C is the set of attribute initialization and updating diagrams and $\mathcal{B}$@C is the behavior diagram.

The denotation of the matrix diagram $\mathcal{M}$@C is a pair composed by a monoid whose set is the set of events $\mathcal{E}$@C and the operation is the parallel composition of events and a set of attributes $\mathcal{A}$@C, as well as the respective codomains.

Consider a generic instance @STOCK of the object class STOCK. The denotation of the matrix diagram $\mathcal{M}$@STOCK is the pair

$$((\mathcal{E}@STOCK, \|_{\mathcal{E}@STOCK}), \mathcal{A}@STOCK)$$

where
    $\mathcal{E}$@STOCK={open,arrival(o),invoice(o),replenishment(n),
                    decrease(o,n):o∈ IORDERI,n∈ IN$_o$ },
    IORDERI is the identification space of the object class ORDER,
    $\|_{\mathcal{E}@STOCK}$ is the parallel operator on $\mathcal{E}$@STOCK
    $\mathcal{A}$@STOCK={quantity_on_hand:IN$_o$,order_queue:queue(IORDERI)}

The denotation of the attribute initialization and updating diagrams $\mathcal{V}$@C is a set of positional formulae like

[u]a=t where u∈ $\mathcal{E}$@C, a∈ $\mathcal{A}$@C, t is an element of the codomain of a.

The denotation of the behavior diagram $\mathcal{B}$@C is a set of safety formulae like

{ after(u)∧F}

where u∈ $\mathcal{E}$@C, after is a temporal operator, F is a formula labelling the arrow in $\mathcal{B}$@C leading to u.

The denotation of the template $\mathcal{T}$@C=($\mathcal{M}$@C,$\mathcal{V}$@C,$\mathcal{B}$@C) is the category $\mathcal{C}$($\mathcal{G}$@C) generated by a graph $\mathcal{G}$@C. The set of nodes is

$$\mathcal{G}@C_0 \subseteq \mathcal{E}@C^* \times [\mathcal{A}@C \rightarrow \cup_{a \in \mathcal{A}@C} codom(a)]$$

indicating that each node is a pair composed by a particular sequence of events and an observation map verifying $f(a) \in \text{codom}(a)$. The value $f(a)$ corresponds to the value of the attribute a after that sequence. A generic node will be represented by $(\sigma, \{(a_i, f(a_i))\})$.

The set of arrows is

$$\mathcal{G}@C_1 \subseteq \mathcal{G}@C_0 \times \mathcal{E}@C$$

indicating that each arrow is a pair composed by a node g and an event e, such that

$$\text{source}((g,e)) = g$$
$$\text{target}((g,e)) = (\text{proj}_1(g)e, \{(a_i, v'_i)\})$$

provided that $\text{proj}_1(g)e$ is according to the behavior diagram $\mathcal{B}@C$, i.e., event e is allowed after the sequence $\text{proj}_1(g)$ and v'_i is according to the attribute initialization and updating diagrams $\mathcal{V}@C$, i.e., v'_i is the value of attribute a_i after the sequence $\text{proj}_1(g)e$.

Consider a graph $\mathcal{G}@\text{STOCK}$ underlying the category that denotes $\mathcal{T}@\text{STOCK}$. Examples of nodes are

$$g = (<\text{open}>, \{(\text{quantity\_on\_hand}, 0), (\text{order\_queue}, \text{new\_queue})\})$$
$$g' = (<\text{open arrival(o)}>, \{(\text{quantity\_on\_hand}, 0), (\text{order\_queue}, \text{enter}(o, \text{new\_queue}))\})$$

An example of an arrow is

$(g', \text{replenishment}(n))$
    $\text{source}(g', \text{replenishment}(n)) = g'$
    $\text{target}(g', \text{replenishment}(n)) = g''$
        $g'' = (<\text{open arrival(o) replenishment(n)}>,$
                $\{(\text{quantity\_on\_hand}, n+m, (\text{order\_queue}, \text{enter}(o, k))\})$
such that
                $m = \text{proj}_2(\text{proj}_2(g'))(\text{quantity\_on\_hand})$ is the value of attribute quantity_on_hand
                $k = \text{proj}_2(\text{proj}_2(g'))(\text{order\_queue})$ is the value of attribute order_queue

For more details about descriptions and denotations of descriptions as graphs see [31].

2.6 Incorporation (inheritance)

So far we have described instances of object classes as independent entities in an object base. However, the usual situation is to have an object base whose object classes instances do interact with each other. Interaction always imposes synchronization between the involved instances. We start by discussing incorporation, which is a very strong form of synchronization.

As an example, assume that we want to make the "total" interaction of a product with the orders involving that product, i.e., a product is synchronized with all the orders of that product. We say that PRODUCT must be incorporated into ORDER. The first consequence of the incorporation is the "code reuse" of PRODUCT in ORDER. That is to say, all the events and attributes of PRODUCT are also events and attributes of ORDER.

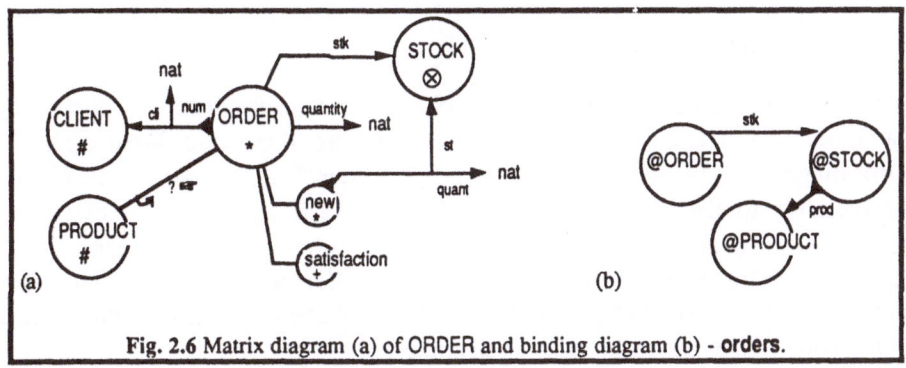

Fig. 2.6 Matrix diagram (a) of ORDER and binding diagram (b) - **orders**.

Incorporations are indicated in the matrix diagram of the target object class of the incorporation by a special hook as the one in fig. 2.6. However we must indicate which are the instances of PRODUCT and ORDER that we want to synchronize. In a sense we must define a condition stating what instances are. This condition is indicated by the symbol "?", the symbol "☞" refers to the value binding diagram also of fig. 2.6.

The entities in a value binding diagram are instances of object classes and event spaces, represented by instance variables prefixed with @, or else data type variables. The purpose of the diagram is to establish bindings to some attributes of the involved instances by using the usual attribute arrows. Other bindings to the variables involved can be represented by expressions in the bottom. When all the bindings presented are true we can say that the implicit condition holds. The binding diagram in fig. 2.6 indicates that the instance @PRODUCT of the object class PRODUCT is incorporated into each instance @ORDER of the object class ORDER whose attribute stk points to an instance @STOCK of the object class STOCK whose value of the key attribute prod is @PRODUCT. Hence, for instance, an event new_price is "seen" by every order of that product. However, a particular product does not "see" an event satisfaction of an order of this product.

In general, we have an incorporation from the object class C_1 into an object class C_2 when the events and the attributes of C_1 are also events and attributes of C_2. There is an incorporation mechanism between the instances of both object classes. The effects of the incorporated events on incorporated attributes are maintained, i.e., we do not have to repeat the respective attribute initialization and updating diagrams. The behavior of an instance in C_1 when incorporated can be further constrained. Note that a new behavior diagram must be given indicating the relationship between the new events and the events that are inherited.

As referred above we can have different kinds of incorporations. In a *safe incorporation* we cannot have events of the target instance that affect the value of the attributes of the argument instance. Hence the values of the incorporated attributes in the target instance are exactly the values of the incorporated attributes in the argument instance. On the contrary, in a *liberal incorporation* the latter restriction does not apply.

The incorporation of PRODUCT into ORDER is a safe one. We do not want events new and satisfaction to affect the values of the attributes of PRODUCT. Moreover, no constraining on events of PRODUCT is indicated.

2.7 Semantics of incorporation

The template of a generic instance @C of an object class C incorporating the instance @D of an object class D is a triple $\mathcal{T}_{@D\to@C} = (\mathcal{M}_{@D\to@C}, \mathcal{V}_{@D\to@C}, \mathcal{B}_{@D\to@C})$. The matrix diagram is $\mathcal{M}_{@D\to@C} = \mathcal{M}_{@C} \cup \mathcal{M}_{@D}$ where $\mathcal{M}_{@C}$ is the matrix diagram corresponding to the new events and attributes. $\mathcal{V}_{@D\to@C}$ is the set of attribute initialization and updating diagrams. These diagrams result from joining the attributes and indicating the effects of the events on the attributes. Events of @C should not change attributes of @D and events of @D must change the attributes of @D as they did before the incorporation. $\mathcal{B}_{@D\to@C}$ is the behavior diagram.

The denotation of $\mathcal{T}_{@D\to@C}$ is the category $C(\mathcal{G}_{@D\to@C})$ generated a graph $\mathcal{G}_{@D\to@C}$ whose definition is along the same lines as we discussed in 2.5.

2.8 Other issues: interaction and abstraction

We have seen the incorporation as a mechanism for synchronizing in a close way instances of object classes. A weaker basic mechanism for synchronization at the event level is *event calling*. Assume also that we have instances O_1 and O_2 of object classes C_1 and C_2, respectively. Assume that we say that event e_1 in O_1 calls event e_2 of O_2. When event e_1 happens in O_1 then event e_2 also happens in O_2. However, it may be possible that event e_2 happens in O_2 with no correspondence to event e_1 of O_1. Hence, calling is an asymmetrical interaction.

Consider again the matrix diagram of the object class STOCK presented in section 2.2 and the (incomplete) matrix diagram of DEPOT in fig. 2.7.

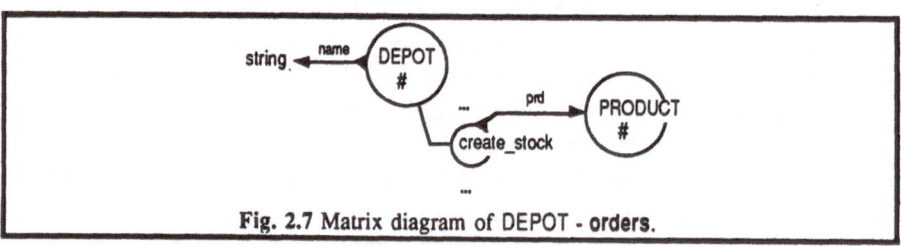

Fig. 2.7 Matrix diagram of DEPOT - orders.

Consider again the matrix diagram of the object class STOCK presented in section 2.2 and the (incomplete) matrix diagram of DEPOT in fig. 2.7.

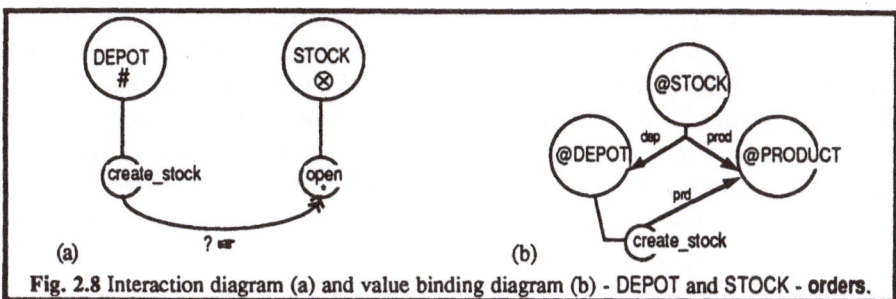

Fig. 2.8 Interaction diagram (a) and value binding diagram (b) - DEPOT and STOCK - **orders**.

Assume that we want to create a new stock whenever an event create_stock occurs in a particular instance of the object class DEPOT. In other words, we want to have an interaction between the event space create_stock of DEPOT and the birth event open of STOCK. This interaction is indicated by an event calling from DEPOT to STOCK. The event create_stock is the argument of the calling and event open is the target of the calling.

Event callings are expressed in interaction diagrams. More than one calling can be introduced in the same interaction diagram. In such diagrams we indicate the object classes involved as well as the argument and the target events of the callings. Arrows indicate the direction of the callings. The presence of the symbol "?" indicates that a condition must be fulfilled. This condition indicates the specific instances of the object classes as well as the specific events that are involved in the calling. Alternatively we can use expressions labeling the calling arrows.

In fig. 2.8 we depict the interaction between DEPOT and STOCK. We impose that an event of the event space create_stock calls an event open. In the binding diagram we indicate the instances of the object classes involved in the calling. Moreover, we indicate the specific event of the event space create_stock that is the argument of the calling.

Instance @DEPOT of the object class DEPOT interacts with instance @STOCK of the object class STOCK. The key attribute dep of @STOCK is @DEPOT. The key attribute prod of @STOCK is the instance @PRODUCT of the object class PRODUCT which is the value of the key attribute prd of the event create_stock.

The abstraction mechanism is yet another form of interaction which is somehow the reverse of incorporation. The result of an abstraction is smaller than the argument object class. The result is obtained by indicating the events and the attributes that we want to retain.

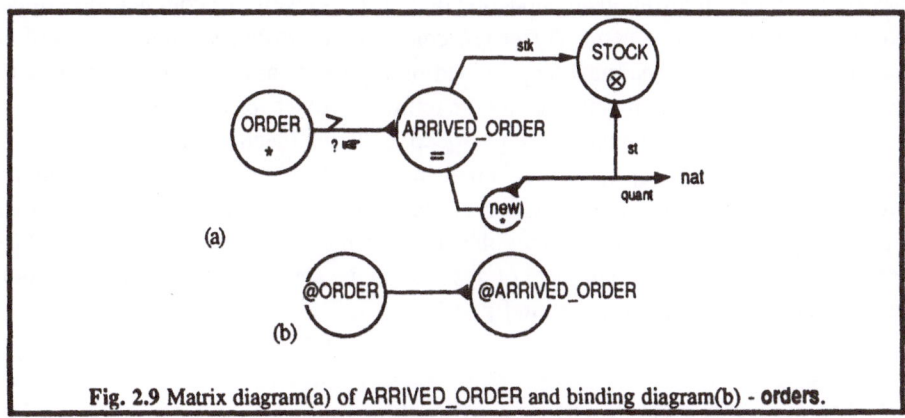

Fig. 2.9 Matrix diagram(a) of ARRIVED_ORDER and binding diagram(b) - **orders**.

In fig. 2.9 we introduce ARRIVED_ORDER as an abstraction of ORDER. Abstractions are indicated in the matrix diagram of the resulting object class. The symbol "<" indicates an abstraction. In the case at hand, we want to keep the event space new and the attribute stk. ORDER is synchronized with ARRIVED_ORDER in the sense that when a new order is created a new arrived order is also created. However, a satisfaction event in a particular instance of ORDER is not synchronized with any event of the respective instance of ARRIVED_ORDER.

3 Reification

3.1 Main concepts

Let us detail the problem at hand. Adopting a pure object-oriented perspective we can understand reification as the way to establish how we can go from an object base schema, called the *abstract object base schema*, into a "more concrete" (*refined*) object base schema, called the *ground object base schema*. As an example consider that we have an abstract object base schema aobs with a single object class. Assume that on the other hand we have the ground object base schema gobs. A *reification* of aobs on top of gobs consists of stating how the object class in aobs is "refined" using object classes of gobs, i.e., how the attributes and the events of the object class in aobs can be "refined" in terms of the attributes and the events of the object classes in gobs.

Two main approaches can be followed in reification: the axiomatic and the constructive approaches. In the *axiomatic approach*, a complete definition of the abstract object base schema must be provided including the complete description of each object class, identification mechanism and template, as well as a complete description of the ground object base schema. A *reification* of the abstract object base schema includes the reification of the attributes and the events of the object classes in the abstract object base schema on top of the attributes and events of the object classes in the ground object base schema by introducing the *reification object base schema*. Finally, the compliance of the reification object base schema against the description of the abstract object base schema must be verified. This verification can be very complicated.

In the *constructive approach* we provide a *partial* definition of the abstract object base schema, composed by the identification mechanism, the events and the attributes (no behavior, attribute initialization and updating diagrams), as well as a complete description of the ground object base schema. A *free reification* of the attributes and the events of the abstract object base schema must be provided on top of the attributes and events of the ground object base schema by introducing the reification object base schema.

Herein, we adopt the constructive perspective. Three mechanisms are essential for defining the reification object base schema: incorporation, as described in chapter 2, *derived attributes* and *transactions*. As a very simplified version of the stock management application we can consider the abstract object base schema dealer composed by the object class DEALER. Hence, at a certain level of abstraction we are only concerned with dealers. The surrogate diagram is introduced in fig. 3.1.

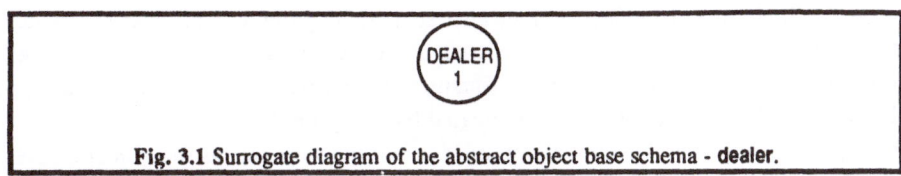

Fig. 3.1 Surrogate diagram of the abstract object base schema - **dealer**.

For simplicity reasons we consider that the object class DEALER has a single instance, as indicated by the symbol "1", and, as a consequence, there is no need to indicate a specific identification mechanism. The matrix diagram of DEALER is described in fig. 3.2. The attribute value_in_stock indicates, for each pair product/depot, the value of the quantity in stock. The codomain is an array whose indexes are strings, referring to the pair product/depot, and whose components are natural numbers. The birth event is start. The update event spaces are order and sale, meaning that the dealer knows of orders and sales.

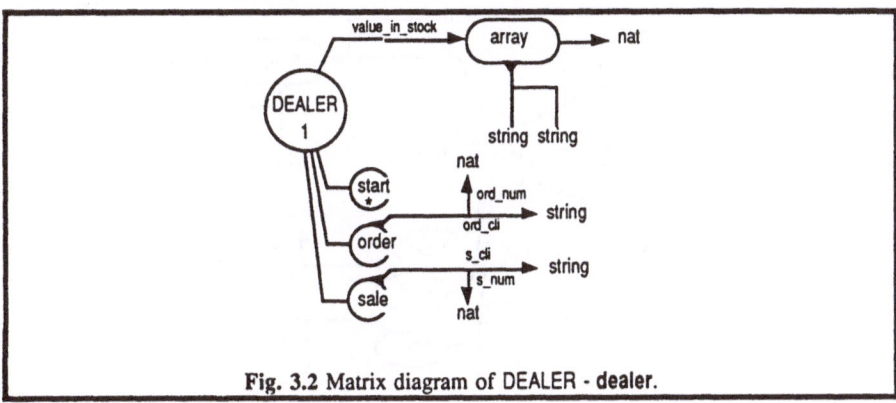

Fig. 3.2 Matrix diagram of DEALER - **dealer**.

In the constructive approach no behavior, attribute initialization and updating must be included since we will define such aspects in terms of the object classes of the ground object base schema. We can say that the object class DEALER in the abstract object base schema is completely described at the template level by the matrix diagram.

The surrogate diagram of orders is presented in fig. 2.1. We want to describe the reification of the object class DEALER (the argument) of the abstract object base schema dealer on top of orders (the target). The first step is to describe the reification object base schema dealer_orders. Let us start by discussing the surrogate diagram presented in fig. 3.3.

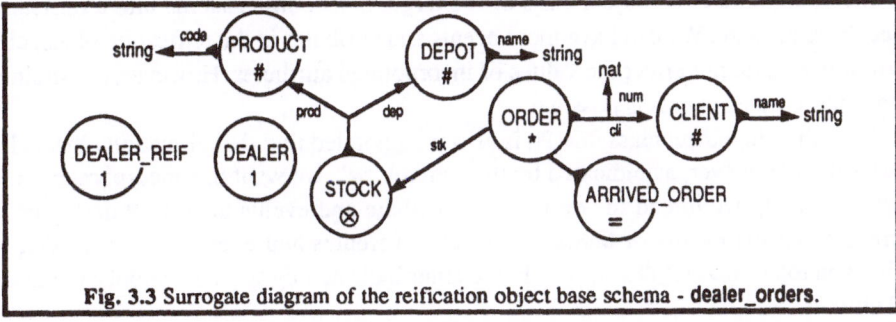

Fig. 3.3 Surrogate diagram of the reification object base schema - **dealer_orders**.

290

We see that both the object classes in the abstract and the ground object base schemata are included in the reification object base schema. Moreover, we see a new object class called DEALER_REIF which corresponds to the reification of the object class DEALER. Again it is an object class with a unique instance as indicated by the symbol "1".

In general, we must have as many *reification object classes* as the object classes in the abstract object base schema that we want to refine. Each class of the latter kind is called the argument of the reification. Of course it is possible to have object classes in the abstract object base schema which we do not want to refine. On the other hand, it is possible to have object classes in the ground object base schema which are not relevant for the reification at hand.

In general a reification object class is a duplication of the argument class in the abstract object base schema. The template of the class DEALER_REIF is introduced in fig. 3.4.

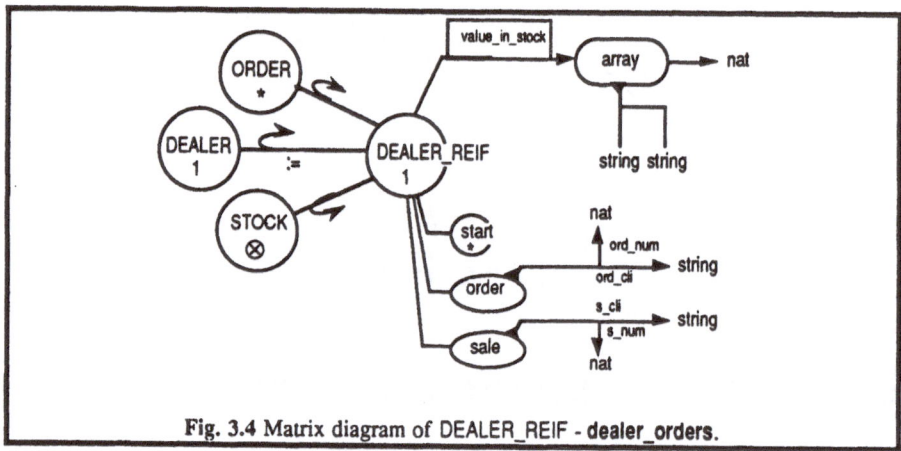

Fig. 3.4 Matrix diagram of DEALER_REIF - **dealer_orders**.

We see that the object classes ORDER and STOCK are incorporated in DEALER_REIF as indicated by the hooks. Since no value binding diagrams are appended we want all the instances of ORDER and STOCK to be synchronized with (incorporated by) the unique instance of DEALER_REIF.

The incorporation of n object classes of the ground object base schema into a reification object class indicates that we need the n object classes to make the reification. Of course it is possible to use different object classes in different reifications. Moreover, it is possible to incorporate the same object class in different reification object classes. The incorporations of an object class of the target object base schema into a reification object class are safe. We can have more events and attributes in the reification object class but new events do not affect the values of incorporated attributes. However, constraining of the incorporated events is possible.

Note that the object class DEALER is also incorporated into the reification object class DEALER_REIF. However, as indicated by the symbol ":=", we want this incorporation to be special. Namely we intend to "define" the attribute and events of DEALER on top of the attributes and the events of DEALER_REIF. The attributes and events of DEALER that are defined on top of DEALER_REIF appear in the latter indicated by special symbols: rectangles and ellipses.

Attributes of an object class in the abstract object base schema are defined through *derivation* upon the attributes of the object classes of the ground object base schema incorporated by the reification object class. Such attributes are derived attributes. The values of a derived attribute are not established by the occurrence of events but by a *derivation expression* involving other attributes, called the *argument attributes*. Of course changes of the argument attributes are indirectly reflected on the derived attributes. We can have constant and state dependent derived attributes. The derivation expression of a constant derived attribute can only involve arguments that are either key or constant attributes. The derivation expression of a state dependent attribute must involve arguments that can be key, constant, state dependent attributes but involving at least one of the latter.

Derived attributes are indicated by rectangles with the name of the attribute inside. Thus, in DEALER_REIF, value_in_stock is a derived attribute. Values of derived attributes are indicated in *derivation diagrams*. These diagrams include the expression involved in the derivation as well as the identification of the instances of object classes whose values are used in such expression.

As an example consider the derivation diagram for the derived attribute value_in_stock presented in fig. 3.5.

The basic idea is to define the value V of the derived attribute value_in_stock for two particular strings S_1 and S_2 as the quantity on hand Q for the stock times the price P of each unit of the product in stock. Hence, the derivation expression is $V=Q \times P$. The diagram shows what are Q and P. The first step is to identify the instance @DEPOT of the object class DEPOT and the instance @PRODUCT of the object class PRODUCT. We state that @DEPOT must be the instance whose value of the key attribute name is S_2 and that @PRODUCT must be the instance whose value of the key attribute code is S_1. Once we identify the instance @PRODUCT, we can say that P is the value of the attribute price of this instance. We can then identify the instance @STOCK of the object class STOCK by saying that the values of the key attributes prod and dep for this instance must be @PRODUCT and @DEPOT, respectively. Finally, Q is the value of the attribute quantity_on_hand for @STOCK.

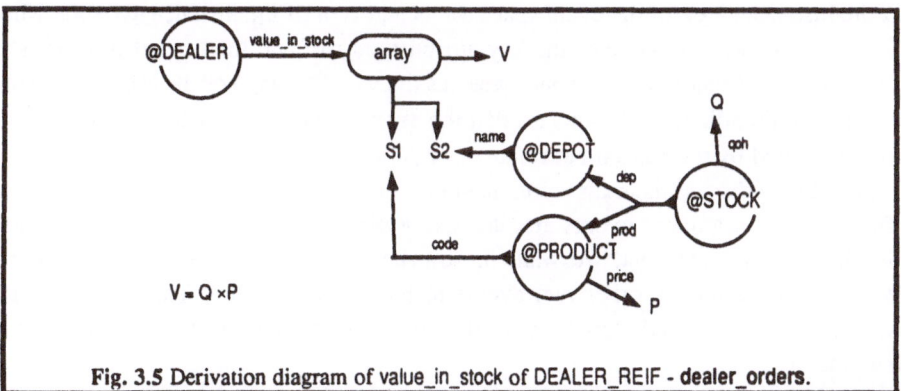

Fig. 3.5 Derivation diagram of value_in_stock of DEALER_REIF - **dealer_orders.**

Events of an object class in the abstract object base schema may be defined by transactions involving events of the object classes of the ground object base schema incorporated into the reification object class. Transactions can involve several events, called the *argument events*, and establish precedence relationships between them. As with events we can have transaction spaces. These spaces are characterized by key attributes. A particular transaction in a transaction space has particular values for the key attributes. When an argument of the reification is an event space then a transaction space must be defined in the reification object class. The basic idea about transactions is that when the event in the abstract object base occurs, then the corresponding transaction must be completed in the reification object base.

Transactions are indicated by ellipses. Hence, as indicated by the matrix diagram of DEALER_REIF, we have the transactions order and sale. Transactions are defined in *transaction diagrams*. Such diagrams are similar to behavior diagrams. The transaction diagram for the transaction space order is indicated in fig. 3.6.

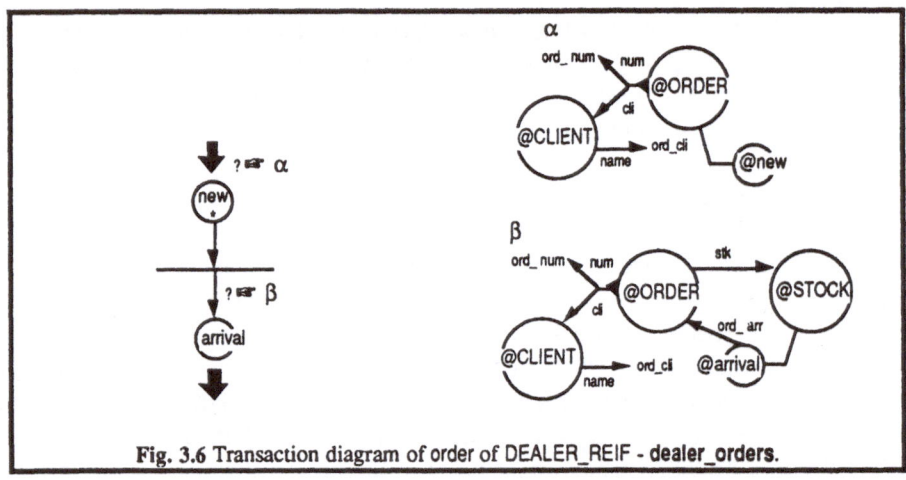

Fig. 3.6 Transaction diagram of order of DEALER_REIF - **dealer_orders**.

We establish that the transaction order has the events new of ORDER and arrival of STOCK as arguments. Bold arrows indicate the way in and the way out as before. The binding diagrams indicated by α and β state, for a particular event order, the instances of ORDER and STOCK where we want to pick up the events new and arrival, respectively. As indicated in α the instance @new of the event space new is an event of the instance @ORDER whose key attribute num is the value of the key attribute ord_num and the key attribute cli is the instance @CLIENT whose key attribute name has the value of ord_cli of the transaction space order. The binding diagram β indicates that the event @arrival must belong to the instance @STOCK pointed by the constant attribute stk of @ORDER.

Let us now discuss the transaction diagram of the transaction space sale as introduced in fig. 3.7. The argument events are: decrease, invoice of STOCK and satisfaction of ORDER. This diagram indicates that we want the transaction to start with an event decrease. Afterwards we want the other two events to happen in parallel. That is to say, it is possible that invoice precedes satisfaction or the other way around, or that they occur at the same time.

The binding diagrams indicated by α, β and γ indicate the instances of the object classes STOCK, ORDER and STOCK where we want to pick up the instances @decrease, @satisfaction and @invoice, respectively. Moreover, in the binding diagram α we also indicate that @decrease is only possible provided that the target @ORDER involves a quantity N that is less than or equal to the value M of quantity_on_hand of @STOCK.

Finally, we must state the relationship between the event start and the transaction spaces order and sale. We can do so in the behavior diagram introduced in fig. 3.8 where we can use both events and transactions.

Hence, the behavior of an instance of DEALER_REIF must start with the event start followed by transactions of the transaction space order and transactions of the transaction space sale.

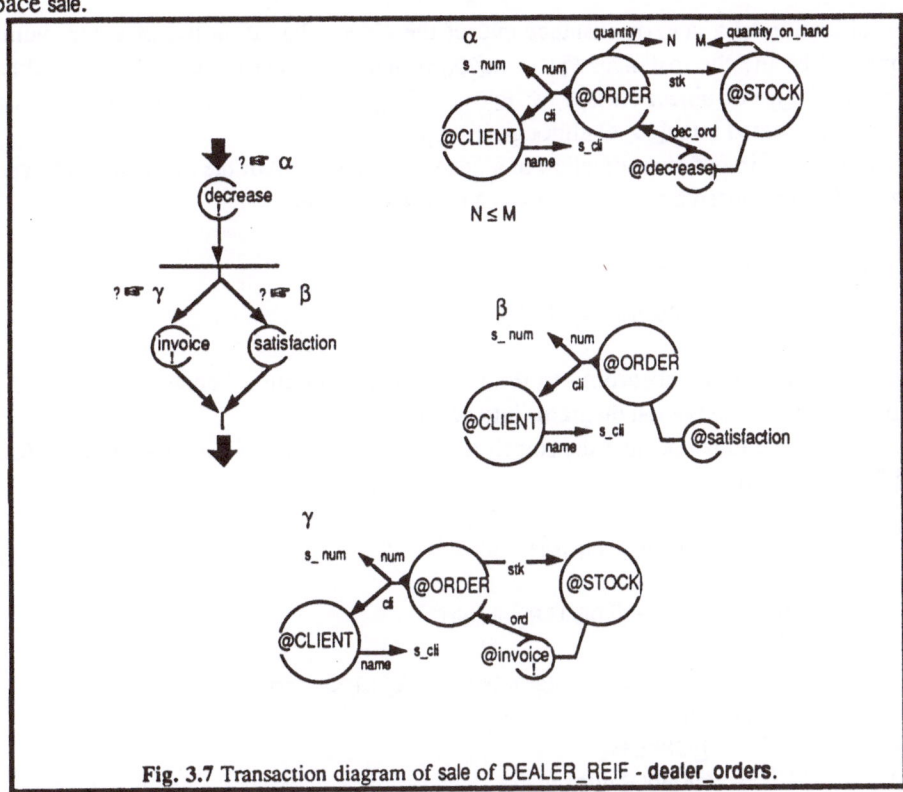

Fig. 3.7 Transaction diagram of sale of DEALER_REIF - **dealer_orders**.

As a conclusion, we can say that in the constructive approach we must start by identifying the object classes in the abstract object class schema that will be refined. A selection of the target object classes of the ground object base schema must be indicated. The schema of a reification object base must be introduced having the object classes referred to above as well as a duplication of each argument object class, called the reification object classes. The matrix of each reification object class must incorporate the relevant target object classes. Moreover, the argument object class must also be incorporated, i.e., all its events and attributes must be events and attributes of the reification object class. The attributes will be defined as derived attributes, and events will be defined as transactions. The reification object class is completed by indicating how events and transactions of the reification object class are related.

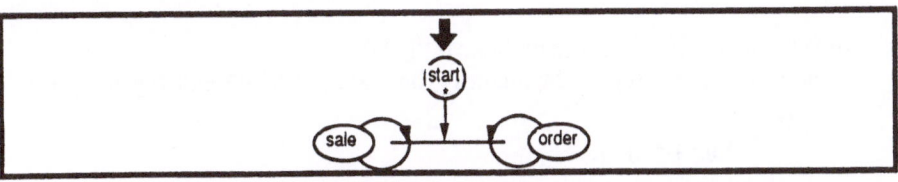

<hr>
Fig. 3.8 Behavior diagram of DEALER_REIF - **dealer_orders**.
<hr>

3.2   Semantics

The reification of a generic instance @C of the object class C on top of a community composed by the the instances @D_1,...,@D_n of the object classes D_1,...,D_n is an object instance @C_reif of object class C_reif. @D_1,...,@D_n are incorporated into @C_reif. Also @C is incorporated into @C_reif although in a special way.

The denotation of the reification of a generic instance @C of the object class C over a community composed by @D_1,...,@D_n is a pair $(h_e, \mathcal{F})$ where

h_e: $\mathcal{E}$@C$\rightarrow \mathcal{E}$@C_reif$^+$
$\mathcal{F}$:$\mathcal{C}(\mathcal{G}$@C$)\rightarrow \mathcal{C}(\mathcal{G}$@C_reif) is a functor

The map h_e is defined according to the transaction diagrams whereas the functor $\mathcal{F}$ is defined taking the derivation diagrams into account.

As an illustration consider the semantics of the reification of DEALER on top of ORDER and STOCK. The map

h_e: $\mathcal{E}$@DEALER$\rightarrow \mathcal{E}$@DEALER_reif$^+$

h_e(@DEALER.start)=@DEALER_reif.start

h_e(@DEALER.order(s,n))=<@ORDER.new @STOCK.arrival(o)>
    such that
        @ORDER=o
        @ORDER.num=n
        @ORDER.cli=@CLIENT:@CLIENT.name=s
        @ORDER.stk=@STOCK

h_e(@DEALER.sale(s,n))=
    <@STOCK.decrease(o,k) @STOCK.invoice(o)||@ORDER.satisfaction>
    such that
        @ORDER=o
        @ORDER.num=n
        @ORDER.cli=@CLIENT:@CLIENT.name=s
        @ORDER.stk=@STOCK
        @STOCK.quantity_on_hand=m
        k≤m

$\mathcal{F}_0$((<e_1,...,e_n>,{(value_in_stock(s_i,s_j),v_{ij})}))=
    (h_e(<e_1,...,e_n>),{(@$STOCK_i$.quantity_on_hand,q_i),(@$PRODUCT_j$.price,p_j)})
        such that
            v_{ij}=q_i×q_j

$$@\text{PRODUCT}_j.\text{code}=s_j$$
$$@\text{STOCK}_i.\text{dep.name}=s_i$$
$$@\text{STOCK}_i.\text{prod}=@\text{PRODUCT}_j$$

For more details about reification see [31,32].

4 Concluding remarks

We discuss the reification dimension in object-oriented data base design. Although an important issue is how to implement object bases in traditional environments we prefer to discuss herein the reification of an object base schema, the *abstract object base schema*, on top of another object base schema, the *ground object base schema*.

The reification involves the definition of another object base schema, the *reification object base schema*. Two possible definitions of reification are introduced: the axiomatic and the constructive perspectives, depending on the definition of the abstract object base schema (complete or partial). Herein we adopt the constructive approach.

The main idea for reification is to introduce in the reification object base schema a new object class for each object class in the abstract object base schema that we want to refine. The reification itself consists in the definition of such object classes. The concepts needed are *incorporation* (inheritance), *derived attributes* and *transactions*.

Consider a particular reification object class. This class must incorporate the relevant object classes of the ground object base schema. Moreover it must also incorporate the object class of the abstract object base under refinement. The attributes of this object are then defined as derived attributes, i.e., they are defined by an expression involving the attributes of the target object classes. The events are defined as transactions involving the events of the target object classes.

For discussing reification we use a diagrammatic notation. Hence we introduce all relevant aspects in diagrams. We start by introducing the diagrams that allow the definition of object base schemata. The diagrams reflect the fact that an object base schema is a collection of object classes plus the interaction (synchronization) between the instances of the classes. Three basic mechanisms for interaction are identified. The basic mechanism has the event as granule and is the event calling. Incorporation and abstraction appear as stronger forms of synchronization. Incorporation provides the different forms of inheritance whereas abstraction is related to the view concept in data bases. For reification we need *derivation* and *transaction diagrams*.

The object-oriented approach that we follow has been under intensive research in the ESPRIT BRA ISCORE (Information Systems - Correctness and Reusability). Several aspects of this research were left out of the paper. Namely the algebraic/categorial semantics [33,34,35,36], the specification language [37,38,39], the calculus for verification and correctness [40,41,42], the proof-theoretic semantics of the specification language constructs [43,44], the query language [45] and the Gentzen-like calculus [46].

Acknowledgements

This work was partially supported by *Junta Nacional de Investigação Científica e Tecnológica* (JNICT) through the OBCALC project and by ESPRIT BRA IS-CORE.

References

[1] Dayal, U. and Dittrich, K. (eds), *Proc. of the International Workshop on Object-oriented Database Systems*, Los Angeles, IEEE Computer Society, 1986

[2] Dittrich, K., *Advances in Object-oriented Database Systems*, Springer Verlag, 1988

[3] Kim, W. and Lochovski, F. (eds), *Object-oriented Concepts, Databases and Applications*, ACM Press, Addison-Wesley, 1988

[4] Lochovski, F., *Special Issue on Object-oriented Systems*, IEEE Database Engineering, 8(4), 1985

[5] W. Kim, J.-M. Nicolas and S. Nishio (eds), *First International Conference on Deductive and Object-oriented Databases*, 1989, 370-395

[6] Fiadeiro, J. and Sernadas, A., "Specification and Verification of Database Dynamics", *Acta Informatica* 25, 1988, 625-661

[7] Gustafsson, M., Karlsson, T. and Bubenko, J., "A Declarative Approach to Conceptual Information Modeling, Olle, W., Sol, H. and Verrijn-Stuart, A., *Information Systems Design Methodologies: A Comparative Review*, North-Holland, 1982, 93-142

[8] Olivé, A., "Dades: A Methodology for Specification and Design of Information Systems", Olle, W., Sol, H. and Verrijn-Stuart, A., *Information Systems Design Methodologies: A Comparative Review*, North-Holland, 1982, 285-334

[9] Rolland, C., Bodart, F. and Leonard, M. (eds), *Temporal Aspects of Information Systems*, North-Holland, 1988

[10] Rolland, C. and Richard, C., "The Remora Methodology for Information Systems Design and Management", Olle, W., Sol, H. and Verrijn-Stuart, A., *Information Systems Design Methodologies: A Comparative Review*, North-Holland, 1982, 369-426

[11] Saake, G. and Lipeck, U., "Using Finite-Linear Temporal Logic for Specifying Database Dynamics", *Proc. CSL'88 2nd Workshop Computer Science Logic*, Borger, E. Kleine Buening, H. and Richter, M., LNCS 385, Springer Verlag, 1989, 288-300

[12] Sernadas, A., "Temporal Aspects of Logical Procedure Definition", *Information Systems* 5, 1980, 167-187

[13] Sernadas, A. and Sernadas, C., "Conceptual Modeling for Knowledge-Based DSS Development", Holsapple, C. and Whinston, A. (eds), *Decision Support Systems: Theory and Practice*, North-Holland, 1986, 121-140

[14] Atkinson, M., Bancilhon, F., DeWitt, D., Dittrich, K., Maier, D. and Zdonik, S., "The Object-oriented Database System Manifesto", *First International Conference on Deductive and Object-oriented Databases*, W. Kim, J.-M. Nicolas and S. Nishio (eds), 1989, 40-57

[15] Bancilhon, F., "Object-oriented Database Systems", *Procs of the ACM Sigact-SIGMOD-SIGART Conference on the Principles of Database Systems*, 1988

[16] Cluet, S. Delobel, C., Lécluse, C. and Richard, P., "Reloop, An Algebra Query Language for an Object-oriented Database System", in [KNN89], 294-313

[17] Khoshafian, S. and Copeland, G., "Object Identity", *Sigplan Notices*, 21[11], 1986

[18] Wieringa, R., "Equational Specification of Dynamic Objects", *Object-oriented Databases: Analysis, Design and Construction*, R. Meersman and Kent, B. (eds), North-Holland, to be published

[19] Cardelli, L., "Semantics of Multiple Inheritance", *Readings in Object-oriented Database Systems*, S. Zdonik and D. Maier (eds), Morgan Kaufmann Publ, 1989, 59-83

[20] Navathe, S. and Cheng, A., "A Methodology for Database Schema Mapping from Extended Entity Relationship Models into the Hierarchical Model", Davis, C. et al, *Entity Relationship Approach to Software Engineering*, Elsevier Science, 1983

[21] De Troyer, O. and Meersman, R., "Transforming Conceptual Schema Semantics to Relational Data Applications", *Information Modelling and Data Base Management*, Springer Verlag, 1986

[22] Ehrich, H.-D. and Sernadas, A., "Algebraic Implementation of Objects over Objects", de Bakker, J., de Roever, W. and Rozenberg (eds), *REX89: Stepwise Refinement of Distributed Systems: Models, Formalisms, Correctness*, Springer Verlag, 1989, 239-266

[23] Ehrich, H.-D., "On the Theory of Specification, Implementation, and Parametrization of Abstract Data Types", Journal of the ACM, 29(1), 1982, 206-227

[24] Ehrich, H.-D., Sernadas, A. and Sernadas, C., "Abstract Object Types for Databases", *Advances in Object-Oriented Database Systems*, in [Dit88]

[25] Sernadas, A. and Ehrich, H.-D., "What is an Object, After All", *Object-oriented Databases: Analysis, Design and Construction*, Meersman, R. and Kent, B. (eds), North-Holland, to be published

[26] Sernadas, A., Fiadeiro, J., Sernadas, C. and Ehrich, H.-D., "The Basic Building Blocks of Information Systems", *Information System Concepts: An In-depth Analysis*, Falkenberg, E. and Lindgreen, P. (eds), North Holland, 1989, 225-246

[27] C. Sernadas, P. Resende, P. Gouveia and A. Sernadas. "In-the-large Object-oriented Design of Information Systems". *The Object-Oriented Approach in Information Systems*, F. Van Assche, B. Moulin and C. Rolland (eds), North Holland, to be published

[28] Sernadas, A., Sernadas, C. and Ehrich, H.-D., "Object-Oriented Specification of Databases: An Algebraic Approach", *Proc. 13th Conference on Very Large Data Bases*, VLDB, Hammersley, P. (ed), 1987, 107-116

[29] Costa, J.-F. and Sernadas, A., *Process Models Within a Categorial Framework*, INESC, 1991

[30] Sernadas, A., Ehrich, H.-D. and Costa, J.-F-, "From Processes to Objects", *The INESC Journal of Research and Development*, 1990, 7-27

[31] Sernadas, C., Gouveia, P., Costa, J.-F. and Sernadas, A., "Graph-theoretic Semantics of Oblog: Diagrammatic Language for Object-oriented Specifications, *Procs IS-CORE Workshop 91*, Saake, G. and Sernadas, A. (eds), to be published

[32] Sernadas, C., Gouveia, P. and Sernadas, A., *Refinement: Layered Definition of Conceptual Schemata*, INESC 1991

[33] Ehrich, H.-D., Goguen, J. and Sernadas, A., "A Categorial Theory of Objects as Observed Processes", *REX90: Foundations of Object-oriented Languages*, Springer-Verlag, to be published

[34] Ehrich, H.-D., Sernadas, A. and Sernadas, C.,, "Objects, Object Types and Object Identity", *Categorical Methods in Computer Science with Aspects from Topology*, H. Ehrig et al, Springer Verlag, 1989, 142-156

[35] Ehrich, H.-D., Sernadas, A. and Sernadas, C., "From Data Types to Object Types", *Journal of Information Processing and Cybernetics*, EIK 26(1/2), 1990, 33-48

[36] Sernadas, A., Fiadeiro, J., Sernadas, C. and Ehrich, H.-D.,"Abstract Object Types: A Temporal Perspective", *Temporal Logic in Specification*, Banieqbal, B., Barringer, H. and Pnueli, A. (eds), Springer Verlag, 1989, 324-350

[37] Jungclaus, R., Saake, G. and Sernadas, C., "Using Active Objects for Querying Processing", *Object-oriented Databases: Analysis, Design and Construction*, Meersman, R. and Kent, B. (eds), North-Holland, to be published

[38] Resende, P. and Rito, A., *A Formal Object-oriented Approach to System Specification—Package Router Revisited*, INESC 1990

[39] Sernadas, C., Fiadeiro, J. and Sernadas, A., "Object-oriented Conceptual Modeling from Law", *The Role of Artificial Intelligence in Databases and Information Systems*, Meersman, R., Shi, Z. and Kung, C., North-Holland, 1990, 305-327

[40] Fiadeiro, J. and Sernadas, A., "Logics of Modal Terms for Systems Specification", *Journal of Logic and Computation*, 1(2), 1990, 187-227

[41] Fiadeiro, J. and Maibaum, T., "Temporal Reasoning Over Deontic Specifications", *Journal of Logic and Computation*, 2(1), 1991

[42] Fiadeiro, J. and Maibaum, T., Describing, Structuring and Implementing Objects, *REX90: Foundations of Object-oriented Languages*, Springer-Verlag, to be published

[43] Fiadeiro, J., Sernadas, C., Maibaum, T. and Saake, G., "Proof-theoretic Semantics of Object-oriented Specification Constructs", R. Meersman and B. Kent (eds), *Object-oriented Databases: Analysis, Design and Construction*, North-Holland, to be published

[44] C. Sernadas, P. Gouveia, L. Silva and A. Lopes. "Objects as Structuring Units for Incorporating Dynamics in Deductive Conceptual Modeling". *Proceedings of the International Workshop on the Deductive Approach to Information Systems and Databases*, 93-110, 1990

[45] Jungclaus, R., Saake, G. and Sernadas, C., "Formal Specification of Object Systems", Abramsky, S. and Maibaum, T. (eds), *TAPSOFT'91*, to be published

[46] Sernadas, C., Gouveia, P. and Lopes, A., "Gentzen-type System for Verification in Conceptual Modeling and Knowledge Representation", INESC, 1990

Database Specification using Transaction Sets

Michael F. Worboys

Department of Computer Science
Keele University, Keele ST5 5BG UK

Abstract

This paper takes an algebraic approach to the specification of relational database systems. It begins by surveying some previous work on model-based and algebra-based approaches to database specification. It then shows how specifications may be constructed using axiomatizations of transaction semigroups which generate database instances. A general class of tuple-based transactions is defined, and it is shown how unconstrained insertions and deletions may be modelled and axiomatically characterized using this class. A general class of integrity constraint is defined, and examples are given to show both static and dynamic constraints within this class. The paper concludes by showing that tuple-based transactions are a strict extension of transactions defined in previous work and points to future areas for study.

Keywords: Transaction, integrity constraint, database theory, algebraic specification.

1 Introduction

Formal techniques for the specification of databases can be broadly divided into two approaches. The first, based upon formal logic, characterizes a database by specifying formulas which hold within its states (static integrity constraints) or between its states (dynamic integrity constraints). The second algebraic approach treats a database as an algebraic structure (abstract data type), consisting of a collection of carrier sets and associated operations and specified by means of identities holding between its operations. In database terms, the former approach is constraint-based, whereas the latter is transaction-based.

A striking distinguishing feature of a database is usually the complex structure of the data within it. Database specialists have traditionally emphasised the structure of the data store as being the paramount notion for database systems. Thus, much of the history of database technology is closely linked with the logic-based view of a database.

This paper presents an algebraic approach to the specification of relational databases in terms of the transactions which generate them. Traditionally, a database is specified by means of integrity constraints, which must be satisfied after each transaction with it. In the transactional approach, the database is specified by prescribing a set of transactions and constraining possible database instances to be generated (in a sense later to be formally defined) from the transaction set. Such transactions act as functions from database instances to instances, and as such have a semigroup structure. However, the dominating notion of 'state' for database specification presents difficulties for formalisation purely within the semigroup. In particular, traditional state-based constraints such as functional, multivalued and join dependencies are not naturally expressed in the transaction semigroup. Some workers have introduced an extra argument to represent state, for example [1]. An alternative approach is to use a specification language specially designed for state-based systems, such as Z or VDM . In this paper, we have chosen not to use any such tools, but to follow a direction using basic algebraic tools. We investigate how far it is possible to go with a bare minimum of state being carried, namely a tuple. By restricting the class of constraints to those which are sufficiently 'localized' (a term to be formally defined later) to tuples, we have obtain some positive results.

Transactions (insertions, deletions and modifications) parametrized by tuples, subject to conjunctions of equality and inequality conditions have been studied in [2, 3]. It is shown that such classes of transactions are sufficient to generate instance sets which are subject to some, but not all, types of classical integrity constraint. This paper generalizes the notion of such transactions to generic tuple-based transactions, and show that further classes of classical integrity constraint may be generated by these generalized transactions. We consider a very simple underlying relational database structure which is untyped and unirelational. Extensions to typed multirelational database schemes are the subject of future work.

In order to place this investigation in context, we begin with a brief survey of related work in the literature. Some of the key papers using the logic-based and algebraic approach to database specification are discussed, before focussing on work more closely related to this paper.

2 Survey of related work

2.1 Logic-based approaches

For the vast majority of the database community, database system specification, (data modelling or conceptual modelling, to use more acceptable database terminology), is concerned with characterizing the acceptable states of the database by means of integrity constraints. Once the integrity constraints are in place, then changes to the database (insertions, deletions and updates) are only permitted if after their action, the database conforms to all the static and dynamic integrity constraints placed upon it. By this means, some control is maintained over the integrity of the system.

The logic-based approach specifies the database by describing its legal states using logical expressions. This is clearly described in [4], where a further distinction is made between the model-theoretic and proof-theoretic views. The model-theoretic view conceives the legal database extension as interpretations of the integrity constaints (usually given as formulas of the first order predicate calculus) in which all the constraints are satisfied. On the other hand, the proof-theoretic view takes the constraints (plus further expressions handling naming, equality, completion, etc.) as the theory within which information to be retrieved from the database may be proved. In both cases, however, the database is specified by describing, using an appropriate logical formalism, its possible states.

This approach has been extended to account for dynamic constraints, using logics extended by modal operators and possible world semantics (each world representing a database state). For example, in [5], the logic is a many-sorted first order logic with modal operators, corresponding to updates. The proof-theoretic approach to databases is adopted. The basic modal axiom system is deontic extended by the Barcan formula. The application of deontic modal logic to database specification have been extensively investigated in [6, 7, 8]. The motivation for using deontic modal logic stems from the realization that integrity constraints often describe a situation that ought to happen, rather than one which necessarily will happen. Thus, an integrity constraint upon a library database might specify the obligation to return a book within a given period but not that the book will be returned within that period. The modalities specifiable in the formalisms of these papers are prohibition, permission, and obligation.

There has been work done on the formal specification of the tools that database designers use to do conceptual modelling. For example, [9] identifies approaches to dealing with modelling abstractions (such as aggregation and generalization). Using category theory, the authors build a formal framework in which abstraction mechanisms may be described. Some of this is presented in the Clear language developed by Goguen and Burstall ([10])

2.2   Algebraic approaches

Turning now to algebraic approaches closer to that of this paper, some early work which defines database schemes using sets of updates is presented by Cassanova, Castilho and Furtado in [11]. In [12], Veloso, Castilho and Furtado contrast a so-called 'query oriented approach' with 'update oriented approach' to database specification. The query oriented approach proceeds by defining allowable states, using predicates. This is precisely the logic-based approach discussed above. It is termed query-oriented by the authors since states can be checked by queries which do not change the contents of the database. States may be specified by predicates (predicative normal form) or sets of relations (characteristic sets). The update oriented approach constructs algebraic specifications as sequences of functions which act upon the database states. This is the same as the transactional approach which we define and use later. The construction starts from the empty state. The state space is a graph, with nodes labelled by characteristic sets and with edges labelled by the single updates. Any given state may be defined by a 'canonical' set of updates which takes the empty state to the given state. A distinction is made between a procedural and an algebraic specification. Although both are based upon updates, in procedural specification, updates are defined by their action on the canonical term sets, whereas in algebraic specification, updates are defined in terms of each other.

In order to provide some formal flesh to our discussion of further related work, we provide details of the usual construction of the relational database model and present Abiteboul and Vianu's definition of a database transaction.

2.3   The relational model

The untyped relational model is constructed in the usual way, as follows. Assume given the countable sets *att* (set of attributes) and *dom* (domain of values). The structure of the database (database scheme) is defined as a collection of relational schemes, where each scheme is a finite set of attributes.

Definition 2.1 A *relational scheme* is a finite subset of *att*. A *database scheme D* is a finite set of relational schemes.

The extension of a database is defined as an instance of its scheme. Database instances are collections of the component relational instances.

Definition 2.2 A *tuple x* over relational scheme R is a function $x : R \to dom$. An *instance* of a relational scheme R is a finite set of tuples over R. The full set of instances of relational scheme R in D is denoted $inst(D, R)$, or $inst(R)$ if D is understood. An *instance* of a database scheme D is a function from D to $inst(D, R)$, such that each R in D is mapped to an instance of R in D. It is denoted $inst(D)$.

2.4   Transactions with the database

Abiteboul and Vianu in, for example, [2, 3] have introduced a notation for describing a simple class of transactions. Each transaction is composed of insertions, deletions and modifications, where these atomic transactions are defined in terms of certain equational and inequational conditions. They make the following definitions.

Definition 2.3 Let R be a given relational scheme. A *condition* is an expression of the form

$$A = a \quad \text{or} \quad A \neq a$$

where $A \in R$ and $a \in dom$.

Definition 2.4 Let R be a given relational scheme. A tuple x over R *satisfies* condition $A = a$, iff $x(A) = a$. We write $x \models (A = a)$. Similarly, $x \models (A \neq a)$ iff $x(A) \neq a$. Let C be a set of conditions, (without loss of generality, assume that each attribute of R occurs at most once in any condition set), then $x \models C$ iff $\forall c \in C, x \models c$. $sat(C)$ denotes the set of all tuples which satisfy C.

Atomic transactions are classified in [2, 3] as insertions, deletions or modifications.

Definition 2.5 Let R be a relational scheme and C be a given set of conditions. An *insertion* based upon C (with respect to R) is written as $i(C)$, and a *deletion* as $d(C)$. Given two sets of conditions, C and C', a *modification* based upon C and C' is written $m(C, C')$.

The semantics of atomic transactions are constructed by allowing each atomic transaction to have an action on the set of all instances of relational scheme R, that is, each atomic transaction has an effect as a function on $inst(R)$. The insertion $i(C)$

will insert into instances tuples satisfying the condition C. To prevent an unconstrained and possibly infinite set of tuples being added to an instance, we stipulate that C must specify precisely one tuple. The deletion $d(C)$ removes all tuples satisfying C. The modification $m(C, C')$ alters all tuples which satisfy condition C so that they satisfy condition C'. Appropriate restrictions are placed upon C and C' so that this makes sense.

Definition 2.6 A *transaction* t is a finite sequence of atomic transactions, written as $t = a_1 a_2 \ldots a_n$.

The semantics of atomic transactions is extended in the natural way to general transactions. Each general transaction has an action on $inst(R)$, which is the composition (leftmost first) of the constituent atomic actions. For our purposes, what is especially to be noted is that the description of each atomic transaction carries with it a limited amount of tuple-based information. This is the notion that we generalize in later sections.

For notational clarity, throughout the remainder assume fixed a relational scheme R within database D. Suppose $R = \{A_1, A_2, \ldots, A_n\}$. Tuples will usually be denoted by letters x, y, z, and transactions by letters t, t', t''. In what follows, where there is no danger of confusion, we will often fail to distinguish between the name of a transaction and its action as a function. If I is an instance and t is a transaction, then It denotes the instance resulting from the application of t to I. In particular, $\emptyset t$ denotes the instance resulting from the application of t to the empty instance.

To continue with the survey, a general treatment of database updates is given by Abiteboul in [2]. There, it is argued that a database update is not just an enhancement of a database query, but a completely different type of operation which requires its own approach. In short, and modifying a well known equation, we have:

$$update \neq relational\ calculus + assignment$$

Among the issues discussed are:

- non-determinism

- safety

- procedural/declarative database languages

- database specification

In [13], Abiteboul and Vianu distinguish between transactions as database specifiers and transactions as database updates. They provide a formal definition of update-completeness with the help of the following definition of genericity.

Definition 2.7 Let D and E be database schemes, and S a finite subset of *dom*. A function $f : inst(D) \rightarrow inst(E)$ is *S-generic* iff for each bijection ρ on *dom* which is the identity when restricted to S,

$$f \circ \rho^E = \rho^D \circ f$$

where ρ is induced in a natural way to bijections ρ^D and ρ^E on $inst(D)$ and $inst(E)$ respectively. (Throughout this paper the convention is followed that in the composition of two functions, the leftmost function is taken to act first).

It is not hard to check that insertions, deletions and modifications are S-generic for some finite S, as are many relational operations (e.g. natural join and select). This leads to the following general definition.

Definition 2.8 A transaction language L is *update complete* iff each computable mapping between database instances which is S-generic for some finite subset, S, of *dom*, is effected by a transaction definable in L.

The paper proposes a transaction language, TL, with base constructs: insert, delete, and while, which is shown to be update complete. The authors define a notion of specification-completeness, (roughly, 'the ability of transactional schemas to enforce any "reasonable" static or dynamic database semantics'), and show that TL is complete

In [14], Karaberg et al give a sound and complete set of axioms for proving whether or not two transactions (in the Abiteboul-Vianu sense) are equivalent, i.e. both have the same effect on each database instance. The paper constructs the 'transition specification' of a transaction. For a given transaction, this comprises the set of its atomic insertions and a directed graph whose nodes are sets of tuples partitioning the entire tuple space in such a way that all tuples in a tuple set are either deleted or updated to tuples in another tuple set by the transaction. Edges of the graph show transitions from one tuple set to another using the transaction. The paper gives a method of finding the transition specification for any transaction. It uses transition graphs to prove the soundness and completeness for the given axiom set.

3 An algebraic framework for database transactions

3.1 The underlying algebra

The underlying algebraic structure in which the transactions are specified is a semigroup with zero element, 0. The zero element has the property that, for all elements s in the semigroup,

$$s.0 = 0.s = 0 \tag{1}$$

where the 'dot' operation denotes the general semigroup operation. The motivation for having a zero element we will see later provides a means of representing 'impossible' transactions, and therefore allows the consideration of illegal sequences of transactions.

The motivation for using this structure arises from the space of partial functions on a set. Let $\mathcal{F}$ denote the set of partial functions on $inst(R)$, including the 'zero' function, which is everywhere undefined. Function composition is defined as usual except that xfg is not defined if xf is undefined. Then, under this extended function composition, $\mathcal{F}$ is a semigroup with zero element. Notice that the composition of a total function with the zero function (either way round) results in the zero function.

Subsemigroups of $\mathcal{F}$ of particular relevance here are the spaces of S-generic partial functions on $inst(R)$, for finite $S \subset dom$.

3.2 Generic tuple-based transactions

The function space $\mathcal{F}$, which includes even uncomputable functions, is too large for our purposes. We restrict attention to narrower ranges of functions which approximate to the actions of certain classes of transactions on a database. In particular, extending the approach taken in [2, 3] to insertions and deletions, we suppose that the transactions are formed from a set of atomic transactions, each of which is parametrized by a single tuple from R. This is made precise in the following definition.

Definition 3.1 A *generic tuple-based transaction (gtt)* t is a computable total function:

$$t : (R \to dom) \to [inst(R) \to inst(R)].$$

The function space $[inst(R) \to inst(R)]$ is taken to be a space of partial computable S-generic functions, for some finite $S \subset dom$. Thus, if $x \in (R \to dom)$ is an arbitrary tuple, then $t(x)$ will have an action as a partial computable S-generic function on $inst(R)$. It is clear that the transaction types discussed in Section 2.4 are gtt's.

Definition 3.2 Let G be a finite set of gtt's. Then let

$$\mathcal{F}_G = \langle \{t(x) \mid t \in G, x \in (R \to dom)\} \rangle$$

denote the smallest subsemigroup of $\mathcal{F}$ which contains $\{t(x) \mid t \in G, x \in (R \to dom)\}$.

3.3 Insertions and deletions

Simple insertions and deletions may be modelled and axiomatically characterized using the above formalism. Let $\mathcal{F}_{ID} = \langle i, d \rangle$ be the substructure of $\mathcal{F}$ generated by gtt's i and d which represent simple insertion and deletion types as follows. For x a tuple of R, $I \in inst(R)$,

$$i(x) : I \mapsto I \cup \{x\} \tag{2}$$

$$d(x) : I \mapsto I \setminus \{x\} \tag{3}$$

$\mathcal{F}_{ID}$ can be algebraically specified by adding the following relations to the semigroup axioms.

$$i(x)^2 = i(x) \tag{4}$$

$$d(x)^2 = d(x) \tag{5}$$

$$i(x)d(x) = d(x) \tag{6}$$

$$d(x)i(x) = i(x) \tag{7}$$

$$i(x)i(y) = i(y)i(x) \tag{8}$$

$$d(x)d(y) = d(y)d(x) \tag{9}$$

$$d(x)i(y) = i(y)d(x) \text{ iff } x \neq y \tag{10}$$

It may be noticed that this axiom set is not independent. For example, (4) may be proved from the equalities:

$$i(x)^2 = d(x)i(x)d(x)i(x) = d(x)^2 i(x) = i(x)$$

using (7), (6) and (7), in turn. We have a soundness and completeness result as follows:

Proposition 3.1 Every equality between members of $\mathcal{F}_{ID}$ which is valid in the set-theoretic model based upon equations (2)–(3) can be deduced from the above axioms, and conversely.

Proof: Soundness is clear, since each axiom is true in the model of i and d as functions. To prove completeness, firstly assume some fixed prescribed ordering of tuples. Now observe that each element $t \in \mathcal{F}_{ID} = \langle i, d \rangle$ may be proved equal, using the above axioms, to an expression of the form

$$\tau_1(x_1) \cdots \tau_n(x_n)$$

where $x_1 < \ldots < x_n$ in the prescribed ordering of tuples, and for $1 \leq j \leq n$, $\tau_j(x_j)$ is of the form either $i(x_j)$ or $d(x_j)$. Furthermore, this expression is unique. Call such an expression a *canonical form* for t. Now, suppose that there exist two transactions, t_1 and t_2, for which the equality $t_1 = t_2$ is not provable from the axioms. Then, t_1 and t_2 must have distinct canonical forms. Suppose that t_1 and t_2 have canonical forms, $\tau_1^1(x_1^1) \cdots \tau_{n_1}^1(x_{n_1}^1)$ and $\tau_1^2(x_1^2) \cdots \tau_{n_2}^2(x_{n_2}^2)$, respectively. Construct singleton instances:

$$\{x_1^1\}, \ldots, \{x_{n_1}^1\}, \{x_1^2\}, \ldots, \{x_{n_2}^2\}$$

Then, t_1 and t_2 will have distinct actions on at least one of these instances. □

It is precisely this kind of soundness and completeness result which allows us to use an axiomatic definition as a specification for a database. We therefore make the following definition.

Definition 3.3 Let G be a finite set of gtt's. Then G is *algebraically specified* by a set of equational axioms whenever each equation $g = g'$ ($g, g' \in \langle G \rangle$) is provable from the equational axioms together with the semigroup axioms if, and only if, g and g' are equal as functions.

Proposition 3.1 may now be rephrased as: $\mathcal{F}_{ID}$ is algebraically specified by the conditions (4)–(10).

4 Specification under integrity constraints

Whilst the work of the previous subsection 3.3 provided a specification of a database
generated by a simple class of transactions, it was unrealistic in the sense that the
instances were completely unconstrained. Invariably in practice, there is a set of
integrity constraints which instances of the database must satisfy. Such constraints
may be static, applying to instances singly, or dynamic, applying to sequences of
instances. The algebraic approach above will handle both types. One class of
particularly tractable constraints are now defined.

4.1 Localized constraints

Definition 4.1 Let G be a finite set of gtt's. Then a *localized integrity constraint*
with respect to G is an conditional equation of the form,

$$t(x)t'(x') = t'' \text{ iff } \phi(x, x')$$

where $t, t' \in G$, $x, x' \in (R \to dom)$, $t'' \in (\{g(x) \mid g \in G\} \cup \{g(x') \mid g \in G\})$, and ϕ is
a first-order logical expression with at most components of x, x' for free variables.

Several classes of classical constraints, well-known in relational database design,
may be algebraically specified by a set of localized integrity constraints. We give
one example, using a well-known class of static constraints based upon functional
dependencies. The expression x_X denotes the restriction of tuple x to $X \subseteq R$.

Example 4.1 Let there be given the set of functional dependencies:

$$\{L_1 \to R_1, \ldots, L_m \to R_m\},$$

with $L_j, R_j \subseteq R$, $1 \leq j \leq m$. Let $\mathcal{F}_{FD} = \langle i \rangle$ be the substructure of $\mathcal{F}$ generated by
the gtt i, which represents a conditional insertion type as follows. For x a tuple of
R, $I \in inst(R)$,

$$i(x) : I \mapsto \begin{cases} I \cup \{x\} & \text{iff } \forall y \in I, \forall j \ (x_{L_j} = y_{L_j} \Rightarrow x_{R_j} = y_{R_j}) \\ \text{undefined} & \text{otherwise.} \end{cases}$$

Then the set of instances:

$$\{\emptyset t \mid t \in \mathcal{F}_{FD}\}$$

is precisely the set of instances which satisfy the set of functional dependencies.
Furthermore, $\mathcal{F}_{FD}$ is algebraically specified by the localized integrity constraints
(11)–(12) below:

$$i(x)^2 = i(x) \tag{11}$$

$$i(x)i(y) = \begin{cases} i(y)i(x) & \text{iff } \forall j, (x_{L_j} = y_{L_j} \Rightarrow x_{R_j} = y_{R_j}) \\ 0 & \text{otherwise.} \end{cases} \tag{12}$$

The proof goes through in a similar fashion to the proof of Proposition 3.1. Soundness is straightforward. For completeness, assume a prescribed ordering of tuples
and construct a canonical form $i(x_1) \cdots i(x_n)$, with $x_1 < \ldots < x_n$, for non-zero
transactions.

4.2 Localized dynamic constraints

Dynamic constraints may also often be represented as localized constraints. We give one example:

Example 4.2 Imagine a company in which salaries of individual employees never decrease with respect to time. Suppose a highly simplified relation scheme $R = \{EmpNo, Salary\}$. Consider the following gtt t, where the action of t is given as, for each x a tuple of R, $I \in inst(R)$,

$$t(x) : I \mapsto I'$$

where:

$$I' = \begin{cases} I \setminus \{y \mid y_{EmpNo} = x_{EmpNo}\} \cup \{x\} & \text{iff } \forall y \in I, \left(\begin{array}{c} x_{EmpNo} = y_{EmpNo} \\ \Rightarrow \\ x_{Sal} > y_{Sal} \end{array} \right) \\ \text{undefined} & \text{otherwise.} \end{cases}$$

Then, the set of all finite sequences of instances $\emptyset, \emptyset t(x_1), \emptyset t(x_1)t(x_2), \ldots$ is precisely the set of instance sequences which satisfy the given dynamic constraint. Furthermore, $\langle t \rangle$, from which the elements $t(x_1), t(x_1)t(x_2), \ldots$ are drawn may be specified by the localized constraints (13)–(14) below:

$$t(x)^2 = t(x) \tag{13}$$

$$t(x)t(y) = \begin{cases} 0 & \text{iff } x_{EmpNo} = y_{EmpNo} \land x_{Salary} < y_{Salary} \\ t(y) & \text{iff } x_{EmpNo} = y_{EmpNo} \land x_{Sal} > y_{Sal} \\ t(y)t(x) & \text{iff } x_{EmpNo} \neq y_{EmpNo} \end{cases} \tag{14}$$

5 Conclusions

5.1 Relationship to earlier work

We have introduced the class of generic tuple-based transactions as a generalization of the class of insertions and deletions studied in [2, 3]. It is clear that both insertions and deletions are gtts, since each effects a computable C-generic function on $inst(R)$, parametrized by a tuple. As an aside, it is clear that the definition of gtts could be extended in a trivial way to have domain $(R \to dom) \times (R \to dom)$, (i.e. parametrized by two tuples), and this would generalize the modification transactions surveyed earlier. Returning to the relationship between generic tuple-based transactions and the class of transactions constructed by Abiteboul and Vianu, the next example shows that the generalization is a strict one.

Example 5.1 Let relational scheme $R = \{A, B\}$ be given. Consider instances of R satisfying the multivalued dependency $\emptyset \twoheadrightarrow \{A\}$. Such instances I are cartesian products $I_A \times I_B$. It is proved in [15] as Theorem 8.3 that transactions, in the Abiteboul/Vianu sense, are insufficient to generate all these instances. However, let i^* be given by:

$$i^*(x) : I \mapsto (I_A \cup \{x_A\}) \times (I_B \cup \{x_B\})$$

Let $\mathcal{T}_{MVD} = \langle i^* \rangle$. Then it is not hard to show that i^* is a gtt and, further, that the set of instances:

$$\{\emptyset t \mid t \in \mathcal{T}_{MVD}\}$$

is precisely the set of instances which satisfy the dependency $\emptyset \twoheadrightarrow \{A\}$. Thus, gtts provide a strict extension of Abiteboul/Vianu transactions.

We may add a corresponding deletion gtt, d^*, given by:

$$d^*(x) : I \mapsto (I_A \setminus \{x_A\}) \times (I_B \setminus \{x_B\})$$

Then $\mathcal{T}_{MVD} = \langle i^* \rangle = \langle i^*, d^* \rangle$. Writing $i^*(x)$ as $i^*(x_A, x_B)$, the following axioms are sound:

$$i^*(x)^2 = i^*(x) \tag{15}$$

$$i^*(x)i^*(y) = i^*(y)i^*(x) \tag{16}$$

$$i^*(x_A, x_B)i^*(y_A, y_B) = i^*(x_A, y_B)i^*(y_A, x_B) \tag{17}$$

5.2 Future directions

Algebraic specification techniques are at their best when dealing with systems where state plays a limited role. With databases, we have an opposite situation, where the state of the database and its internal structure dominate. Therefore there is no natural way to use pure algebraic structures. However, for databases whose constraints are sufficiently localized to tuples, we have given some examples to show that the standard algebraic approach can be applied. This is true for both static and dynamic constraints. There is scope for a more systematic investigation and more general results. For example, the definition of localization could be generalized to cover any bounded strings of transactions. Furthermore, the precise power of generic tuple-based transactions in relation to other previously defined transaction classes is yet to be determined. Another interesting question is the implication that the transaction sets have for the logical design of the database (corresponding to normalization in the classical theory). These are matters for future work.

Acknowledgements

The author is grateful to Nick Measor, University of Leicester, U.K. for many helpful discussions, and to Petros Bofakos for commenting upon an earlier draft.

References

[1] T.S.E. Maibaum. Database instances, abstract data types and database specification. *Computer Journal*, 28(2):154–161, 1986.

[2] S. Abiteboul and V. Vianu. Equivalence and optimization of relational transactions. *JACM*, 35(1):70–120, jan 1988.

[3] S. Abiteboul and V. Vianu. A transaction-based approach to relational database specifications. *JACM*, 36(4):758–789, oct 1989.

[4] R. Reiter. Towrds a logical reconstruction of relational database theory. In M.L. Brodie, J. Mylopolous, and J.W. Schmidt, editors, *On Conceptual Modelling*, pages 191–238. Springer-Verlag, 1984.

[5] S. Khosla, T.S.E. Maibaum, and M. Sadler. Database specification. In Steel and Meersman, editors, *Database Semantics (DS-1)*, pages 246–271. North-Holland, 1986.

[6] F. Dignum. *A Language for Modelling Knowledge Bases*. PhD thesis, Vrije Univ., Amsterdam, 1989.

[7] F. Dignum and R.P.van der Riet. Knowledge base modelling, based on lingusitics and founded in logic. *Data and Knowledge Engineering*, 1990.

[8] R Wieringa, J.-J.Ch. Meyer, and H. Weigand. Specifying dynamic and deontic integrity constraints in databases. *Data and Knowledge Engineering*, 4(4), 1989.

[9] C Sernadas and A Sernadas. Conceptual modelling abstraction mechanisms as parametrized theories in institutions. In Steel and Meersman, editors, *Database Semantics (DS-1)*, pages 121–140. North-Holland, 1986.

[10] J.A. Goguen and R.M. Burstall. The semantics of clear, a specification language. In D. Bjorner, editor, *Abstract Software Specifications*, pages 294–332. Springer-Verlag, 1980.

[11] M.A. Cassanova, J.M.V. de Castilho, and A.L. Furtado. Properties of conceptual and external database schemes. Monografias em Ciencias da Computacao 11, Dept Informatica, P.U.C. do Rio de Janeiro, 1981.

[12] P.A.S. Veloso, J.M.V. de Castilho, and A.L. Furtado. Systematic derivation of complementary specifications. In *IEEE*, 1981.

[13] S. Abiteboul and V. Vianu. A transaction language complete for database update and specification. In *Proc. 6th Symposium on Principles of Database Systems*, pages 260–268, 1987.

[14] A. Karaberg, D. Karaberg, K. Papakonstantinou, and V. Vianu. Axiomatization and simplification rules for relational transactions. In *Proc. 6th Symposium on Principles of Database Systems*, pages 254–259, 1987.

[15] J. Paredaens, P. de Bra, M. Gyssens, and D. Van Gucht. *The Structure of the Relational Database Model*, volume 17 of *Monographs on Theoretical Computer Science*. Springer-Verlag, 1989.

Working Group Sessions

Is a Picture Worth a Thousand Words?

In this session, we discussed the role of graphical notations in database specification. The discussion focussed on two main points: the usefulness of graphical notation and whether or not a graphical notation can be considered formal.

The session began with participants discussing various graphical notations and their uses. The use of graphical description is prevalent in the specification of database application systems both for structural and behavioural description. These descriptions are useful for communication with the customer in establishing system requirements, as a graphical specification of part (or all) of the system and as part of the final documentation of the system.

The point was raised that some people do not regard a graphical description as formal. In fact, some researchers (both in database-related research and in other areas) appear to scorn those in the database community who "only draw pictures rather than writing mathematical formulae". It was agreed that there is no reason why a graphical notation should not be formal provided that the graphical description language is unambiguous and precisely defined. However, it was pointed out that it is easier to have an unambiguous graphical description language for state as opposed to behaviour.

Then the issue of representing constraints in a graphical description was raised. Clearly, if only a few fixed forms of constraints are supported, then a particular graphical notation can be introduced to represent these constraints. For example, graphical notations were introduced into the entity-relationship model to represent specific forms of dependency constraints and totality constraints on relationships. If a general constraint language is available, then the form of "graphical notation" adopted could be annotating the diagrams with boxes containing the constraint rule. This then led to much discussion on the question of what counts as "graphical" and what counts as "textual" .

It was agreed that graphical notations are particularly useful for providing an overview of a system: in other words they are useful at a high-level of abstraction. There was less agreement as to whether a detailed graphical description of a system was desirable. Some felt that the benefits of graphical description is lost if a diagram is overly complex or large: once a diagram has to be decomposed into a number of diagrams over several "pages", then they felt that textual representation would be preferable. Others felt that effective systems had been developed in which everything was graphical - and that the use of good browsing techniques, graphical query languages etc. can make graphical working feasible.

Indeed, the group wondered if we are too restricted in our thinking by only considering current technologies and systems. In the future, the use of animation, colour and sound might be much more effective in supporting graphical descriptions of system behaviour.

It seems that there will always be those who prefer "pictures" and those who prefer "words". In our small working group, it tended to be the "database" people who fell into the first category and the "formal specifications" people who fell into the second. But, interestingly, some of the formal specifications people did admit to sometimes drawing diagrams while developing a system specification: however, this was considered as something purely for personal use and not part of the specification or refinement process.

Given that there is a large percentage of people who do find diagrams helpful, it seems reasonable that they be included in the documentation of a system. It is particularly true of the eventual end users of a system, that they are unlikely to be very familiar with a given formal specification language. Good graphical notations are fairly easy to grasp and provide a useful basis for agreeing on user requirements. Such graphical notations may also have a precise semantics which means that while the resulting specification may not be complete in itself, it will be a step ahead of the purely informal textual description.

Moira Norrie
Ivan Tabkha

Mixing and Matching

This discussion was meant to centre around heterogeneity, seen by several of the participants as the feature of database systems that most sharply distinguished them from other software. The topics proposed for discussion were: Sources of heterogeneity; semi-formal techniques; formal techniques; and the uses of formal specifications.

1. Sources of heterogeneity These were easy to identify: Heterogeneous software components of DBMSs and DBMS applications; Different data models used by designers from different DBMS cultures; Different modellings of the same domain, even within the same formalism; Heterogeneous hardware, operating systems, programming languages.

2. Semi-formal techniques

These are a mixture of abstract formalisms and specific tools for managing heterogeneity:

Standard components: these include operating system standards like Unix, POSIX, and microkernels; object managers like WiSS; the X.500 name service standard; and integration platforms like Comandos.

Standard languages: in the database world, these include the standards for SQL and its relatives, and the various data models in use. But these don't go nearly far enough yet - we should be able to pick up a standard and agreed specification of the relational model as easily as the GNU Emacs source code.

Interface descriptions: The most common technique for interface description is the header file. This is nowhere near enough - for example, in one system several of us have used, the call interface is well defined, but the protocol for using it isn't (there is more state than the manuals tell you about) - misunderstanding this is a common source of programmer errors. Other techniques for interface description include ANSA-style encapsulation, ("wrapper technology"), RPC standards like XDR and ASN.1, and IDL (for passing structured information between program modules)

Tools for generating "standard" components There are tools for generating code to do syntactic manipulation such as Yacc, lex and Cornell's Synthesizer Generator. The optimizer generator which is provided as part of the EXODUS database system "toolkit". One way of fixing a standard is by the adoption of an unspecifiably complex tool like an Ada compiler - this ensures compliance ultimately with a validation suite rather than a formal model.

3. Formal techniques

We asked participants what formalisms they had actually used, and obtained the following list:

- The relational model itself: not in the same league as Z for handling transitions and error behaviour, but good at describing the state space.

- The Calculus of Constructions; two people were using this - powerful but unwieldy, with far too much explicit detail when you don't want it.

- Model-based Z-like methods: these specifications "expanded like popcorn" as afterthoughts about the problem domain accumulated. The Z schema calculus did assist in controlling complexity, though (with the caveat that this feature of Z can be more fun for the writer than the reader).

- Constructive algebraic definitions in an ad hoc formalism. This was a useful guide to implementation.

- VDM and CSP (the latter not used for DB work)

- Logic programming in the abstract via slightly-souped-up first-order predicate calculus; these mathematical techniques are becoming more prevalent because "programmers are becoming more intelligent".

- Conventional data models, succeeded by an object-oriented language with added temporal logic to capture system dynamics.

- Denotational semantics. This is elegant for expressing both DB state and queries, extensional and intensional information. It's easy to set up multi-level descriptions. On the other hand it's rather verbose: 45 pages for a very simple DBMS. (Is this so bad? If the specification is used to direct software development, as with David Schmidt's denotational-semantics-driven compiler generators, or used to provide executable prototypes via a denotational semantics interpreter, that's fairly compact code by usual standards.)

- Executable specifications in Prolog using a denotational methodology; the executability made development much easier. This used formal methods purely as a source of transformationally derived programs, not as a source of theorems about the system.

Some surprising things were missing from this list: The high-profile algebraic systems: OBJ (Eqlog, FOOPS, ...), Larch, LOTOS, ACT ONE; Executable rewrite systems: REVE, ERIL; Higher-order functional languages: ML, Miranda; Categories, sheaves, toposes, ...; CCS, SCCS; Pure temporal logics, dynamic logic; Petri nets; Graph grammars; Deontic logic.

4. Roles for specifications

We identified the following roles a formal specification can play:

- Interpretation or execution as a prototype

- Generation of implementations

- Documentation: external (for the client internal) of the design

- Derivation of properties: transformations coverage (do we handle all cases?) consistency of the specification feasibility

- Reverse engineering: specifications usually aren't kept in step with the implementation

- Self-description: Data models can be represented by metaschemas; it is important to prove that operations (like database merging) or transformed code respect these schemas; see also Moira Norrie's paper in these proceedings...) Metaschemas can be useful within a running application, as with a scientific data model associating pedigree and accuracy information with numerical data.

- Design insight

- Standardization: But in practice, about the only system everyone agrees on is regular expressions (or, to be *slightly* more charitable, BNF)!

5. What specification issues are peculiar to database work?

In developing standard approaches for specifying databases, it isn't yet clear whether the specification of DBMSs or of database applications should come first. Both have been tried.

There are two differences between formal methods in database work and in software engineering generally that affect the way systems have to be specified:

DB work is already more abstract than most SE - the relational model is a long way from its implementation - and heterogeneity (specified explicitly or left for the reverse engineer) is ubiquitous.

Jack Campin
David Harper

Are Database Programmers Capable of Formality and Refinement?

The discussion focused on formal development approaches employed by database application programmers. We presented the following questions about the process of formal database application development:

1. What is the role of formal specifications in the development of database application systems?

2. What should be the development process from requirements specification to application system?

3. What are the various layers involved in database system specification?

4. What specification techniques are appropriate and who should be using these techniques?

We began by considering what characteristics of database applications distinguish them from other kinds of applications, and whether in fact there is anything special about applying formal techniques in developing database applications.

Persistence: We observed that database systems are characterized by longevity of data. They usually involve a large volume of data that can last for a considerable period of time. Furthermore, the longevity of data and its impact in the long term made it a valuable asset that had to be well managed. Given the longevity of the data it is difficult to foresee all of its possible uses, and hence it is impracticable to define a specific interface that would satisfy all applications developed during its lifetime. This might imply that to allow the applications to evolve comfortably over time, only the data structures and constraints needed to be specified and nothing else. Object-oriented models may suffer from this problem in the long term, requiring too much to be fixed in advance when dealing with long-lived data. On the other hand, formal specifications can and are used for purposes other than documentation and description. For example, they can be animated for fast prototyping, used to reason about the behaviour of a system, or reified to obtain an implementation.

The implementation model: Another characteristic which distinguishes database application development is that the application designer is provided with a target model, either logical or physical, to which the real world is mapped. The conjecture was that this may make the route from requirements to implementation more amenable to formal specification techniques.

Granularity: Further, the granularity of its operations makes a database application different. Relational database systems allowed operations on collections of similar objects while traditional file systems used a record-at-a -time approach. Novel applications, like CAD, require the ability to handle both collections of objects and individual objects. What are the implications, if any, for the database application development process?

Data modelling versus OOP: Given the same application, would an approach starting from a data model using some kind of semantic hierarchy, deliver the same result as an approach employing object-oriented design and programming techniques? Replies suggested that this presupposed incorrectly that OOP classes and the entities in data models were comparable. In OOP, classes are used for both classification and the organization of computation. The purely computational classes in an implementation might not appear in the data model of the application. In an object-oriented framework, the notion of *collection* - an extension, or group of objects - was distinct from that of *type* (or class) - a behaviour-based concept describing the interface to objects of that type. In the database world, lumping the two concepts together the way Smalltalk does may limit reusability.

Levels of specification and implementation: It was generally agreed that specification should start at an abstract level independent of any specific database management system. For example, different relational database management systems (implementations) may give different meanings to the same operation (in their treatment of nulls, for example), and will certainly support different subsets of the relational model constraints. Some papers presented in the workshop advocate such an approach. Concern was expresssed about how easy it was to implement a system from a high level specification, if the specification model was very different from the implementation model. It could be very difficult to reify the specification on relatively low-level database implementation models.

Requirements specification: The central demand on a requirements specification is that the customer should be able to understand it. Full executability is not needed, but animation is a great help. Logic programming environments are a useful tool for this; some database development systems integrate requirements languages. A problem with these languages is that their semantics is itself badly underspecified.

Verification and the state of the art: One participant asked "What is the state of the art in program correctness in database applications?" and "Can one write database software and prove that it is correct?". Four responses to this were (1) that large-scale verification was no more feasible for database work than for other areas of software engineering; (2) that refinement methodologies, with integrated correctness proofs, can work in practice; (3) that mapping a requirements specification to a system specification was straightforward, while mapping the system specification to an implementation was a big leap; (4) that we need larger building blocks that let us specify an entire database system.

Reusability: Database applications don't seem to be as reusable as the generality of software (such as numerical libraries or the Smalltalk-80 system classes). Standard SQL does not seem to help very much in this respect. On the other hand, database systems do well at making data reusable. Why are data reuse and code reuse so different?

Pressures for formalism: There are economic reasons why formalism is likely to become prevalent in the database world. One is reverse engineering of existing code for reimplementation mediated by formal description: Bachmann's experience with this has already shown it to be viable. The other is in safety-critical systems: while the military and aerospace industries are the main forces presently insisting on safety- critical software, financial and health databases have a comparable impact on human life, and it can't be long before legally enforced requirements for proven safety are the norm for them too.

Jack Campin
Daniel Chan
David Harper

Where do we go from here?

There are three general aspects of database systems to which formal specifications may be applied. Firstly, there is the formal theory of data models and query languages. Secondly, they may be applied to certain aspects of database management systems designed to support a particular data model - such as transaction management systems. Thirdly, we can consider the process of engineering database applications using formal methods.

In this working group session we considered how prevalent the use of formal methods is and considered ways in which database researchers could be encouraged to use formal methods.

Members of the group reported that both in the U.S.A. and in the U.K., the use of formal specification techniques in the database community is very limited. The work on formal specification techniques in these countries is mainly in connection with deductive databases and logic as applied to databases. The trend is that the database community tends to be market-driven rather than theoretically motivated.

It would appear that many "traditional" database researchers are rather cautious about the use of formalisms in database sytems. Further, for those who gain an awareness of the necessity and benefits of formal specifications, it may be difficult to know where to start. A whole range of formalisms might be employed to specify various aspects of a database system. These formalisms include: various logical systems, many-sorted algebras, temporal logic, state transitions, transitional logic, process specification, term and graph rewriting and refinement calculus.

It is not even the case that any one technique is adopted for a particular aspect. For example, if the literature is examined for specifications of data models, the reader is confronted with a whole mix of techniques - ranging from established specification techniques and languages to those devised by the authors of that particular paper. Not only does this make it difficult for the data model designer to select a good specification formalism for his model - but it also makes it much more difficult for the reader to appreciate the similarities and differences among existing models.

Clearly, it would be difficult for database researchers to acquaint themselves with all of these techniques - particularly to such a level of understanding where they could appreciate the relative merits of the various techniques.

Some members of the group expressed disappointment that it is not always easy to find theoreticians of computer science who are interested in the database domain. The area of databases is often regarded as an application area - rather than central computer science. Hopefully, this situation is changing in that, as systems become larger and more complex, it is realised that it is not only the traditional record-processing type of applications that require databases.

It would seem that the situation is improving with more conferences on theoretical aspects of database sytems taking place both in Europe and the U.S.A. Formalism is becoming more accepted by the database community and theoretcal computer scientists are turning to it as a fertile area.

The group agreed that it would be desirable to agree a common set of techniques for the formal specification of databases. Furthermore, it would be beneficial to develop widely acceptable specifications of widely-used data models so that the database community would use common expressions and notation and thereby increase the understanding and interaction among its researchers. It should be emphasised that we are not advocating formal standards and wishing to preclude the investigation of alternative and new techniques: rather we are looking for the sort of general agreement that seems to have been reached in other research communities.

Petros Bofakos
Moira Norrie

Author Index

Published in 1990